THREADS OF EMPIRE

THREADS OF EMPIRE

A History of the World in Twelve Carpets

Dorothy Armstrong

WEIDENFELD & NICOLSON

First published in Great Britain in 2025 by Weidenfeld & Nicolson,
an imprint of The Orion Publishing Group Ltd
Carmelite House, 50 Victoria Embankment
London EC4Y 0DZ

An Hachette UK Company

The authorised representative in the EEA is Hachette Ireland,
8 Castlecourt Centre, Dublin 15, D15 XTP3, Ireland (email: info@hbgi.ie)

1 3 5 7 9 10 8 6 4 2

A CIP catalogue record for this book is
available from the British Library.

Map by dkbcreative

ISBN (Hardback) 978 1 3996 1422 1
ISBN (Export Trade Paperback) 978 1 3996 1423 8
ISBN (Ebook) 978 1 3996 1425 2
ISBN (Audio) 978 1 3996 1426 9

Typeset by Input Data Services Ltd, Bridgwater, Somerset

Printed in Great Britain by Clays Ltd, Elcograf, S.p.A.

MIX
Paper | Supporting
responsible forestry
FSC
www.fsc.org
FSC® C104740

www.weidenfeldandnicolson.co.uk
www.orionbooks.co.uk

For my family: You are the pattern in the carpet

Contents

A MAP OF THE WORLD IN TWELVE CARPETS

SIBERIA

RUSSIA

Ngorno-
Karabakh

GEORGIA
Gori

CASPIAN SEA

ARMENIA

AZERBAIJAN
Shusha

TURKEY

AZERBAIJAN

Tabriz

Ardabil

IRAQ

IRAN

RUSSIA

KAZAKHSTAN

• Novosibirsk

Pazyryk
Valley

Altai
Mountains

MONGOLIA

UZBEKISTAN

Turkmen Nomadic Territories

CASPIAN SEA

Bukhara

KYRGYZSTAN

TURKMENISTAN

TAJIKISTAN

• Geok Tepe

Kyber
Pakhtunkhwa

CHINA

W CAUCASUS

• Ardabil
• Tabriz

• Kashan

• Herat

AFGHANISTAN

IRAN

Kirman

Lahore

• Amristar

Q

Hormuz

PAKISTAN

NEPAL

SAUDI
ARABIA

UAE

INDIA

BANGLADESH

OMAN

YEMEN

ARABIAN
SEA

BAY OF
BENGAL

GULF OF ADEN

Preface

One of the first carpets to share my life was loaned to me by a friend who was a translator of Arabic literature. Too big for his flat in Cairo's Garden City, it arrived in my pale, neutral Cambridge sitting room like a deliberately disruptive aesthetic intervention. Serried rows of abstract designs marched down the intense, high-contrast red and dark blue of its length. Its geometry was almost perfect, but not quite, the tantalising waywardness of the human hand destabilising the eye and mind. The motifs insisted on their meaning without ever revealing it, conjuring a hallucinatory state of half-knowing. I couldn't walk across it without staring down the shaft it offered into the past, the lives of its weavers, all the places it had lain before. It was a *coup de foudre*, like infatuation. There was no way back.

I was in love at first with exoticism, fantasy and folklore, the world of flying carpets and old magic.[1] The ancient story of Sheba's gift to Solomon of a rug made of green silk and gold which could carry his entire army entranced me – God, in a rage at the king's pride, shook the carpet, throwing the soldiers to their deaths. I devoured the folk tale of the flying carpet made by the Russian witch Baba Yaga for Ivan the Fool, to help the simple soul on his journey to power. I was thrilled to find more recent magic carpets: Mark Twain's Captain Stormfield was unfortunately abandoned in the wrong part of heaven after his death but flew to his proper sector of paradise on a flying carpet, actor Sabu as Aladdin flew on a magic rug over a twinkling Hollywood Baghdad. I was impressed by their subversive power, so great that stories have come

1

down through time of the destruction of enchanted carpets by Mongol and Sassanian emperors. The sense of that dangerous and alien power persists – among the panoply of wands, broomsticks, mandrakes, potions and spells available to its students, flying carpets were forbidden at Harry Potter's Hogwarts.

But as I lived alongside them, the carpets themselves, rather than fantasies of them, took a grip on my imagination. I began to visit Bruce Lepere's famous rug room at Liberty in London, where he was often still in his shorts after an adventurous buying trip. The advice he gave on collecting rugs was not easy to follow. The best place was Peshawar, he explained, where a buyer should be sure to take plenty of packs of American cigarettes and be prepared to sit all day chain-smoking with sellers in the bazaar. Through dealers like Bruce, I began to understand the arcane hierarchy of carpets, a set of beliefs about the quality and origins of rugs which determines market prices. A natural contrarian, I had my doubts about this hierarchy even before I fully understood it.

My taste in carpets went in phases. I began with a strong preference for geometric designs executed in strongly contrasting colours like those found in Caucasian village carpets, and was less inspired by the naturalistic designs, complex palette and fine materials of Persian carpets. Then I developed a recherché interest in the austere and sometimes inaccessible carpets of Turkmen nomads. But it was always the most storied carpets which compelled my attention. As I write, my two favourites among my own carpets are ones that embody real and imagined memories. The first is from Azerbaijan, home to a great and ancient weaving tradition. It was bought by my son in Baku, over a cup of mint tea with the dealer (he tells me), and for which he asked me to wire the money (immediately) by Western Union. The other was described to me by the great carpet scholar Jon Thompson as a rug made by a Turkmen bride and her mother-in-law as part of the dowry the girl would take to her husband's tent. The girl would have woven from childhood. Her fingers would be nimble, her taste sophisticated. She was accustomed to the weaving of complex textiles in the dim light of a tent or sitting outside in her tribe's steppe encampment as children and animals vied for her attention. Nevertheless, I tremble with her at the thought of the weeks spent working on this rug alongside a mother-in-law who, minute by minute, scrutinised her as a weaver, wife and mother.

Women have mostly been the weavers of the world, and carpets are one of their most highly evolved art forms. When I encounter an unfamiliar carpet, my first questions are about what the weaver was thinking when she made it, what else was going on in her life, what was happening in the world around her tent or village or workshop, and how it affected her. These are the questions of a historian rather than a connoisseur, and none of them have much to do with any hierarchy of quality.

As the years passed and the carpets on my floors started to overlap each other, this question of what is a better or a worse carpet started to perplex me. One rug can please me more than another, but then one brand of coffee can please me more than another, and it doesn't mean it's the best coffee in the world. Carpets are fabulously diverse but can seem to be part of a secret body of knowledge, policed by specialists and dealers, who define what is good and bad, and more insidiously what it is good or bad to admire. I began to see that carpets were readily susceptible to being interpreted in support of ideologies of taste, which themselves were part of ideologies of power.

The issue would not leave me alone, and in 2010 I took a leap of faith and decided to try to resolve it, at least to my own satisfaction. I went back to school to educate myself in the material culture of Asia, then pursued an academic career investigating the role of carpets in Asian history. The School of Oriental and African Studies in London, the Royal College of Art, the Victoria and Albert (V&A) Museum, the Ashmolean Museum and the University of Oxford have all offered hospitable homes to the person who is sometimes referred to as 'the carpet woman'.

The story I have been chasing for more than a decade now is not how old or how good is a particular carpet, where does it come from, how valuable is it, or even how was it made and by whom. The question was always about the historical role carpets have

played, and why they lend themselves to that. This book arises
from that long process of questioning the way we talk and think
about carpets and looks at them as agents in historical events, and
particularly at their strong relationship with power.

The world beneath our feet tends to be less observed than the
world at eye level. Once we begin to look, we can see carpets in
every environment which celebrates power. In a moment from
the TV series *The Crown*, the observant and astute screenwriter
has Gillian Anderson as Margaret Thatcher point to the floor of
a state room in Downing Street and say to the foreign dignitary
accompanying her, 'Lovely, isn't it?' The carpet does indeed lie
in Downing Street. It is a high-quality replica of the legendary
Ardabil made for the great Iranian Shah Tahmasp in the sixteenth
century, bought for the V&A, then known as the South Kensington Museum, at the height of the British Empire in 1893. Off she
walks across it in her high-heeled pumps, swinging her handbag,
to rule an empire of her imagination.

I was primed for an interest in textiles by my childhood in
industrial Lancashire. Most of the women in my family were
makers, particularly seamstresses and knitters. But my particular
North was also that of the cotton mills, and in my family's past
were men and women who worked in spinning and weaving
factories, swept along by industrialisation. Those earlier generations had participated in the sometimes-desperate story of
nineteenth-century textiles, recorded in anguished detail in Engels' 1845 *The Condition of the Working Class in England* and Mrs
Gaskell's 1855 novel about the Manchester textile industry, *North
and South*. The textile industry has a long history of exploiting the
vulnerable, and carpets are no exception. Carpet-weavers are often
illiterate, poor, young, female. Carpets celebrate power but also
illuminate powerlessness, and this book examines both sides of
that coin.

I have looked at thousands of carpets over the last fifteen years,
and hundreds before that, and have seen, touched, smelled and
studied some of the greatest in the world. But the choice of carpets
for this book was not about the 'best', it was about the most storied,

those that can give us insight into how the world has turned over the almost ten thousand years the book covers.

Edinburgh, 2024

Introduction

This book is about the relationship between carpets and power. That relationship has a discrepancy at its heart; that an ancient technology practised by the humblest of peoples should produce some of the world's greatest symbols of authority and control.

The story of carpets is the story of transformations, of simple practices turned into great art, of domestic objects changed into the apparatus of politics, wealth and religion. The rugs in this book show how these textiles came into being and then were reinvented as they moved in the slipstream of powerful warriors, colonists, missionaries, intellectuals, merchants and industrialists. Along the way we find tricksters, fraudsters and conspiracists. From the fifth-century BCE contents of the tombs of Scythian chieftains, to the carpets under the boots of Stalin, Roosevelt and Churchill at the 1945 Yalta Peace Conference, they uncover a different version of the past.

Carpets are travellers in time and space. The spotlight in these chapters falls repeatedly on three zones and three time-periods of intense significance for the relationship between carpets and power. The geographies are the territories along the Silk Roads that facilitated the movement of goods and ideas across Asia; the West, Central and South Asian regions where the world's great carpets were made; and a Global North which has had a fascinated hunger for them. The book also visits the places in which these carpets have come to rest in our own time: the imperial grandeur of the V&A and Berlin's Pergamon Museums, the opulence of the

Getty Museum, the reflective atmosphere of temples in Japan and churches in Romania.

The first of the book's three time-periods is the continent-changing movement west of nomadic tribespeople out of the Petri dish of Central Asia from around 500 BCE. They brought a transformation of the way of life in much of Eurasia, along with the carpet-weaving practice that was central to nomadic cultures and beliefs. The second is the Eurasia-wide resurgence of the fifteenth, sixteenth and seventeenth centuries, and the explosion into Eurasian consciousness and geopolitics of a new art form, the courtly carpets of Anatolia, Iran and Mughal India. The third period is what historian Eric Hobsbawm called the Age of Empire, the peak of Western colonialism in the nineteenth and twentieth centuries, when Asian carpets were used as propaganda for diverse holders of power, in dramatic acts of cultural appropriation. This book is not a geography-by-geography narrative or a traditional chronological history; instead the story repeatedly returns to these different geographies and periods as it explores moments of signif-icance for the relationship between individual carpets and power.

The power in these chapters takes many forms. The reader will find Scythian, Seljuk, Mongol, Mamluk, Ottoman, Safavid, Mughal, Tokugawa, Hapsburg, British, Soviet and US Empires. The power of religions is here, including varying sects of Chris-tianity, Islam, Buddhism and Animism. Mercantile and industrial systems, and what we now call the 1 per cent, private individuals who through time accrue to themselves an exceptional proportion of the world's resources and wealth, are present. The reader will also encounter the power of those who create knowledge for the rulers of their times, and those who subvert it through trickery.

The discussion of power is also a discussion of the powerless, and throughout the story of carpets we hear the drumbeats of oppression, war, climate change and consequent human migration and loss. We are always in the presence of the skilled, patient, inventive weavers who made these carpets. They are creators of artefacts which are part of our global cultural heritage, but they rarely share in power. We can't usually hear or read their words, but we can begin to understand their vision and experience if we look hard at their work. The back of a rug can show us the line where two weavers sitting together on the same bench each turned back along their half of a row of knots to weave the next row. The sequence of a complete row is as abstract as computer code, but they integrated their two halves perfectly between them. The sometimes bizarre corner motifs at the end of the rug which was woven last, where the design seems to have been abandoned, remind us that the weaver was managing stretchy threads on a loom, working through a mathematical prediction she had made when she began the rug, and that those things sometimes got away from her. Where possible I retrieve fragments of the lived experience of weavers in their own time, often from details like this: an act of imaginative conjuring. Weavers often belong to groups that have been marginalised since text replaced song as the primary way of recording the past, and the literate began their long ownership of records.

The geographical and temporal range of this book is wide, but at its heart are twelve carpets. They give the book its structure, which proceeds from the oldest carpet to the youngest. Their biographies dictate the places, time-periods and events each chapter explores. Some end their lives burned in bombed-out basements, some are preserved for the future in frozen tombs. Some warmed the legs of Lutheran worshippers during the European Reformation or became armour for medieval Japanese warlords, or decorated Jazz Age parties in the US. They are repeatedly used as props at moments of historical change, symbolising the beginnings and ends of wars and the rise and fall of emperors. They are woven and traded by their makers as a way out of persecution, dispossession, expulsion, collectivisation, population exchanges and forced settlement. But whatever the drama of their biographies, they all have the same origin, the hand of a person in a tent, village or city workshop, patiently interweaving fibres day by day to bring the object in her imagination into being.

That is what the book is about. There are some things it isn't. This is not a handbook or a history of carpets. Nor is it a guide to the 'greatest' carpets in the world, whatever that might mean (although some very great carpets are discussed). It begins with a carpet dating to around the fourth century BCE, but it does not track through what we know about carpets from then on. Many specialist writers have done all this, and their work can be found in the Endnotes and Bibliography to this book. Instead, it is a selection of carpets that are intrinsically interesting in themselves, but are also turnkeys to histories of power, and mirrors to the deeply held values of the cultures that have collected them.

It is also a particular form of history. In broadcaster and author Mary Beard's words, historical writing is subject to a 'Big books by blokes about battles syndrome',[1] or, to extend the trope, about scientific breakthroughs, or discussions of other white males, mostly dead. The tone of these histories, she suggested, was expected to be authoritative, brooking no disagreement. Meanwhile she described an expectation that histories written by women should be intimate, offering an inner journey, relying on authenticity rather than authority, herstories. Professor Beard may have been exaggerating for effect, and in any case some wonderful histories and herstories have been written about both battles and inner journeys. Nevertheless, there is some truth in her comments.

But the question of what a reader can expect from a historian need not be so fixed. I offer here a history which is episodic and eclectic, responsive to my own interests and experience, personal, but not an inner journey. It is not an attempt at a conclusive single narrative with winners and losers, heroes and villains. Instead, it represents history as a kaleidoscope, where fragments of knowledge shift into new patterns each time they are turned by an object, an event, a person. The carpets I discuss each represent a turn of that kaleidoscope, showing what are sometimes the same fragments of knowledge in a different light, creating a new version of the old story. It kept surprising me. I expected episodes of struggle between itinerant and settled communities, the dark pattern of exploitation whenever carpet-weaving comes into contact with the market, the impact of the egos and agendas of the great of the world. But I did not expect to find Stalin so often at the centre of

my vision, or the mountainous and landlocked province of Transylvania in modern Romania, or conspiracists and fraudsters. Our
understanding of the past is provisional, continuously remade by
the filters placed on it, and it is global, subject to continuous ebbs,
flows, fusions and separations.

The Italian writer Italo Calvino commented that 'the curse
of our century [the twentieth] is that every cognitive interest is
transformed into an accusation . . . in search of a crime to try, a
disgrace to report, a secret to violate'.[2] By this definition, there are
parts of this book that Calvino would see as cursed, in search of
the crime to prosecute. The history of textile production has long
been one of exploitation of the vulnerable. Carpets are associated
with the enormities of war, and the cruelties of the powerful. Their
makers are often refugees or nomads, or groups trying to scrape a
living from fragile ecosystems.

While the crimes, disgraces and secrets are undeniable, they
live alongside the enduringly life-affirming skills, not to mention
the beauty, of the artefacts weavers make. That beauty and skill
echoes evocatively through the old writings of Ibn Battuta and
Al-Tabari, Xenophon and Homer; in the records of less eloquent
early modern figures like Thomas Wolsey and Lorenzo de Medici,
who nevertheless took the trouble to ensure their precious carpets were recorded in detail in their inventories; in the works of
late-nineteenth and early-twentieth-century European and North
American scholars like Wilhelm Bode and Arthur Upham Pope,
who were shocked into lyricism by the unfamiliar loveliness of
old rugs. This book offers a contribution to that long history of
celebration of the beauty of carpets and the skill of their makers.

Chapter 1
Chieftain

KNOTTED-PILE CARPET, THIRD OR FOURTH CENTURY BCE, PLACE OF PRODUCTION UNKNOWN

Twenty-eight horsemen gaze out at us as they troop ceaselessly around the sides of a square textile. A few have been lost in one tattered corner, but the remainder march into our present from their ancient world of clashing weapons, blinding sun reflected from metal, the clamour of adrenaline-fuelled warriors, the savoury perfume of blood. Their formation is disciplined: the men sometimes mounted on the horses in domination, sometimes walking humbly alongside, the horse to the forefront. With their decorative fringed blankets and intricate headgear, the horses are more magnificently attired than their riders. The horsemen have nothing to fear from us, soft products of an easy time. They walk on by with their fierce, unblinking stares.

Close by them, moving in parallel, are rows of deer. These horsemen may be ready for battle, but they are also herders. Their deer are beautiful: tenderly dappled, magnificently antlered. They are transparent, their interiors displayed, X-rayed like animals in the earliest cave paintings.[1] Their liver, lights, heart and reproductive tracts are fully visible, in celebration of all they offer: the nourishment of milk and meat, hide and antlers for protection and materials for art, new life in fawns and calves. There is a powerful connection between the horsemen and the animals whose great hearts and lungs withstood the challenges of travelling long distances in extreme conditions on their behalf, moving to new pastures or riding to war.

The warrior-herders and their animals are hemmed in on all sides by forces they cannot control. On the narrow inner and outer borders are griffins, mythological animals with the heads of eagles, king of birds, and the bodies of lions, king of beasts. Griffins are ancient symbols of majestic authority across civilisations in Asia, but also vibrate with the power of undomesticated nature. At the centre of the rug is a field of stars and crosses, each with a pale dot at its heart and lotus buds at the end of the arms. These motifs connect the rug with ancient religious systems, encountered by its weavers as objects and ideas moved across Eurasia through trade and warfare. The dots are a Central Asian animist symbol dating back to the Neolithic and may represent the sun; the lotus bud is one of the most powerful symbols found across Hinduism, Buddhism and other Asian religions from at least the fifth century BCE. Its many meanings include the womb of the universe. There are powers evoked in this artefact that are greater than man and his actions, but the pulse at the heart of the rug is the intense communion between these ancient horsemen and their beasts.

This evocation of a lost world view and experience was not sculpted or rendered in brushstrokes. It was produced through a far more indirect and unpredictable process. Short lengths of wool were looped around vertical threads strung on a loom, its warps, and secured by beating down horizontal threads, its wefts, to create a velvety surface and a pattern. Each row of multicoloured loops, usually called knots, was only a few millimetres wide and the pattern emerged very slowly, at the rate of a few inches per day. The patient layering of one narrow row of loops on another eventually gave us the indomitable gaze, the slow-moving deer, the grimacing griffon and the harmonious unity of colour and design. This is the creative mystery of the technique of knotted-pile carpet-weaving. It is a mirage created by tiny loops of different-coloured wool or silk.

The colours have faded with time, and the old carpet is only ever photographed under the dimmest of light to protect it from becoming brittle and turning to dust. We must rely on our imagination to see the reds, greens, creams and black of the vegetable and insect dyes as they originally sang out. One of the few living people who has handled the rug, a Russian museum curator, describes it as 'soft and velvety, the wool lustrous and silky'.[2] Despite the physical stresses it has endured in its long life, the lanolin-rich wool has retained its suppleness, and the rug is still an object of deep sensuality.

Despite its age, the physical jolt I felt when I first saw images of this carpet was not because it looks strange and archaic, but because it looks so familiar. Its multiple borders around a central field, its red, green and light-brown wools, its geometric motifs and representations of animals and vegetation are designs and colours continuously used in the carpet-weaving areas of Asia through to modern times. In it, the past speaks to the present in a shared language. This time-travelling rug is known now as the Pazyryk, an almost complete knotted-pile carpet from the fourth-century BCE Iron Age, of greater antiquity than any found before or since. It is a unique and precious clue to the origins of these entrancing artefacts, who made them and who they were made for. But its survival long hung on a thread, and we have it now only by repeated twists of fate.

Pazyryk is on the Ukok plateau of the Great Ulagan plain of the Altai mountains, a poem of names on the far edges of the imagination of people in the West. It is around three hundred miles south-east of Novosibirsk, 'New Siberia', the nearest modern Russian city. Cold and remote, the plateau is 8,000 feet above sea level, and is surrounded by 14,000-foot peaks as high as the summit of the Sierra Nevada in the US and dwarfing Britain's highest mountain, Ben Nevis.

Pazyryk is remote in both space and time. At the edge of the permafrost reaching down from the Arctic, the plateau is the last remaining fragment of the mammoth steppe, the vast and ancient ecology of edible grasses, herbs and shrubs which spread across Eurasia from Spain to China during the last Ice Age, between around one hundred and twenty thousand and eleven thousand years ago. The Ice Age steppe supported woolly mammoth, bison and reindeer. Today the plateau is home to vanishingly rare species like the snow leopard, black stork and steppe eagle, their presence a testament to the region's continued remoteness and lack of human presence. The way in and out is through passes which are recognised as very dangerous even by contemporary enthusiasts for extreme travel, snow-covered and avalanche-prone for most of the year.[3]

It has long been a desolate place. No remains of ancient forts or domestic settlements have ever been found there. But it is home to the dead. Pazyryk was the numinous site chosen for the burial chambers of their royalty by the Scythians, a group of Iron Age tribes found across the steppe from the Black Sea in the west to Siberia in the east between 700 and 200 BCE. The high, windswept plateau was the point of departure into the afterlife of their chieftains and queens.

The spell cast by the Altai mountains of Siberia over Russian archaeologists was as strong as that of Troy over Europeans, and the Lost City of the Incas over North Americans. From the eighteenth century, Russian archaeologists had been excavating burials in the Altai, at the point in the vastness of Central Asia where Russia, China, Mongolia and Kazakhstan converge. But it was not until 1924 that a team from the Russian Museum in Leningrad made the explosive discovery at Pazyryk of five Scythian *kurgans*, ancient barrows or burial mounds, in one of the most important finds in modern archaeology.[4]

The leader of the excavations was Sergei Rudenko, head of ethnography at the museum and a specialist in Siberian societies and cultures. As excavations began in the late 1920s, Rudenko was in his early forties and at the height of his powers as a respected ethnographer. He was a veteran of fieldwork with remote Central Asian tribes and a member of a thriving international community of ethnographers and archaeologists.[5] Rudenko was a scholar-adventurer, switching between the classroom, the museum and the wilderness and its tribes.

Excavating the Pazyryk tombs was a primal encounter with ice and cold. The last snow falls there in mid-June and the first frosts occur in mid-August. Rudenko and his team sheltered in felt tents, the traditional *yurts* (Turkic) or *gers* (Mongolian) of the Altai, during the cold nights of the summer digging season. Earlier archaeologists lit fires on top of frozen tombs to melt the impenetrable ground ice into mud, but Rudenko and his team preferred to pour boiling water over them, in what they saw as a modern improvement.[6] They worked in slush and inhaled the methane smell of ancient vegetation that arises from melted permafrost, as steppe eagles with eight-foot wingspans wheeled above them hoping for pickings. Despite the severity of the environment Rudenko wrote later with lyrical nostalgia of their lonely eyrie, saying: 'In the early spring, when the iris, Altai anemone and campion are flowering, the ground is covered by a blue-grey carpet; in summer the varied steppe-meadow grasses flower luxuriantly.'[7] He even had an evocative phrase for the soil with which they struggled daily: 'Under a thinnish layer of chestnut-coloured humus the bottom of the valley is filled by fine-grained white quartz sands.'[8]

The Altai mountains had been known since ancient times as the mountains of gold, and expectations were high when work began on the Pazyryk burial mounds in 1929. From the early eighteenth century, Scythian digs sponsored by Peter the Great had uncovered glittering gold armour, horse trappings and jewellery combining refined craftsmanship with animal motifs which leap and hunt with the vitality and ferocity of the natural world. Many of these treasures had found their way first to Peter the Great's private cabinet of curiosities and then to the Hermitage Museum in St Petersburg. Pazyryk was not part of these early expeditions and so its barrows were expected to be sealed and their contents intact, but when Rudenko began excavating he found that grave-robbers had already stripped the tombs of all metalwork – even removing the tin and gold foil from decorative motifs on belts and clothing.

The archaeologists were often hungry. It was difficult to sup-plement the provisions they brought with them, as any extra food had to be brought in over dangerous passes. They were always tired in the thin air of the high Altai. The sun beat down during the day as they bent low to the ground under it, picking fragments from the soil. They now had to summon their will and courage to continue in the face of disappointment. But the graverobbers had inadvertently protected even more precious remains than jewellery and gold. When the thieves had opened the tombs, muddy water had poured in, creating a robust seal of yellowish ice.[9] That dirty ice preserved the rarest of archaeo-logical finds: organic matter, including bodies, wood, plants and textiles. The 1929 Pazyryk dig uncovered the bodies of ten horses with their saddles, bridles, blankets and headgear, preserved for two millennia, ready for the chieftain's glorious procession into the afterlife. The remaining Pazyryk mounds promised equally thrilling discoveries. But the geopolitics of the 1930s and 1940s abruptly closed down the excavations at Pazyryk, and for almost twenty years the long silence and emptiness of the royal tombs was restored.

Rudenko did not return to Pazyryk until 1947, by which point he was in his sixties. His youth was gone, but the great adventure which had awaited him so long was finally about to begin. In his scholarly account of the excavation, *The Frozen Tombs of Siberia: The Pazyryk Burials of Iron Age Horsemen*, Rudenko wrote as a disciplined scientist. But we can imagine how profoundly moved he was as he returned to work in the deep chill of the tombs among the flickering lamps and the hushed mutterings of his fellow archaeologists.

His patience was rewarded. The remaining burial mounds yielded up mummified remains of the leaders of Scythian society: their khans, tsars, kings, queens and princesses. Frozen with them were their fine horses and artefacts of wood, horn, leather, fur, felt and woven textile. These were not exclusively homely domestic objects and tools, but included works of great craftsmanship and creative inspiration, chosen by connoisseurs. Their fine artistic qualities could be recognised now that the intruding archaeologists' eyes were not blinded by the glitter of gold. Other traces of the Scythian world were also found, including food, drink, drugs, false hair, tattooing implements and musical instruments. The Scythians were distant in time and place, but shockingly familiar, with their hemp and cheese, their vanity and love of life.

The most remarkable items were found two years into the post-war dig, in *kurgan* (barrow) five, excavated in 1949. A tall, well-built warrior was found alongside what Rudenko called his concubine, a small woman with long brown hair, recognisably a handsome and powerful couple even after almost two and a half thousand years. As the excavation of their rich grave goods progressed, the team found an outer chamber containing the remains of the chieftain's nine horses and their tack, and alongside them a scrunched-up frozen ball. This seemed an unpromising discovery compared to the warrior and his concubine. But the frozen detritus turned out to be the unique object which is now celebrated across the world as the Pazyryk carpet, dating back to at least 300–400 BCE, when the chieftain was interred.

This most ancient of surviving carpets almost never saw the light of day. The period between 1929 and 1947, when the Pazyryk excavations were closed, was a time of the utmost jeopardy for Russian archaeologists. In 1929 Rudenko had faced down nature and graverobbers to open up the past at Pazyryk. But he could not face down the Russian politics of the 1930s, or the impact of global war in the 1940s.

After the 1917 Bolshevik Revolution, Rudenko, like many other

Russian scholars, was gradually separated from his international intellectual community and instead had to work within a Russian echo chamber, negotiating the ideological demands of Marxism on ethnography and archaeology.[10] A new government department came into being to supervise these disciplines. The Institute for the History of Material Culture was named by Lenin himself to emphasise Marxism's central belief in historical materialism, the idea that the ultimate cause of historical change is a struggle driven by economic pressures among social classes. The pre-revolutionary archaeology which focused strongly on objects belonging to elites was to be replaced in the USSR by an archaeology which would focus on the social relations of the proletariat. This was a very difficult agenda for Rudenko to satisfy. No humble settlements have ever been found in the Pazyryk valley. His excavations uncovered exceptional artefacts in the graves of wealthy and powerful chieftains. The Pazyryk valley was the sacred burial ground of kings, where they met eternity not in company with the proletariat but with eagles, snow leopards and solitude – and with their royal treasure.

Alongside this remodelling of prehistory, archaeologists and ethnologists also faced the challenge of Soviet ideas about nationalism and ethnicity. Marxism-Leninism believed that socialism was international, not bound by nation states. But as the fledgling USSR came under threat internally and from other European and Asian powers, nationalism and the idea of a pure shared ethnicity reaching into prehistory became important to the state. Again, Rudenko was in trouble. The Scythians had been claimed by eighteenth- and nineteenth-century Russian archaeologists as Slavs, and hence the 'little brothers' of Russians, as Stalin had it. But at the time of Rudenko's excavation, scholars believed that Scythians were likely Iranian in origin.[11] Meanwhile it was clear from artefacts in the tombs that Scythians had travelled, fought, traded and married across thousands of miles of steppe, picking up and incorporating influences as they moved. They were very much the product of cultural and ethnic exchange, rather than being a pure bloodline. The USSR's insular, Slavic-Russian focus was as difficult for Rudenko to fulfil as its emphasis on the social and economic lives of ordinary folk. His position, like those of many of his archaeological colleagues, was becoming precarious.

In 1929, Rudenko was at work excavating Pazyryk barrow one with his colleague Sergei Teploukhov and his Siberian student Mikhail Gryaznov, in the high and empty Ulagan plateau surrounded by the Altai mountain peaks, almost two thousand miles away from the political hotbed of Moscow.[12] The excavation of other enticing barrows lay ahead of them. But the tectonic plates of history were shifting, and as the archaeologists carried out their delicate work of recovery, Stalin was consolidating his position on the ruling committee of the Communist Party. In 1929 he became, in effect, dictator, and soon began the purges of non-conforming elements in Russian society which eventually became the Great Terror. The impact on Rudenko's intellectual community was immediate. Collaboration with overseas scholars, particularly those from then-enemy Germany, was forbidden. Russian archaeologists were arrested as spies and enemies of the state, and many perished. Historian of Russian archaeology Leo Klejn lists nine of the dead, with the caveat that there were many more.[13] More than fifty curators at the Hermitage Museum were deported or executed in the early 1930s.[14] In 1929, the scholarly archaeologists far away in the Altai mountains were about to be denounced by Komsomol, the influential youth wing of the Communist Party, as 'enemies of the people' and 'wreckers' of the Soviet dream.[15]

Rudenko had the double misfortune of being born in both interesting times and an interesting geography. He was from Russian Kharkov, currently Ukrainian Kharkiv, bitterly disputed throughout the twentieth century by nationalists of various stripes. The forced collectivisation of Ukrainian agriculture between 1928 and 1933 and the subsequent devastating famines known to history as the Holodomor, the Hunger-Death, had inflamed Ukrainian nationalism. Consequently, Ukrainian intellectuals were under suspicion. Rudenko was arrested in 1933, accused of setting up an underground Ukrainian nationalist organisation, and for 'pointless investigations and ethnographic idealism' at Pazyryk.[16]

He was set to work digging Stalin's notorious White Sea Canal to join the Arctic and Baltic Seas, a high-profile component of the first Soviet Five Year Plan. One hundred thousand political prisoners from the gulags dug the canal by hand, an estimated twenty-five thousand of whom died. Meanwhile Rudenko's student Gryaznov was exiled internally, accused of being an underground fascist working with Ukrainian and Russian nationalists. Gryaznov's sentence was reduced when, after eleven interrogations, he finally gave information against Rudenko. The third Pazyryk archaeologist, Sergei Teploukhov, committed suicide in prison.[17]

Rudenko and Gryaznov seemed lost to their families, to archaeology and to the world, as tragic Teploukhov was. A fragment in this landscape of loss, the Pazyryk carpet and the other extraordinary grave goods in the barrows looked set to remain locked in the ice of their underground darkness. All were victims of a profound ideological struggle about the nature of the past, the present and the future.

But history is a complex and unpredictable system. As a result of his work on the frozen burials, Rudenko deeply understood ice, and this knowledge saved his career and his life despite the tightening of Stalin's grip. Rudenko's useful skills were recognised as he dug Stalin's canal in the Arctic Circle. He was promoted and, to some degree, protected. During the intense suffering of the siege of Leningrad by German forces between 1941 and 1944, as the city's population gradually died from starvation, the archaeologist joined 'The Road of Life', the team that supplied the besieged city across frozen Lake Ladoga. Rudenko was responsible for ice forecasts indicating when it was safe for heavy sleds loaded with food to move across the lake.[18] An agitprop poster for the White Sea Canal construction had declared, 'Canal army soldier, The heat of your work will melt your prison term!', and for Rudenko, that was one thing Stalin said which proved true. Leo Kleijn knew Rudenko in old age and said: 'This prickly old man with his walrus moustache was a living legend and proof that fate could be resisted.'[19] Just like the carpet, Rudenko was saved by the ice.

When Rudenko returned to Pazyryk in 1947 to continue the excavations, the government ensured that his team included a former member of the Cheka, the earliest form of the Soviet Secret Police, and a member of its replacement, the KGB. The lengths the state was willing to go to control the dangerous archaeologist are striking. Despite this scrutiny, the establishment that had defined the Pazyryk excavations as 'pointless' examples of 'bourgeois ethnographic idealism' and that had threatened to bury forever both the archaeologist and the carpet had shifted its position. The rug would be brought up to the surface of the earth after all and redefined as an icon of the Russian origin story, representing Russia's beginnings in an imagined collective society lost in time.

The Pazyryk carpet's discovery in 1949 overturned mainstream thinking about knotted-pile carpets, which at that time were believed to have reached their artistic peak in urban communities in West Asia – first in Anatolia from around the fourteenth century, then in Iran from around the sixteenth century. This beautiful and sophisticated carpet was more than a thousand years older than the carpets of the Seljuks, Ottomans and Safavids. It proved that by the fourth century BCE, the technology, design structure, palette and motifs of the knotted-pile carpets that we are familiar with now had already been brought to a high level of accomplishment. It is hard not to be struck by a surprised frisson of recognition when first encountering it. The Pazyryk carpet was not the remnant of a rudimentary early stage in carpet-making but the product of a mature art form, and pointed to even more ancient origins for the practice. Controversy began immediately, when one of the greatest twentieth-century Islamic art historians,

Kurt Erdmann, challenged whether the Pazyryk was in fact a knotted-pile carpet at all. In an effort to protect his theory that carpet-making had reached its peak in sixteenth-century CE Iran, Erdmann declared it 'a rug-like textile', describing it as a cousin of velvet with a nap made from loops cut after manufacture, and consequently different design technology. He later acknowledged that the Pazyryk find was a rug, saying ruefully, 'The starting point for my carpet knowledge may well have been disproven.'[20]

As soon as Rudenko discovered it in 1949, commentators focused on where the carpet was made. This was no neutral discussion: the rug's aesthetic and conceptual sophistication was guaranteed to elevate the modern perception of whichever culture could be shown to have produced it. The first hypothesis came from Rudenko himself. Rudenko's sense of the Scythian way of life, their abilities, attitudes and skills was based on his experience as an ethnographer with early-twentieth-century Altai communities, who had not impressed him. Rudenko believed the carpet was beyond the craft skills of such semi-nomadic unlettered folk, and that it must have been made much further west in Iran, among what he regarded as more highly developed settled communities whose weaving traditions were described in ancient textual records.[21]

He backed this up with an analysis of the motifs in the carpet, which he identified as being reminiscent of the ornamental style of the Persian Achaemenids. This early Persian Empire, in power between 550 and 300 BCE, was one of the great forces of Eurasia and fought, traded and exchanged ideas with Scythian tribes. Rudenko proposed that the Pazyryk carpet was woven in a settled Iranian workshop either as an export carpet made for trade, a diplomatic gift, or a commission by the Scythian chieftain. He ruled out the idea that the carpet could have been made by the people who buried it, semi-nomadic horse-herders with apparently no written history or literature. He held this position even though he himself had unearthed many examples of the highly evolved material culture archaeologists now call the 'Scythian triad': superb horse trappings, finely wrought weapons and metalwork, and animal designs so vivid they seem to graze, leap, fight and kill before us.[22] He also put to one side the long history of exchange of ideas and artefacts across Eurasia, which continues to make it difficult to pinpoint the origin of a particular design.

Rudenko's account of the Pazyryk makes the same assumptions that we will see repeatedly in this book about the environments and makers deemed appropriate for the production of great carpets. While modern carpet specialists recognise the weaving skills of both wandering pastoral peoples and settled rural communities (often describing their products as 'tribal' and 'village' rugs respectively), there is less willingness to see these weavers as the makers of the great named carpets associated with both religious and secular empires. Carpet specialists are sometimes disturbed by the paradox that the practice of weaving – an ancient and basic craft form practised by the humble, poor and illiterate, many of them women – has produced some of the world's great emblems of political, military, financial and cultural success, among which are remarkable works of art. Specialists often prefer to situate the production of such iconic carpets in environments which they consider more evolved, such as urban workshops or the ateliers of the wealthy and powerful. They hold to this even though the materials and equipment of carpet-weaving – fibres like wool, dyes from boiled plants and insects, and the simple frame of the loom – are common to weavers in tents, villages, workshops and studios.

Buried under these assumptions about carpets is the ancient conflict between the settled and the nomadic. The start of human settlement ten thousand years ago in the Neolithic period saw an existential struggle begin between settled farmers, seen as legitimate targets for plunder after their appropriation of previously shared territory and resources, and wandering nomads, seen as savage raiders unsettling the possibility of progress.[23] Records tend to be kept by the settled, and the midnight terrors of settled storytelling are often nomads: Goths, Huns, Mongols,

North American indigenous peoples. This fundamental conflict arises from the profound suspicion among people who
stay in one place about people who, out of choice or necessity,
move, whether they are called pastoralists, nomads, gypsies,
invaders, migrants, refugees or rough sleepers. The shadow of
this conflict is always present in a history told through carpets.
Neither Rudenko nor many of the specialists who examined the
Pazyryk carpet after its discovery were disposed to see this elite
and refined artefact, the prized possession of a powerful Iron
Age chieftain, as the product of semi-nomadic tribes who spent
their lives harrying the settled world and providing it with its
monsters.

This left the field open for commentators to choose their preferred geography for the origins of the enigmatic and beautiful
carpet, representative of an art form which must have already
been fully developed two and a half thousand years ago. Along
with Rudenko, many within the European and North American
tradition of carpet studies claimed it for Iran. The academic
tradition, which had developed from the mid-nineteenth century
onwards, consistently held Iran as an imagined homeland of all
that is great in carpet-making. These scholars backed the settled,
cultivated, literate and courtly society of the Persian Achaemenid
Empire as either the carpet's place of production, or the place
where its design originated.[24]

For Russians, the carpet had and continues to have more
explosive potential, as an emblem of their imagined Scythian
ethnic origins. The question of where and by whom it was made
was literally much closer to home. Mikhail Gryaznov, the Pazyryk
archaeologist who in the 1930s had been forced to buy his freedom
from Stalin's interrogators by denouncing Rudenko, suggested
Turkmenia (modern Turkmenistan) as the source of the carpet.[25]
When Gryaznov suggested this Turkmenia was still part of the
USSR, and he was in effect claiming the Pazyryk for Russia.
His suggestion for the rug's provenience has a strong rationale:
Turkmen are still prodigious rug-weavers, and Bronze Age rug

knives excavated in Turkmenistan attest to the longevity of carpet-weaving in the area.[26]

The carpet is now housed in the Hermitage Museum. In their 2022 online catalogue entry, the museum's curators, who live both alongside the carpet and within Russian culture, offer a nuanced and understated version of this same story, marginalising Iranian influence and placing the carpet's makers in Central Asia:

> The exact origin of this unique carpet is unknown. There is a version of its Iranian provenance. But perhaps it was produced in Central Asia through which the contacts of ancient Altaians with Iran and the Near East took place.[27]

A broader church of imaginative enthusiasts takes the story in some surprising directions, demonstrating the malleability of this enigmatic object. In 2004, Bevis Longstreth, a successful corporate lawyer and trustee of the Textile Museum, Washington, read the carpet's motifs through the filter of Judaic numerology, and suggested that itinerant Jewish weavers moving from Anatolia to Central Asia could be the makers of the Pazyryk. In 2005 he published a novel based on this research,[28] inventing Rachael, a beautiful Jewish weaver from the Persian settlement of Sardis in what is now Anatolia. Rachael fell in love with the fictional Targitus, a muscular and tattooed Scythian warrior, and eloped with him across the Caucasus and steppe to the Altai mountains, where she wove a fabulous carpet. Once again, the story circumvents the idea that the Pazyryk was made by the nomads who buried it or by others of their kin.

The fragmentary nature of the evidence, and the heavy reliance on received wisdom in biographies of the Pazyryk carpet mean we can't say positively who made it. We can, however, remind ourselves of some objections to the prevailing view. Central Asian nomads have for centuries been among the world's great carpet-weavers. It seems from finds of Bronze Age weaving implements in the Murghab region of Southern Turkmenistan that they had the skill early. And while the carpet's motifs may indeed be reminiscent of Achaemenid ornament, the long history of movement across Eurasia undermines the idea of a single place of origin for a design. Transfer and mixing are fundamental characteristics of the continent-wide grass corridor of the steppe. For millennia, people have moved across it for war and trade, carrying objects, ideas and technology with them. The Scythians might have dipped independently into the rich shared ornamental heritage of Eurasia, rather than copying a Persian model or simply buying an Iranian carpet. Nevertheless, carpet specialists continue to entertain themselves by debating whether the animals on the Pazyryk carpet are Siberian reindeer and elks or Iranian fallow deer, and whether Scythians always rode with saddles and the Iranians always bareback like the riders in the Pazyryk carpet. In addition to this fog of interpretations, scientists find it difficult to isolate specific Iron Age wool or dye types from Iran, Central Asia or Siberia which might settle the matter. Analyses describe the Pazyryk's yarn only as 'primitive hairy wool',[29] and there is no definitive proof as to whether the dyes were shared Eurasian types or if they were made from specific steppe plants and insects.[30] Meanwhile, the Pazyryk is more than a thousand years older than any confirmed Iranian carpet in existence, so we simply have nothing to compare it with.

The struggle for ideological and emotional ownership of the Pazyryk carpet continues, but Ludmila Barkova, former curator of Scythian treasures at the Hermitage Museum, calls for a broader perspective, honouring the makers rather than undermining the claims of some in favour of others:

The exact place of manufacture of the Pazyryk carpet is perhaps not as important as the fact that the pile carpet technique developed so early and spread so rapidly throughout the nomadic civilisations of the steppe corridor, reaching a very high level of sophistication comparable to the greatest woven masterpieces of more recent times.[31]

Modern commentators may fight over what kind of deer, what kind of wool, whether nomads had the necessary skills, but somewhere in Asia, around two and a half thousand years ago, perhaps during the dark winter season when outdoor activities slowed, a group of people – almost certainly women with exceptional skills developed from childhood experience weaving alongside their mothers, as they do to this day – produced a remarkable artefact. They worked from imagination, memory, drawings, or other carpets, in a tent, log cabin or brick workshop. They lived simply, somewhere on the margins of the world of politics and conquest, and left no personal traces. But their carpet found its way to the chieftain of a nomadic empire and became part of the celebration of the horses that were at the centre of his culture and life.

The chieftain found in Pazyryk barrow five alongside the woman now known as his concubine was around fifty-five years old at the time of his death, five feet nine inches tall, well muscled and with black wavy hair.[32] He had the physical charisma and strength required of a tribal leader who ruled by might. His body had been decorated with tattoos, possibly to indicate nobility and courage, possibly to offer him supernatural protection in battle.[33] They had been created by sewing or pricking soot into his skin during his youth. The tattoos now lay under the fat of a lifetime. This refined body art was found on many of the warrior men and women preserved in the Pazyryk barrows. It used motifs of the animals with whom they shared their lives – horses, deer, hares, domestic fowl and birds of prey – and those which haunted their dreams – tigers and wolves. Some were composite fantasy animals with the hooves of horses, the talons of eagles and the heads of leopards, which embodied the strength, cunning and danger of all.[34] The chieftain in barrow five wore earrings and was clean-shaven, although carefully dyed and constructed false beards were found in the barrows. The smaller female body with long, fine chestnut hair lay alongside him, both their faces to the

west, where the sun sets and where we assume the Scythians believed the afterlife lay. Rudenko's archaeological reports describe
him as Mongoloid and her as Caucasian, using the peculiar ethnic
terminology inherited from nineteenth-century European racial
theory. This difference between them continues to intrigue and
even titillate commentators.[35] She is described in the literature
as his concubine, on the assumption that his wife would have
lived to marry another senior member of the chieftain's family. The concubine gave her life to be the chosen companion of
this tall, dark, powerful man with his many horses, before and
after death.

The carpet was not found in the intimate joint grave of the
chieftain and his concubine, but in the separate burial chamber
of the horses. Almost square, the rug measures seventy-two by
seventy-eight inches (one hundred and eighty-three by two hundred centimetres) and the archaeological guess is that it was the
chieftain's horse cover, visible beneath his rudimentary Scythian
saddle. Its iconography, colours and sheer glamour would identify
the chieftain to the rest of the tribe as he herded their horses across
the steppe or galloped into battle. The carpet was the artefact of
the public man, the powerful leader and warrior, not of the private
man and lover.

The burial mounds at Pazyryk were built over the course of
fifty years in the fourth century BCE for three generations of the
leaders of a tribal confederation, a group of tribes which would
mobilise if under military threat or if new territory were needed
for their herds. Although the Altaic Scythian tribes also reared
sheep, goats and yaks, horse-breeding and horse-herding were at
the heart of their specialised form of semi-nomadic pastoralism.
They were economically outward-looking, trading animal pelts
and their highly prized horses for export goods like oil-rich
coriander seeds and lustrous Chinese silks along what came to be
known as the silk and fur routes.

Nomadic steppe peoples who bred and herded horses from
the Black Sea to the borders of China are described in Caucasian
folk histories from the seventh century BCE, and associated with

archaeological remains from the ninth century BCE onwards.³⁶
By the fourth century BCE, the Central Asian Scythians who
buried their dead at Pazyryk were no longer fully nomadic. Their
environment supported their grazing needs comfortably enough
for them to live in settlements of log cabins, and while herders
sometimes moved animals to new grazing sites, the community
no longer needed to practise the intricate ecological management
which required the transhumance of entire populations of no-
mads.³⁷ On the other hand, they were not a settled culture. They
did not farm and instead fought for grazing territory and animals.
Basing his observation on ethnographic work with Central Asian
nomads in the nineteenth century, Sergei Rudenko asserted that
'driving off cattle was not regarded as a felony, and rustling
was regarded as a special kind of profession'.³⁸ The perceived
disregard for the farmer's view of property by nineteenth-
century nomads was transferred by Rudenko to fifth-century
BCE Scythians. He may well have been right. Throughout recorded history, the conflict between land as individual property
and land as a common good has been widely observed, and
continues into the present day. It is one of the deeply embedded
causes of the antipathy between nomads and settled peoples the
world over.
    Rudenko suggests that in peacetime the life of a Scythian
warrior was an indolent one, given over to play fights, hunting
for pleasure, gaming, drinking and getting high. Certainly, the
remains of cannabis – in the form of burned hemp seeds – and
of fermented mare's milk were found in the Pazyryk tombs. But
even the rigorous Rudenko was susceptible to the construction
of stories which supported his own preconceptions. His account
of the social life of the ancient Scythians was coloured by his
fieldwork with Altai men of his own time, and by a scholarly and
possibly wider prejudice against them. Vasily Radlov, director of
the Russian Museum of Ethnography and the man who revolutionised the Russian study of Central Asia in the later nineteenth
century, is reported to have said that the men of the Altai were
in a constant state of either 'getting drunk or being drunk'.³⁹ The

lives of Scythian women on the other hand seem to have been highly active. Weapons were found in the burial mounds of high-status Scythian women. Women may have played a role in both government and war. They may also have been among the craftspeople carving wood and bone, and smithing gold. They were certainly tattoo artists and their tools were buried with them. This would, of course, be alongside their relentless and gruelling domestic responsibilities of child-bearing and -rearing, caring for animals, cooking, cleaning, nursing. Scythian women also shared the pleasures of Scythian men, if the hemp found in their tombs is anything to judge by.

Despite the great emphasis on gold in lore about the Scythians and the awe-inspiring gold artefacts discovered in some previously excavated Scythian tombs, they were an Iron Age people. The new iron weapons made and used from around 700 BCE were invaluable for the Scythians, who were constantly scrapping for grazing rights and seeing off large-scale settled armies like those of the Persians. The chieftains of Pazyryk had six-foot-long spears tipped with iron, iron swords, and arrows with iron barbs which they shot from technologically advanced composite bows of wood and gut. They fought with these menacing weapons at high speed from horses that DNA research has shown were among the strongest then available. They were mostly black or dark brown, colours traditionally associated with the hard hoofs necessary in a society that did not shoe its horses. When an army faced the Scythians they faced a huge, fast-moving cavalry with glittering gold armour and fearsome iron weapons, mounted on dark horses, roaring across the steppe.

Combat, victory, revenge and death were at the centre of Scythian culture and its art (although art may not have been a concept for them). While their artefacts draw on a shared Eurasian aesthetic vocabulary of naturalistic and mythological animals, they have a distinctive and brutal Scythian twist, evoking a fearful and bloody natural world where carnivores leap on herbivores, prey hangs from the mouth of predators, the strong destroy the weak. The visceral impact of Scythian animal motifs is intensified by a surreal distortion which arose as craftspeople applied them to strangely shaped objects like buckles, bridles, sword belt holders, arrowheads or as tattoos to their living human hands. As well as gold, tin and other metals, they worked their strange bestiary on felt and textiles, wood, bone, lacquer and dead human skin, which, ancient observers reported, 'is thick, and has a tremendous sheen, more brilliant, and whiter than almost any other kind of skin'.[40]

Archaeologists suggest that this art of violent animal combat allowed nomadic makers and their audiences to explore the idea of rebirth through death, in the threatening world where they lived.[41] The Pazyryk carpet stands apart from this conjuring of darkness before the return of light. Instead, it is a poised and calm celebration of the duality of the life shared by the warrior-herder and his animals. The horsemen and their steeds are prepared, well equipped, in motion but not in battle. Only the tattered corner of the carpet is wounded, not the fighters. The well-fleshed deer with their healthy internal organs graze securely in their environment. The mysteries which surround them, in the form of griffins, sunspots and lotus buds, are benign invocations of royal authority and the fecundity of nature. The Pazyryk chieftain went out into the world seated on an evocation of the success of his way of life.

And that is all we know. The Scythians left no texts. The best recorded insight we have into their social and imaginative world is the *Legend of the Narts*, the origin story of their north Caucasian cousins, the Ossetians.[42] This imagining of the heroes, witches, and fever-dream beasts of the steppe is believed to date from between the seventh and fifth centuries BCE, an oral tradition first recorded – and inevitably distorted – in the nineteenth century.

But as early as the fourth century BCE, when the chieftain in barrow five acquired the Pazyryk carpet to demonstrate his identity as a cultural, political and military leader, commentators from other societies were already at work defining an outsider's idea of a Scythian. They wrote in what is sometimes called the Axial Age, the period between 500 and 300 BCE which produced some of the world's great religions, alongside, it is suggested, a dawning of human self-awareness.[43] The idea of 'Scythian' was defined at a time of intense intellectual and spiritual exploration, when the creation and solidification of group identities was of great importance. In the absence of written records by Scythians themselves, an imagined composite came into being, from histories composed by writers in settled societies.

The most enduring invented Scythian is that imagined by the fifth-century BCE Turkish-born Greek historian Herodotus. His Greece was a constellation of cities orbiting the Athens of Pericles, still regarded as a triumph of human civilisation. The Greeks' strong sense of identity and exceptionalism was reinforced by the attacks they faced down from intimidating enemies like the Spartans and the Persians, and by their sharp awareness of the threat from nomadic peoples across Eurasia.[44] Herodotus turned his mind to the strangeness and terror of the world surrounding the small, vulnerable Greek republic. He was particularly compelled by the Scythians, who, although barbarian nomads, had, like the Greeks, held back the mighty Achaemenid Persian Empire.

Herodotus wrote from his usual pose of the even-handed scholar, balancing multiple sources, including what he claims were first-hand experiences travelling among Scythians living around the Black Sea. But his neutrality was a performance. Doubt was cast on his histories by his contemporary Thucydides (b. 460 BCE), then a century later by the great Aristotle (b. 384 BCE), and persisted for half a millennium until the first century CE, when he was called 'the father of lies' by Plutarch (b. 46 CE).* In the late 1970s an article in *Harvard Studies in Classical Philology* entitled

---

* While it is an amusing parlour game to collect insults against Herodotus, he has a number of defenders among modern historians.

'Did Herodotus ever go to the Black Sea?' reached the conclusion that 'Either he did go and remained content to give readers what they expected to hear in the first place even though it was not true, or he did not go at all.'[45]

Herodotus' Scythians came from the same imaginary landscape as *The Legend of the Narts.* He was drawing from a rich brew of hearsay and legends regarding not only Scythians and Ossetians, but Issedonians, Alans, Samartians, Massagetae and 'Bald People' (probably Mongols) from across the Caucasus and Central Asia. Into the mix went his Amazons, mythical one-breasted female warriors who may have been an echo of the fighting women of the Scythians, whose weapons were buried with them in their tombs.

In fourteen chapters of Book Four of his *Histories*, five pages in a modern paperback,[46] Herodotus offers us Scythians who wear cloaks made from the scalps of their enemies, drink blood out of those same enemies' skulls, feast on casseroles of the remains of their chieftain's body mixed with animal meat. He describes elaborate ritual strangling of animals and humans, and the punishment of false soothsayers by being burned alive. A few pages earlier he gives us the blinding of slaves to stop them stealing the cream from the top of the mare's milk, and the practice of blowing into a mare's vagina with a bone reed to facilitate milking.[47] He conjures a death cult where tribesmen who had failed to kill during the year were excluded from communal rites and shamed, and sexual practices where women were shared. His Scythians are drinkers and smokers of cannabis, which he tells us 'makes the Scythians howl with delight'.[48] Archaeologists have discovered enough evidence in the Pazyryk tombs for some of these elaborate stories to stick, and Herodotus' savage Scythians have come down through history. It is only with some effort that we recover the careful horse-herders with their deep understanding of the resources and environment of the steppe, their taste for beautiful metalwork, carvings, felts and carpets, and their exceptional craft skills.

Herodotus' evocation of a gore-fest has stuck for more than

two millennia, but his writing also relishes much that is Scythian - their highly evolved material culture, their kings and complex social system, their sophisticated technology, with its wheeled carts and innovative weapons. The military historian in him, as opposed to the mythographer, researched and recounted their battle tactics in some detail. He enthused about the Scythian manoeuvre of pretending to retreat in disarray, then reassembling to face down the enemy's disorderly chase. His Scythians are often tricksters, gleefully pulling the wool over the eyes of the Persians.

Herodotus' Scythians were also sexy. He was strongly impressed by the Scythian look, from the infamous cloaks of scalps to his lubricious account of the cleaning rituals of Scythian women involving a paste of cypress, cedar and frankincense spread over their bodies and left for a day: 'Not only does this endow them with a delicious scent, but it leaves them cleansed and gleaming.'[49] He seems not to have been the only one to register the sex appeal of both male and female Scythians. Glamorous Scythian warriors were found on Athenian pottery in their slender, close-fitting armour and dress. It is still easy to be enticed by accounts and representations of their tight fur trousers, short kaftans covered with leather plaques gilded with metal foil, and extravagant wooden millinery carrying bird and animal forms. Their tattooed legs and the soft boots covering them were decorated with the same motifs.[50] The griffins, horses and elks on the Pazyryk carpet were among them, alongside the ferocious Scythian reworking of an animal vocabulary shared across Eurasia.

The Scythians we inherit from Herodotus are a potent combination of creativity, slyness, beauty, sensuality, courage, intellect, savagery and ferocity. In the words of historian François Hartog, 'The Athenian, that imaginary settled being, had need of an equally imaginary nomad. The Scythian conveniently fitted the bill.'[51] They had become the buried id to the Greeks' morally controlling superego. As this invented Scythian gradually penetrated European consciousness, the Pazyryk chieftain slept on, and his carpet lay discarded in a dark corner of his tomb.

These imagined Scythians, who have left us their hoards of gold and horse trappings, their furs and intricate artefacts carved from bone, horn, wood and metal, their body art and their felts and carpets, have continued to be a powerful instrument of identity formation into the modern world. Their artefacts are still in play and at risk.

Although there is no clear historical or archaeological line of descent linking Russians, Slavs and Scythians, the Janus-like Scythians, at once dark and glittering, nomadic and yet deeply connected to Siberia and the steppe, were part of the idea of Russia from the eighteenth century, and became integral to Soviet identity from the very beginnings of the Bolshevik Revolution. In 1917, as the First World War continued to rage, the fragile new Russian government sued for peace with Germany and the Central Powers. The Germans negotiated aggressively with a weakened Russia, demanding it give up Ukraine and the Baltic states. In January 1918, the Russian poet Aleksander Blok wrote one of his most famous poems in response to the confusion and pain these negotiations caused in a Russia whose identity was already vulnerable. In 'The Scythians', Blok issued a warning to Europe that Russia was an Asian as well as a European power, and called up the Scythians as a reminder of that latent Asian power:

You are but millions. Our unnumbered nations
Are as the sands upon the sounding shore.
We are the Scythians! We are the slit-eyed Asians!
Try to wage war with us – you'll try no more![52]

Blok's Scythians borrow heavily from Herodotus; 'we love raw flesh, its colour and its stench', 'we know how to play the cruel game of breaking in the most rebellious steeds and stubborn captive maids', 'we call you to the ritual feast and fire'. The long-dead tribespeople are the most profound symbolic threat Blok can summon to warn the European powers against messing with Russia. It is not the sophisticates of Leningrad, the politicos of Moscow, or even the regular European-style Russian military who will mobilise to protect the motherland, Blok tells us, but numberless tribes from the East, whom he has condensed into one invented nomad, the Scythian.

This appropriation of the idea of the Scythian continues into contemporary Russian politics. After the collapse of the Soviet Union in 1991 and the loss of its European and Central Asian Soviet satellite states, two-thirds of the territory of the new Russian state lay in the permafrost of the Arctic.[53] It had become a northern nation. As post-Soviet Russia struggled for a new identity, a northern origin story developed among a loose network of nationalists, amateur historians and the Russian press. Its central assertion was that the source of all Eurasian cultures lay in a prehistoric Slav-Aryan population which had moved south from the Arctic.[54] In this story, steppe pastoralists – and most importantly the Scythians – were the forebears of the Slavs and consequently progenitors of the whole of civilisation. They were, however, transformed in the twentieth-century Russian populist imagination from Blok's 'slit-eyes Asians' into blond, blue-eyed Aryans. Siberia and its Scythians returned to the centre of Russian national identity.

The power of the Scythian story in Russian political life is demonstrated by images released by the Kremlin in 2009 of President Vladimir Putin's holidays during the short, intense Siberian summer. Published in the state-run tabloid RIA Novosti, they show Putin riding horseback and bare-chested by Lake Baikal, the heart of Scythian territory, and spearing pike in Lake Tuva, less than a hundred miles from Pazyryk. The oldest Scythian sites so far identified are at Tuva, dating back to the ninth century BCE, and back up folklore suggesting it was the origin place of the Scythians.[55] The images represent Putin as a virile leader, a man of stratagems and guile, a warrior and hunter, the protector of a great culture with its roots in the Arctic North. He is our Pazyryk chieftain made new.

The objects made by these idealised ancestors are of great value to the regimes which use them for identity formation. The museums in which they are preserved are active rather than passive agents in the creation of national stories, and museum curators and their collections are consequently at significant risk. The Scythian collections in Russia's museums are highly prized, but Ukraine also has a well-established Scythian prehistory, and great collections of Scythian finds in its museums illustrating that past. Indeed, some Ukrainian populists have their own variant of the Scythians-as-the-progenitors-of-civilisation story, although for them the diaspora expands from the Urals out into the rest of Eurasia, rather than from the Arctic.[56] But in 2022, the precious Scythian antiquities in Ukrainian museums moved out of the world of myth-making and fantasy into realpolitik, becoming participants in Ukraine's defence against the Russian invasion. The UK's *Guardian* reported that Scythian objects in Ukrainian museums had been seized in large quantities by Russian soldiers as spoil. The director of the museum in Kharkiv, birthplace of Sergei Rudenko, explained to the paper that curators across Ukraine were sleeping alongside their Scythian artefacts to protect them. When confrontations finally broke out between museum staff and the Russian military, two curators in Kharkiv died defending their treasures.[57] Contemporary Ukrainian curators now brave the fallout of revolution and war, just as Rudenko and his team had done a century earlier – tenacious scholars facing the rage of those modern chieftains, Vladimir Putin and Joseph Stalin.

For the time being, the Pazyryk carpet is protected from this turbulence. The gilded and pastel beauty of Peter the Great's Winter Palace is home to the most prestigious galleries in Russia's most prestigious museum, the Hermitage. The museum contains glamorous Scythian finds from Central Asian tombs, and first among equals is the unique carpet from Pazyryk barrow five. Even in that environment of past luxury and historic drama, and under the dim and unrevealing light museums use to preserve precious textiles, the drab and tattered six-foot-square carpet inspires awe.

It communicates with us across twenty-three centuries, evoking the life of a nomadic tribal leader and the woman who shared her life with him, the jeopardy endured by people who work to preserve human heritage in turbulent political times, and above all, the women who spun, dyed, designed and wove this outstanding piece of Iron Age art.

Chapter 2
Sultan

KNOTTED-PILE CARPET, SIXTEENTH
CENTURY CE, WEST ASIA OR
NORTH AFRICA

I had ordered up a rare old rug from its nest in a Glasgow store-room. Normally protected by darkness, it was briefly exposed to the bright light of a conservation studio. Unrolling it on an examination table seemed an intrusion into its privacy, and a step into the unknown. No one had touched this carpet for seven years,[1] but now I felt its crumbly fringes, its dry wool. I tentatively stroked my nitrile-gloved hand across the intertwined mesh of its warps and wefts, revealed to the touch now that the velvety knotted pile had mostly worn away. I smelled the old lanolin of its wool, bosky, sour and un-fresh. Precious carpets are usually protected by the glass of a museum vitrine or seen only in images. They can seem purely visual, like cartoons. Meeting a carpet in person radically tilts perception. This rug insisted to my senses that it was a physical object constructed by human beings a long time ago from the products of nature, not simply an elegant design.

But it is also an elegant design – indeed more than that. The carpet's surface is divided into small compartments, within each of which is an intricately knotted light-blue star with a yellow cross at its heart. Tiny cypress trees and stylised motifs fan out from the central star, each precise and defined when observed close up, but transforming when viewed as a whole. I looked, and as my brain caught up, leaned closer to look again, wondering what I'd actually seen. The carpet seemed to operate in phase space, the multiple resolutions of its pattern somehow all present at once. Such moments of transmutation are not found in the orderly graphic repeats of Anatolian and Central Asian rugs, or the multi-layered and representational designs of Iranian and Mughal Indian carpets, which instead seek to delight us with their clarity and precision.

The palette is red, light blue and turquoise with a little yellow, on first sight the traditional colours of Asian carpets. But here it is used to achieve not the usual sharp contrast which clarifies outlines, but tonal modulations so close and subtle that they tease the eye, dissolving firm boundaries. The diffusing and coalescing palette and phase-space design give a tantalising shimmer to the old carpet. That shimmer does not depend on the luxuriousness of its materials, as does the radiance of silk, but arises from the weavers' inspired management of colour and the tesserae of motifs.

After the long depredations of time, the shimmer conjured by the original weavers of this Glasgow carpet is evanescent. But enough of it remains to show that the rug belongs to a very rare group of carpets which have been keenly desired across Asia and Europe since their making more than six hundred years ago. With an aesthetic impact quite distinct from more familiar Turkish, Persian, South and Central Asian carpets, for more than a century this group of carpets has been the subject of red herrings, scholarly blind alleys and failed attempts to identify them. Where these iridescent carpets were made, who made them and for whom is still a mystery. They are blossoms of a plant which appears to have no roots.

The Glasgow rug is misshapen and patched. Modestly sized at five feet (150 centimetres) long and four feet (120 centimetres) wide, its bottom edge is distorted through centuries of changing humidity, the varying elasticity of its wool stretching and shrinking to different degrees. It had been so badly worn that 20 per cent of its surface has been repaired.² Unprepossessing as it might at first glance seem, the carpet has two kinds of enchantment: the last flickering of that shimmer, and the almost magical skills of the restorers who repaired it so that it seems single and whole.

I gently turned the rug over and gazed meditatively at its back. It became clear as I looked that a quadrant of the carpet had been copied at some point in its history, then cut up and rewoven into the original rug to repair damage. The repair was likely carried out in the late nineteenth or early twentieth century, when museums and collectors grew intensely interested in Asian carpets as artworks, and when a market premium was placed on complete, undamaged carpets.³ On the carpet's front, as expected, I encountered the artisanship and aesthetic vision of its long-dead weavers, but its back presented me with an extra gift: the craft skills and ingenuity of its more recent repairers.

There is criticism now of the over-restoration of old carpets carried out in the late nineteenth and early twentieth centuries. There is an understandable sense that an old object should wear its wounds proudly, rather than be artificially restored to perfection. But rug repair is a remarkable craft in its own right – it is hard enough to weave a new rug, let alone reanimate an old one. Often, restorers simply cut out the damaged section of the original rug, leaving a shortened carpet. But with discerning eyes and trained fingers, the repairers of the Glasgow carpet had woven a replica of a section containing the main components of the rug's design, having calculated that this would give them all the motifs they needed to make the carpet whole. Someone in the team found dye shades and wool of the right texture to match the carpet. The quadrant they constructed was not a copy of the original when it was first produced, with its full pile and newly dyed colours, but of the rug at the stage of wear and fade it had reached by the nineteenth century – a sophisticated application of technical skill which almost defies the imagination of non-weavers. The 'new' patches were then woven invisibly into gaps and holes which were irregular and ragged. Even if rug-repairers can achieve all this, there is often an aspect they can't predict or control – the fading of the dyes they have used for the patching. If the dyes of the patch fade at a different rate to the dyes of the original, over time they become visible. When I encountered the Glasgow carpet in 2023, the patches were visible only from the back. The colour matching of the front was still perfect.

We know a little more about the repairers of these carpets than their invisible weavers. This highly skilled work may have been carried out by artisans in Asia, where carpet-weaving skills were indigenous. It is thought possible, for instance, that the V&A's world-famous Ardabil carpet was repaired in Turkey, rather than the place where it was found and woven (Iran) or the place it now makes its home (the UK).[4] That 'perfecting' also happened in the late nineteenth century. But rug-dealers across a Europe increasingly hungry for fine carpets also set up their own local repair workshops. Indeed, from 1896, an accomplished dealer and restorer had a shop in Sauchiehall Street, Glasgow, six miles away from where I stood looking down at the old carpet.[5]

Victor Behar had emigrated from Istanbul to Scotland in the late nineteenth century.[6] Europe was then a place of commercial opportunity for Turkish rug-dealers, but at home the Turks were suffering political repression, savage victimisation of religious minorities and ethnic cleansing as the Ottoman Empire moved towards its bloody and difficult end. Not only carpet entrepreneurs but skilled weavers such as Turkey's persecuted Armenians fled or were driven out in huge numbers.[7] An image published around 1912 shows apparently Asian craftswomen, in Eastern dress with their hair covered, at work in Behar's Glasgow workshop. We don't know for sure who repaired the carpet, but they may well have been refugees fleeing to Scotland from persecution three thousand miles away.

Museums usually have more objects than they can display, a phenomenon recently critiqued by sociologist Malcolm Gladwell as 'dragon psychology' – hoarding.[8] As a result of the centuries-long generosity of donors, the choices curators must make about what the public will see are fraught, sometimes with emotion, and sometimes even with conflict. In the 1960s, pre-eminent carpet scholar May Beattie had examined the carpet and recommended that, given its exceptional rarity, it should be moved out of storage and put on display.[9] However, what is conventionally regarded as its poor condition has meant that it has been long assigned to the stores rather than the galleries. Consequently, I had visited the carpet in a warehouse in a wet and windy post-industrial Glaswegian suburb. Leaving the train at a lonely station, I walked across a piece of wasteland pocked with pools of rainwater and passed uneasily under an unlit nineteenth-century railway bridge, finally arriving at the reassuringly well-equipped modern building which is home to the stores of Glasgow's Burrell Collection.

Ten miles away from its store, the display space for the Burrell Collection is in a very different environment: a graceful modernist building butting up against the woods of a large park in the leafy Glasgow suburb of Pollokshaws. In the entrance, tree-dappled light filters through a glass wall on to a life-size fifteenth-century Chinese Luohan, a disciple of Buddha, and inside the museum are examples of what is arguably the most exceptional personal collection of art in Britain, gathered together by Sir William Burrell (1861–1958) and his wife Constance (1875–1961). As visitors move through the elegant, luminous building, they can see examples of the six thousand objects the Burrells gave to the city of Glasgow and its people in 1944, and the more than two thousand they contributed after the gift was made. The limpid spaces are filled with fine paintings from the Dutch Golden Age, French Impressionists and their followers the Glasgow Boys, lucent early Chinese, Japanese and Islamic ceramics, imposing bronzes, and a whole creative world of medieval European tapestries, furniture, sculpture and stained glass. Alongside them are great examples of carpet art, ravishing and in pristine condition.

Burrell is now regarded as one of the great modern carpet connoisseurs. One dimly lit room contains the world-famous Wagner

Garden Carpet, woven in seventeenth-century Iran during the culturally glorious period of the Safavid emperors. It depicts a garden in paradise, its explosion of birds, animals, butterflies, trees and blossom made orderly by the water channels that segment it. Lulled by this vision of paradise, visitors walking a couple of metres around the corner move from heaven to hell as they encounter a group of equally exceptional but grotesque animal carpets, made in northern India and Afghanistan in the late sixteenth century under the Mughal Empire. In these rugs fantasy animals hang from the mouths of other nightmare beasts in disturbing chains, perhaps being devoured, perhaps mating, perhaps being born.

We don't know when Burrell bought the shimmering carpet now banished to the storerooms – object number 9-67 – or what he thought he was buying. This is a piece of bad luck, as Burrell was meticulous in keeping orderly and unusually complete purchase books. These, along with his extensive correspondence, are a remarkable resource for researchers, although, as it turned out, not for me. He began collecting in the last decades of the nineteenth century but did not begin keeping his purchase books until 1911. Carpet 9-67 is not mentioned in the purchase books, so it was most likely bought before 1911. Even if Burrell's records of the purchase had survived, carpet scholarship in the West was still in its infancy in the late nineteenth and early twentieth centuries, so he may have known little about it to pass on to us.

However, we know a good deal about Burrell as a man, a collector and a major shipping magnate in the great imperial port of Glasgow. It's possible to reconstruct the frame of mind in which he might have approached the purchase of 9-67. Burrell was not a collector outwardly possessed by sweaty lust for artefacts. He was a cool customer and liked to keep a low profile. He did his research. Robert Lorimer, Burrell's friend and architect, accompanied him on his exhaustive and exhausting shopping trips in the art centres of Europe. Burrell came armed with a list of all the antique shops in the towns they visited, which he systematically ticked off. He visited local museums and galleries to understand the art-historical context.[10] His library at the Burrell Archive contains the wide range of texts he consulted, a thorough representation of the aesthetic thinking of the time, which bear his hand annotations. On the day I visited the stores, I had to be gently separated from Burrell's notes in Arthur Upham Pope's seminal works on Persia's carpets, so that the curator had time to show me more of her treasures. Burrell was a tough negotiator in a tough business, shipping, and he transferred that skill into his collecting. Eminent art historian Kenneth Clark remembered: 'His stories of how he outwitted art dealers are too numerous to be repeated; but the funny thing is that they rather liked him. He was playing their game, and they knew where he stood.'[11] Presbyterian, Northumbrian-born and Glasgow-raised, he was the definition of hard-headed.

But this should not be taken to mean that he was cautious. On the contrary, he was audacious. Burrell was the third generation of a shipping dynasty in Glasgow. When he joined the company in 1876, it had only seven ocean-going tramp steamers. Making bold commercial judgements, by 1885 William and his brother George had built Burrell's into a world leader in shipping, supporting Britain's huge international extractive and trading empire.[12] Tough and driven mercantilists like Burrell delivered the British imperial project quite as much as did soldiers and government officials.[13] The source of the wealth that empowers collectors is rarely innocent.

Burrell was a substantial spender. At the peak of his buying in 1936, he purchased £7 million ($9 million) worth of art in today's money, which bought a lot of treasures in an art market that was far less inflated than the one we live with now.[14] The wealth that enabled him to become a prince of culture, however, did not come from the quotidian running of an international shipping fleet – profitable as that was – but from a daring financial manoeuvre. Developed economies in the late nineteenth and early twentieth centuries suffered from booms and busts. The Burrell brothers commissioned and bought ships cheaply in the bust, described by a contemporaneous commentator chillingly as 'soup kitchen times – everyone starving for a job'.[15] They then held their nerve as the ships lay unused in Glasgow's docks. When the next boom arrived, they sold their ships at inflated prices as trade revived.[16] Robert Lorimer observed that their approach 'sounds like a game anyone could play at but none of them have the pluck to do it'.[17] Burrell was a risk-taker.

There is always hazard for successful entrepreneurs who try to become cultural leaders, competing for social prestige and cultural dominance as they do for competitive edge. They must be seen to be buying skilfully, out of their own superior taste and knowledge, and to be buying well in terms of price. Otherwise they risk being lampooned as gullible fools in a market they don't understand, manipulated by dealers who prey on their vanity. But Burrell was an expert rather than a novice purchaser when he bought carpet number 9-67 sometime before 1911. As early as 1901, he was already so distinguished and trusted a collector that he was the largest single lender of artefacts to the Glasgow International Exhibition, contributing more than two hundred works, including carpets.[18] Clearly, the sophisticated Burrell did not buy the patched and beaten-up rug I saw in the Glasgow storeroom by mistake. Indeed, it survived his vigorous and regular culling of his collection, holding its own against the glamour of his other acquisitions. It was Burrell the risk-taker who bought and kept his conviction purchase despite its damaged condition, ongoing scholarly uncertainty about the family of rugs to which it belonged, and its potential to undermine confidence in his judgement, both as a connoisseur and a businessman.

The Burrell Archive's object file for carpet 9-67 is nothing more than a cheaply printed form, but it has resonance.[19] Even before we read the words on it, the pressure of the pencils and pens of generations of curators and their repeated crossings-out as they struggled to clarify where and when the rug was made alert us to the fact that this is a problem carpet.

The first hand on the form is likely that of William Wells,

the keeper of the Burrell Collection from 1956 until 1978. Wells took over the year after carpet 9-67 was moved into the public collection from Burrell's home, Hutton Castle, in the clean coastal Northumberland air, a hundred miles from dirty Glasgow, despoiled by industrialists like himself. With firm pen strokes, Wells confidently describes the carpet as Rhodian, associating it with the Mediterranean island of Rhodes. This may be what Burrell himself understood it to be, although by 1956, at the age of ninety-five, he had less of a direct hand in cataloguing. In 1947 he had warned Wells' predecessor, Andrew Hannah, not to expect much input from him, saying: 'Now Mr Hannah, I am an old man and get very easily tired . . . so please work out the details as well as you can.'[20]

The island of Rhodes in the eastern Mediterranean was a Christian bulwark against Islamic forces during the twelfth- and thirteenth-century crusades, and home of the Knights Templar and the Knights Hospitallers of St John. Describing the carpet as Rhodian distanced it from Islamic associations and turned it into a potentially Christian artefact. Although it is often assumed that fine carpets of the period were the product of Islamic societies, Christians like Copts and Armenians were also exceptional weavers. Meanwhile, descriptions of similar-seeming carpets in European inventories from the fifteenth century onwards were identified as Rhodian. Early carpet scholars suggested that the crosses at the centre of the stars in such carpets, yellow in the case of Burrell 9-67, might be the emblem of the Knights of St John.[21] Wells's suggestion of a Rhodian connection was plausible.

However, no evidence has yet been found of the carpet industry on the island of Rhodes, and rugs formerly described in this way are now thought to have been woven in south-west Turkey. From there it is believed that they were exported to Rhodes, leading to the assumption in early European inventories that they were also made there.[22] They may have been woven for the Knights of St John and borne their insignia, but they were not, it seems, woven in Rhodes. While the question of a Christian origin for Asian carpets is often politicised – as can be seen in the current geopolitical crossfire between Muslim Azerbaijan and Christian Armenia, where claims of ownership of the tradition of carpet-weaving are part of political propaganda – William Wells's identification seems more likely to have arisen from the patchy misconceptions of the carpet scholarship of the time than from ideology.[23]

With a much lighter and perhaps uncertain touch, a second, unknown hand faintly proposes Central Asia as the home of the carpet with the shimmer. The curator who made this amendment may have read mid-twentieth-century German research asserting that Rhodes was an entrepot rather than a weaving centre, and so cast around for a more likely origin for the carpet.[24] But by choosing Central Asia, a huge territory of tribal weavers with their own ancient local weaving and religious traditions, many of which are still little understood outside their own communities, the second curator sent the carpet to the equivalent of the dark spaces on old maps inscribed 'here be dragons'. Central Asia is firmly crossed out by hand three, that of Noorah Al-Gailani, curator at the Burrell Collection at the time I visited in 2023, who had replaced it with Syria or Anatolia, re-situating it in the heartland of the West Asian carpet-weaving belt.

The dating of the carpet caused no less anguish to its curators. William Wells's 'early eighteenth century' has been crossed out and replaced by Noorah Al-Gailani's 'sixteenth century', moving the carpet's date of production back in time from what is often regarded by carpet specialists as a period of decline in carpet-making to what is regarded by that same community as a golden age.

The Burrell object file for carpet 9-67 maps the struggles faced by generations of curators as they tried to pin down the origins of these enigmatic iridescent carpets. But while curators can cross out and change their assessments on internal records, as they do their best with scant historical records and the divergent opinions of more than a century's carpet scholars, the published record of a collection must place a bet. The most recent record of the carpet published by the Burrell Collection dates rug 9-67 at 1500–1600, and suggests that it was made in Damascus, Syria, or over the modern border in Anatolia.[25] This puts it in a group of rugs currently believed to have been produced under the cultural influence of Mamluk arts in the waning years of the slave empire and for some time after its defeat by the Ottomans in 1517. By settling on a Mamluk rather than a Rhodian origin the curators at the Burrell switched the cultural background of the carpet and its makers, from Christianity and its crusaders to Islam and its *jihad*, literally 'struggle', to preserve Islam. They also moved it to a deeply unfamiliar and unresolved part of the history and geography of carpets.

Museum-building and empire-building moved forward in lockstep in the second half of the nineteenth century, as curators who are now at work disentangling the connection know to their cost.[26] Prestigious museums, sometimes new, sometimes built on older collections, offered a way of understanding and celebrating the rapidly expanding global reach of European and North American nations, both in trade and territory.[27] This is the period when the V&A Museum in London, the Metropolitan Museum of Art in New York, the MAK in Vienna, the Musée des Arts Decoratifs in Paris, the Art Institute of Chicago and the Kaiser-Friedrich-Museum in Berlin came into being. It was a tremendous environment for the creation of knowledge. From the late nineteenth century, a group of talented young scholars in Austria and Germany took the opportunity it offered. They turned their minds to the study of the material culture of Islam, which had been obscure to European art historians but was increasingly claiming public and scholarly attention. It was an exciting and under-explored world in which they could make their name. At the heart of it was the study of old carpets.

In seizing the artefacts needed for their art-historical projects, European scholars could be as ruthless, if not as directly violent, as the European colonial armies of the period. One of the global reference collections for the study of carpets is now in the

Pergamon Museum in Berlin. At its core are the rugs acquired for it by a foundational scholar of carpets, Wilhelm von Bode (1845–1929), founder-curator of the Kaiser-Friedrich-Museum. Bode made the intuitive leap that since Eastern carpets appeared in European Renaissance religious paintings, they might still lie ignored and unvalued in European church repositories. He was right. He bought many examples of rare, centuries-old Asian carpets at exploitatively cheap prices from cash-strapped churches in late-nineteenth-century Italy. Rejecting the knowledge-sharing ethic of academic work, Bode kept his treasure trove secret for a generation, so that prices would stay low for the benefit of German scholarship, the museum, the kaiser and Germany.[28] He did not go unrewarded. The Kaiser-Friedrich-Museum was ultimately renamed in his honour, and the first thing visitors now see as they approach Berlin's peerless Museum Island is the title 'Bode Museum' carved and gilded on to the massive neoclassical building.

The way in which the Berlin Collection came together may trouble our scruples, but it was rocket fuel for the development of carpet studies in Germany. Bode and other early carpet scholars set to work reverse-engineering the story of Asian carpets. They had little personal or experiential knowledge of how carpets were made or used in Asia, relying instead on the collections in Berlin and elsewhere in Europe, collectors' inventories, travellers' reports, court records, and the representation of carpets in European paintings. Despite these constraints on their knowledge of the places and people who made rugs, they felt confident enough to develop classifications of type and quality. Fifty years ago, Edward Said transformed thinking about this taxonomic urge, pointing out that to categorise knowledge of an ancient or alien culture is a way of attempting to control and reinvent it.[29] Said called this Orientalism, and anxiety about it haunts the modern world. But Bode and his colleagues set to work in a different intellectual and political climate. Major groups of carpets from Iran, India and Turkey were neatly slotted into the Austro-German taxonomy. But as the recipe card for these groups was defined, anomalies appeared.

Some carpets just wouldn't fit into the rules devised by European and, as time went by, North American scholars. Among these anomalies was the family of carpets to which William Burrell's 9-67 belongs.

These rugs were visually quite distinct from the traditions German scholars had classified: Safavid Iran (1501–1736 CE), with its medallions, floral tracery and courtly scenes of the hunt, Ottoman Anatolia (1299–1922 CE) with its repeating geometries, interlacing and designs derived from calligraphy, and Mughal India (1526–1857), with its painterly and lifelike representations of nature. In 1901, Bode tried to pin down the distinctiveness of the anomalous rugs, describing their 'restrained palette' and 'peculiar lustre', creating 'soft light reflections blended through the nature of the design' which 'can truly be characterised as a kaleidoscope translated into textile form'.[30] The mystery of who made these carpets and where was catnip to late-nineteenth- and early-twentieth-century scholar-curators. The hunt was on to discover the creators of the unique iridescence of which Burrell's 9-67 now retains only a trace.

Several generations of Berlin's art historians interrogated their date and place of making, including Bode himself, his protégés Ernst Kühnel (1882–1964) and Friedrich Sarre (1865–1945), and their heir Kurt Erdmann (1901–64), all at some point directors of the Berlin Museums. The answer this tight and powerful group of knowledge-builders came up with was the fifteenth-century Mamluk Empire, which at its height ruled Egypt, Syria, the ports and holy places of Arabia and the south-east of Anatolia. Bode and Kühnel suggested Mamluk Damascus as the centre of production, as carpets whose descriptions matched those of the unidentified group appeared in early European inventories as 'damascene' rugs.[31] Sarre followed up by pointing out the visual relationship between the carpets and Mamluk woodwork, mosaics, book bindings and ceilings in Cairo.[32] Erdmann interrogated the fragmentary textual sources,[33] and the traces of Mamluk Egypt were there to be found. In 1474, the travelling Italian merchant Barbaro had mentioned that carpets from Tabriz were superior to those he had seen in Cairo. A sixteenth-century Medici inventory listed a carpet from Cairo. Ottoman records told that in 1585 Sultan Murad III had asked for eleven weavers from Cairo with their wools. Meanwhile, carpet motifs were examined to establish relationships across media and geographies. Were there, for example, echoes of ancient Egyptian palm trees and hieroglyphs in the designs? Gradually the compass settled on Mamluk Cairo as the place where the iridescent carpets with their kaleidoscopic patterns were made.

The German School's pride in and sense of ownership of the knowledge they had built about these enigmatic carpets was powerful. It is illustrated by Erdmann's remark in the 1950s that if a previously unknown Mamluk carpet came up for sale, however expensive – and they are rare and almost always very expensive – the Berlin Museums should buy it in celebration of the role of German scholars in identifying the group.[34] It would have been quite a stretch. The Baillet-Latour Mamluk carpet auctioned by Christie's in 2014 sold for £782,500 ($1,299,733) against an estimate of £250,000. The Burrell Collection insured its battered rug 9-67 for £150 in 1954, but it's doubtful that the modern equivalent of £1,600 could now replace it.[35]

But despite their careful work, the arguments made about Mamluk carpets by Bode, Sarre, Kühnel and Erdmann didn't have the clear and sometimes irrefutable historical basis available for Persian, Mughal and particularly Anatolian carpets, where the miracle of Ottoman record-keeping keeps us honest. Detailed timelines and locations for their production couldn't be confidently established. Like the patterns in the shimmering kaleidoscopic carpets, we see evidence for who made them and where, but if we look again we see something different.

The story of the Mamluk Empire and its culture begins with Yusuf ibn Ayyub ibn Shadhi, nicknamed Salah-ad-Din, 'Righteousness of the Faith', known in the West as Saladin. From 1171 Saladin was the Ayyubid-dynasty sultan of Egypt, Syria and its wider territories. Even in his own time, Saladin was a legendary Islamic military leader and antagonist of medieval Christianity, leading his armies in jihad against Europe's crusaders. As Muslim and Christian armies struggled during the Third Crusade for control of territories in the Middle East, the decisive intervention was Saladin's seizure of Jerusalem in 1187 from the European armies who occupied it.[36] Unsurprisingly, he was and is a heroic and inspirational figure in the Islamic world.

His adversary in the bitter five-year stand-off over the holy city was the man variously known as Richard the Lionheart, Richard Coeur de Lion, Richard I of England and Duke of Aquitaine. The struggle for Jerusalem was viewed as existential by its participants and was embodied in the figures of Richard and Saladin, who are mythologised in their evocative titles and nicknames. The pair can still be either bogeyman or holy hero depending on the ethnicity and religion of the parent telling the bedtime story.

The loss of Jerusalem was a tremendous psychic blow to Christendom. Whoever seized it must surely have been in some way beyond the norm of good or evil. A European Saladin came into being, at first in medieval romances, who was the model of the chivalrous knight and consequently a worthy adversary.[37] This Saladin of the imagination is a shapeshifter who often appears disguised, then is revealed in glory. He is characterised by his flashing, biting scimitar and his magisterial dignity. He has a physicality which is sensually threatening as well as menacing in battle. He is Saladin the generous, the virtuous, the just, the strong, a wise leader, creative diplomat and conqueror, but also Saladin the earthy and ferocious. For Europeans, he *was* Egypt, just as Cleopatra was.

Saladin may have believed that God was on his side in battle, and Europeans may have believed he was invested with the sanctity of chivalry, but the military success of Saladin's sultanate depended heavily on the elite fighting machine he had established. These were the Mamluks, made up of enslaved people trained to absolute loyalty and martial prowess.[38] By 1259 the Mamluk military had become so strong that they superseded Saladin's successors and took direct power in Egypt and Syria. The new rulers immediately secured their control in the most dramatic way imaginable at the time. In 1260, at Ayn Jalut near Galilee in Palestine, the Mamluks succeeded where all the great armies of Asia had failed. They turned back the terrifying nomadic Mongol horsemen who in the previous fifty years had carried out what has been described as 'an ecological war of destruction' against settled peoples, poisoning their wells, sowing their fields with salt and creating the largest land empire Eurasia had ever seen.[39]

As they had been under Saladin, the Mamluks at Ayn Jalut were again the saviours of the settled communities of Islam. From 1250 to 1517 CE Mamluk sultans ruled a huge Islamic empire from Anatolia in the north to Sudan in the south, from Libya in the west to the Arabian peninsula in the east. The empire's cities included Cairo and Alexandria, Damascus and Baghdad, Mecca and Medina. This vast and largely Arabic geography was not ruled by Arabs but by Turkic and European slaves.

At the heart of Mamluk military and political control was a systematic and remarkable programme of social engineering.[40] Mamluk soldiers were bought as children or adolescents in the great slave markets of the Black Sea ports. Many were Turkic and many were Christian. Their original homes were in the western steppe and the northern Caucasus. Taken to Egypt and Syria, they were apprenticed to a Mamluk master, who trained them up in political and military arts and in the practice of Islam. The natural emotional bonds of the young slaves were forcibly broken, and they were re-educated in absolute and exclusive loyalty to their master and to the Mamluk sultanate, rather than to their families and communities of birth. When they completed their training they were freed, but only to join the Mamluk army and administration. For most of the period of the Mamluk Empire, natural male children of Mamluks could not inherit their father's status or possessions or lead the army and the empire. New slaves were bought and placed as apprentices with the Mamluk master instead. Ten generations of slave children and the biological children of

Mamluks experienced this ideologically driven way of life, and ten generations of locals lived under their rule.

Among the most successful commercial nations of the medieval period, for two hundred and fifty years the Mamluks traded and interacted with other powerful material cultures in medieval Europe and Asia. They developed a great material culture of their own. Wealth, power and competition for prestige drove the development of Mamluk arts, in common with other empires, but their social programme left them with a unique need. Their arts had to help them come in from outside. Each generation of Mamluk rulers was chosen on merit from a group of men who had been brought to Egypt as slave children from geographies much further north and west. There was no inheritance by right, no primogeniture, no handing down from father to son among great families. There was no shared ethnicity. Many were not Muslims from the cradle but converted as part of their training. Consequently, every generation of Mamluk rulers had to re-establish their right to rule.[41]

The Mamluks set out to remind the world that despite their original status as slaves, immigrants and often Christian infidels, they were the rightful rulers of Egypt and the holy places of Islam in Syria and Arabia. Their monumental architecture, particularly mosques, madrasas and tombs, their intricate woodwork, glittering metalwork, radiant lamps and windows, beautiful painted books and glamorous textiles and carpets acted as declarations of both their Islamic piety and their power. Their arts communicated their living and irresistible strength.

At the same time, trade was never far away from their minds, and they consciously created a distinctive Mamluk style – a brand which played well in rich European markets. Their art shored up Mamluk identity in a fragile ecosystem of belonging but was also unafraid to differentiate itself in the interest of commerce. The unique dynamic of the Mamluk period brought about what has been described as the Renaissance of Islam, six hundred years after Muhammad's *hejira* and revelation.[42]

However, this Mamluk story runs counter to the expected arc.

It is easy to assume that a renaissance is a beginning, as it was in Europe. But the Mamluk Renaissance and its blaze of cultural glory came not at the height but at the end of their empire, from around 1468, under Sultan Qaytbay and his successors.[43]

History, ecology and technology had by then moved against the Mamluks.[44] The massive death toll of the fourteenth-century plagues had led to a restructuring of trade and agriculture in a depopulated Eurasia. Egypt's irrigation system collapsed, and areas of fertile land in Mamluk territories were left uncultivated, their inhabitants returning to Bedouin pastoral nomadism. Their dominance of the great Indian Ocean trade, which made landfall in Mamluk ports in Arabia, ended in the late fifteenth century with the Portuguese discovery of direct sea routes from Europe to the Indian Ocean. The rise of new regional superpowers like the Ottomans, and profound changes in military tactics after the adoption of gunpowder, undermined Mamluk dominance on the battlefield.[45] When they faced the Ottomans in their final campaign at the beginning of the sixteenth century, Mamluk knights, with their complex medieval codes of honour inherited from Saladin, still preferred to fight with weapons which were fundamentally the same as those used by the Scythians in the fifth century BCE. The Ottomans carried muskets.

As the Mamluks grew vulnerable, the need of their sultans to advertise their claim as rightful rulers grew even more intense. Rituals were instituted to demonstrate loyalty to the sultan, some practised daily. These ceremonies were dressed with glamorous props, including textiles and costumes.[46] As their domestic economy failed, the export trade in Mamluk artefacts became more important, and sultans invested in their creative industries. In that last burst of creativity, the use of carpets as a tool to perform power at home and abroad, and as a highly valuable export commodity during the economic misery of the later fifteenth century, seems to have begun.

It is unsurprising that the Mamluks, with one eye on geopolitics and the other on the market, should have sponsored the weaving of carpets. We know they commissioned them. Some of the carpets we describe as Mamluk include the personal blazons or symbols of individual emirs, found on other types of artefacts made in Cairo and Damascus in the fifteenth century.

Indeed, the roots of Mamluk connection with carpets went very deep. These Turkic, West Asian and European arrivals had come as children or adolescents from the carpet-weaving areas of the Caucasus and the Balkans. Before they were taken to the Black Sea slave markets, they lived with mothers and sisters who wove rugs. Their childhoods were spent sitting on, eating off and sleeping under carpets. We can imagine them carrying around small, tattered pieces of rug as children the world over drag their security blankets and rags.[47] Carpets were integral to the lives they had left behind, and it is hard to believe these psychologically powerful objects did not exert a pull, even after the slaves' re-education by Mamluk emirs.

Nor is it a stretch to believe that the Mamluks invented a specific style, rather than adapting an existing tradition. The carpets they were familiar with in their youth would have been woven in the many local design idioms of their original homes, so no simple preference for a region or style can be safely assumed. It is easy, on the other hand, to imagine that the Mamluks wanted a visual and sensory vocabulary for their carpets which would integrate seamlessly with their other grand imperial arts, woodwork, bookbinding, tile and glass, a carpet style that was a coherent part of the Mamluk brand. And if those carpets were to compete in European and Asian trade with the products of Ottoman Anatolia, which was already a great weaving centre by the fifteenth century, they had to be aesthetically different to Anatolia's clear geometries. They needed something provoking and arresting like the shimmering colour harmonies and phase-space design I had seen in Glasgow.

The doubts and difficulties about the idea of a highly developed Mamluk pile-carpet-making industry lie not so much in the idea that Mamluks would want carpets, or that they had reason to create a new form of design, but in the questions of where they were made and by whom.

One of the reasons it is so hard to place these carpets in time or geography is because we don't have the whole plant, just the blossom. We don't know anything about its root system, in the form of earlier carpets from which the tradition grew, carpet fragments or even early representations of them in paintings or books. In neither Mamluk Cairo nor Mamluk Damascus are there the traces of makers, workshops and equipment that support our understanding of other ancient carpets, or fragments of carpets. Even now, more than a century after the debate began, the evidence about them is mostly indirect and textual: inventories, tax records, edicts, using confusing and inconsistent terminologies. In terms of the historical record, these carpets – which some believe surpass all others, and which found their way to the Italian and Hapsburg elite, the Ottoman court and the collections of imperial museums – apparently came from nowhere. In the words of a contemporary historian of Islamic art, they are 'that rarest phenomenon in the history of Islamic art, a synthetic artistic tradition without embedded social roots'.[48]

The idea that they were made in Cairo presents particular problems. The great Eurasian carpet-weaving belt of the northern hemisphere lies between the thirtieth and forty-fifth parallels, in the world's temperate and sub-tropical zones, where Eurasia's sheep and their shepherds are found. Cairo, in the far north of Egypt, just scrapes in at 30 degrees north. Even that greatest of Mamluk carpet scholars, Kurt Erdmann, was uncertain about Cairo as the physical site of production, saying: 'for lack of a better alternative, scholars today accept that Mamluk carpets were likely produced in Cairo'.[49]

The absence of carpet fragments in Cairo raises further doubts because there is a treasure trove of other textile fragments at the archaeological site of Fustat. This 'city of tents' was the predecessor to Cairo, established after the seventh-century Muslim conquest of Egypt by the followers of Mohammed. Five hundred years later, in 1168, it was deliberately burned to save its wealth from the approaching European crusaders. When Mamluk rule began in the

mid-thirteenth century, the Mamluks used the scorched ruins of
Fustat as their rubbish tips.[50] The modern inhabitants of Cairo do
so still, and it is now a desolate lunar landscape in the Old Cairo
quarter of the modern city. Since the beginning of the twentieth
century, excavations there have yielded extraordinary evidence of
daily life. Egypt's dry air and the low acidity of its soil help preserve fibres, and Fustat's finds are particularly rich in fragments
of late antique and early medieval cotton, linen and silk made by
Islamic and Coptic Egyptians and also traded from India.[51] But the
very few remains of carpets found in Mamluk middens at Fustat
are too fragmentary and ambiguous to allow us to understand
what they are, where their materials came from, or the lives of the
people who made them.

Ernst Kühnel, one of the foundational group of German carpet
scholars, offered a flash of insight into the spinners of Mamluk
carpets, and a rare piece of evidence that they were at work in Cairo itself. With his colleague Louisa Bellinger, Kühnel analysed the
techniques used to spin the wool of the great collection of Mamluk
carpets in the Textile Museum, Washington.[52] They observed that,
unusually for anywhere else in the Eurasian carpet-weaving belt,
the wool of the mysterious carpets was spun counterclockwise, in
the direction of the downstroke of the letter S, rather than clock-
wise, in the direction of the downstroke of the letter Z. One of
the most important textiles in Egypt is linen, made from a native
plant, flax. When flax dries it naturally turns counterclockwise.
So, they hypothesised, Egyptian spinners would follow the habit
developed when spinning flax and would spin all fibres, including
wool, counterclockwise. They concluded that Mamluk carpets,
or at least the spinners of their wool, might therefore have been
Egyptian, labouring in the Cairo heat or in dusty rural villages to
produce yarn for Mamluk textiles, as the economy of the declining empire collapsed around them, prices soared and the silver
required to buy food and pay rent disappeared from circulation.[53]
This fragile evidence of the S-spun wool has become a smoking
gun, a fundamental proof, for the story of a carpet-weaving industry in Mamluk Cairo.

Meanwhile, the vacuum of 'carpets from nowhere' has been filled by the idea that they were made by incomers, migrants. Some specialists propose that master weavers were brought from Iran to Egypt by the Mamluks to set up a new carpet-making industry.[54] Others suggest an influx into Mamluk territories of refugee artisans disrupted by wars and politics in fifteenth-century Iran and Anatolia.[55] The spotlight among these scholars falls on Turkmen tribesmen, whose highly developed tradition of carpet-weaving uses the same asymmetrical knots as Mamluk carpets, looped round one warp thread, rather than symmetrical knots, which loop round two. Specialists also point out that the two carpet traditions share a design of repeated *guls*, abstract flower or star motifs, often repeated in rows.[56] Turkmen tribal confederations ruled parts of Iran and Anatolia in the fifteenth century, and the names of the two most significant tribes, the *Akkoyunlu* White Sheep and *Karakoyunlu* Black Sheep Turkmen remind us of how closely the lives of these sophisticated and powerful nomadic groups were intertwined with their flocks, the wool their sheep produced, and with the practice of weaving. Inter-tribal rivalry led to civil wars, and in 1468 the Black Sheep were defeated by the White at Tabriz. Their diaspora, scholars suggest, may have ignited an unprecedented blaze of carpet art in the late Mamluk Empire.[57]

When we unpick this hypothesis, it offers a bleak story. Displaced Turkmen weavers, it suggests, travelled overland to Cairo and Damascus from fifteenth-century weaving centres such as Tabriz in modern Iran or Diyarbakir in eastern Anatolia, both centres of the conflict between the Black and White Sheep Turkmen tribes. This is a journey of more than a thousand miles to Cairo and around five hundred to Damascus. Turkmen were nomads, inhabitants of what geographers call the sub-Arctic nomadic zone, from the Mediterranean coast to Anatolia, Iran and on to Central Asia. Historian of nomadism Resat Kasaba tells us: 'tens of thousands of tribes moved constantly across this belt of high mountains and dry steppes and deserts for millennia'.[58] The refugee Turkmen would have known how to organise for transhumance, the movement from pasture to pasture of the whole tribal group and its flocks, but they would have been in flight rather than following their established routes. The journey would have been made at the speed of laden horses and camels, and the smallest walking child. Along the way the refugees could face lack of food and water, exposure, threats from animals, suspicion from locals. Some would be lucky enough to find themselves welcomed by communities on their route who valued their crafts and skills. We cannot avoid the idea that many would have perished.

But the story of a Turkmen diaspora is yet another historical deduction, based on the regional geopolitics of the time. We still don't know the truth, any more than the curators of the Burrell Collection did, or the German School of carpet studies. The lives of the unknown weavers of the carpets we now describe as Mamluk are lost to history and buried under layers of sediment created from our ongoing recalibration of the scant facts.

In 1517, Ottoman Sultan Selim the Grim crushed the Mamluk military of Sultan Tuman Bay and ended the Mamluk Empire. The Ottomans absorbed Mamluk territories, transforming themselves from a marginal Islamic entity in Anatolia and the Balkans to the dominant empire in Eurasia, rulers of Cairo, Damascus and Alexandria, and guardians of Islam and its holy places in Arabia.[59]

From at least the fifteenth century CE, the knotted-pile rugs of the settled Ottoman Empire were one of the global carpet industry's great aesthetic and commercial successes.[60] They were in demand among Ottoman trading partners across Eurasia. Their dramatically abstract designs, some geometric, some derived from calligraphy, some with striking motifs of stylised animals, mesmerised the European elite. European Renaissance painters used them as props to demonstrate the magnificence of Tudor monarchs, Medici popes and princes of the Church, and the astonishing wealth of merchants in Renaissance Italy and the Low Countries.[61] Turkey carpets were highly desirable symbols of power and prestige. There was no particular need for the Ottomans to become involved in the dying textile tradition of a dead empire which they had just conquered, yet they did.

Textual records showing that Mamluk-style carpets were woven well after the fall of the Mamluk Empire. They are interpreted as proof that after the slave empire's territories fell into their hands in 1517, a series of Ottoman sultans supported and patronised workshops employing Mamluk weavers in the greatly enlarged Ottoman Empire.[62] As late as 1585, almost seventy years after the Ottoman defeat of the Mamluks, Sultan Murad III issued an edict that eleven weavers from Cairo with a large quantity of their wool be sent to Istanbul.[63] Murad's motivation is subject to much scholarly speculation. His command is sometimes interpreted as a glimpse of the foundation of the first Ottoman court carpet workshop, where excellent Cairene weavers were needed to elevate local production to the standard of refinement the great empire now demanded.[64] Another suggestion is that elite Ottoman weavers were already at full capacity producing carpets for an imperial project celebrating continent-spanning Ottoman power, the Selimiye mosque at Edirne in Ottoman Europe. Completed in 1575, it was considered by imperial architect Sinan to be his masterpiece. Its dome was symbolically larger than that of the Byzantine Hagia Sophia in Istanbul, and its huge internal spaces needed many luscious carpets for the performance of Ottoman power.[65] The sultan's weavers, the story goes, were completely occupied and he consequently needed more. Whatever the reason for Murad's edict, almost seventy years after the collapse of the Mamluk Empire, there were carpet-makers in Cairo, and the sultan of all the world wanted them for his court.

There are many explanations for the perhaps counter-intuitive Ottoman preoccupation with Mamluk carpets. Keen commercial calculation, an Ottoman strength, would have been one of them. The European 1 per cent bought what they thought of as Damascene or Cairene carpets at high prices, and in some Italian centres like Venice and Florence they were sometimes held in higher regard and cost more than Turkey carpets.[66] It may also have been a simple acknowledgement by one of the world's great carpet cultures that the aesthetic of these rival Mamluk carpets was truly exceptional. Many Mamluk-influenced Ottoman court carpets ended up in the imperial repository at the Topkapi Palace in Istanbul.

But the Ottoman interest in the exotic Mamluks is also a form of intra-Islamic Orientalism, the appeal of the closely related Other. Conquerors are often powerfully and perversely attracted to the cultures they have brought low. In a famous example, the devotion of the ferocious nomadic Mongols to the settled courtly arts of defeated Iran and China transformed Mongol society in the thirteenth and fourteenth centuries.[67] The sultans of the enormous Ottoman Empire at the height of their power, and with their own esteemed carpets to hand, were fascinated by the carpets of the strange, fading and collapsed Mamluk Empire. What emerging centres of power perceive as aspirational is often a puzzling and puzzled reimagining of lost superpowers.

The sponsorship of Mamluk weaving by the Ottomans after the fall of the Mamluk Empire has muddied the waters further in our search for the home of Burrell's carpet 9-67. It greatly extends the range of potential times and geographies of its making. Some specialists suggest that carpets sharing the Glasgow rug's design of repeating compartments were made in this period of intimacy between Turkish and Mamluk weaving in sixteenth-century Ottoman Damascus or Anatolia.[68] Again, we don't know. Anna Beselin, currently curator of Bode's great collection of carpets in Berlin, observes about a similar carpet in the museum's collection: 'Unfortunately, a final localisation cannot be definitively undertaken.'[69] Her words are understated, but her sigh of frustration is almost audible.

The house of cards we build about Burrell's carpet 9-67 repeatedly collapses. It remains a deeply enigmatic object which illustrates how difficult it is to construct histories of rugs. They wear, rot, burn and fray, are cut up and reused, and this vulnerability leaves many gaps in the physical evidence offered by their remains. Meanwhile the circumstances of their production, by illiterate and nomadic weavers in shifting empires, mean that textual records are few and far between. The truth is hard to come at, and we often have little more than wandering designs and details of types of knots, direction of spinning, or warp and weft structures to construct a carpet's history. The labour is sometimes too heavy for the fragile evidence.

The carpet lying in the twilight of a museum storeroom has not yet yielded up its secrets. We don't know whether it was woven in the last blaze of the slave empire of Saladin's Mamluks, or the Ottoman Empire at the height of its power across the continents of Europe, Asia and Africa, or indeed somewhere else. We don't know where its originally lustrous wool came from, who its weavers were or their experience of the world in which they wove it. But William Burrell's commitment to it, despite the insecurity of its provenience, shows the power of a confident collector who trusts his own judgement. He liked the look of the misshapen, worn old rug, stuck with it and so provided us with a thorn in the side of received wisdom. Meanwhile, the rug sleeps on in its dark nest in rainy Glasgow.

Chapter 3
Shahenshah

KNOTTED-PILE CARPET, SIXTEENTH CENTURY CE, IRAN

For seven years I worked at the V&A Museum in London. Every day, I walked past a huge glass box at the centre of the Islamic gallery. It is forty feet long, twenty feet wide, and taller than an adult. As I passed it usually lay in darkness to protect its contents from damage, but on lucky days I would catch the ten minutes out of every thirty when the lights are turned on and join the crowd who had waited for the moment of illumination. The box, or perhaps shrine, contains a huge carpet.

The dim lights in the shrine glimmer over the carpet like stars on a wide sea, illuminating the undulating waves of pattern that float across its blue depths. On the dark-blue surface unfurl overlapping skeins of blossom, like strands of preternaturally beautiful seaweed. But then, with a click of the brain, the sense of looking at an ever-changing sea recedes and in its place emerges a highly structured array of large motifs overlaid on multiple levels of flowering stems on a dark-blue field, reconciling mutability with order. An elaborate central medallion hung with golden pendants provides a still anchor among the movement. Quadrants of the medallion's design fill each corner of the field like heavy chased gold. Deep borders of lozenge-shaped cartouches hold us stable. Despite that first impression of a dark-blue sea, the colours of the large motifs arrayed on it are not freshly naturalistic but the suave colours of a dusky palatial interior. The cartouches are woven in a subdued range of soft clarets and sage-greens, the medallion and corner quadrants in dull golds. The shapes belong to the design lexicon of Asia, and the colours to the spaces occupied by princes. The carpet transports us away from South Kensington to wherever our personal Arabian Nights dreams are located.

As the first visual and imaginative shock recedes, the carpet returns us to the spiritual world of Islam. Medallions are often interpreted as the sun, or Allah's divine radiance at the centre of the universe, or the pool at the centre of the garden of paradise – all perhaps ways of saying the same thing.[1] The tendrils of foliage and blossom appear to wheel round it, like satellites. At each end are precise and elegant representations of mosque lamps. In a touch which reveals a highly self-aware maker, the design reflects the lamps which would have hung glowing from the ceiling above the carpet as it lay on the floor of a consecrated space. The field design could be infinitely repeated in both directions, the corner quadrants forming new central medallions without limit. Art historian Robert Hillenbrand suggests that this is the source of the design's aesthetic and spiritual power: 'The design is deliberately not complete but is only a portion of an unimaginably large but thoroughly disciplined composition. Hence the viewer receives intimations of infinity, even eternity, all the more affecting because they are not explicit.'[2]

In an emotional leap, the carpet takes us from the universal to the personal. Above one of the mosque lamps is an inscription, a message from its own time and place, woven as if handwritten. It is an intimate gesture, but unless we can read its ancient language and decorative calligraphy, the inscription only serves to emphasise our distance from the world the carpet represents. The sponsors and makers of the carpet speak to us, but we can't hear what they say.

As we look, the desire to compare and classify kicks in. It is said that when fourteenth-century peasants first viewed Giotto's naturalistic church frescos, they did not understand that they were seeing depictions of people. When the shrine's lights come up, it is hard at first to adapt to the idea that what is inside is a textile, a carpet. Despite the radical difference in scale, the design is more reminiscent of an illuminated painting or a gorgeous, tooled book cover. The rug signals that it is the product of a high culture, and first cousin to other high art forms.

The huge rug is an unfathomable expression of human skill and vision, constructed by the slow-building, loop-by-loop precision of knotted-pile carpet-weaving and the manual and cognitive dexterity of its weavers. A potent combination is at work in it of awe, beauty and fascination with the Other, a culture distant in time and place. The commanding carpet in the glass shrine is the world-famous Ardabil, believed to have been made in the reign of Shah Tahmasp I of Iran (1524–76), as the Safavid dynasty moved towards its towering cultural peak.[3]

The Ardabil's glass shrine was built during the three-year redesign of the V&A's Islamic gallery between 2003 and 2006. It was manufactured by Italy's Laboratorio Museotechnico Goppion, the firm that made both the glass protection for Leonardo da Vinci's *Mona Lisa* at the Louvre and the cases protecting the Crown Jewels in the Tower of London.[4] Why, among so many precious and culturally irreplaceable objects, did the rug deserve such exceptional care and protection?

The gallery contains other precious carpets, including a very old rug from Ushak in Anatolia, believed to have been made around 1500 and woven to a design specified by Ottoman Sultan Mehmet (1451–81), the conqueror of Constantinople and the Byzantine Empire. It too is a beautiful carpet, with monumental medallions, delicate floral tracery across its field and a rich ruby palette with blue highlights. A penumbra of pinkish-camel-coloured wool around the claret of the central medallion disconcertingly evokes an eclipse of the sun. Perhaps this medallion is suggestive of secular authority interposing itself between us and a greater divine power – although one wonders if even Ottoman emperor Mehmet the Conqueror would dare that.

Despite its beauty, age and historical resonance, Mehmet's Ushak carpet is not allocated its own bulletproof, light-controlled shrine and hangs on the gallery walls alongside other objects. It apparently does not warrant the level of reverence afforded to the Ardabil. The Ardabil commands the imagination of carpet connoisseurs like no other rug. Since its arrival in the V&A in 1893, it has become the standard against which other carpets are measured and has helped sustain an idea that Persian arts and culture are superior to those of other Islamic geographies and communities.[5]

A Google search today would deliver descriptions of the Ardabil as the most beautiful, the largest, the oldest, the most finely woven carpet in the world. Some of the popular claims made for it are simply wrong. It is not the largest carpet in the world. That title was claimed in 2018 by a modern carpet in the opulent Sheikh Zayed Al Nahyan mosque in Abu Dhabi, which at 60,546 square feet is the size of a football pitch. There are many antique carpets which are also larger than the Ardabil, like those made in nineteenth- and early-twentieth-century India for *durbars*, princely gatherings. It is certainly not the oldest carpet we have still in existence; there are carpets almost a thousand years older. This claim may be a popular misinterpretation of the fact that it is currently the oldest known carpet with an inscription. Nor is it the most finely woven; the V&A's Ardabil has an average of 340 knots per square inch, which, while high, doesn't match the unimaginable thousands per square inch achieved by Mughal weavers. As to the question of whether it is the most beautiful, that claim is always an equivocal mixture of personal taste, fashion and prestige. The Ardabil attracts hyperbole, as if those who encounter it must grasp after reasons to explain its exceptional status among carpets.

What is certain is that the carpet's weavers were highly accomplished and aesthetically ambitious. They used natural or cream-coloured silk for the warps and wefts. These fine foundation materials allowed the tight packing together of its woollen knots, permitting intricate detail in the design. They used asymmetric knots, which loop round only one warp thread, rather than symmetrical knots which loop round two, in modern terms a series of single rather than double pixels. It's to those single-pixel asymmetric knots that we owe the sinuous curves of the foliage in its design. The asymmetric knots which deliver graceful and naturalistic drawing are found so often in Iranian carpets that they have come to be called Persian knots. The two-pixel symmetrical knots looped round two warp threads deliver the more angular geometries of Anatolian carpets and are often called Turkish knots.

The Ardabil's weavers seem not to have worked mechanically from knot plans which told them the colour of each individual knot in the carpet's entire sequence, or followed knot-by-knot instructions sung or intoned by a team leader. Had this been their practice, the two lengthwise halves of the rug would have been perfectly symmetrical. But small differences in design between one half and the other – a leaf which blows in its own direction, a blossom which has opened more fully than others – suggest that the weavers were working by eye, possibly converting a design on another artefact or following a drawing.[6] This is one of those moments when the non-weaver's imagination fails, defeated by the level of cognitive and technical skill needed to hold a complex design in the mind and at the same time build it up line by line over a surface thirty-three feet long by seventeen feet wide, making adjustments all the while.

The first impression of the carpet is of golden, sage and claret designs on a dark-blue background, but the weavers actually worked with a palette of sixteen colours to achieve its rich and glowing effect and its dynamic natural movement. The dye masters and mistresses who supported the weavers derived the carpet's shades from plants, animals and insects, an advanced craft developed across the Eurasian rug-weaving belt from ancient times. These natural dyes, so called to distinguish them from those synthesised in factories from around 1850 onwards, have become a touchstone of modern beliefs about what is admirable and valuable in an Eastern carpet, and the Ardabil carpet is an object lesson in their use.

The carpet's patron had commissioned a fashionable carpet

from its makers, as well as a pious one. The central medallion began to be a favoured motif of elite buyers during the fifteenth century and is strongly associated with the artistically refined courts of early modern empires in the region, in particular the Mamluks, the Ottomans and the Safavids. It was used across various art forms, but most famously in carpets and bookbinding. The Ardabil carpet was to represent both the secular power of its patron and the sacred power of the universal divine.

Excellent as the carpet is, none of this is unique to the Ardabil. There are many rugs in the world's collections of which this is also true. Other factors impelled the Ardabil to its totemic status as emblem of all carpets – and of Persia's cultural dominance.

As the Ardabil carpet arrived at the V&A, multiple revolutions were taking place in Western thought. It was a time of great steps in the physical sciences, but also new ideas about the nature of humanity, its development and history, many triggered by evolutionary theory.[7] This new intellectual world was threatening as well as exhilarating. An important way of managing the uncertainty it created was to take comfort in taxonomies. And there was no end of material to slot into these comforting categories. As well as an expanded sense of historical timescales and a more granular and microscopic understanding of the physical world, this period was also marked by a much wider exposure to diverse geographies and cultures, as colonialism and globalisation took their inexorable path forward. In the ferment, it was important for the populations of the metropoles of Europe and North America to know where both things and people fitted into taxonomic hierarchies.

Colonisation was a process of coercive extraction of the wealth of those other peoples and geographies. It was rooted in hunger for power, territory and wealth. But intellectually and morally engaged colonisers also urgently sought a rationale for their right to dominate. Ideas about 'the white man's burden', their predestined responsibility to bring Christianity and what they saw as enlightened Western values to more 'primitive' groups, were part of this rationale. Its substrate was racial theory enabled by evolutionary theory.[8] A taxonomy of races came into being which put white men of northern European extraction at the top of the racial hierarchy. In this mental model, colonialism was an inevitable consequence of that racial superiority.

If you weren't a white northern European man, the next-best thing was to be Persian. From the eighteenth century, Enlightenment philologists had defined an Indo-European language group and racial type they dubbed Aryan, which was distinct from Arabic and Semitic groups.[9] In this schema, Aryan Persians – with their Indo-European language and their 'European' physical attributes – were the first cousins of the world's natural leaders. From this mix of eighteenth- and nineteenth-century racial, linguistic and evolutionary theory an idea of Iranian exceptionalism developed. It proposed that Iran was the dominant agent in the development of Central, South and West Asia, at least before Europeans and Russians involved themselves in those geographies. To believe in that exceptionalism it's necessary to ignore not only the constant flux of peoples across Eurasia and the millennia-long Turkic diaspora, but also the history of Afghan, Uzbek and other Central, South and West Asian peoples – which, quite often in the West, we still do. But for upstart new European empires of the nineteenth century who desired to associate themselves with great empires of the past, Europe's close Aryan cousins the Persians were ideal candidates.

Mid-nineteenth-century French writers such as Arthur de Gobineau were early Persophiliacs, but the focus on Iran and the racial theory of which it was a part soon spread across Europe.[10] Persian literature had been translated into European languages in the eighteenth century, and poets like Hafez struck a deep chord as Europe and North America moved towards Romanticism.[11] In the later nineteenth century a flood of artefacts was sold into expanding global markets by hard-pressed Persians, giving Persia a rich, unfamiliar and luxurious visual identity beyond Asia.[12] Novel objects arrived in Europe and North America, including

ravishing illuminated paintings, exquisite books and book bindings, intricate metalwork and woodwork, vibrant and lustrous
polychrome ceramics and, of course, fine textiles and carpets. As
the nineteenth century progressed, a generalised concept of an
exotic, sensual and louche Orient was replaced by a more specific
idea of a refined Persia of intellectual clarity and unmatched visual
inventiveness.[13] Artist, connoisseur and cultural commentator
William Morris (1834–96) reflected the zeitgeist when he said in
1882, 'To us pattern designers, Persia has become a holy land, for
there in the process of time our art was perfected.'[14]

Part of the story which late-nineteenth-century Europeans
constructed was that Persian culture was both the source and the
most consummate expression of the whole of Islamic culture, and
by the beginning of the twentieth century leading German scholar
Friedrich Sarre could confidently declare that Persian culture was
'the most important branch of Mohammedan art'.[15] Carpets were
at the heart of this art-historical pivot to Persia, particularly the
carpets made for the courts of the Safavid imperial shahs who
ruled Iran between 1501 and 1736.

Ottomans and Mughals were also great weavers of elite court
carpets. In Britain and the Netherlands there was a strong demand
for Mughal carpets as early as the seventeenth century, through
trading links with South Asia. Meanwhile, before the nineteenth
century, the generic term used in European textual records for any
ornately patterned knotted-pile carpet had been 'Turkey rug'. Nevertheless, while Ottoman and Mughal carpets had an important
place in the taxonomy of rugs which developed in the West during
the nineteenth and early twentieth centuries, they came to be less
highly regarded – and indeed, less costly – than Safavid carpets.[16]

This was not a purely aesthetic judgement, although it was often couched as one. The loaded assumptions about ethnicity which
placed Iranian art in its own class also inevitably coloured the
assessment of its carpets. Trade and economics played a part too,
bringing unfamiliar and therefore exciting Persian carpets into
a late-nineteenth-century European marketplace where Turkish
and Indian carpets were already well known.[17] Meanwhile, the

complicated and conflicted political reputation of the Mughal and Ottoman Empires affected nineteenth-century European opinions of their material cultures.

The Mughal Empire was a spent force by the mid-nineteenth century, but the nominal Mughal emperor, Bahadur Shah Zafar, frail and elderly as he was, was co-opted as the figurehead of the 1857 Indian uprising against the rule of the British East India Company. The rebellion so unsettled British assumptions of their rights to India's land, population and resources that direct rule from Westminster was imposed and the British Raj established.[18] The uprising of the colonised against the coloniser created a frisson across other European imperial nations. Meanwhile, the Ottoman Empire was regarded by nineteenth-century European politicians as 'the sick man of Europe', a phrase attributed to Tsar Nicholas I. Given what lay ahead for the Romanovs, the tsar's comment is bitterly ironic. Nevertheless, the Ottomans created a tangled web of political, military and territorial problems for European states which lasted until its collapse in 1922.

The political fallout of these events played into perceptions of the culture of the Mughal and Ottoman Empires, and their great carpets were not immune. The Safavid Empire, safely extinct since the eighteenth century, could no longer participate in the politics and armed conflicts of Western colonialists in the ways the Mughal and Ottoman courts and their armies did. The Safavids were sealed in their glorious cultural past, and they and their carpets offered a highly manicured cultural parallel for the aspirational new empires of Europe.

By the beginning of the twentieth century, the global domination of Safavid carpets was simply an accepted fact. In his still-influential *Survey of Persian Art*, published during the 1930s, leading curator and scholar Arthur Upham Pope summed up his lifelong lobbying for Safavid carpets, saying:

This world verdict on Persian carpets as the finest that have been made is amply sustained. In this medium Persia has suffered no rivalry [. . .] the great carpet that is shared between the

Cathedral of Cracow and the Musée des Arts Decoratifs, Paris, the Anhalt, and the Ardabil carpets are quite unapproached by anything to which they can be compared. [They] offer unlimited scope for the Persian genius for pure design [. . .] guided by an unfailing intellectual clarity which is characteristic of the Persian spirit.[19]

By the time Pope was writing, and with his help, Iranian carpets of the Safavid sixteenth and seventeenth centuries had become a superclass of rugs in the view of Europeans and North Americans and the Ardabil had been crowned as its pre-eminent example. Despite the many political, social and economic factors quite extraneous to the carpets themselves which had influenced this judgement, and the scintillating examples of rugs from other regions, the assessment remains unchallenged. The Ardabil and its Safavid cousins are still taken to be the apex of carpet art and are seen as primary evidence of the supremacy of Iranian culture.

In the constrained economic circumstances of Britain in the early twenty-first century, and amid the post-imperial crisis of confidence which the British have been experiencing for the last fifty years, it is hard to summon the atmosphere of the late nineteenth century. Huge wealth was extracted from Britain's colonies overseas and its industrial working classes at home. Colonisation, globalisation and industrialisation brought suffering to many and a degree of intellectual anxiety and scruples to some. In Britain, these anxieties were notably articulated by thinkers such as William Morris and Friedrich Engels and novelists like Charles Dickens and Elizabeth Gaskell. But for capitalists, the ruling classes and the majority of the bourgeoisie in Britain it was a time of drive, experiment, bold assurance and spending. One of the ways in which this expressed itself was in the building of impressive civic homes for growing imperial collections of artefacts. An outstanding example among them was London's South Kensington Museum, now the V&A

Museum. Founded in 1852, the original purpose of the V&A was to provide excellent examples of decorative arts to improve the quality of British manufacturing design, supporting Britain's aspiration to dominate an increasingly global trade. By the 1890s it had amassed a remarkable collection of objects from domestic and European designers for this purpose.

The V&A also collected energetically from across Britain's formal and informal empires, by fair means and foul. In just one example, the V&A's China gallery contains a crimson lacquer throne made around 1780 for the travelling palace used by the Qing emperors in their hunting grounds south of Beijing. In a violent and undisciplined occupation of Beijing carried out in 1900 by soldiers of an alliance between the US, UK, Russia and Japan, Russian soldiers looted the Qing imperial throne. It was then brought to London by a tsarist Russian diplomat during the 1917 Bolshevik Revolution. In a bathetic end to this international drama, the stolen Qing throne was bought for the V&A by one of the UK's biggest potato-dealers. But that 'major figure in the wholesale potato industry', as the V&A catalogue has it,[20] offers a dramatic illustration of how everyday commerce, high politics, colonial ruthlessness and human loss came together in the objects collected by nineteenth-century imperial museums.

Throughout the V&A, Asian loot sits uneasily alongside trade goods, and demonstrations of colonial power alongside the museum's original utilitarian aspiration to improve manufacturing design. Its galleries still map the encounter between nineteenth-century Britain and the world it sought to dominate. Old Persian carpets became part of that apparatus of domination. They helped represent the imperial Britain of steam, iron, coal and manufacturing as an empire comparable in cultural glory to the lost Safavids.

The V&A had acquired carpets from its beginnings, buying examples from the Great Exhibition of 1851 as part of its foundational collection. There was a particular emphasis initially on India. Britain had strong historic trading and political links there through the British East India Company, which until 1857 governed large parts of India to the financial advantage of British shareholders, including the British government. The V&A also collected the Turkish carpets known from Renaissance paintings and the centuries-long trade between Europe and the Ottoman Empire. As the museum began building its collection in the mid-nineteenth century, the carpets of Persia were rarer and much less familiar.

In 1878 a paradigm shift occurred among European museum curators. France, leaving behind the traumas of the Paris Commune and the Franco–Prussian War, organised an impressive international exhibition. The 1878 Paris Exposition Universelle was housed in the purpose-built Palais de Trocadéro on the hill of Chaillot overlooking the Eiffel Tower. There visitors encountered rare centuries-old Persian carpets from private collections, whose owners had previously kept them for their own pleasure.[21] A report written by Caspar Purdon Clarke, who would later become director of the V&A, evokes the shock of his encounter there with 'a high-class branch of fine art production that had hitherto been utterly ignored by Museum administrations'.[22] We can only imagine his mixture of delight at the carpets and embarrassment at the gaps in the knowledge of the mighty V&A, whose curators were at work separating the good from the bad, and setting standards of creativity across nations and media.

When Purdon Clarke expressed his wonderment at the old Persian carpets in the Oriental gallery of the 1878 Exposition Universelle, he did so in a building whose other wing contained France's newly established Museum of Ethnography. There, objects from non-Western cultures were arranged in stages to indicate their level of development towards Western civilisation.[23] The pivot to Persia and its carpets by Europe's cultural establishment was soundtracked by the drumbeat of racist theory in the background, down the stairs, along the corridor, just next door.

In the later decades of the nineteenth century, the old Iranian carpets shown in the 1878 Paris Exposition and others of their kind were on the move from their declining European aristocratic owners, who began to trade family heirlooms for the new money of industrialists and bankers in Europe and the US.[24] These arriviste owners in turn traded in their rugs as they upgraded and developed their collections in an inflationary merry-go-round. Demand outstripped supply from both European and Iranian sources of old Persian carpets. Museum curators were hungry for opulent Iranian rugs and had to find the money to play this new and very expensive game.

The V&A was relatively slow off the mark. The Musée des Tissus in Lyon had bought an early Safavid silk and precious metal brocaded carpet directly from the 1878 Exposition, its showily luxurious materials irresistible to bling-seeking European colonialists. But throughout the 1880s, as market prices inflated, the V&A held back from the necessary investment.[25] William Morris, a great carpet enthusiast, tried to cajole the V&A into spending the money required to buy old Iranian carpets. Morris's voice was respected in the museum, and in 1884 he was made a formal referee for purchases made by the V&A. But despite his advice, it was not until a full five years after the Paris Exposition, in 1883, that the museum finally paid £308, the equivalent in 2024 of about £36,000 or $45,000, for a sixteenth-century Iranian carpet with a central medallion and complex field of animals and vegetation.[26] Subsequent opportunities to buy complete museum-quality examples of old Iranian carpets were few and far between, and despite intensifying efforts throughout the 1880s the V&A seemed to have missed the boat.

Then they hit the jackpot. The V&A learned that a London art importer and dealer, Robinson and Company, was offering a previously unknown, large, well-preserved and beautiful Iranian carpet dated to the mid-sixteenth-century Safavid era. It was displayed in their shop in London's Wigmore Street, where a team of Victorian gentlemen from the V&A in frock coats and eyeglasses travelled the two and a half miles from South Kensington to examine it.

The carpet was originally priced at £7,000,[27] the equivalent in today's money of almost a quarter of a million pounds, or

$300,000. After a good deal of horse-trading the V&A paid £1,750, and a private donor made the price up to £2,000. During the museum's discussions about buying the carpet, Caspar Purdon Clarke, by then one of its directors, commented: 'I consider the carpet a bargain at £1,500. The only modern carpets combining that fineness of count, 676 knots to a square inch, with artistic workmanship are those made by Aubusson in imitation of the old things of the Goupil collection.'[28]

The V&A, still mindful of its pocketbook, felt it had made a good deal. As Purdon Clarke implied, it got the carpet's antiquity and Safavid connections effectively for free, as per square metre it was cheaper than high-quality contemporary French Aubusson copies of rare old carpets. With perfect circularity, the Goupil collection mentioned by Purdon Clarke was the group of carpets brought together by Paris dealer Albert Goupil for the Paris Exposition Universelle in 1878, which had kicked off the scramble for old Persian carpets in the first place.

The arrival of a sixteenth-century Safavid carpet in Robinson's Wigmore Street shop was more than a fabulous opportunity for consumption in one of the wealthiest cities in the world. It was a cultural event that made the pages of the London *Times*,[29] and a call to battle for the museum's advisors and curators. Here was the opportunity to glorify Victoria's empire by close association with the much-admired, ethnically and culturally impeccable Safavid golden age of Persia, through the medium of what quickly came to be acclaimed as the world's finest carpet.

The carpet in the shop on London's elegant Wigmore Street was the Ardabil, and it began its journey into myth as soon as it was launched into the culturally inquisitive London of 1892. To justify its eye-watering initial asking price, Edward Stebbing, the managing director of dealers Robinson and Company, needed to create a compelling marketing story imbuing the carpet with the necessary allure. The story he came up with is captured by

the title of an illustrated pamphlet on the carpet which he published in 1892. He called it *The Holy Carpet of the Mosque at
Ardebil.*[30]

The royal city of Ardabil was a sacred centre in Safavid Iran;
indeed it is still a site of pilgrimage today. It is the burial place of
Shah Ishmael I, the founder of the Safavid dynasty, and shrine
of his holy ancestor, Shayk Safi al-Din Ardabili, founder of the
Safaviyya School of Sufism, after whom the Safavids were named.
In his pamphlet, Stebbing says of Shah Ishmael I, 'Almost all of his
ancestors were regarded as holy men, and some of them as saints.
They had long been settled at Ardebil, where they lived as retired
devotees.'[31]

Ardabil was the familial and religious heart of the Safavid
dynasty. By claiming the shrine at Ardabil as the place where the
carpet was used and found, Stebbing associated it indelibly with
the imperial family, and the exceptional blaze of cultural glory
over which the Safavids had presided. But the title of Stebbing's
marketing pamphlet went even beyond this positioning of the
carpet as an exceptional product of royal patronage suitable for
use in its dynastic spiritual heartland. He did not describe the
mosque as holy, but the carpet itself. The Ardabil was offered to the
V&A by Stebbing as a sacral object invested with a power beyond
the material, the utilitarian or the ceremonial.

Stebbing had another tool to ratchet up the glamour and mystique of the carpet he was trying to sell. His pamphlet contained
a translation of the inscription and date on the carpet: 'Except for
thy threshold there is no refuge for me in all the world. Except
for this door, there is no resting place for my head. The work of a
servant of the court, Maqsud of Kashan. 1539–1540.'[32]

To have this amount of information woven into a carpet is
vanishingly rare. Alongside the evocative couplet from the poet
Hafez, beloved among the many poets of Persia, the inscription
offers historical information, the apparent date of making and
the apparent maker. The inscription meant that the Ardabil
was not only an exceptional artefact from a revered place and
time, but that it articulated its own historical significance.

Stebbing had put together a package that was mouth-wateringly attractive to the gentlemen of the V&A, even if wasn't enough to part them from the £7,000 he originally asked. Nevertheless, he had drafted the outline of the heroic story which solidified around the Ardabil in the late nineteenth and early twentieth centuries

In his letter to V&A director Thomas Armstrong recommending the purchase of the Ardabil, William Morris explained: 'I am sure that this is far the finest Eastern carpet which I have seen (either actual carpets or reproductions of them)',[33] which a headline in the London *Times* escalated to the claim that it was the finest carpet in the world.[34] Fake news never depended on social media. Morris continued: 'For firstly it must be remembered that this carpet has no counterpart, whereas the finest carpets hitherto seen . . . belong to a class of which there are many examples.'[35]

Both Stebbing's marketing and Morris's recommendation laid stress on the carpet's uniqueness and its excellent state of preservation. These claims proved to be shockingly false. It soon became clear that a second Ardabil carpet existed, sold by the same dealer, Edward Stebbing, in the previous year, 1892, to a US collector, Charles Tyson Yerkes, on the condition that it should not return to Britain.[36] Yerkes was the prototypical US robber baron, a super-rich financier and entrepreneur who whitewashed his dubious business dealing through cultural investments and philanthropy. Stebbing took a risk in entrusting his secret to this slippery character. It was also soon evident that this second Ardabil had been cannibalised to repair the tattered borders of the V&A's Ardabil. Still-unknown artisans in a still-unknown location wove and stitched sections from the border of the second Ardabil into the London Ardabil.[37] The repairs are very clear now we know they are there, but the referees and curators seemed blinded to them at the point of sale by the psychological impact of the carpet and their deep desire for it. Curators and carpet specialists now mourn the repairs as an act of vandalism carried out in the interests of a market which preferred a perfect object to one which preserved its historical integrity, its wounds and losses.

If anything, these suggestions of conspiracy around the holy carpet added to its cachet and power over the public and scholarly imagination. When the second Ardabil was sold on by Yerkes in 1910, the auction catalogue made capital of the confusion, saying salaciously that 'A greater or less measure of mystery has for years surrounded the Ardabil carpet of South Kensington, a dark suggestion of some truth hidden, and even furtive intimation of *chicane*.'[38]

The intimation of chicane stuck to the carpet. As late as 1966, Kurt Erdmann, one of the twentieth century's pre-eminent scholars of carpets, suggested that senior officials at the South Kensington Museum were complicit in concealing the history of the two carpets and the repairs before the Ardabil's arrival in the museum. Erdmann said: 'Mr Stebbing did not tell the truth about its excellent state of preservation. This of course was known to the director of the Museum.'[39]

The repairs were uncovered, but the route by which the rug had come to the V&A remained a mystery. In 1914 A.F. Kendrick, Keeper of Textiles at the V&A, tried to investigate its provenance. It was twenty years since the carpet's acquisition and Kendrick belonged to a new generation of curators who had no part in the purchase, or Erdmann's proposed conspiracy. Kendrick wrote that year to Stebbing enquiring after what he knew: 'I have lately been collecting what facts are recorded about the history of the Ardabil Carpet. So far, I cannot trace how or when it left Ardabil. The carpet is of so great interest that it seems essential to record all that can be known about it while the facts are in the recollection of people living.'[40]

The V&A file indicates that there was no reply from Stebbing, and it was stamped 'no further action'. It seems that all parties were willing to let the investigation lie dormant. As leading late-twentieth-century carpet scholar May Beattie put it, 'The one fact that remains is that valuable historical information has been distorted and lost in the tangled web of the carpet trade.'[41]

The strong presumption among historians now is that the answer to Kendrick's question is that in the 1880s Hildebrand Stevens, dealer and on-and-off British consul in Tabriz, bought the two carpets from the shrine at Ardabil, which was raising money for repairs to the mosque complex after earthquake damage. It is proposed that Stevens sold them to Anglo-Swiss carpet-manufacturers and dealers Ziegler and Company, who had operations in Iran. Sections from what became Yerkes' Ardabil were then used to repair the V&A Ardabil, and the historical consensus is that the repairs were managed by Ziegler and Company, using artisans either in Tabriz or Turkey.[42] Then it was acquired by that inventive, psychologically acute salesman Stebbing, who wove a story the museum and the public wanted to hear.

Meanwhile, *pace* May Beattie, there was another indisputable fact. There were two carpets, not one, and that changed everything. The patron of the carpet could no longer be envisaged even by the most sceptical as someone merely wealthy, aristocratic and educated. The scale of the project to weave two identical elite carpets during his reign suggested the patronage of Shah Tahmasp I himself. What the V&A's Ardabil lost in uniqueness it gained in prestige.

The previously unknown Safavid carpet offered a home for many disparate strands of British feeling about Iran. It was commissioned and produced by what had come to be known as northern Europe's Aryan cousins in Persia, who had dominated their region as the British now dominated the globe. It was made during what the West increasingly judged to be the sixteenth- and seventeenth-century Safavid peak of Persian culture, a fitting parallel to the peak the British believed their empire had achieved. It was associated with both the Safavid royal family and with a highly pious, even if not Christian, tradition. And in a further benefit for the patriarchal imperialists of 1890s London, the name in the carpet's inscription was a man, Maqsud Kashani, neatly eliminating any suggestion that women, the world's weavers, might be behind this sacred masterpiece.

At the same time, the carpet was a celebration of Eastern sensuality and luxury – traits with which the British struggled during the nineteenth and early twentieth centuries. Desire for these experiences threatened British moral rectitude at home and sapped Britain's moral authority in its colonies and among its distant trading partners. The fear of 'going native' haunts late-Victorian literature, and a dissipated East was often cast as the shadowy twin to the brisk, daylight Victorian and Edwardian eras.[43]

A powerful and enduring origin story developed for the Ardabil out of these complex associations and suggestions of conspiracy. It tells us that Persia, in decline and thoughtless of its own past treasures, left the world's finest carpets to moulder in a shrine to an exotic medieval holy man. The rugs, royal and sacred, were rescued by intrepid Europeans, who might be mercenary but had the clear-sightedness to recognise their value. They fell into the hands of ruthless Western capitalists, who collaborated with wily Eastern artisans to create a single apparently perfect but disputed carpet. The museum, greedy for Oriental treasure, conspired in the mystery and the hoax.

The story has many powerful archetypal components: the object of high material and spiritual value rescued from a neglectful East by the West, the jeopardy of its mysterious, potentially dangerous route to its new home, and the West's taking control of it and its powers, religious and political.[44] The story also suggests the beginning of a backlash to this romantic exoticism, in the strand which dwells on the idea that European power brokers deceived to get what they wanted. It feels like fiction, harking back to Wilkie Collins's 1868 novel *The Moonstone*. You could imagine Steven Spielberg using it as a plot for an Indiana Jones movie.

These stories about the carpet express the values of the British Empire at its noontide, as much as, if not more than, the lost glamour of the extinct Safavids. The Victorians and Edwardians believed they were talking about a Persian rug when they talked about the Ardabil, but they also talked about their own Orient-haunted selves.

The Ardabil, its patron and its makers have a history as well as a mythology. Its inscription dates it to the reign of Shah Tahmasp I. The Safavid dynasty was established in 1501 by his father Shah Ishmael, a charismatic and successful leader, who was hailed as Shahenshah, King of Kings, by his people. But when Tahmasp came to the throne as a boy of ten, his family dynasty and its hold over a previously politically fragmented Iran had only existed for thirteen years. The new empire and its young emperor were vulnerable.

Tahmasp had a struggle to secure the new Iran. He had to settle civil wars at home between the scrapping and plotting Black Sheep and White Sheep Turkmen tribes. He also had to fight off incursions from Iran's traditional nomadic Uzbek enemies on its eastern and northern frontiers, and at the age of fourteen led an army which decisively defeated them at Jam in 1528. Meanwhile the great Ottoman Empire to the west had reached its height with the rule of Suleyman the Magnificent, who became Ottoman emperor in 1520, just four years before Tahmasp became Safavid emperor. The two men – the experienced Ottoman leader with his mature empire, and the Safavid emperor, young and precarious like his dynasty – fought and vied for territory and influence in the region. But by the early 1530s, Tahmasp, still barely out of his teens, had stabilised the new Iran, and a period of high courtly art and culture flowered.

Tahmasp's and the Safavids' claim to authority in Iran rested not only on political acumen and military success, but on their claim to a special role in Islam, and a special relationship with its Prophet. Ishmael and Tahmasp were believed to be seyyida, descendants of the Prophet. They were members of the Safaviyya, based in Ardabil, who were followers of the Prophet's cousin, son-in-law and close companion, Ali. In the modern world we call these followers of Ali Shia Muslims. Part of their belief is that Ali will return in the form of the Mahdi, and indeed Tahmasp's father Ishmael had declared himself the Mahdi, Ali reincarnated. Under Ishmael, Shia Islam became the official religion of Iran, replacing the multi-faith but predominantly Sunni Islam of pre-Safavid times, often by forcible conversion. The great schism which sets modern Shia Iran apart from many of its Sunni neighbours and complicates and embitters politics in the Middle East today dates back more than half a millennium to 1501. Like many religious hatreds, it is dizzyingly ancient.

Ishmael had the charisma, but Tahmasp had the political creativity. From around 1533 he repositioned the relationship between religion and emperor. Rather than claiming to be the reincarnation of Ali as his father had done, a positioning likely to provoke dissent in his less compelling hands, Tahmasp developed the idea of a Safavid king as a pious servant of Shia Islam. He built and redeveloped centres for the performance of kingship which were at the same time holy places.[45] It was as if the British monarch carried out not only his coronation and worship, but also his audiences with prime ministers, dinners with foreign dignitaries and garden parties at Westminster Abbey rather than Buckingham Palace. Of particular significance to Tahmasp was the shrine at Ardabil in north-west Iran, dedicated to Shayk Safi al-Din Ardabili, his link with Ali and the Prophet.

At the date woven into the Ardabil carpets, 1539–40, textual records show that Tahmasp was extending and rebuilding the shrine complex at Ardabil, adding a grand audience hall, the Jannat Saray. Its dimensions are just big enough to hold both Ardabils. The idea that the twin Ardabil carpets were commissioned by Tahmasp I for his newly built Jannat Saray is supported by much circumstantial evidence, but is ultimately a scholarly historical deduction. Nevertheless, the compelling image of the two huge and beautiful carpets unrolled there for the shah's audiences with powerful political figures of the era, like the refugee sons of the Mughal and Ottoman emperors, Humayun and Bayezid, the great of Iran itself and diplomats from all over Eurasia, is too enthralling to resist.

When it arrived in the West at the end of the nineteenth century, the Ardabil was believed to have been made in the Iranian artistic centre of Kashan, largely because the carpet's woven inscription describes it as being the work of Maqsud Kashani. But it seems likely that Maqsud's name describes his personal connection with Kashan, rather than the place the carpet was made. Ardabil itself isn't an exceptional carpet-making area, so has also tended to be rejected as the place it was woven. Tabriz is often offered as the most likely possibility. Just over a hundred miles from Ardabil, it was a centre for the weaving of impressive silk floral carpets with intricate central medallions. Historians now believe that Tahmasp and his court were based at Tabriz at the date of the Ardabil carpet's inscription. But this discussion seems beside the point given that Shah Tahmasp, riding high on sixteenth-century Safavid imperial success, could have commanded weavers and designers from anywhere in his territories to create carpets which glorified both his reign and his dynastic shrine.

Cold water was thrown early on the idea that Maqsud singlehandedly wove the two carpets himself, which would have been the work of decades. It was replaced by the proposal that he was overseer of a team of carefully selected artisans, as has traditionally been the case in the handweaving of special carpets. The assumption now is that a team of weavers worked on it for several years, offering a welcome period of security and stability for the artisans involved and their families. They were temporarily freed from weaving without any guarantee of sale, unpredictable short-term commissions, and the interference of trade associations that controlled production and pricing in urban Iran in the sixteenth century.[46] It's possible that they participated in the creative exchange between artists working for Tahmasp in other media.[47] There is a long scholarly tradition which attributes the designs of elite carpets like the Ardabil to bookbinders and painters.[48] If the Ardabil's weavers were indeed part of such a vibrant artistic

community, it is possible that it raised their aspirations for the
carpet, as they worked for many months, perhaps amounting
to years, knotting the sixteen colours of wool on to individual
silk warps.

Although the world's weavers are mainly women, part of
the story that grew in Europe from the late nineteenth century
onwards about the weaving of elite Safavid carpets was that they
were woven by highly skilled men.[49] A handful of Western visitors
to sixteenth-century Iran note the absence of women in weaving
sheds,[50] but as May Beattie points out, any female weavers would
have been hidden away from the eyes of visiting Western non-
Muslim men.[51] Meanwhile, even a figure such as Donald King, the
V&A's highly respected Keeper of Textiles in the 1970s, pointed to
'common sense' as the source of the belief that men designed and
wove Safavid carpets.[52] This is a phrase which always suggests that
there is no hard evidence. Whatever the historical truth, the idea
of male Safavid weavers suited a nineteenth-century Western view
which held that if an object was art then it was created by men,
and that what women practised was a lesser form of creativity
described in the West as craft.[53] The Ardabil's great significance to
colonial ideology has created such powerful stories that they cloud
our reading of history.

The rescued and repaired icon became the centrepiece of the Islamic collection in one of the world's leading colonial museums, the
V&A. The twin carpet, its borders removed to realise the dream of
the single perfect artefact, suffered a significant reduction in status
and went into private ownership as a rich man's ornament. Even as
he promoted the uniqueness of the Ardabil to the London market
in 1892, Stebbing was busy selling the cut-down twin to Charles
Tyson Yerkes. The second Ardabil was one of the great prizes
in the competitive world of late-nineteenth and early-twentieth-
century collecting, and Yerkes was only the first of its owners. In
1939 it was sold to its last private owner, John Paul Getty. It is now

shared between the Los Angeles County Museum of Art and the Getty Museum, Malibu.

There are not enough original Ardabils to go around the power-hungry men of the world. But fortunately, fine replicas of it are considered appropriate for rooms that contain and embody power. As well as the copy in Downing Street, there was one in Hitler's Reich Chancellery. A story that may be apocryphal tells that one of the reasons for John Paul Getty's gift of the cut-down Ardabil to LACMA was that even he, then the richest man in the world, should not be walking on a genuine Ardabil. The aura of this carpet is so intense that even a copy of it reinforces the status of great men and perhaps the original sometimes has too much power for them.[54]

Meanwhile, the display of the London Ardabil in the V&A's Islamic gallery completes a process which has taken it beyond mere demonstrations of private status by the wealthy and powerful, or of national status by great museums. That process began in 1892 with Stebbing's marketing pamphlet, which launched the idea that the Ardabil carpet is holy. The holy carpet in its glass shrine in turn now frames the V&A's Islamic gallery as an environment for worship, although not that of religion as conventionally understood. The worship it provokes is that of a Western-defined hierarchy of material culture. The Ardabil has become the supreme totem of a superclass of Persian carpets, reigning over all other carpets and exemplifying the superiority of Persia over all other Islamic culture.

But while it is endlessly desirable and apparently available to its viewers, the carpet is also endlessly out of reach. The lights in the Ardabil's glass shrine are switched on for only ten minutes out of every thirty, and the viewer's encounter with it is as much about darkness and withholding as about illumination and revelation.[55] The V&A's congregation gathers, waiting for the lights to go up. As they wait, they see their own faces in the dark glass, an intimation that, just like the Victorians, what they will see in the Ardabil is a reflection of their shadow selves.

Under the dim illumination the viewers judge the carpet for themselves. I have long been fascinated by this moment of encounter and a few years ago conducted a vox pop of the visitors. Their responses suggest that expectations are not always met: 'I thought it would be gold.' 'I thought it was supposed to be the oldest carpet in the world.' 'I thought it would be very bright.' 'I can't see the pattern in it.' 'It's just a carpet.' The wait in the darkness gives the viewers time to invent their own Ardabil story, a sometimes unfulfilled dream of unimaginable antiquity, opulence and potency.

The V&A's Ardabil is a powerful example of what is meant by the appropriation of one culture by another. It illustrates the political and psychological power available in the reinvention of objects. The Ardabil's appropriation helped validate the exploitative aspirations of one empire, the British, by tying it to another, the Safavid, sanctified by age and extinction.

The carpet was transformed into a fetish object in the nineteenth-century West, which, instead of illuminating the culture and religion of the Safavid Empire in which it was made, served to reinforce the identity of a different age and nation, imperial Britain. The mythology built around it eliminated the experience of the Ardabil's sixteenth-century makers and nineteenth-century repairers, human beings with lives and stories of their own. These histories are being challenged by modern scholarship, but their impact on thinking about carpets broadly has been more difficult to mitigate. The appropriation of the Ardabil has been instrumental in the building and consolidation of a hierarchy of carpets based on racist nineteenth-century thought, a hierarchy which still persists and echoes through this book. The racial framework proposing that northern European white men and their Persian brothers were the world's civilisational leaders has been discredited, but its impact on how we think about carpets remains.

In popular understanding, Persian carpets now trump the claims to greatness of other rugs, and an Iranian origin is the default imagined for fascinating carpets that we don't fully understand. Iran was one of the suggestions as the place of making of the fourth-century BCE Pazyryk carpet found in Siberia, and diaspora weavers from Tabriz in Iran as the makers of fifteenth- and sixteenth-century Mamluk rugs. Carpets from other regions are often described generically as Persian, as if there are no others, and despite the distinguished and diverse history of carpet-making across Eurasia. Indeed, it was hard to keep the word Persian out of the title of this book. Students often ask me, 'Which carpets are the best?' Before I have time to reply, they answer their own question: 'It's Persian, isn't it?'

Chapter 4
Samurai

FLATWOVEN KILIM, SIXTEENTH CENTURY CE, IRAN

Sometime in the mid-sixteenth century on a ruined agricultural field, a huge army of peasant foot soldiers fought with swords, spears, bows and matchlock guns, roaring, bleeding and dying in the Japanese mud.[1] Their samurai leaders moved around the battlefield, fighting both on horseback and on foot, urging their men to greater efforts in the face of exhaustion, fear and pain. Samurai armour was designed to give them mobility for the martial arts in which they were skilled, and for this they sacrificed the protectiveness of the solid metal armour used in Europe. Instead, scales of metal, boiled leather or lacquered wood were interlaced together, allowing the knights to dance as they fought. To help their foot soldiers identify them as they moved nimbly around in the storm of the fight, samurai wore elaborate headpieces and *jinbaori*, highly decorative campaign jerkins. These battles raged as Japanese warlords struggled to dominate the fractured country after more than a hundred years of the Warring States period, the Sengoku. Among the most powerful of them was Toyotomi Hideyoshi (1537–98), one of Japan's three 'Great Unifiers'. Artefacts preserved for almost five hundred years conjure him as he appeared to his troops. A hallucination amid the smoke and noise of the battlefield, his soldiers identified him by his yellow-cloaked horse guards, his standard of golden gourds, his black helmet with its black-lacquer sunburst crest and his jinbaori, among them one decorated with brilliantly coloured silk images of ferocious animals engaged in the primeval battle between the weak and the strong.[2]

Samurai armour is among the most chilling in global warfare and has inspired a powerful modern expression of good fallen into evil: the insect-like carapace and monstrous headpiece of Darth Vader in George Lucas's *Star Wars*. But jinbaori often strike a different note to this dehumanised and terrifying killing machine: instead, part of their purpose was to encourage foot soldiers in battle. They displayed the glamour, personality and prestige of their wearer, sometimes even their humour. They were often fantastical creations using wild colours, opulent fur and feathers, intricate embroidery, gold and silver thread, precious-metal embossing and rare textiles. Silk from continental China was highly prized in their making, as was imported wool in a region with few sheep.[3] Hideyoshi had a wardrobe of jinbaori crafted from this rich diversity of materials and techniques, which evoked for his soldiers different aspects of his charisma.

But one jinbaori was exceptional in both message and material. It insisted on the barbarism of battle and death rather than the life force of the leader, and it achieved this by adopting and adapting the iconography of a little-known and half-imagined society five thousand miles to the west. In a culture which had no tradition of fine carpet-weaving, it was tailored from an imported silk kilim, made during the sixteenth-century starburst of weaving in Safavid Iran. No other surviving jinbaori uses imported carpet as its source textile, let alone a rug produced by weavers who are still among the world's most revered. Hideyoshi's campaign coat is unique. It poses the question of what Hideyoshi wished to project through this alien object – what Iran meant to the resurgent Japan of the sixteenth century.

After five hundred years, the jinbaori's vividly drawn and brightly coloured animal motifs still glow and glitter on their background of gold-coloured silk embellished with silver and gold thread. Animals in Persian carpets are often represented as participants in an Iranian courtly ritual of the hunt, leaping away with courage and grace from men on horseback, or resting in paradise gardens. But Hideyoshi didn't select a textile displaying these echoes of Islamic spirituality and the sophisticated social habits of sixteenth-century Iranian aristocrats for his war gear. Instead, from the repertory of Japanese ideas about Iran he chose a Persian kilim which materialised the savagery of an existential struggle. As his foot soldiers watched for him in battle, they saw animals clambering on each other, fangs bared and claws unsheathed in a savage fight for survival, or prowling across the field of the carpet looking for prey.

The tailors who transformed the kilim into a jinbaori for their great military patron emphasised this struggle, using ten framed motifs of fighting animals as the centre of their redesign: three pairs on the front of the jinbaori and two pairs behind. The murderous savage beasts are placed over Hideyoshi's chest and back, and their visceral power protects his heart, lungs, liver and lights. Some of the fighting pairs are lions and spotted deer, others are eerie and supernatural *qilin*, the flaming deer of Chinese mythology, motifs which travelled west from China to Iran during the thirteenth and fourteenth century Mongol Empire. Now they travelled back east to Japan. Around these scenes of animal warfare are arranged lion masks and mythological birds associated with Asian royalty. The more peaceful pastoral aspects of the kilim's original design are literally marginalised, deployed only around the edges. Deer gambol among blossom and leaves in the narrow borders flowing down each side of the front opening of the jinbaori and along the base of its back. They are the dream held in peripheral vision as the struggle for survival takes place on the main body of the vest. We are left in no doubt that this is war gear.

When Hideyoshi chose a Persian carpet for his most psychologically important piece of battledress, he appropriated Safavid culture for his political agenda – just as the V&A did in its reinvention of the Ardabil carpet. It's easy to assume that Orientalism is solely enacted by the West on the East, but both intra-Asia Orientalism, the exoticisation of East Asia by West Asia, and Occidentalism, the reimagining of West Asia by those further east, are common. Hideyoshi's jinbaori shows us Occidentalism in action, an appropriation and reimagining of Persia, in distant West Asia, for the circumstances of Warring States Japan. The V&A's appropriation of the Ardabil had glamorised sixteenth-century Iran as a successful cultural and imperial peak, and a model for imperial Britain. In sixteenth-century Japan, Hideyoshi summoned from his Persian carpet a vision of beautiful barbarism, celebrating the seemingly endless war in which he was engaged. Both Orientalism and Occidentalism are instruments for turning history into propaganda.

The jinbaori was not simply an ideological object. It was meant to be worn. Hideyoshi has the reputation of being an ugly man, and this is borne out by contemporaneous portraits. It has been suggested that the boy who had suffered poverty, privation and hardship in his peasant childhood grew into a small and emaciated adult.[4] Oda Nobunaga, the ruler in whose service he rose to eminence, called him 'a bald rat', and when in 1585 Hideyoshi became *kampaku* (imperial regent ruling Japan on behalf of the emperor), graffiti described him as 'the monkey regent'.[5] The glowing gold jinbaori was tailored and padded into a substantial shape, suggesting a powerful and elegant physique. We can't know now how he appeared to his soldiers as he loomed towards them on the battlefield or marched in victory parades. Perhaps the jinbaori transformed the damaged man into an impressive hero, or perhaps his physical limitations were instead highlighted by the outrageous borrowed glamour of his war gear.

Unlike most campaign coats, whose embellishment is extreme and competitive, Hideyoshi's allows the exceptional textile to do the work of glorifying its warlord without further ornament. This unusual restraint on the part of both the makers and their patron suggests a respect for the artefact and an acknowledgement of its aesthetic and imaginative power. The carpet from Safavid Persia was fascinating to its Japanese hosts in a way that a bolt of fine silk from their continental Chinese neighbours wasn't.

The transformation of the Iranian kilim into the Japanese jin-baori may have taken place in one of Hideyoshi's many castles, or in Kyoto, the ancient Japanese capital. The artisans who worked on the transmutation are more accessible and known to us than the Persian weavers of the kilim, because there are extensive records and images of craftspeople in sixteenth- and seventeenth-century Japan. Painters and historians recorded the practice of crafts as activities of interest in themselves, rather than of value only for what they produced. This different perspective towards makers and making had philosophical and religious roots. In the Buddhist tea ceremony the focus is not on the final cup of tea, but on the ritual and craft of making it and the tools of that craft, the tea-pots, tea bowls and whisks. Equally, Confucianism's engagement with society's productive activities, many of them crafts, and its emphasis on salvation through work was part of its pragmatic appeal. The phrase 'Find a job you like, and you will never have to work a day in your life' is attributed to Confucius. Painters such as Kanō Yoshinobu (1552–1640) could readily find audiences and patrons for series like his *Paintings of Various Professions*. Indeed, one of the patrons of the famed Kanō family of painters to which Yoshinobu belonged was Hideyoshi himself.

Artists of the period illustrate castle ateliers where exceptional needlework is being carried out, but it is equally likely that the artisans who were given the task of making the jinbaori worked in the Nishijin area of Kyoto, whose grid of streets close by the Imperial Palace is still the textile quarter of the city to this day. Hideyoshi had saved and restored the ancient capital after its battering and near-destruction in the Sengoku civil wars. It is still revered as one of the world's great cultural centres. In Kyoto, the exotic and unique kilim would have been repurposed into an emblem of Japanese military culture in a specialist workshop housed in a *machiya*, one of the traditional wooden townhouses of Kyoto, with their sliding screens and cool courtyard gardens.

Both men and women would have been involved in the transformation. Craft guilds in Kyoto were the exclusive preserve of
men, so the route to textile entrepreneurship was closed to women,
but sixteenth- and seventeenth-century painters show women in
workshops stitching, binding and hand-painting garments. Wom-
en's hands are also present in these garments as suppliers of work
done in the seclusion of their homes, where they made the braids
and cotton wadding used in jinbaori.[6] Meanwhile, the palace was
a privileged if constrained home to highly skilled male and female
artisans, and it was a high honour to be invited to join their number.

Whether women or men, in a palace or a Kyoto workshop, a
jinbaori's makers needed a high level of technical and sensory
understanding to make these wild and fantastical garments. Some
aspects of the process were familiar to them: the structure of the
popular *kosode*, the forerunner of the kimono, and its shorter
version the *dobuku* were often the base shapes of a jinbaori. They
were skilled in, or able to source, appliqué and embroidery, special
buttons, fastenings and braid. But they also needed the expertise
to work with extraordinary materials like yak hair, bear fur, tiger
and leopard skins, paper, gold and silver leaf, and the wide range
of feathers used in jinbaori, or as in this case, a heavy carpet.[7]

A kilim is a flatwoven textile whose pattern is constructed by
the interweaving of warp and weft threads. It has no knots added
to it, and no pile. Its structure and its design are inseparable.
While not so thick and heavy as a wool pile carpet, a silk kilim
is a substantial textile and could not have been easy to handle. Its
weight, stiffness and fixed size may account for the unusual shape
of Hideyoshi's jinbaori, which is narrower than the more usual
flared silhouette. As the tailors worked, the wefts and warps would
fray and shed fibres, some of them silk thread wrapped in precious
metal foil. One wonders what happened to those glittering and
valuable shards in the clean and frugal environment of the workshop, and whether their spiky remnants scratched Hideyoshi's
neck when he wore the jinbaori.

The artisans who cut, padded and lined the kilim with saffron-
dyed silk needed to transform an object which was effectively

two-dimensional, like a painting, into a three-dimensional artefact whose meaning could be deciphered as a human body moved
within it. To do this, they had to dismember the kilim. This would
not have been an unusual or unwelcome requirement: Japan has a
long and highly valued practice of repair, recycling and repurposing.[8] The kimono of Hideyoshi's widow Onene, for instance, was
unpicked and reassembled as an altar cloth for the Kodaiji temple
in Kyoto, where Hideyoshi's jinbaori is now also preserved. Off-
cuts of precious textiles were recycled into *meibutsugere*, albums of
'celebrated fragments', or into bags and pouches for tea ceremony
utensils, or as mounts for hanging scrolls.[9] These practices of
revivification were not restricted to the wealthy and their prestige
possessions; everyone recycled textiles. The poor used crafts like
boro and *sashiko*, decorative top stitching by hand, to patch and
reinforce the rags they wore. These historic Japanese techniques
are increasingly practised now in a West waking up to its own
profligacy when it comes to the use of resources.

But the rare kilim from which the war vest was cut was an
object which in Persia was intended to be viewed whole. Its ar-
rangement of motifs and borders had been thought through as
a single integrated composition, just as Japanese screens were.
Did the tailors who made the jinbaori pause their scissors before
cutting into the design? The interiors of our homes are now clut-
tered with chairs, sofas, ottomans, stools, cushions and bedheads
cut from carpets. We do it all the time. Yet the cutting into and
repurposing of a carpet from another culture is a profound act
of appropriation, arguably even more so than inventing a new
history for it or having yourself painted standing on it in a pose
of domination. The physical slicing into the artefact carries with it
the frisson of a taboo act.

Orientalism and Occidentalism gain their power not solely from
the thrill of one's difference from the Other, but from what is
shared. The kilim, with its violent and aristocratic iconography,

was produced for the Safavid elite. The first Safavid shah, Ishmael, had come to power in 1501, and by the end of the century his dynasty had forged a unified and regionally ascendant Iran. The borrowing of iconography and materials from Iran could not have been better suited for the battle gear of Hideyoshi. In the same period that the Safavids established stability at home and Iranian dominance in large parts of West and Central Asia, the arriviste Japanese general had brought more than a century of anarchy and civil war in Japan to its bloody end and was now looking to expand his and his country's influence. The empire he planned involved a decisive step westwards, first into the Korean peninsula and then into China. From China, empires had rolled west across Eurasia for centuries. Hideyoshi invaded Korea twice, in 1592 and 1597. It was the obsession that haunted his final decade of life. Hideyoshi's dream of marching victoriously westwards in a jinbaori made from the carpet of an existing West Asian superpower, Iran, was a superbly confident act of possession, reinvention and threat. It was also an act of hubris. His Korean campaigns failed, and Hideyoshi's vision was not realised until Japan's twentieth-century colonisation of Korea. In today's Japan and Korea he is still an emblem of the controversial legacy of that modern occupation.[10]

Hideyoshi was born a peasant in Nakamura, near the Pacific coast of Japan, into a sixteenth-century world of violence and turmoil, but also of volcanic change. Hideyoshi took the opportunities afforded by those fractured times to become a great general and then de facto ruler of Japan. His ascent – from the boro-stitched rags of the impoverished, powerless and malnourished boy to the Persian jinbaori of the aspirant overlord of a westwards-moving Japanese Empire – was steep.

In 1467, the ruling Ashikaga shogunate had collapsed. A century of civil wars followed. During this Warring States period, Japan's *daimyo*, the feudal lords ruling personal territories, fought among each other with their private armies of samurai warriors and peasants. It was a savage and tragic time for Japan and left a powerful desire for stability which has deeply marked Japanese history. That stability was delivered by three men of the same generation, but with very different temperaments and outcomes for themselves and Japan – Oda Nobunaga (1534–82), Toyotomi Hideyoshi (1537–98), and the first Tokogawa Shogun, Ieyasu (1543–1616). Traditional rhymes invoke the very distinct personalities of the three 'Great Unifiers' and their role in the creation of early modern Japan.

If the songbird won't sing, kill it – Nobunaga
If the songbird won't sing, make it – Hideyoshi
If the songbird won't sing, wait – Ieyasu.[11]

Nobunaga ground the rice
Hideyoshi baked the cake
Ieyasu ate the cake.[12]

Nobunaga began the process of unification through fear and military violence, grinding Japan just as he ground rice for the cake. By the mid-sixteenth century, many of the warring daimyo had accepted his rule of terror. But bloodshed begets bloodshed, and Nobunaga could only maintain his military peace by means of escalating violence. Ultimately, he was caught in the trap himself, and after a military defeat committed ritual suicide, *seppuku*, his sword carving up his belly. The peasant Hideyoshi had risen up in Nobunaga's service from being his sandal-bearer, and on his death stepped forward as Japan's military and civil leader. A famously brave and fierce warrior, Hideyoshi was known for his strategic abilities in both war and statecraft and, unlike Nobunaga, also for his mercy. As regent for the emperor and leader of the government, the hugely energetic Hideyoshi baked the cake, transforming Japan from a military to a civil state, one with the stability, confidence and curiosity to look outwards to the West. On Hideyoshi's death in 1598, the spectre of civil war rose again. Now it was time for Tokagawa Ieyasu to eat the cake. Within five years Ieyasu had pacified and gained control of Japan, establishing the Tokugawa shogunate which ruled a stable and peaceful Japan until 1868. But during the three hundred and fifty years of the shogunate, Japan turned inwards. No leader stepped forward to try to create a westward empire or to intensify the westward connections which had brought Hideyoshi's jinbaori into existence.

Hideyoshi had engineered a settlement between Japan's classes which endured until the nineteenth century. Peasants were no longer to bear arms, and in a richly dramatic realisation of this he initiated a sword hunt throughout the nation to disarm them, promising to reforge them as a giant Buddha. The role of peasants was now to stay in their communities, which Hideyoshi had had carefully mapped and surveyed, and to tend to agriculture, making it possible for their daimyo to pay taxes. Meanwhile, the daimyo were required to accept Hideyoshi's centralisation of taxation and foreign policy, in exchange for significant autonomy in their own domains.

Hideyoshi understood the potential of both religion and culture for maintaining peace and stability, and energetically encouraged them. He supported Shinto, Buddhism and Confucianism – indeed, he built and restored so many temples that he contributed to the ecological crisis of deforestation in sixteenth-century Japan.[13] He ruled over a cultural explosion, the Momoyama period, named after the flowering peach blossom at his great castle at Fushimi outside Kyoto. The period, which is sometimes called Japan's Golden Age, has been described as 'contrapuntal',[14] containing more than one melody. The first was the deep spirituality of Shinto, Confucian and Buddhist values, and the *wabi* aesthetic of the tea ceremony: simplicity, rusticity, humility. The second was the equally deep financial and cultural investment in beauty, glamour and prestige. This was both civic, in the rebuilding of cities like Kyoto and the construction of castles and palaces, and individual, in personal adornment and the decoration of interiors, gardens and tea-houses.

But it was not only the culture that pulled in two directions, but the man. There was a fracture between the beaten-up, unpredictable and wizened warrior, with his humble origins, and the splendid and pious leader of a peaceful and culturally vibrant Japan. On the one hand he desired to personify *bun-bu*, the warrior code of the samurai, in which the arts of life, *bun*, and the arts of war, *bu*, are held in harmony. He became both a poet and a Noh actor, and was deeply versed in the tea ceremony. Modern historians sometimes regard the idea of the low-born 'bald rat' and 'monkey regent' practising these refined Japanese traditions as slightly humorous, which gives us an idea of what might have been whispered about Hideyoshi behind his back in his own time, and what the peasant-boy-turned-general then imperial regent had to face.

But Hideyoshi was no new-age, one-love hippy. He was given to unpredictable bouts of violence amid the textiles, gold, lacquer, poetry, tea-making, moon-gazing and peach blossom. He committed strategic atrocities when he believed them necessary to achieve his objectives or redeem his standing.[15] He forced relatives and close advisors to commit suicide and used vicious exemplary punishments. He crucified Japanese Christians as a warning to Jesuit missionaries. He cut off the ears, or possibly the noses, of Korean prisoners of war and buried them in the Mound of Ears, Mimizuka, which can still be found opposite the Toyokuni shrine in Kyoto where Hideyoshi himself is buried.

He was also deeply interested in bling. Described by a Western art historian as 'an aggressive plebian genius',[16] Hideyoshi promoted a glamorous cultural theatricality designed to cover up his humble origins and validate his role at the head of the Japanese army, government and society. A great party-giver, he held some of Japan's most spectacular and self-aggrandising celebrations, some of which are still remarked on today.[17] At these gatherings, Hideyoshi and his entourage displayed themselves in fabulous garments as his pageants wound through local streets into scented and blossoming woods, lit by lanterns in the dusk, passing over artfully designed bridges, viewing golden fish and elegant birds.[18] Those garments had to hold their own in fashion-obsessed Momoyama Japan, and the regent had to surpass all.[19] Few of Hideyoshi's social competitors or detractors could have topped the impact of a jinbaori made from a unique textile brought five thousand miles from an almost imaginary Persia. But, like Momoyama culture and Hideyoshi himself, the jinbaori was contrapuntal, bringing images of animals in savage struggle, echoes of another world, into the peace and beauty that Hideyoshi had created.

In 1974, May Beattie was at a meeting of the assembled scholars of the Royal Asiatic Society in London, among them specialists on Japan.[20] She had just given a paper on sixteenth-century Persian carpets and asked the assembled Asianists if anyone could tell her whether Hideyoshi had ever actually worn his famous Iranian kilim jinbaori in battle. No one knew. This culture-fusing artefact was also contrapuntal – it is as likely that its life was one of parties and competitive consumption as that it was one of war and bloodshed.

It's unlikely that the common folk of Kyoto who watched Hideyoshi parade through the streets or the soldiers who fought alongside him had a well-developed idea of Iran. His Persian kilim would have primarily impressed them with its deluxe exoticism. But for the sixteenth-century Japanese elite, Iran was beginning to come into focus.

There is some evidence of an ancient connection between the two countries, despite the five thousand miles which separated them. A pale-green Iranian glass bowl from the fifth century was found at Nara, one of Japan's early capitals, east of the coastal city of Osaka on the Seto Inland Sea. The bowl's survival for more than fifteen hundred years suggests that it was regarded as a treasure, its Iranian aesthetic appreciated. In the sixth century an Iranian mathematician is recorded as living in Japan and teaching imperial staff.[21] He was clearly regarded as a talented and trustworthy person. Nara was also the furthest point east of the Silk Roads, the overland trading routes which criss-crossed Asia. Between the fourth and the eighth centuries, the flow of goods, people and ideas through these arteries was mediated by Sogdians, a powerful trader-nation who were Iranian in extraction. Over time Iranian became the *lingua franca* of the Central Asian steppe and deserts which separated East Asia from the rest of Eurasia. Persia, its language, culture and values were part of the connective tissue between Japan and the world, but for centuries Japan's relationship with Iran was distant, fragmentary and indirect.

So it remained until the 1500s. From the birth of the Safavid dynasty in 1501, Iran had become an international diplomatic hotspot under the Safavid shahs, receiving embassies and religious missions, and exchanging news from Europe and Asia. Japan was not a direct participant in Iran's diplomatic system, and Iran had no stake in Japan's wars or internal politics. But from the mid-sixteenth century sea routes proliferated, increasing trade and bringing international merchants and Jesuit missionaries to Japan. Faster long-distance ships increased the speed of communications, and with fewer handoffs came fewer Chinese whispers.

News began to reach Japan of an Iran which was no longer almost mythological, but instead the home of a real-world Safavid Empire. That faraway dynasty had come from nowhere in the early sixteenth century, uniting their country and dominating their region in a foreshadowing of Hideyoshi's aspirations for Japan. It's likely that the elites of Japan knew more about Iran in the later part of the fifteenth century than they had ever known. What they had described to them was a Safavid Empire which, despite its remoteness and its unfamiliar religion, was a superbly successful military and cultural regime, fit to be thought of alongside Japan. What they saw with their own eyes and felt with their own hands was the beauty and sensuality of Safavid artefacts.

It is one thing to desire a fine carpet from the small production of a rising empire five thousand miles away, and quite another to gain possession of one. Two barriers stood in Hideyoshi's way: price and supply.

The kilim would have been an extremely costly purchase. More than a century of civil war had damaged Japan's prosperity, and expensive military campaigns were still ongoing in Korea. However, against the odds, Hideyoshi and his daimyo were rich. A crisis six thousand miles away provided Hideyoshi with the means for his luxurious Momoyama splendour, its expensive materials, the labour of artisans, architects and builders and the import of exclusive artefacts like Persian carpets.[22] In the fifteenth and early sixteenth centuries, Europe's growing trade with Asia led to an outflow of European gold and silver coins in exchange for Asian spices, textiles and ceramics. Europe did not have adequate sources of new gold and silver in its mines, and in the fifteenth century this bullion crisis became so acute that Europeans began to return to a barter economy. Europeans also began looking for new sources of bullion, a problem which Spain, for instance, solved for itself by its rapacious seizure of gold and silver objects and mines in the Americas.

Japan was the beneficiary of this European problem. In 1530, a rich vein of silver was found at Iwami, south of modern Tokyo on the island of Honshu. Iwami silver has been compared in quality to that mined by the Spanish at Potosí in Bolivia. Advanced mining and smelting technology was brought to Japan from China and Korea in order to exploit further extensive silver finds made during the sixteenth century. The Japanese elite paid for their expensive luxuries with the silver coins Europe needed to oil the wheels of its exploding international trade. Hideyoshi could buy whatever he wanted with his silver, including a silk kilim from an elite workshop operating in the sophisticated and refined textile culture of faraway Safavid Iran.

He had the money, but he also needed access to the products of a culture with which he had no direct contact. Transporting goods between East and West Asia was never easy. Goods could arrive in Japan from Iran by land across the mountains and deserts of the Silk Roads, or through the challenging seas of the Maritime Silk Road, which stretched from Japan and China, along the coasts of South East Asia, India, the Arabian peninsula, the Persian Gulf and the Red Sea. These trading systems had been in operation for more than a millennium, the vast distances broken into shorter, more manageable journeys by local Asian and Arab merchants.[23] But by the early sixteenth century both Silk Road systems were less secure than they had been.

The overland Silk Roads had become vulnerable to breakages in their enormously long chain of connections after the fourteenth-century fall of the Mongol Empire which had protected them through what Latinate Western scholarship calls the *Pax Mongolica*. Meanwhile, the security offered along the Maritime Silk Roads in the early fifteenth century by China's Ming dynasty was short-lived. Between 1405 and 1433, Admiral Zheng He had led a fleet of Chinese state-sponsored treasure ships which visited ports as far west as Mecca and Aden on the Red Sea, Mogadishu on the east African coast, Calcutta in India and Hormuz in the Persian Gulf. Territory was not the objective, but trade and power.[24] Zheng is almost always referred to by modern writers as 'the eunuch Zheng He', as if his genitalia had a material impact on his seamanship, and even though many Chinese government officials were eunuchs. The Ming dynasty abandoned its navy and its maritime aspirations after 1433 and, like the overland Silk Roads, the Maritime Silk Road lost its imperial security. Private trade continued to thrive, but long-distance commerce like that between Japan and Iran became more difficult.

The consequences of the Chinese withdrawal in terms of the shift in the balance of international economic, political and territorial power towards Europe were dramatic. In 1497 Portuguese ships under Vasco da Gama sailed into the Indian Ocean for the first time. In the words of global historian Janet Abu Lughod: 'When Portuguese men-of-war finally breached the zone in the early decades of the 16th century and violated the "rules of the game" of mutual tolerance that had prevailed in that region for a thousand years, there was no-one to stop them. The rest, as they say, is history.'[25]

It has taken more than five centuries for China to return decisively to a maritime expansionist policy through its current

'One Belt, One Road' project, which includes heavy investment in ports along the coasts of Eurasia, Africa, Latin America and Australasia.[26] Control of international trading routes is once again part of a shift in the global balance of power.

The Portuguese merchant ships which infiltrated the Atlantic and Indian Oceans and the China Seas in the sixteenth century were in effect the gunboats of a foreign power.[27] Their infamous *cartazes* system was a protection racket that limited trading rights and safe naval passage to those who paid off the Portuguese. They turned traditional trading posts which had until then been peaceful international entrepots along the Persian Gulf, Indian Ocean and China Sea into colonies organised to extract profit.[28] Portugal may not have been a major player in the territorial wars and politics of sixteenth-century Europe, but its merchant ships allowed it to punch above its weight along the littorals of Africa and Asia, building a vast coastal empire which lasted from 1415 to 1999.[29]

By the early sixteenth century, the Portuguese controlled Hormuz Island in the Persian Gulf, Goa on the west coast of India and Macau in southern China. Consequently, when shipwrecked Portuguese sailors first arrived in Japan in 1543, the Portuguese merchant ships which followed them already had the basis of a fast, seaborne trading link between Iran and Japan. The Portuguese traded European and Asian goods into Hormuz, and Iranian goods out of it both to Europe and as far as the edge of the Pacific Ocean. They became important brokers of the world's relationship with Safavid Iran and its seductively attractive and exotically unfamiliar material culture.[30]

The hulls of the Portuguese carracks, *nau de trata*, were water-proofed with black pitch. They were described by the Japanese as *kurofune*: black ships, and Portuguese traders arriving from Macau in the south as *namban*: southern barbarians. This leaves us in no doubt as to how the Japanese viewed the cultural status of their European visitors. A beautiful screen in ink, coloured paint and gold leaf by Kanō Naizen (1570–1616), an artist patronised by Hideyoshi, shows the black ships with their huge sails billowing as they enter the port of Nagasaki, a natural harbour on the west coast of Japan's southernmost island, Kyushu. Kanō's screen shows the apparently irresistible energy of the transformation of a Japanese village into an outpost of the Portuguese Empire. As the menacingly large and heavily armoured black ships on Kanō's screen move across the sea to the harbour, the busy town of Nagasaki is shown alive with European and Japanese traders and shopfronts, European missionaries and their Japanese followers. Boxes of goods and rolls of textiles are shown in the arms and over the shoulders of porters. As Hideyoshi gathered around him the performative apparatus of his supreme role in Japanese politics and society, Portuguese merchant ships arrived in Nagasaki carrying desirable goods collected from their trading colonies – including Hormuz in the Persian Gulf.[31] It had taken a revolution in the seaborne balance of power between Europe and Asia to give Hideyoshi access to his Iranian silk kilim, just as it had taken a European currency crisis to give him the funds to buy it.

The jinbaori is now in a mortuary temple in Hideyoshi's restored Kyoto, 'the central stage of the Momoyama period'.[32] Its journey can be traced back via Nagasaki to the Portuguese trading station at Hormuz. But it is difficult to track it from that island in the Persian Gulf further through Iran's patchy records of sixteenth-century crafts. During the late nineteenth- and early-twentieth-century development of carpet studies, carpets showing animal combat like the kilim in Hideyoshi's jinbaori were believed to have been made in Kashan, long known as a great weaving centre.[33] Investigations made by May Beattie in the 1970s suggested they were made in Kirman, and so extensive was her review of existing animal combat carpets, their structure and the scant textual records she had access to that Kirman has come to be accepted.[34] These issues of where carpets were made have always been the source of burning controversy in carpet circles, and often remain unresolved. Current work led by curator Jessica Hallett at the Gulbenkian Museum in Lisbon is re-examining the history of Persian carpets traded through Portuguese merchant routes, so a new story may yet emerge.

Whichever of those famous Iranian rug-weaving towns was the kilim's original home, its expensive materials, sophisticated design and skilled artisanship suggest it was part of a small-scale production in a quality-controlled environment like a workshop or studio, made by weavers whose gender is unclear (but which Western commentators prefer to think of as men). The large investment in time, labour and yarns would not have been borne by individual weavers. More likely it was a commission by a merchant, or a speculative investment by the workshop owner. There was a strong guild organisation in urban Iran, so the workshop would have operated within mutually agreed commercial rules.[35] Equally, it is possible that it was part of a personal collection and was sold on as a liquid asset when the owner hit difficult times or upgraded their collection. There has been a modern suggestion that the kilim was a special commission reflecting the taste of Japanese consumers, possibly even Hideyoshi himself, since it contains motifs very similar to the Japanese *hanabishi* motif, a flower which is also a diamond.[36] The claim is based on the assumption that the diamond flower is not part of Iran's own decorative vocabulary. But the range of floral motifs in Iranian carpets is extremely wide, and it would be difficult to prove this exemption.

The most solid ground amid these uncertainties is that the kilim was made during the reigns of Safavid Shah Tahmasp, who reigned between 1524 and 1576, or Shah Abbas, who reigned between 1588 and 1629, in a period of creativity and refinement in Iranian carpet-making which still fascinates us.

Fifty years earlier or later, the Iranian kilim might never have found its way to Japan, the textile workers of Nishijin or Hideyoshi's wardrobe. The Iranian-Japanese jinbaori is the product of the century between the opening of Eurasia to a new era of international trade and the beginning of *Sakoku*, literally 'closed country', the foreign policy of a Tokugawa shogunate that sought to control the forces of external influence in Japan. Japan could have become part of the new world system which was coming into being in the sixteenth and seventeenth centuries under the pressure of intense European, West, South and Central Asian imperial expansionism, and facilitated by revolutions in the technologies of warfare, but it chose not to.[37]

One of the catalysts for Japan's withdrawal was a taste of what interventionist empires could bring alongside trade. Roman Catholic missionaries, particularly Jesuits, travelled with Portuguese traders and actively sought to make Christian converts. Theirs was a Church Militant, not only actively fighting sin in themselves and others but building educational and political influence to make sin's defeat more likely. This caused severe tension with Hideyoshi, and later the Tokugawa shoguns, to whom the stability they had created after the anarchy of civil war was extremely precious. They were prescient. In the sixteenth and seventeenth centuries, Europe was upheaved and transformed by the religious wars of the Reformation.

Japanese leaders passed laws banning Roman Catholic missionaries and their activities and occasionally carried out violent purges, for example Hideyoshi's crucifixion of European priests and Japanese converts in 1596. But these laws were generally weakly enforced. Relationships remained cordial between late-sixteenth- and early-seventeenth-century Japanese rulers and the Portuguese who brought European guns and gunpowder, Chinese silk and porcelain, Indian textiles and spices and Iranian carpets. Trade and highly desirable objects trumped the dangers of a foreign religion.

That changed in 1639 when the Shimabara rebellion blew up in Kyushu, the province where the 'black ships' port of Nagasaki was located. Local peasants, many of them Christian converts, were outraged by their daimyo's unreasonable demands and rebelled against him with the support of Portuguese missionaries and *ronin*, wandering masterless samurai. They were opposed by as many as one hundred and twenty-five thousand Tokugawa troops and the gunboats of Protestant Dutch traders, who saw where their best interests lay. It turned out to be the largest rebellion the Tokugawa shoguns were ever to face. After it had been crushed, the shogun Iemitsu expelled all Portuguese from Japan – missionaries and traders alike. He rewarded the loyalty of the Dutch with trading rights on the island of Dejima, off Nagasaki, where they remained until 1853, almost as long as the Tokugawa shogunate lasted, providing Japan with a carefully controlled flow of foreign goods and ideas. After the rebellion, Sakoku began to be enforced more intensely. As Europe pushed out into the world, seized territories and spread its cultural influence, Japan began, if not to close altogether, at least to tightly control its interactions not only with Europe but with its neighbours China, Korea and the northern Ainu islands of the archipelago. Migration out of and into Japan became difficult.

Western commentators have tended to see Sakoku as a negative for Japan, pointing out the extraordinary rate of Japanese internationalisation, industrial and economic development after it was forcibly opened by the US in the nineteenth century. This is recognisably a Western capitalist view, based on the idea that technological progress and economic growth are worth any cost. But Sakoku offered Japan two centuries of stability and peace, in which its culture took its own directions and thrived, and when it avoided the wars, social disruption and some of the misery of parts of the world where globalisation and industrialisation took hold. In Japan itself the Sakoku period is often regarded as a golden age. Meanwhile, twenty-first-century views on the impact of developed-world mercantilism and colonialism and the capitalist drive for growth across the globe are less benign than in previous centuries. We are increasingly aware of the costs involved, and the withdrawal engineered by the early Tokugawa shoguns begins to be seen in a different light.[38]

Hideyoshi's jinbaori came into existence just before the rulers of Japan rethought and ultimately resisted the game of empires developing across Eurasia and the Americas. The kilim brought from Hormuz to Nagasaki by late-sixteenth-century Portuguese

Catholic mercantilist-imperialists is a reminder of the last moment before Japan's withdrawal from the early modern globalisation and colonisation which has defined the way we all live now, and whose consequences we continue to struggle with.

From 1639, it became even harder to lay hands on an Iranian carpet. Nevertheless, Japanese elites were driven to acquire these beautiful, charismatic and prestigious artefacts however they could. Kyoto textile guild members worked around the restrictions to amass seven Safavid rugs for their guild collection. These relatives of Hideyoshi's kilim are displayed every year on floats participating in the ancient Gion Festival, passing through Kyoto to the Yasaka shrine, their colours shimmering more than half a century after they were made, still objects of awe and mystery to the gathered crowds.[39]

Meanwhile, Hideyoshi's campaign coat has embedded itself permanently in the Japanese cultural imagination. It has been carefully preserved for centuries in the Kodaiji temple and designated by the Japanese government in more recent times as *Juyo Bunkazai*, an Important Cultural Property. In the later twentieth century, the Miho Museum in Kyoto bought two of the jinbaori's close cousins: the Figdor silk kilim and the Sanguzsko knotted-pile carpet. The Miho carpets are believed by some carpet scholars to have been woven in the same Iranian workshop and possibly from the same original drawing as the carpet from which Hideyoshi's campaign coat was made.[40] The undisclosed prices the Miho Museum paid for them must have been a king's ransom in the overheated late-twentieth-century international market for Safavid carpets. Even when the charisma of Hideyoshi and the historical significance of his jinbaori are stripped away, Iranian carpets cast an enduring enchantment in Japan. Orientalism and Occidentalism form a two-way street, leading both east and west. Safavid fever travelled east into Asia as well as west into Europe and endured there for as long.

Chapter 5
Priest

One Sunday in the mid-1540s, an eager multitude shivered as it waited to hear a preacher. The Black Church in Braşov, Transylvania, was south-east Europe's largest, with room for five thousand worshippers. The congregation were almost all new Protestants. They had rejected the teaching of the Roman Catholic Church and come to listen to their spiritual leader, one of the first priests to take the risk of following the teaching of Martin Luther. In Braşov, the new religion of Lutheranism was now accepted, and the terrors of the European Reformation had begun to retreat. The preacher had much to explain to his listeners about their new relationship to God, so his sermon took time. They would have been very cold indeed.

Braşov lies high in the snowy Carpathian mountains. As Luther recommended, the church was unadorned, with nothing to come between the worshipper and the worshipped – and little to distract the congregation from the bitter chill. The valuable paintings, opulent priestly robes, gold and silver crucifixes, bejewelled censers and candlesticks had all gone. But it wasn't altogether bare. Beneath the priest's hand a small crimson carpet with deep pile was draped over his pulpit, glowing like a ruby in the dim light.

Some prosperous-looking groups within the congregation had marked their territory with similar carpets, draping them over their pews. These offered the plain-living Protestants some illicit comforts. It would have been easy to flip the soft, warm rugs over their cold feet, or let their children lie down on them.

The carpet under the preacher's hand was a small, vibrant rug, only five feet four inches long by three feet eight inches wide (113 by 162 centimetres), with a dense knotted pile into which his fingers could sink to escape the Carpathian chill. Contemporary visitors to the stores of the Black Church in Braşov can still experience the rug as it appeared to those long-ago worshippers, Despite its great age, the colours and pile are beautifully fresh, perhaps a result of being kept in the cold and dark of the mountain church, brought out only to be draped over pulpits and pews rather than trodden underfoot.[1] The wool held its dye particularly well, endowing it with a rich and vibrant blood-red field, and highlights of bright blue, yellow and an inky blue-black. All the colours are boldly contrasted: this is not the subtly modulated palette of Mamluk or Iranian work. The borders reverse the colour scheme, and the carpet's flatwoven kilim ends are the blue of washed denim.

The weavers used sharply differentiated dark wool to pick out the outline of a large lozenge on the red field, with an ornate hexagonal medallion at its centre. Within the outer lozenge and above the central medallion lies a lamp, knotted in dark and pale wool as if illuminated, a naturalistic flash amid the rug's sober and restrained abstraction and its coded hieratic drama of diamond, medallion, amulet. The carpet has likely been in the collection of Braşov's Black Church since the early sixteenth century.[2] It lay in the church in celebration of the European Protestant Reformation, but the wool from which it was made did not come from Carpathian sheep, or its dyes from Transylvanian plants. Its design was not formed by the radical agenda of Lutheranism. It was made in Asian Anatolia by Muslim women, and thrums with an Islamic sensibility.

The first tell is its size. Small rugs like this are prayer rugs: *sajja-dah* (*seccade* in modern Turkish). Worshippers knelt on them to pray or hung them on a wall where their designs evoked the physical and spiritual environment of a mosque: the *mihrab*, or prayer niche, whose pointed arch orients the worshipper towards Mecca;

mosque lamps which dimly illuminate the atmospheric space; and sometimes mosque pillars with their echoes of Muhammad's first prayer hall in his home in seventh-century CE Medina. Over time all these references were translated into an abstract design vocabulary. A peculiarity of the Braşov carpet is that rather than one prayer niche, as would be found in a physical mosque, it has two, mirroring each other in the two halves of the carpet. They come together to form its elongated lozenge with pointed ends, described in carpet lore as a double-ended niche. The design quirk has given the name 'double-niche' to the family of Anatolian rugs to which the Braşov carpet belongs.

We can rarely date the emergence of individual carpet motifs, and even more rarely have a historical record which apparently explains it, but the double-ended niche is one of these rarities. In the fifteenth and sixteenth centuries, the Anatolian province of Kütayha was a great centre for the weaving of carpets for export to Europe. In 1610, Sultan Ahmed I and senior Islamic cleric Shayk-al Islam sent an edict to the carpet-dealers and weavers of Kütayha province, forbidding them from using religious iconography such as the mosque prayer niche, Quranic script, or representations of Mecca's Ka'aba on artefacts made for export.[3] The weaving of rugs showing the prayer niche but intended for sale to *kafirs*, infidels who did not follow Islamic teaching, was suddenly potentially blasphemous. Scholars suggest that ever-adaptable weavers responded by weaving not a single pointed niche on their rugs but abstract double pointed lozenges derived from the original design.

The weavers could avoid serious religious crime by this change, but perhaps they also sought to resist the clerical and political authorities who tried to control their creativity. There is a long history of the subversion of male authority by female weavers.[4] By doubling the niche, perhaps they privately doubled up on the piety of their rugs. These highly capable women were mostly illiterate, and we only have the evidence of their rugs. Even if they had left us written records, it is unlikely they would have recorded such an act of resistance. We don't know what motivated them to begin weaving this innovative design or when they began. Meanwhile the scholarly theory of the origin of the motif is not itself watertight. Some double-niche carpets have traditionally been dated before the 1610 edict.[5]

Within the lozenge shape formed by the two prayer niches sits a central medallion, and above it a lantern with the distinctive shape of a mosque lamp. There is debate among scholars as to whether mosque lamps in carpet design are in fact motifs from pre-Islamic magical beliefs representing amulets to ward off the evil eye, like the blue-eyed tokens which so fascinate modern visitors to Turkey and West Asia. Indeed, carpet motifs are often derived from the ancient symbols of nature cults like animism, or other early spiritual practices. Yet the Brașov rug's ornament is convincingly a lamp: we see the links on the chain from which it hangs, the decorations suspended from it like droplets, the sparkle of its glass.

The corners of the carpet's field are filled by shapes often described as arabesques. That term suggests curving and proliferating vegetation, but the Brașov carpet's motifs are halfway to geometry and to the intricate ribbon-like interlacing known as strapwork, which was one of the many impressive innovations of the makers of fifteenth-century Anatolian carpets. The decorated corners are called spandrels, the architectural term for the almost triangular space between the outer curve of an arch and a wall in a mosque. Both the designs and the ways of talking about prayer carpets echo the Islamic religious spaces in which they are found. The carpet is replete with sacred potential, albeit a potential it fulfilled on a different continent, within a different religion.

In the late 1520s, a young teacher at the University of Vienna reached a crossroads in his life. Immersed in the new ideas about man and God expressed in the humanism of Erasmus and the theology of Martin Luther, Johannes Honterus suddenly found himself at the very edge of Christendom. The Ottoman Empire had defeated Hungary at the Battle of Mohács in 1526, then marched on Vienna, besieging it in 1529. The mighty Roman Catholic Hapsburg Empire of Charles V, which stretched from Spain across Germany and the Low Countries to Hungary (and which increasingly dominated South America), was under immediate threat from the Islamic Turks. Vienna was right on the fault line: an uncomfortable position. Johannes moved further west, and by 1530 he had found his way to Basel in Switzerland. He was following in the footsteps of Erasmus himself.

The Roman Catholic Church and its Hapsburg imperial sponsor in northern Europe were doubly beleaguered. As the Ottomans approached the gates of Vienna, the Church was already fighting the Protestant Reformation at home. In Germany's Wittenberg in 1517, Martin Luther had launched an attack simultaneously on the corrupt practices and fundamental teachings of the established Church. His radicalism galvanised people of all social and educational levels across Europe, causing rebellions, wars, persecution and political upheaval that lasted for more than thirty years. Stability was restored only with the Settlement of Augsburg in 1555, which adopted the crude but somewhat effective principle that each ruler should decide the creed of his people, be it Protestant or Catholic. Johannes Honterus may have fled the history-defining clash between the Ottomans and the Hapsburgs by moving to Switzerland, but he continued to dwell within another conflict, a strenuous and often violent battle for the human soul. Indeed, he was a combatant.

In Basel, Johannes deepened his study of Lutheran theology, which exhorted a personal religion based on 'God's love alone, faith alone, and scripture alone'. In practical terms, this rejection of Roman Catholic priests as holy intermediaries created a need for Bibles at reasonable prices translated into living languages, rather than the exclusive Latin of the Church. It also required pamphlets explaining the new theology. Basel already had a well-established paper-making industry when one of Gutenberg's apprentices set up a press there in 1468, just a decade after his master first printed his revolutionary Bibles. In Basel, Johannes studied engraving,

printing and paper-making, the great new communications technologies of the era. He also became a renowned cartographer.[6]
He was determinedly acquiring the portfolio of skills needed by a
missionary for Lutheranism.

Despite its victory in 1526 at Mohács, which gave it possession
of a large chunk of Hungary, the Ottoman Empire never did take
Vienna. Neither did it take that part of the Hungarian Empire
which was Johannes' original home, Transylvania. So in 1533 he
was able to return to his native town of Braşov, where he set up
a paper mill, a printing press and a humanist school, the last of
which still exists today. After ten years of teaching the new theology and printing his own books and those of like-minded scholars
– and despite repeated attempts by the parliaments of Hungary
and Transylvania to violently repress the new faith – Johannes had
made Lutheranism the dominant religion of his community. In
1544 he was made First Priest of the City, becoming the founding
Lutheran pastor at the Church of the City, now known as the
Black Church, its large stone blocks darkened by past fires and
more recent pollution. His profound theological understanding
and missionary work was praised by Martin Luther, who called
him 'The Lord's Evangelist'.[7]

The name 'Johannes Honterus' gives little clue as to his ethnicity.
Like many humanist scholars, and despite his work commission-
ing, printing and distributing vernacular Bibles, he was at home in
Latin, and took a Latin version of his name for his own published
works. But he was born plain Johann Hynter, a descendant of a
diaspora from the Low Countries that arrived in Transylvania in
waves from the twelfth century onwards, and he grew up speaking
a German dialect influenced by the origins of his forebears in
Luxembourg.

These settlers were first described in 1206 as *hospites Teuton-
ici and Flandrenses*, our guests from Germany and Flanders.[8]
From the twelfth century, the kings of Hungary invited western

European builders, farmers and miners to settle in Transylvania, develop its industry and agriculture, and strengthen its defences against the threat from the east. Transylvania is ringed by the Carpathian mountains, but its borders were porous to Eurasian nomads. During the thirteenth century the Mongol Empire was at its height and Hungary, one of central Europe's great medieval principalities, was a glittering prize. Nogai, the great-great-grandson of Chinggis Khan, led the Golden Horde on invasions in 1241 and 1258, battling through the province of Transylvania, where the city of Braşov was a strategic target. In the first incursion, the region fell easily, but by the time of Nogai's return in 1258, aiming to use Transylvania as a base from which to push his territories further west, the population knew what to expect and had worked assiduously to prepare their defence. Nogai's troops encountered strongly fortified towns and stiffer resistance and were turned back. Crucial to this reversal were the efforts of the 'guests from Germany and Flanders', and in particular the town of Braşov.

In one of history's attractive but befuddling misnomers, the ancestors of Johann Hynter have come down to us as Saxons of Transylvania, though Saxony, on the border between the east of modern Germany and Poland, was not where these so-called Saxons began. Rather they came from the borderlands of south-west Germany and the lowlands of modern Belgium, Luxembourg and the Netherlands. Many of them have moved on from Transylvania in the twentieth century, but, scattered as they are, they still proudly call themselves the oldest German diaspora community in the world (ignoring population movements that go back to the earliest human development).

For eight centuries they remained a remarkably distinct population in Transylvania, distinguished by language, religion and culture, and forming one of the country's most prosperous and powerful groups. But the upheavals of the twentieth century changed their fate. Romania fought alongside Nazi Germany in the Second World War. Marshal Stalin sent divisions of the Red Army into Romania in 1944, driving out the German Wehrmacht and ending Nazi rule there. Stalin was a severe threat to the

Transylvanian Saxons. They identified as German, so were on the losing side. They were capitalists and property owners, their values and activities inimical to the communism which now entrenched itself in central Europe. Thousands of Transylvanian Saxons were deported to Russia and the Soviet Zone of Germany as forced labour. Those that survived and were released mostly found their way to Germany.[9] Saxons who had managed to retain their freedom and some of their wealth made their own way out of Transylvania, seeking refuge in West Germany, Austria and North America, where they found shelter as Cold War victims of communism.

For many centuries before this diaspora, Transylvanian Saxons were successful merchants and artisans with a deep interest in trade. Their commercial success gave them increasing power over their host nation. At the height of their success, they established seven thriving and well-defended citadels where they could carry out their profitable business in security. These Saxon fortified cities became the customs centres for Transylvania, controlling its international trade, and also led the defence of the country. In Romanian their resonant names are Brașov, Sibiu, Bistrița, Sighișoara, Mediaș, Sebeș, Cluj-Napoca, in German, Kronstadt, Hermannstadt, Bistritz, Schassburg, Mediasch, Mulbach, Klausenberg. Together they inspired the name that stuck for the wider region: Siebenbürgen, the seven citadels, described in a local song-cycle, the Siebenbürgerlieder, as the land of blessings. During the medieval and early modern periods the Siebenbürgen Saxons, with their Flemish-Luxembourg dialect and their northern European outlook, were the controlling group in this territory, dominating the Romanian-speaking, Christian Orthodox population. In 2005, a Romanian historian called them colonisers, overreaching their original invitation as guests to become an extractive and repressive minority.[10]

The threat from the east to the prosperous burghers of the Saxon cities of Transylvania remained, but it shape-shifted. The power of the Golden Horde Mongols in Europe and Russia fragmented during the fifteenth century, and its end was symbolised by the

Horde's decisive defeat by Russian Tsar Ivan III on the banks of a tributary of the Volga in 1480. The Mongols in Asia went into decline even earlier, vanquished by the Mamluk Slave Empire in West Asia in 1260, defeated by the Ming dynasty in China in 1368. Decimated by the mid-fourteenth-century Black Death, and gradually assimilating into local communities, the empire broke into smaller khanates. Meanwhile, the Ottoman Empire, the hard work against the Mongols done by others, had begun its seemingly inexorable rise, reaching its greatest territorial extent between 1522 and 1566 under Suleiman the Magnificent. In the fifteenth century it had begun to press decisively into Europe.

On paper, the Ottomans might seem to fit the European nightmare of the rapacious infidel horde from the east perfectly; a new edition of the Huns and the Mongols. Yet the relationship between the Ottoman Empire and Europe was more equivocal. For instance, even during times of outright conflict, groups of Protestants and Muslims co-operated to protect their business interests. Ottoman sultans had long valued the territory now known as Romania as an access point for Ottoman trade into Europe. As early as 1456, Ottoman Sultan Muhammad II issued a *firman* permitting exchange between Istanbul and Moldavia, Wallachia and Transylvania. Although the Ottomans directly controlled most of Hungary after the 1526 Battle of Mohács, Transylvania was such a productive economic trading partner for the Ottomans that it was left to its own devices, remaining an autonomous Hungarian principality until around 1570, when it became an Ottoman tributary state 'of the most loose and generous kind'.[11] Thus the Siebenbürgen cities established themselves as wealthy trading posts along the Ottoman roads into Europe.

Carpets were one of the great Ottoman trading commodities, and neither geopolitics nor war could stop them from finding their way into Transylvania. They were exported across the Black Sea from Anatolia and up the Danube to the port of Brăila, transported on mules through the arduous mountain tracks of the Carpathians to the Transylvanian customs centre at Braşov. Records show a vigorous trade dating back to at least 1480.[12] In

1503 five hundred rugs came through Brașov, although this high number might have been partly because the passage from Asia to Venice closed during the Venetian–Ottoman War of 1499–1503.[13] During the 1530s and 1540s, as Johannes Honterus was working tirelessly to spread Luther's teaching and remove the Roman Catholic priesthood from the relationship between God and man, customs documents show that the trade in 'Oriental' textiles through Brașov reached an average value of fourteen thousand gold florins per year, a substantial volume compared to other commodities.[14] Many Ottoman textiles and carpets were traded on into Europe and Russia, but some stayed in Transylvania, forming an unlikely accompaniment to Martin Luther's austere new creed.

The earliest records of purchasers in Brașov are dated 1480–81. They included Endres Broleders, a leather merchant, who bought one rug, and Michael Messerschmidt, who bought a lavish eight.[15] But we are not talking here about a handful of rarities. In the early twentieth century, almost four hundred Anatolian prayer rugs made between the sixteenth and the eighteenth centuries were recorded in Transylvania's churches and museums.[16] It has been described as the largest concentration of small-format Anatolian carpets in the West.[17] The Black Church in Brașov has the biggest single holding, of around one hundred and forty carpets. They were reverently preserved over the slowly passing centuries by severe black-clad clerics, as they enacted their devotions in the cold of the huge blackened church, battered by the winters, storms and winds of the Carpathian mountains. The relationship between the Lutheran Protestants of Transylvania and the prayer rugs of Anatolia was deep and enduring.

Johannes' compatriots, the Siebenbürgen Saxons, converted early and enthusiastically to Lutheranism, and in 1553 the Transylvanian Diet became the first European parliament to legislate for freedom of religious conscience. The Saxons took control of the religious spaces in their towns and transformed them for their new vision of God. Before it became Johannes' base in 1544, the church in Braşov was the Roman Catholic Church of St Mary, one of south-east Europe's biggest religious centres. The building was constructed in the fourteenth century, with the stained glass, painted murals, statues of holy figures and paintings typically found in Roman Catholic Gothic cathedrals.

It has been subject to layers of restoration and redesign over the centuries and it is difficult today to conjure what the space looked like after Johannes transformed it into a Lutheran chapel in the mid-sixteenth century. Lutheranism was less extreme than Calvinism or Puritanism in its objection to ornament in its religious spaces, and Lutherans tended not to purge them of decoration to anything like the same degree. Nevertheless, it is likely that Johannes' church shed its original grandeur to become some kind of simple white space, the statues and paintings sold or placed in storage, the coloured window glass removed. Today the church is still glazed with clear glass, and there are traces of murals that have been scraped off the walls. Yet the rugs remained. Why did these plain Lutherans keep so many elaborate Islamic prayer rugs safe for so many years? It is a mystery.

There are no records of Saxon churches buying carpets for themselves, but many of carpets being donated. Anatolian carpets were valued among the Saxons of Transylvania much as they were elsewhere, and wealthy individuals liked to collect them, as did various guilds and trading associations. There are Transylvanian folk memories recorded by late-nineteenth- and early-twentieth-century travellers of carpets being used at engagement ceremonies and as drapes for coffins, then being donated in thanks to the church.[18] They were often left to churches in wills, and over time there seems to have arisen a custom of using rugs to demarcate the sitting area of wealthy families and guilds in the church, with the carpets presumably left there after their owners'

deaths. In the monastic church at Sighisoara we find a rug with an inscription written in ink on the kilim end: 'Having obtained two benches after long persistence, in gratitude and in honour of God the fraternity [guild] has given [illegible]'.[19] What the fraternity guild had given was an Anatolian rug with which to mark out their longed-for permanent space in the belly of the Saxon Lutheran kirk.

Under the new theology, such donations were fraught with questions of conscience. In the Islamic world carpets were seen as highly suitable pious gifts, and carpets donated by devout Muslims have piled up in mosques over the centuries, offering scholars an archaeology of weaving techniques and designs. This Islamic practice translated readily into the tradition of donations to Roman Catholic churches, a priesthood which was happy to accept fine gifts of all kinds, including precious carpets, and for whom nothing was too fancy for their sense of the divine. There was, however, a significant glitch in the process for Lutherans. Central to the Ninety-five Theses that Luther nailed to the doors of the Castle Church of Wittenberg in 1517 was the assertion that no one, either alive or waiting in Purgatory, could buy salvation through money or gifts to the Church. Luther's insistence that priests and Popes could not fulfil their promise of divine indulgence in return for such donations was the battering ram that demolished Roman Catholicism in northern Europe.

Early Protestants believed that gifts offered in exchange for forgiveness of sins were not only useless, but emblems of clerical corruption. The conviction that salvation could not and should not be bought was at the centre of the Protestant revolution, and in its early years led to the rejection of pious gifts. Donations of money, land, property, paintings, sculpture, sacramental objects made from gold, silver and jewels, costly and elaborate clerical vestments and furs, tapestries and other forms of precious decorative textiles were all suspect. Yet even during the austere sixteenth-century beginnings of Lutheranism, gifts of carpets were accepted in Transylvania. The seductions of beauty, sensuality and prestige may have played a part, but it is equally possible that Anatolian prayer rugs communicated their own inherent spirituality to the devout Lutherans.

As the Transylvanian church collections became known to the international community in the early twentieth century, the juxtaposition between Lutheran Christianity and Islamic weaving seemed so strange that a narrative developed identifying them as local production. In 1985, Charles Grant Ellis, a noted North American commentator, suggested that the carpets were not in fact made by Anatolian weavers but in Wallachia, one of the provinces of modern Romania.[20] Scholars now reject this. As always, the deduction rests partly on textual records, and partly on sometimes fragile commonalities of techniques of spinning, knotting, setting of warps and wefts, end finishes, and resemblances observed by eye between dyes and wool. Any skilled weaver can copy a pattern, of course, so that tells us little; but on balance the evidence suggests that the 'Transylvanian' carpets are Anatolian.

Once opinion on this question had settled, other stories came into being to explain their presence at the heart of Lutheran Christianity. One was elegantly expressed at a meeting of leading carpet scholars in 1996, where it was explained that the carpets were 'theologically neutral', a repository of sacred power that was generic and non-sectarian.[21] This is hard to square with the powerful particularity of the religious imagination in the Reformation. It's hard to imagine Johann Hynter, his black robes smeared with dust and whitewash from the holy frescoes he had just consigned to the night of time, thinking to himself 'This theologically neutral Anatolian rug is just the job'.

Reflecting in 2005 on this conundrum, the then head of the Evangelical Church of Romania, Dr Christoph Klein, wrote:

> The phenomenon must certainly be related to the taste and love of culture of the Transylvanian Saxons. These, together with their natural love of order and care and respect for their

patrimony, have been decisive elements in the safeguarding of the Ottoman carpets. The fact that this was possible despite their provenance from a different religious and cultural environment again confirms the traditional tolerance of Transylvanians. It was precisely this tolerance and the humanist openness initiated by the Reformation and nourished by the Enlightenment that defeated the sporadic attempts, for example in Braşov, to remove these so-called 'unchristian' symbols from the church.[22]

It is striking that this portrait of an open-minded people makes special reference to the intellectual breakthroughs of fifteenth-century humanism, a pan-European return to ancient Greek and Roman philosophical texts, and the eighteenth-century Enlightenment, a similarly continent-wide efflorescence of concern with individual liberty, religious tolerance and the sovereignty of reason. Yet there is no hint at all of the religious intensity of early Protestantism – even though we know from customs records that many of these rugs arrived in Braşov just as Europe was torn apart by the early Reformation. One might wonder whether the enduringly tolerant Transylvanian disposition implied by Dr Klein's historical summary is being asked to bear an unreasonable weight. On the other hand, perhaps there really is something to the Saxons' 'natural love of order and care and respect for their patrimony'. This rings true to their origins as burghers and peasants in Flanders and Luxembourg. They looked after their stuff, wherever it came from.

There is another possibility. A widespread opinion was held among beleaguered Protestants in Britain, France and northern Europe – even during the Ottoman imperial invasions of Europe – that the sultan was preferable to the pope, and that it was better to be Muslim than Roman Catholic, both in life and death.[23] Protestants and Muslims were not only both 'peoples of the book', in common with all Christians and Jews, but the two communities shared an austere commitment to the direct relationship with God. *Sola fides, sola scriptura* – faith alone, scripture alone. As in many unlikely marriages, the relationship between Transylvania's

Lutheran churches and the rugs of Islamic Anatolia is built on a shared view of what at bottom really mattered.

Bram Stoker never actually went to Carpathia or the Sieben-bürgen, but the books he read about them gave vivid first-hand accounts. The Transylvania that he depicts so indelibly in *Dracula* drew from sources such as Emily de Laszowska-Gerrard's travel memoir *The Land Beyond the Forest: Facts, Figures, and Fancies from Transylvania* (1888) and Major E.C. Johnson's *On the Track of the Crescent* (1885). Stoker has his protagonist Jonathan Harker arrive in Bistritz, the German name for Bistrița, whose church has its own collection of carpets. Stoker tells us that Bistritz was 'the post town' for Dracula's castle,[24] although this is often identified by vampire fans as Bran Castle, just outside Brașov, more than two hundred miles away. May Beattie, travelling around the Transyl-vanian Saxon Lutheran churches in 1964, said bluntly of Bistrița, 'Only carpets would bring us to such a place',[25] and Jonathan Harker in 1898 was even more chilled by it. Stoker has him say, 'I read that every known superstition in the world is gathered into the horseshoe of the Carpathians, as if it were the centre of some sort of imaginative whirlpool.'[26]

That whirlpool among the unvisited and often forgotten dark forests and remote peaks of Transylvania contained the cycle of Dracula stories which were to form the centre of Stoker's novel, alongside other ancient tales of tall red-haired *Solomonars* – Cloud Chasers who rode dragons and controlled the weather – and se-ductive *Ielele*, who lured men with enchanted dances and could bring good or evil depending on their whim. Powerful charms for protection were required against these superhuman threats: garlic rubbed on doors, poppy seeds sprinkled round entrances, beech-wood broomsticks wedged across doors, broken mirrors buried underground, regular communal rituals of exorcism and respect.[27]

Against this background of eerie folk stories and protective magic, it may be less difficult to imagine a union of two austere and rigorous religions of the book. People who live at the centre of a whirlpool of superstitions might be glad to marshal spiritual resources from any feasible source. They might be doubly reassured by the protective symbolism of Anatolian carpet motifs. A mosque lamp which could also be read as an amulet against the evil eye, such as the one found on the double-niche carpet in the Black Church, had the power to satisfy multiple spiritual needs. Meanwhile, Transylvanians had been accustomed to a rich spiritual broth, while Lutheranism was a religion with little fantasy. Perhaps the association with Islam through its carpets opened up a wider sacred and imaginative landscape.

The question of how evangelising Lutherans lived with the prayer rugs of their evangelising Islamic rivals prompts an equally unanswerable query about the imaginings and accommodations of Muslim weavers making rugs for Transylvania. They were weaving for their traditional enemy, and for *kafirs*. There was evidently an awareness in the Sublime Porte, the centre of Ottoman government, that their valuable carpets were part of a discordant religious encounter. Why else would it have issued its edict forbidding the use of Quranic inscriptions, representation of the Ka'aba at Mecca and the mihrab on export carpets? Such edicts may have accelerated adaptations in the weaver's designs, as she dodged the injunction against explicit Islamic religious references. Yet it is difficult to believe that an Anatolian carpet-maker felt that the motifs and designs of her carpets and her practice of weaving them were 'theologically neutral' or lacking in religious imagery, explanations given by Western scholars for the acceptability of Anatolian carpets within Lutheranism. Her designs might be abstract and non-figurative, or constrained by the sultan's edict, but they were still the symbols of her Islamic faith.

At the same time, like the Lutheranism of Transylvania, that faith and its symbolism had a wilder spiritual hinterland, in the pre-Islamic animism and nature worship which in many carpet-weaving areas continued to live alongside Islam. When Lutherans looked at an Anatolian carpet in the half-darkness of an old Transylvanian church they saw symbols derived from a religion of the book, but also from an Islamic culture which was as haunted by ancient nature-forces as that of the Transylvanian backwoods.

The relationship between the Saxon Lutherans and Anatolian carpets was an intimate accommodation. The rugs arrived because of the everyday business of trade, which both the Transylvanian Saxons and the Ottomans prioritised, and stayed because of an unexpected fit with the spirit of their new religion. They were absorbed into Saxon daily life without being deliberately redefined. But elsewhere in Europe a conscious process of appropriation of Anatolian carpets was taking place. They became propaganda tools in European art.

Anatolian carpets are the 'Turkey' rugs of the European Renaissance and Reformation, sought after by kings, emperors, popes and great merchants. Their purchases are memorialised in the works of European Renaissance painters. Anatolian rugs could be expensive, so they were a good way to signify the status of their subjects; but their complex colours, patterns, textures and lustrous glow also gave innovative Renaissance artists a chance to show off their abilities to prospective clients. Some successful painters, such as Lotto and Holbein, built their own carpet collections.[28] Indeed, identification of carpets in European Renaissance paintings is one of the core tools in the dating and grouping of old rugs for academic and commercial purposes and is how Western carpet studies began, in Julius Lessing's pioneering late-nineteenth-century work.[29]

In modern Western carpet terminology these Anatolian carpets are called the Painter Group, and individual pieces are named after the artists who used them: Holbein carpets, Lotto and Memling rugs. This is surely cultural appropriation if anything is, but it seems immovable in carpet discourse. When Charles Grant Ellis wrote his *tour d'horizon* of Anatolian carpets only forty years ago he called it 'Ellis in Holbeinland', renaming not only its carpets but the geography and its people for the sixteenth-century German-British painter.[30]

In European Renaissance painting, Turkey carpets became important symbols of both earthly and heavenly power and are often present when an unassailable combination of the sacred and the secular was required. Around 1500, the Master of St Giles painted the ninth-century Holy Roman Emperor Charlemagne kneeling on an Anatolian carpet as he was shriven for a transgression too heinous to be forgiven by his priest alone (the sin was rumoured to be incest or necrophilia).* The painting illustrates a traditional story of God using an angel as postman to deliver a personal letter of absolution for Charlemagne.[31] The first Holy Roman Emperor needed the full firepower of the Roman Catholic Church to weather the outrage his sin had created, and the sixteenth-century painter chose a Turkey carpet to ground this explosive fusion of political and religious power.

Catholic artists used the same Anatolian props in their anti-Protestant propaganda. Lorenzo Lotto's *The Alms of S. Anthony* was begun around 1525, ten years after Martin Luther published his Ninety-five Theses, and completed in the early 1540s, as Johann Hynter converted Transylvania to Lutheranism. In the painting, St Anthony sits on a throne surrounded by angels, while deacons of the friary that commissioned the painting give alms to the poor, leaning down to them over a balustrade covered with an Anatolian carpet.[32] The painting reminds any potential Protestant converts of the Church's charitable vocation, on which many of the poor depended. But the juxtaposition also sends a warning: a faith that could command the precious carpets of the empires of Asia could certainly see off a rabble of Protestants.

Yet symbols can be fickle. In 1534, Henry VIII of England broke with the Pope and with Roman Catholicism and declared himself

---

* Not, I should say, on the strength of specific reports, but simply because either might have qualified as 'a sin so terrible he would rather die than name it', per an intriguing reference in the twelfth-century *Kaiserchronik*. This text is our sole ground for supposing that he did anything outstandingly unsavoury at all. If he was by nature prone to embarrassment, perhaps a lesser indiscretion would have been enough to silence him.

supreme head of the Church in England. Two years later Hans Holbein painted a mural of the king for the Palace of Whitehall in London. At this terrifying moment, as Protestantism became England's official religion, Henry's chosen painter used the most charged signifier of earthly and spiritual power in his prop box to send his anti-Catholic message: he had the king stand on a carpet from Anatolia.[33]

This symbolic ambivalence is most noticeable when the same carpet type operates in the iconography of both Protestantism and Roman Catholicism. In Tintoretto's *The Discovery of the Body of Saint Mark*, produced between 1562 and 1566, the artist painted a crimson double-niche rug like the one in Braşov's Black Church on the floor under the saint's body. This provides the saint with a suitably dignified protection from the marble floor, but also emphasises the violence of the episode, the red of the rug echoing the saint's spilled blood after his body was dragged through the streets of Alexandria. Tintoretto's work is part of a cycle of paintings that forcefully celebrate Roman Catholicism, yet the actual carpet he paints shares its design with the double-niche carpet in the Lutheran Black Church at Braşov. And in a final irony, though that rug had been absorbed as a component in the minimalist machinery of Lutheran worship, it has nevertheless been renamed by modern Western carpet scholars after a Roman Catholic painter of anti-Protestant propaganda. The square of fabric woven by Muslim women in Anatolia and conserved in a Lutheran church in Transylvania is now known as a Tintoretto carpet.

And how should we think of it?

Modern Ushak is a city of around two hundred and fifty thousand. Hot and dry in summer, snowy in winter, it is around a hundred and thirty miles inland from Izmir and more than three thousand feet above sea level. Visitors today (there aren't many) find a dusty, industrialised and mercantile community, its Ottoman mansions often in disrepair, its mosques modest, but you can't miss the factories for sugar beet, leather and woollen goods. Ushak's museums now celebrate the early Greek civilisations that settled there, and Mustafa Kemal 'Atatürk', the twentieth-century father of the Turkish people. Anatolia was the base from which Atatürk defeated the Greeks in the Turkish War of Independence and established the modern Turkish Republic in the early 1920s. Ushak was also the family home of his wife Latife Hanim Usaklig-il, a lawyer educated in Paris and London, who until their divorce in 1925 was the embodiment of the emancipated woman of the new secular Turkish state.

A casual visitor might come away with the impression that between the Phrygian and Lydian Empires in the eighth century BCE and the early-twentieth-century establishment of the Turkish Republic, nothing much happened here. On the contrary, Ushak was a centre of creative innovation for four hundred years. From at least the fourteenth century, a rich and diverse art form developed here from the traditional weaving practices in the town and its surrounding communities. Carpets from Ushak are now regarded by carpet scholars as one of the pillars of the classical design tradition in Turkish carpet-weaving, and one of the most important of the Ottoman Empire's many contributions to international culture.[34]

Safavid Iran and Mughal India's hour of carpet-making supremacy began in the mid-sixteenth century, yet as early as the 1300s Ushak rugs were coveted throughout Eurasia, as carpet remnants in collections, inventories and correspondence attest. Buyers of Ushak carpets came from a wide range of social and economic classes and locations. Rugs were sold to middling domestic customers and exported along Ottoman trade routes west, east, south and north. Weavers also made rugs for themselves.

Behind this fashion lies a vigorous international market, and an industry which responded by making some of the first steps towards mass production. Ushak carpets were not one-off items crafted in ateliers for super-elite individual patrons. They were commercial products made in high-quality workshops, or in villages with close relationships with dealers. Like the production of Ottoman ceramics at İznik, and silk at Bursa, fifteenth- and sixteenth-century Turkish carpets were most likely high-quality batch production, even if we now revere them as unique art objects. It has been suggested that between the fifteenth and the eighteenth centuries 'the largest production of commercial carpets in history' was woven at Ushak.[35] This hard-to-prove claim has likely been overtaken since the beginning of the nineteenth century, but indicates the sense among carpet historians that the scale of Ushak's early modern carpet industry was exceptional.

The Braşov carpet could have been made in a workshop in Ushak itself, in a quality-controlled environment in which wool, dyes and weavers were expected to meet standards set and overseen by an *ustad*, a skilled supervisor, or in a local village, either as a commission from a dealer or, speculatively, in hope of a buyer. The designs were the result of some form of negotiation between the weavers, who understood the design and weaving process, and dealers and workshop owners, who understood customers and markets. Photographs taken by twentieth-century students of carpet-making in Anatolia show the participation of the whole village in loom-building – men, women and children – and the strong presence of male villagers in discussions with visiting dealers. These fundamentals have likely remained the same over time. Women were the weavers and often also the dyers, although commercial workshops like those at Ushak sometimes had their own dye-houses. The women may have woven the carpet from memory, from earlier rugs or, as some scholars suggest, from cartoons derived from other fashionable carpets. The geometric vocabulary of these weavers, distinct from the fluid naturalism of Iranian and Mughal carpets, their use of symmetrical knots looped round two warp threads rather than the single-warp loops of Iranian carpets, and their earthy palette based around the reds produced by the madder plant continue to identify a carpet as Turkish to the present day.

One of the most characteristic forms in Ushak carpets is the six- or eight-sided medallion, built up with varying levels of complexity from smaller motifs and sometimes exploded into stars. The more basic medallions are first cousins to the stylised hexagonal and octagonal flower called the *gul*, which is the ancient foundational design of the great nomadic Turkmen carpet-weavers of Central Asia, who moved westwards from the eleventh century. Repeating geometric medallions were central to Anatolian carpet design from the fifteenth century onwards, which may be a technological as well as an aesthetic choice. Walter Denny, a leading scholar of Anatolian carpets, suggests that the natural rectilinear grid of the loom favours the creation of these hexagonal and octagonal forms: that they arise from the medium of weaving itself.[36]

As these *guls* marched across the field of the rug, one of the great innovations of Anatolian weaving developed to fill the carpet's borders. Interlace, or *girih*, is a complex and precise linear style of strapwork, weaving in and out on multiple levels, requiring enormous precision and visual acuity on the part of the weaver. It echoes a spiritually resonant version of Arabic script known as *kufic*. Pseudo-*kufic* or kufesque symbols, with the look of the sacred script but no meaning, were an important border design in fifteenth- and sixteenth-century Turkish carpets.

Medallions and strapwork were integrated into carpets of different sizes used for differing purposes. Important among them were small prayer rugs, which placed the Anatolian design vocabulary within a decorative structure evoking the architecture, light and atmosphere of a mosque. Columns, prayer niches and mosque lamps were all rendered abstract and geometric, and integrated with the idiom of *gul* and *girih*. In a leap of imagination, the weaver married together her religious sensibility, what she knew she could do with the loom and what the design and purpose of the rug required. The carpet from the Black Church at Brașov is an example of this transmutation.

In the later nineteenth century, European and North American interest in the carpets of Asia had reached a new level of intensity, and scholarship began.[37] The carpets in the Siebenbürgen Saxon churches came late to this party, hidden away between the Danube and the Carpathians in small medieval cities far from the centres of early Western research in Paris, Vienna, Berlin and London. They were first exhibited in 1914 in Budapest, and first catalogued in 1933. Since then, carpet specialists, as sectarian on occasion as the Protestants of the Reformation, have expressed different views on the carpets of Transylvanian churches. Some have seen them as a pure expression of vigorous traditional craft skills and of a spirituality that transcends creeds and sects. Others have declared that all but the earliest are tacky export products that not only failed to represent Anatolia's true creative and spiritual tradition but actively corrupted it, by offering the temptation of export profits. In the carpet world this is sometimes seen as a sin as unspeakable as Charlemagne's.[38]

It is always a useful corrective, in the midst of these heated debates between scholars far removed from the production of these artefacts, to turn our minds to the weaver. For three hundred years, in the summer dust and winter snow of villages around Ushak or in workshops in the town itself, early modern Anatolian women fashioned carpets for an unknown community six hundred miles to the west. Once in a while they might have encountered a European intermediary of the trade, a non-Muslim man speaking an incomprehensible language. For a mix of cultural and religious reasons, it is likely that they would have stayed out of his way, and in any case, his craving for their rugs might have been as difficult to understand for the women as it is now for us. Perhaps they were buoyed by the popularity and commercial success of their craft, part of the confident surge towards Eurasian domination carrying the Ottomans forward; it's nice to be on the winning side. Perhaps they were troubled by the fact that conflict with the very Europeans they were weaving for took their village men away to Ottoman wars. In the main they kept weaving, each woman as she had done since she was a child, to the best of her abilities. Was all this really nothing more than a drive to the bottom of a booming export market?

Textual evidence describes a vigorous trade from the late fifteenth century, and Anatolian carpets continued to arrive in Transylvania until the eighteenth century. Yet few of the carpets in Transylvanian churches and museums are believed to date from before the late 1600s. The discrepancy implies immense losses, far beyond the natural degradation of textiles over time.

Two episodes might explain this. In 1689 a fire blazed through Braşov, damaging many buildings including Johann Hynter's church and destroying many of its carpets. Locals attribute the name of the Black Church to this fire, although it has also been suggested that later industrial pollution is the real culprit. In the 1960s May Beattie made a tour of Siebenbürgen. In her view there were few very old Ushak carpets in Braşov; 'one wonders', she writes, 'if any of the rugs are pre-fire'.[39] Despite her scepticism, other scholars have thought they found examples from the early sixteenth century, although, as is often the case, the dates are provisional.[40]

Carpets that survived the fire were then subject to the depredations of voracious late-nineteenth and early-twentieth-century European dealers and collectors, who are reputed to have devised cruel and extraordinary means of getting hold of them. A legend has them bribing grave-digging sextons to cut them up and feed the fragments through small holes in the walls, to avoid the scrutiny of churchwardens.[41] Facing fire and theft, the 'Tintoretto' double-niche carpet in the Black Church starts to seem like a lucky survival.

What remains of their Anatolian collections now casts a spell over the Siebenbürgen towns. Twentieth-century scholarship was dominated by locals who were drawn in from unlikely professions to become students of their towns' carpets. During her 1960s tour, May Beattie noted that her most knowledgeable informant was Albert Eichorn, 'the local pharmacist who seems to repair rugs for the church'.[42] Meanwhile, the first and until recently most complete catalogue of the Transylvanian rugs was produced by Emil Schmutzler, a Siebenbürgen textile industrialist.

Since the turn of the millennium major work has been done to catalogue the collection, and Transylvania's Anatolian carpets have become a *cause célèbre*. They are gradually moving into Romanian museums and the care of modern conservation departments. Yet it is still possible to tramp across the snow of the main square of Braşov's Old Town, and under the eyes of the wary guardians slip into the chill of the blackened church to see some of them, hanging from their wrought-iron rails, bright postage stamps in the vast, cold darkness from which so many messages have been erased.

Chapter 6

Tycoon

KNOTTED-PILE CARPET, SIXTEENTH CENTURY CE, INDIA OR IRAN

In 1970, John Paul Getty, the seventy-eight-year-old business magnate and art collector, reputed to be the world's richest man, was immured with a pair of mistresses at his English estate, brooding over his legacy.[1] On 14 April he recorded in his diary, 'Apollo 13 in trouble. Take samples of dyed wool from carpet for test. Wear my [slimming] belt. Walk.'[2] The heroic drama of the rocket crew's struggle to save their own lives and US national pride, finding their way home by the line between the Earth's light and dark sides, took priority in Getty's characteristically telegraphese account of his day's events. Third and fourth places went to his daily fight to maintain his youth, looks and virility. But the second item was a surprise. Getty had taken a pair of sharp scissors and snipped small pieces of differently coloured wool from the pile of an old rug, in preparation for laboratory analysis of its dyes. Getty cared enough about this carpet to trust no one else with the job. He found time to attend to it despite the demands of running what he liked to describe as the world's largest personally controlled oil company and grappling with the personal tragedy of his son's heroin addiction.

The carpet he cut into was strikingly large: almost twenty-six feet long by ten feet wide. Its brilliant wine-red field was bordered by a dramatic contrasting border of black or darkest blue, and the motifs adorning it were picked out in shades of saffron and yellow, dark, mid- and denim-blue. All its colours were fresh and vibrant, as if made yesterday. It was luxurious: woven from silk and fine, lustrous wool.

The rug's designs were layered on top of each other: scrolling vines, sprays of small blossoms, sprigs of leaves. Superimposed on this fecundity were quartets of palmettes, which formed the main structure of the design (a palmette is an asymmetric motif, a fan shape of radiating petals like a bisected plant). The four palmettes in the quartets on the carpet each pointed in a different direction; in carpet parlance they are 'in-out palmettes', creating a series of diamond shapes marching down the length of the rug. This motif has a long history; indeed one of the founding fathers of carpet studies, Alois Riegl (1858–1905), used it as an example of what he regarded as universal principles of design evolution, found across cultures and through time.[3] It may have evolved from the lotus flower, with its powerful associations of purity and spiritual transformation, or perhaps it sprang from Egyptian representations of palm fronds. Its echoes of the reproductive organs of a bisected plant may connect it with fertility. Over time this rich composite of nature symbolism became a pan-Eurasian favourite, used east to west and north to south across the carpet-weaving belt. Like its palette and materials, the rug's design proclaimed itself as classic and opulent. It was attractive to someone who wanted to make a big statement.

John Paul Getty was one of the twentieth century's great private carpet collectors. He was the last personal owner of the twin to the V&A's legendary Ardabil, claimed by many commentators to be the world's finest carpet. So rich was his collection that in the late 1940s and early 1950s, he was able to donate not only his Ardabil, but a second sixteenth-century Safavid carpet, known as the 'Coronation Carpet', to the Los Angeles County Museum of Art.

The rug from which he snipped the wool samples was a handsome, skilfully woven and beautifully preserved carpet, but it wasn't among his most prized. The reason Getty's attention was now focused on it was that its authenticity had been challenged, and with it his judgement as a connoisseur and dealmaker. Almost as bad was the nature of his challenger: an outsider to his world of wealthy art-dealers and their exclusive clients.

John Paul Getty's antagonist was none other than Dr May Beattie. By 1970, May Beattie had catalogued major public and private collections in the UK and abroad, organised groundbreaking exhibitions and advised collectors and curators. Her learned articles were widely published.[4] She was highly respected by collectors and dealers, publishers and museum curators. In contrast with John Paul Getty, her life was notably modest. Getty took his scissors to the palmette carpet in the dim light filtering through the famous painted glass of Sutton Place, his Tudor mansion outside London, where he was surrounded by a lifetime's accumulation of the world's artistic treasures, his dysfunctional family and multiple lovers. May Beattie, on the other hand, was working quietly and painstakingly to codify her encyclopedic knowledge of carpets ancient and modern in the sub-urban house she shared with her husband in the UK steel city of Sheffield.

Born in Edinburgh in 1908, May Beattie was educated in Can-ada and Scotland, and had the flintiness and shy charm common among Scots from those two geographies. Her interest in carpets began in the late 1930s. In 1937 her husband, Colin Beattie, was ap-pointed head of the Pasteur Institute of Bacteriology in Baghdad. Soon after the newlyweds moved close to the remains of Nineveh and Babylon their house was robbed,[5] and May began visiting the city's bazaars to replace their furnishings. Drinking mint tea in the souk as dealers unrolled carpet after vivid carpet, revealing a previously unknown lexicon of design and craft, May discovered a lifelong obsession. After the Second World War spread to Iraq, she evacuated from Baghdad with other British women and children, the refugees strafed by Axis planes as they made their slow way by bus across the two thousand miles to what was then British India. It is not clear what happened to the rugs belonging to the young married couple as the war drove them apart from each other and their property.[6] The Ashmolean Museum in Oxford is now home to May Beattie's personal collection, and it would be a spine-tingling moment of connection to the past to find one of her Baghdad carpets there, an experience for a researcher akin to May's own in the souks of Baghdad. So far the archives have not yielded up such a secret.

Over the decades, she built a reputation for knowledge and integrity among curators and publishers, carpet-dealers and collectors. She did so without the protection of an institution: her last academic affiliation had been in the 1930s as a bacteriologist at Edinburgh University, where she gained her PhD. As she became seriously interested in carpets in the 1950s, her husband Colin issued a warning, telling her that without the standards of intellectual rigour and detachment she had learned as a scientist, she would remain just one of the hordes of amateur enthusiasts, spinning tales about rugs without evidence.[7] She took the hint. But in her effort to set the history of carpets on a solid footing, she valued her intellectual independence even more than the scientific method. She deliberately positioned herself outside the power structures of the world of carpets so that she would not be beholden to anyone. She became the conscience of the field of carpet studies, a voice that sought to be detached from both the commercial market and carpet mythology. In 1970, her insistence on her integrity and autonomy put her on a collision course with the richest man in the world. And John Paul Getty, power broker of the global oil economy, was no less jealous of his reputation for connoisseurship than she was of hers.

In December 1969, Sotheby's in London held a sale of Asian rugs, the first of two selling a single collection. The auction company described it as 'A Collection of Highly Important Oriental Carpets: Sold by Order of the Kevorkian Foundation'. It is worth pausing on this language. 'Foundation', with its association with charitable rather than commercial purposes, is a useful word to establish a collection's integrity. 'Highly important' is dealer-speak for old, rare carpets of historical and aesthetic significance, appropriate for the private collections of wealthy buyers who seek to be recognised as connoisseurs, and public collections whose excellence is designed to reflect the power of states and institutions. Sotheby's also stressed the exceptional nature of the collection's provenance: the owner, Hagop Kevorkian (1872–1962), was one of a generation of able young Armenians who fled to Europe and North America from Ottoman persecution. They included famous names in the worlds of international business and collecting such as the oil baron Calouste Gulbenkian (1869–1955) and the art-dealer Dikran Kelekian (1868–1951). As it moved westwards, this Armenian diaspora was instrumental in introducing collectors and museums in the West to Middle Eastern artefacts.[8]

Kevorkian was described by a leading twentieth-century art historian as a 'powerful and mysterious' figure in this early Western encounter with Islamic art.[9] He consciously created a mystique which differentiated him from other Armenian art-dealers, deliberately obscuring both his early background and his complex web of financial dealings, positioning himself instead as an objective archaeologist and scholar. Consequently, the provenance he described for the artefacts he sold had strong authority. However, Kevorkian's claim to scholarly independence has been repeatedly questioned. The form of archaeology he practised was excavation at commercial digs, whose prime objective was to uncover artefacts for the art market rather than to understand the past. Modern scholars point out that 'a detrimental consequence of commercial digging was that it obscured the origins of items and encouraged the use of vague terminology'.[10] Kevorkian did not dig his carpets out of the ground, but there is the possibility that they shared his loose way with provenience, provenance and classification. Despite these questions, Sotheby's positioned his carpets as beyond reproach and worthy of the most discriminating buyers, while at the same time trading on Kevorkian's pioneering, adventurous personality. Collectors readied their bankers.

Meanwhile, May Beattie contracted a bout of flu. Nevertheless, loath to miss the advance viewing of this important collection and made of stern stuff, one bleak December day in 1969 she took her handkerchief and notebook to examine the carpets. She was immediately suspicious of some of them, noting in her records that not all the carpets matched their catalogue descriptions.[11] A representative of John Paul Getty also visited the Sotheby's pre-auction viewing to help his employer select the carpets he would buy from this exceptional collection with its glamorous provenance. Getty bought four in total: a pale silk rug with gold and silver embroidery made in Safavid Iran for central European clients, and hence called 'Polonaise'; two carpets with an all-over design of naturalistic blossoms on a ruby-red background made in Mughal India, of a type called 'Millefleurs'; and the palmette carpet from which Getty ultimately snipped the pieces of wool for dye-testing.

The catalogue described the palmette rug as being 'of remarkably fresh colour and fine state of preservation, the rich wine-red field woven with Shah Abbas design. Probably woven at Herat'. The motif is elevated from its position as an old favourite across Eurasia and North Africa to a design specifically associated with the Safavid Shah Abbas, who reigned in Iran between 1588 and 1629. As interest and trade in Asian carpets had accelerated in Europe and North America from around 1850, the most prized were increasingly those of sixteenth- and seventeenth-century Iran, made in court ateliers at the height of the success of the Safavid Empire under Shahs Tahmasp and Abbas. Sotheby's naming of the rug's design for Shah Abbas is like naming all traditional South Asian *achkan* or *sherwani* Nehru jackets, after their most famous wearer.

Meanwhile Herat, where Sotheby's suggested the carpet was made, is now in western Afghanistan, but in the sixteenth and seventeenth centuries was situated across an earlier border in eastern Iran. Safavid carpets from Iranian Herat, Isfahan, Kirman and Kashan were particularly esteemed in European and North American readings of carpet history. Calling the rug Herati further reinforced its claim as one of the West's most desired carpets. Sotheby's catalogue description gave the rug a closer association with the Iranian imperial family and the peak of Safavid carpet production than it may have deserved.

Getty's public collection had been housed since 1953 in a wing of his ranch at Malibu. Among those artefacts was a group of iconic carpets. Getty was now in the midst of moving his collection into a purpose-built museum, the Getty Villa, and setting up a Getty Arts Foundation to secure it in perpetuity. His ambitions were not modest. The new Getty Villa was modelled on the Villa of the Papyri at Herculaneum, which had belonged to Julius Caesar's father-in law. On his death, Getty intended that the Getty Museum in Malibu should be the richest in the world, leaving the majority of his vast personal and business assets to the museum in his will. He achieved his objective. In 2020 it had a staggering endowment of $7.7 billion, surpassing all other museums.[12] Ground was broken on the Getty Villa in 1970, and Getty ramped up his collecting to match the ambition of the building.

As part of Getty's masterplan, a complete catalogue of the objects in his collection was planned for publication in 1972, with contributions by respected experts. In the summer of 1969, Burton B. Fredericksen, chief curator of the Getty Museum, invited May Beattie to write the section on Getty's carpets.[13] The recommendation probably came from elsewhere, perhaps from the German industrialist (and Getty's friend) August Thyssen (1842–1926), whose family collection May Beattie was about to catalogue. Fredericksen was himself a scholar of Western painting, and in the events that followed he became increasingly uneasy in the combative arena of rug connoisseurship.

Mrs Beattie's first response to Mr Getty's approach was 'What is the fee?' Behind this blunt request was a desire to protect her independence. She believed that advisors and dealers who took a percentage of the price paid by the rich purchasers of fabulous carpets could not maintain their objectivity. She demanded instead that she be paid as a professional scholar.

Her second question was 'Will all expenses be defrayed?' She wished to physically examine the carpets to ensure accurate analyses, and that might involve extensive travel to Getty's various homes. Getty, however, believed that only fourteen of his carpets were of a quality worthy of cataloguing. 'The size of the collection', Fredericksen told Beattie, 'does not warrant the expense of a trip to California.' Beattie insisted, explaining that she needed to examine the Malibu carpets at the heart of the collection 'in the wool'. Getty finally capitulated on that but refused to underwrite a trip to his palace near Rome. As Fredericksen informed Beattie: 'None of the three in Italy are worth even $1,000' (just over £6,000, or around $8,000 today). 'Money value does not always indicate the importance of a rug,' May Beattie wrote back sharply.

Although they were already in discussion via Fredericksen about the catalogue, Mrs Beattie did not know that Mr Getty intended to bid in Sotheby's 1969 auction. A few weeks later, in early January 1970, she heard for the first time that Getty had bought the four Kevorkian carpets. The purchases were a shock to her. Among them was one which on her rheumy visit to Sotheby's pre-sale display had raised her suspicions.

Mrs Beattie wrote at once to her intermediary, Fredericksen, by return of post, the best she could do given Getty's reluctance to pay up for transatlantic phone calls or even airmail.[14] She began by tactfully describing one of Getty's Kevorkian purchases, the polonaise silk rug from Safavid Iran, as 'a very pretty piece', and the two Mughal carpets Getty had bought as 'good, honest, attractive rugs'. But there was a sting in the tail. 'What I am writing about is no 20,' she warned. Kevorkian number 20 was the large wine-red rug with 'Shah Abbas' palmette designs, attributed by Sotheby's to late-sixteenth-century Herat. Bluntly, she wrote to Fredericksen that she 'would not be able to catalogue that as earlier than the nineteenth century'. She expressed the hope that 'Mr Getty may very well be aware of all this'.

As it happened, Getty had consulted the Queen's carpet-dealer, C. John, about the Kevorkian carpets. Fredericksen was distraught: 'I thought since the prices were substantial, and because he evidently had C. John's advice, that they would be something of very high quality. I am utterly unversed in carpets.' May attempted to reassure him. 'Don't be despondent about rugs, dealers say quite frankly that they say rugs are older than they really are.' Her acknowledgement that dealers sometimes lied was no comfort to Fredericksen, who wanted to avoid his employer's wrath. 'I don't see much point in telling Mr Getty now: I gather he has met you and has approved of your participation in the catalogue, so we will just hope for the best.' Perhaps aware of the weakness of this strategy, he offered Mrs Beattie a somewhat hazy incentive to bury her doubts, saying: 'If you can convince him sufficiently, he may ask you to play a greater role in future acquisitions.'

Fredericksen did not have the measure of his correspondent. 'I am slightly uneasy about your wish not to mention the dating of No 20 at present,' Mrs Beattie replied, stealthily uncloaking her determination. 'If it should come about that I had to discuss the rug and was asked why I had not mentioned the dating earlier I have only one answer.'

At this point there was a pause of five weeks in the correspondence, which the imagination doesn't strain to fill. 'I took your advice and told Mr. Getty your opinion about Kevorkian No 20,' Fredericksen wrote at last from California. 'Mr Getty was very upset about it.'

Getty faced a dilemma. If he accepted May Beattie's verdict, his strenuously won name for acumen in the field of carpet-collecting would take a tumble just when the imperial museum bearing his name was rising above the waves at Malibu. On the other hand, what did scholarly authority come down to, in the end? What indeed, besides agreement with other authorities? Would the giant who had made his first million by the age of twenty-three, bought a sixty-year interest in half of all the oil in the neutral

zone between Saudi Arabia and Kuwait, built the world's largest
private oil company and done it all at bargain-basement prices
now meekly accept as fact the state of opinion just as he found it?
Was he so lacking in savvy and manly strength that he would be
routed by a posse of women, rug-dealers and museum curators?
Whatever his inner turmoil, his diary for the five-week pause in
communication records only that he continued doggedly packing
objects for transportation from Sutton Place to California, walking, wearing his slimming belt and eating meagre dinners with his
coterie of mistresses.

Between January and April 1970, Mr Getty went to work. He
recruited luminaries of the carpet world to support his belief
that Kevorkian number 20 was made in sixteenth-century Herat.
George Wingfield-Digby, Keeper of Textiles at the V&A, supported
Sotheby's provenance. As a specialist in European tapestries rather
than Asian carpets, he may have preferred to follow the opinions
of what he perceived as more established combatants in the debate
rather than Mrs Beattie. Meanwhile, C. John offered to buy the
carpet back at the auction price, a flamboyant gesture of the firm's
faith in the carpet. Money might at that moment have played a
part in Getty's decision, as it did during the negotiations over his
grandson's kidnap in 1973, when his tough bargaining led to the
loss of the child's ear. But apparently there was something more
at stake in the row over the carpet than financial issues, and he
did not take advantage of C. John's offer. Meanwhile, Mr Webb at
Sotheby's claimed to have consulted fifteen experts who told him
the rug was made in the sixteenth century. One of them, he said,
was Mrs Beattie herself. The controversy was becoming a farce.

May Beattie suggested cutting through the impasse by testing
the dyes. Synthetic aniline dyes first came on to the market in
1850, so if the rug contained any, it had to have been made after
that. She urged Fredericksen to ensure that 'someone who has Mr
Getty's interests at heart should take the samples of wool from the
carpet for testing'. Getty trusted no one but himself. He personally
took the sample and entered the fact in his diary. Yet there is a
question of whether we can trust him. He was careful to record

One of the oldest rugs in existence, the Pazyryk carpet can be found at the Hermitage Museum in St Petersburg.

In this detail of the Pazyryk carpet, the internal organs of animals important to the way of life of its makers and users are picked out in different coloured knots.

Russian archaeologists recovered the Pazyryk carpet from the frozen tomb of a Scythian chieftain in the remote Altai mountains of Siberia in 1949.

There is mystery around where and when so-called chequerboard carpets were made. They are often associated with the Mamluk slave empire centred in Cairo. This example is in the Burrell Collection, Glasgow.

Reg. no. 9/67
Inv. no. ....
Cat. ref. ....
Object ... "Rhodian" carpet with cartouche and arabesque border
....
....
.... Syria or Anatolia
Provenance ... Central Asia
.... 16th c.
Date .... early 18th cy.
Artist ....
            h.   w;   d.
Size : ft/ins. ..6.1".. 4'
    : metric ..185.4.. 121.9 (cm)
Colour .... red centre

For seventy-five years, the curators of the Burrell Collection have repeatedly changed their mind about where and when their chequerboard carpet was made.

The chequerboard carpet demonstrates the skills of both its original weavers and later restorers. This restoring workshop is Behar's, Sauchiehall Street, Glasgow.

'Singular perfection . . . the finest I have seen.' The late-nineteenth-century judgement of William Morris has helped determine the modern reputation of the V&A's Ardabil carpet.

The twin to the V&A's Ardabil was cannibalised to repair its tattered borders. The borderless carpet became a rich man's trophy until it was given by John Paul Getty to the Los Angeles County Museum of Art in 1949.

A war vest, or jinbaori, belonging to Toyotomi Hideyoshi, leader of Japan in the later part of the sixteenth century. The vest was made from a silk kilim imported from Safavid Persia and is currently held at the Kodaiji Temple in Kyoto.

Satiric cartoon showing Japan's sixteenth- and seventeenth-century leaders jointly making the cake of a unified Japan. At the front, the warlord Nobunaga grinds the rice, in the centre the 'bald rat' Hideyoshi bakes the cake, and in the upper right, the first Tokugawa Shogun Ieyasu eats it.

May Beattie was one of the leading carpet scholars of the twentieth century. She asked many penetrating questions about the carpets in this book, including Hideyoshi's jinbaori.

A rug of diverse spiritual potential. Woven with the design of an Islamic prayer rug, collected by the devout Lutheran churches of Transylvania between the sixteenth and eighteenth centuries, and used as a prop in sacred paintings by Roman Catholic artists, such as Tintoretto, during the Renaissance. This rug is in the collection of the Black Church in Brasov, Transylvania.

Within the austere interiors of the Lutheran churches of Transylvania, Anatolian prayer rugs hang like bright postage stamps, as seen here in the Black Church, Brasov.

A carpet made either in India or in Persia, in either the seventeenth or the nineteenth century. The ambiguity about this type of rug creates difficulties for collectors of high-status carpets. This carpet is in the Getty Museum, California.

Weavers have used samplers for centuries. This example contains moti from more than fifteen different carpet designs, from wide-rangir periods and locations. The mobility of designs and their persisten over time make it difficult to identify when and where a carpet is mad the taking of samples, but we do not have any evidence of what happened to those old fibres between his hand and the laboratory.

No aniline dyes were found in the chemical analysis of the fibres which made their way to the lab. No smoking gun, but no clarity in the other direction either. Because there was no switchover moment when all weavers moved to aniline dyes, and some weavers never used them, their absence proved nothing. The dating remained unresolved. As is so often the case, the carpet offered up no answers to the kinds of questions its owner wanted to ask of it.

In April 1970, curator Fredericksen wrote his last letter to Mrs Beattie: 'The most unfortunate result of all this is that Mr Getty, C. John, et al felt it necessary to marshal their forces against your opinion, and although it was your idea to put it to the test, Mr Getty now distrusts your expertise. I do not think, as I am sure you will understand, that the catalogue of carpets can now be written without some ill feeling, so we had best give up the attempt.' Her reply conveys relief at her sacking: 'I suspect that there may have been worse trouble ahead.'

Attempts to write the history of a carpet often hit a brick wall. There are few written records. Village and nomadic weavers tended not to keep inventories, and the records of larger workshops and aristocratic ateliers are frustratingly patchy. Carpets are fragile; they decay, burn and are cut up for other uses, so we don't have enough rugs to construct reliable series back through time. Their weavers and the technology of the loom don't need heavy fixed equipment and buildings and so rarely leave archaeological remains. If we compare the situation to, for example, the great ceramics industries of İznik in Turkey, Arita in Japan and Jingdezhen in China, with their kilns, government co-ordination and often rich textual and material remains, it's clear that carpet history has a special problem. The basic questions of when, why, where and by whom carpets were made often go unanswered in a way that is not so acute for other artefacts and structures, unless they are very old indeed. Enthusiasts and specialists get stuck on those basic questions, with very little evidence to help them.

But rugs abhor a vacuum. The people who have most information about a carpet are often the dealers who are selling it. They know something about the route by which it has come into their hands and have heard the stories attached to it by its previous owner. Consequently, commercial activity and the creation of knowledge about carpets went hand in hand. This was true to a lesser extent of many antiquities and artefacts, but the presence of rich textual, archaeological and material sources means that scholarship in universities and museums could develop alongside dealers' know-how and acted as a counterweight to the stories told in the marketplace. The lack of comparable sources about rugs meant that during the twentieth century, commercial knowledge dominated independent scholarship.

Many carpet-dealers were and still are very knowledgeable, but even the most elevated have vested interests. What we believe about the Ardabil carpet, for example, is deeply conditioned by the marketing drive which dealer Edward Stebbing undertook in the 1890s to ramp up the price he could get from the V&A. Sotheby's auctioneers are a great repository of knowledge about carpets and apply the highest commercial standards to themselves; nevertheless, their marketing of Kevorkian number 20 in the 1969 auction also made a glamorising appeal to a royal provenance and overstated their confidence about where and when it was made. Less scrupulous dealers have also had significant input to histories of carpets. This misalignment between the imperatives of commerce and intellectual rigour has created a vicious circle, the shady reputation of carpet history discouraging scholars from entering the field and improving it. When May Beattie and John Paul Getty locked horns over Kevorkian number 20, they were fighting about who owned the truth.

May Beattie was so convinced about her conclusion that she was willing to face down Getty, refuse Fredericksen's inducements, and go to war with many of her associates in the carpet world. But

it isn't crystal clear that she had strong foundations for her conviction. In an effort to bring clarity to the confusion and distress felt
by Getty and his team, she wrote a formal report on her doubts for
them in March 1970.[15] It is not an analytically rich document, and
she makes only four points. She believed the carpet's condition
was too 'mint', unfaded and unworn, and quoted a dealer looking
at it alongside her at the sale preview in Bond Street who said
'it looks new'. Nor did she like the palette and dyes: 'the colours
were hard, and in particular I did not like the yellow'. She implied
in this comment that the dyes might be chemically synthesised,
although the dye test ultimately proved this not to be the case.
She did not approve of the execution of the design, which struck
her 'as being curiously pulled out' compared to other examples
of the so-called Shah Abbas design. She was one of the world's
great practitioners of the analysis of weaving technique, but in her
report she says only that it was 'correct for its type'.

Of course, she had a wonderfully extensive visual and material
knowledge of carpets, but we understand very little about the
carpet from what she writes. This is not to say she was wrong,
but the high-stakes analysis offered by the scientist of carpetology
was based primarily on her highly educated eye. She thought the
carpet was 'off', one of her favourite words. She acknowledged
this in her report to Getty, saying, 'It is frequently difficult to put
one's finger on what is wrong.' This was possibly a dangerous level
of candour, given her adversary, but it is an important reminder
that in this struggle over who owned knowledge about carpets,
scholars as well as dealers and collectors were often on shaky
ground.

In 1972, Beattie went a step further than challenging the date
of the Getty carpet. That year she published her catalogue of the
carpets amassed by August Thyssen and his family.[16] In the two
years since her set-to with John Paul Getty, she had reflected further on the group to which Kevorkian number 20 belonged, and
in her Thyssen-Bornemisza catalogue she suggested that whenever
they were made, some of these carpets might have been woven
not in Persia at all but in India. Both of Sotheby's claims for the

Getty rug's exceptionalism, its date and its place of making had now been challenged by the carpet sage from Sheffield.

May Beattie didn't like the look of the carpet, but she also had an agenda.

An important part of the modern story about rugs is that those made in elite ateliers during the sixteenth and seventeenth centuries in Safavid Iran are the best in the world. They are indeed thrilling objects of great accomplishment and beauty, but the focus on them goes beyond that. Since the end of the nineteenth century, they have been viewed by the international carpet market not as first among equals but as the measure of all other carpets. Underneath Mrs Beattie's struggle with Getty lay a desire to police the boundaries of these revered rugs.

Once an elite group has been identified, people become interested in what is part of the group and what isn't. This is not a straightforward exercise. Both India and Persia were great centres of carpet-weaving from the sixteenth century onwards. The aesthetic tastes of the Safavid and Mughal Empires were intimately related. One story tells us that Mughal carpet-weaving was born when Mughal Emperor Akbar brought a team of Iranian weavers to his capital at Fatehpur Sikri.[17] Among the styles the Persian and Indian industries developed was a shared idiom sometimes called Indo-Persian carpets. It was characterised by a design of palmettes, blossoms, spiralling connecting tendrils, often on a rich-red field, like Getty's Kevorkian number 20. Such carpets continue to be woven today.

The confusion around Indo-Persian carpets is not an exceptional case. It is often difficult to pin design down tightly to a place or time. We are accustomed to the idea that industrial production borrows and reassembles patterns and motifs from elsewhere and from different times. The late-nineteenth- and early-twentieth-century design archives of Glasgow carpet-manufacturers Templeton and Stoddard contain patterns foraged from museums like the V&A, artists like William Morris and Frank Brangwyn, and ephemera such as decorated Japanese fans. Those designs can be tracked through the industrialists' records to the final knot plans used in setting their huge, noisy industrial carpet-making machines.[18] Yet we often resist acknowledging that this *bricolage* is not an exclusively industrial practice.

Pre-industrial handweaving does not use the heavy machinery of industrialisation but shares a similar approach to design. Textile weavers and designers have always been magpies repurposing motifs and patterns from the objects and media that happen their way. Handweavers of carpets past and present take inspiration from other rugs, paper patterns bought in the marketplace or provided by artists, and carpet samplers known as *wagireh*. Surviving wagireh are dated as early as the eighteenth century, and the tradition may be older. They offer multiple unrelated carpet motifs in the same piece of weaving, from which the weaver of a new rug can make her selection. The motifs are often drawn from places and times distant from her own.

Given the fluidity of design, weaving technique and dyes are often offered as a better tool for identification of the place and time of the production of a carpet. But Eurasia is famous for technology transfer. Trade and travel offer the opportunity for sharing ways to make dyes, spin and weave. Even modern technology like dye analysis and carbon-dating can only give the rough outlines of a carpet's history. It is unsurprising that Getty's carpet did not readily reveal its secrets.

The storm in Malibu about where and when Kevorkian number 20 was made is at its heart a fear of deliberate fakes and misrepresentations, and an uncertainty about the status of the legitimate variants that an old tradition throws up over time. While cases of workshops which deliberately fake iconic carpets are rare, versions of classic motifs and designs are often made in carpet-weaving communities far from their presumed original places of making. Meanwhile, the ageing of new rugs has long been part of carpet-weaving – they are washed and left out in the hot sun to dry and fade. These practices are part of a living, changing craft.

They do, however, complicate the question of provenience when a carpet hits the pricing mechanisms of the market. If I buy a nineteenth-century Indo-Persian carpet under the impression that it is a sixteenth-century Safavid carpet, and pay a sixteenth-century Safavid price, it's a problem – otherwise it's simply a beautiful and interesting nineteenth-century carpet.

Why did John Paul Getty care so much about Kevorkian number 20? He seemed to have little to prove. His worldly success was extreme. He controlled the Getty Oil Company alongside a spider's web of other businesses. He was at the heart of the oil politics of the time. Business associates regarded him as an exceptional negotiator. He was the model of the twentieth-century tycoon.

Yet there were shadows in his persona. The world saw him as eccentric. A 1986 headline in business magazine *Fortune* neatly summarises this public image: 'Mr. Getty: The possibly richest man in the world was mean, miserly, sexy and fearful of travel and detergents'.[19] His oil-pioneer father had doubted his business acumen and expected his son to lose the inheritance the older Getty had created. The sense of jeopardy was intense as John Paul Getty grew up among stories of dramatic ascents and ignominious falls from grace of oligarchs who benefited from the extraordinary transformation of the US into a world superpower. That the son ultimately exceeded the success of the father may not have healed the original wound, and he may indeed have had much to prove.

Getty grew up a careful observer of the interplay between commercial and cultural power, intensely aware of the role of culture in glorifying and redeeming rapacious businessmen. He bought his first notable work of art (a Dutch landscape by Jan van Goyen) in 1931, but his memoirs talk about earlier experimental purchases going back to his teenage years.[20] He came to see culture not only as a way of glorifying his own image, but as part of an almost messianic mission to lead American men away from their 'uncultured barbarism'.[21] He was a genuine enthusiast and well-informed art lover, but his enthusiasm carried a taint of obsession.

By the time Getty began collecting, the previous generation of robber barons and captains of industry had inflated prices beyond his pocket for artefacts that they had particularly valued, among them carpets. Getty had to wait for the financial and geopolitical shocks of the 1930s to become seriously involved in the rug market. Art prices were already weakened by the effects of the Great Depression, when it became clear that a second war in Europe was likely. In the late 1930s there was a buyers' market in art and artefacts, particularly if the collectors were buying in dollars. After the 1935 Nuremberg Race Laws this high-end buyers' market was intensified by the availability of artefacts belonging to Jewish families whose property had been seized by the Nazis. In his book *The Joys of Collecting* Getty describes a trip to buy sequestrated Rothschild property, and the advantageous prices available.[22] He hunted the deal like a shark scenting blood. The Getty Research Institute and its Getty Provenance Index have now carried out significant work to identify and return John Paul Getty's acquisitions of Nazi-era cultural property. But Getty seized the moment and joined the merry-go-round of purchasers of exceptional carpets during the upheavals of the 1930s and 1940s. His diaries record his glee at dealing in a market where fire-sale prices could be achieved. After participating in a 1939 auction at Parke-Bernet in New York, he wrote: 'Got all 4 rugs for $9922, about 23 per cent of their former value.'[23]

The satisfaction went beyond dealmaking. Public auctions of the belongings of dead oligarchs were Getty's Colosseum, where he fought not only for good prices and the world's most exceptional carpets, but with the ghosts of the most successful men of recent generations. In his diary, Getty made a list of the carpets he bought at the 1939 Parke-Bernet sale, describing not their most recent owners but the buyers whom he was most gratified to have outdone:

67. $2000 Indo-Isphahan Hunting Carpet c.1600 [. . .] sold at Wm. Salomon sale 1923, $9,000
69. Polonaise $3900 c.1600 [. . .] Yerkes 1910 $12,300

70. Isphahan $1200 late sixteenth century [. . .] Clarke [*sic*] 1925, $8,000

71. Polonaise $2350 c.1600 Benguiat 1925 $13,500.

In the auction, Getty had bested 'copper king' William A. Clark (1839–1925, mining, banking, politics) and the original robber baron, Charles T. Yerkes (1837–1905, railways, banking), who were both nineteenth-century super-rich industrialist collectors. He also paid knock-down prices for carpets belonging to William Salomon (1852–1919), the famous financier, and leading art-dealer and carpet connoisseur Vitall Benguiat (1860–1937). The provenance of Getty's collection of carpets eventually also included bankers Jacob Schiff, J.P. Morgan, financier-industrialists John D. Rockefeller and Clarence Mackay, two Rothschild counts and the wealthy dealers Duveen, Kevorkian and Kelekian. In this game of prestige, an elite carpet attached a new name, in this case J. Paul Getty, to the exclusive club of its owners.

A narrative Getty spun about his 1939 acquisition of one of the legendary twin Ardabil carpets casts light on how collectors can reframe a carpet's reputation in the service of identity creation. So important was this story to Getty that he gave it two entire pages in his memoir, *The Joys of Collecting*. In 1938 he opened negotiations with Joseph Duveen, by then Lord Duveen, whom Getty described as a 'titan amongst art dealers' – an appropriately god-like adversary for the imperial Getty.[24] Duveen owned the twin to the V&A's revered Ardabil carpet. Getty tells us that the great dealer had bought the second Ardabil in a piece of brinkmanship, turning his back on the seller by taking a transatlantic ship, then closing the deal by ship's telegraph when the seller crumbled. Getty presents Duveen as not only a titan but an inventive dealmaker to match Getty. He then explains how he outfoxed Duveen, after the dealer refused to sell him the second Ardabil. Getty waited patiently for circumstances to darken in Europe, offering $70,000 as war broke out, a price described by Getty as 'virtually a gift'.[25] This story has been repeated through scholarly literature until it has begun to have the feel of solid fact.[26]

Having won in the amphitheatre of the deal, Getty then attempted to overturn connoisseurial and scholarly assessment of the relative merits of each of the twin Ardabils to present himself not only as the master dealmaker, but as the culturally dominant owner of the finer of the two. As we have seen, the London Ardabil was bought for the South Kensington Museum, now the V&A, in 1893, on the urging of a party of enthusiasts including William Morris, who declared he had never seen a finer carpet. Great emphasis was laid on its completeness and uniqueness.[27] Both these characteristics were soon shown to be false. It was revealed that the carpet had a twin, later Getty's Ardabil, and that the twin's borders had been used to repair the London Ardabil. But the cultural authority of the South Kensington Museum alongside the fact of the London Ardabil's completeness has tended to lead to the assumption that the carpet which lies in a glass shrine at the centre of the V&A's Islamic gallery is the superior of the two.

In the 1960s, Getty attempted to reverse this assumption: 'In 1890, the [. . .] rugs came into the possession of an English art-dealer named Robinson. The dealer, aware of the value of his treasures, proceeded cannily. He offered the lesser of the two large carpets to the British authorities, at a very high price, handily neglecting to mention that he owned its superior companion piece.'[28] The 'superior companion piece' is, of course, the carpet bought by Getty from Duveen in 1939, now shared between the Getty Museum in Malibu and the Los Angeles County Museum of Art. Getty set out to reframe the assessment of the relative aesthetic, historical and commercial value of the two carpets. However, despite his efforts, the reputation of the London Ardabil remains intact. Just as he was unable to reverse the view offered by May Beattie on Kevorkian number 20, Getty could not undermine the supreme standing in the West of the London Ardabil. But that did not stop him promulgating his version. The tycoon accepted no authority higher than himself when it came to telling the story of his artefacts.

The planned Getty Museum catalogue which kicked off this episode proved difficult to bring to fruition, and eventually the project dissolved into a series of specialist catalogues on parts of the collection entitled 'Masterpieces of the Getty Museum'. No specialist masterpiece catalogue about Getty's carpets was published by the Getty Museum, with the single exception of a 1972 pamphlet by Rexford Stead, curator of the Los Angeles County Museum of Art, on the Ardabil carpets.

In fact, 1970 turned out to be the peak of Getty's interest in Asian carpets. He seems to have been burned by Kevorkian number 20 and the Oriental rug market. He couldn't be sure of the carpet, but he couldn't sell it either, because the market might be affected by Mrs Beattie's views. To be humiliated on price in a deal and not to be able to fully retrieve the situation was against his nature.

Although the Getty collection continued to expand, and his diaries for the period very frequently record 'another buying day', Asian carpets ceased to be his focus after 1970. In 1969, Getty curator Fredericksen had written to May Beattie about the timing of her visit to Getty's carpets in Malibu, stressing that she should 'delay the trip as far into next year as you conveniently can, because there is a good chance that more acquisitions will be made'. Mr Getty's dream of his legacy as an emperor of culture had clearly included rooms of ravishing imperial carpets from sixteenth- and seventeenth-century Persia and India. But that dream was unfulfilled, because the oligarch could not on this occasion bend an artefact and an expert to his will.

In 1976, the year that J. Paul Getty died, the handbook to the Getty Museum contained no references to Asian carpets. At a Sotheby's auction in 1990 the Getty Museum sold many of its rugs, 'leaving one of Getty's few genuine predilections unrepresented in his own museum', as curator Fredericksen elegiacally puts it in his memoir.[29] In this 1990 cull, Kevorkian number 20 wasn't sold. Despite the twenty years that had passed since Mrs Beattie's assessment, the museum did not risk testing the questionable carpet against the market. It's still in the Getty collection, but the online catalogue entry which matches its dimensions and Sotheby's description of its provenance until recently had no image. As those of us who have worked in museums know, getting to the head of the queue for photographs is a sure sign of how much an object is valued. Fifty years on the Getty Museum seems still embarrassed by Kevorkian number 20.

The carpet's reputation has been permanently overshadowed by a conflict between a North American plutocrat intensely concerned about his cultural standing and a contrarian and independently minded British carpet scholar who thought the carpet was 'off'. The carpet was consequently withdrawn from the Getty Museum's galleries, the international carpet market and the world. It became one of history's disappeared artefacts.

Who were the weavers of the carpet at the centre of this late-twentieth-century dispute? Were they Iranian or Indian? Did they work in nineteenth-century factories or sixteenth-century workshops? Were they men or women, children or adults? Whatever the answers, their lives would not have been easy. The weavers of a high-quality carpet using expensive materials like Kevorkian number 20 would have been subject to intense quality control and rigorous discipline.

We know very little about the lives of the sixteenth- and seventeenth-century weavers of the court carpets of Safavid Iran, but we are told that weavers in Mughal Indian carpet workshops of the time lived in virtual slavery, at the whim of nobles and officials.[30] If the carpet was made in the nineteenth century, its weavers experienced no easier a life. In 1900, pioneer carpet specialist John Kimberley Mumford – whose carpet book was a set text in the art history departments of Ivy League colleges in the US – likened nineteenth- and early-twentieth-century Indian carpet factories to prisons.[31] Life was no picnic for weavers in Iran either. No less a commentator than Vladimir Lenin, who visited the urban carpet factories of Persia as he prepared himself intellectually for the 1917

Bolshevik Revolution, commented on the high development of the division of labour there, resulting, he observed, in deep alienation of the weavers.[32]

But weavers have a trick of reclaiming agency in difficult circumstances and producing work which resists both its historical context and later distortions of its reputation. Despite the punitive conditions in which Kevorkian number 20 may have been made, its later failure to support a tycoon's self-fashioning, and its rejection by modern connoisseurs, it remains the case that at some point now long ago a team of women, girls, men or boys in Iran, Afghanistan or India wove a handsome and culturally resonant carpet whose story and intention were only truly known by the people who commissioned and made it. We would have to travel to the stores of the Getty Museum to see it in the wool, and photographs of it are few and far between, but we can be confident that, hidden away somewhere in the dark, the artistry of the rug's invisible, unknown and anonymous makers still resists the standards set by later connoisseurs and what those experts might regard as 'off'.

Chapter 7
Goddess

FLATWOVEN KILIM, EIGHTEENTH CENTURY CE,
ANATOLIA

In 1992, the leading UK interiors company Habitat launched its
'tribal' collection, at the heart of which was a series of specially
commissioned carpets featuring large geometric motifs and arresting colour combinations such as electric blue and terracotta.
Describing the campaign's provocative TV ad soon after its first
broadcast, textiles scholar Pennina Barnett wrote:

> A well-dressed man sits on a cushioned rattan sofa, one leg
> crossing the other. He is reading a hard-backed book. The
> camera focuses on his face. 'Habitat's new collection is inspired
> by tribal cultures,' he says, in well-modulated tones. The cam-
> era moves to his polished brogue, resting on a designer rug.
> We hear the sound of the vacuum cleaner, as he lifts both feet;
> an elephant trunk slides into view, followed by a middle-aged
> woman directing it towards the carpet . . . 'Mrs Living Room
> I presume?'. Monochrome photographs flash onto the screen,
> savages with cutlery-pierced noses, and lips elongated with
> sgraffito-decorated plates. The scene knowingly evokes stereo-
> types: jungle, discovery, gender, subservience; but there's a
> twist: while the cleaner is blonde, her employer, the epitome
> of Culture and Civilisation – is black, and the 'savages', young,
> trendy and white.[1]

Barnett calls the carpet vacuumed by an elephant's trunk a 'designer' rug. This was a trigger word for affluent and aspirational consumers in the 1980s and 1990s. The concept is still vigorously present in the idea of the designer handbag or designer jeans, utilitarian objects elevated by their association with an individual creator. But while the carpets in the collection were artfully 'designed' to stimulate consumer appetites, they also borrowed from a creative tradition defined by its age and anonymity. Many of the rugs in Habitat's tribal collection were kilims: flatwoven textiles without any velvety pile. Traditionally, kilims were the products of wandering nomads and isolated village weavers, often made for their own use. The savvy advertising agency that put the Habitat campaign together counted on their target consumers seeing these brightly coloured, abstract flatwoven rugs as emblems of the remote and alternative ways of living conjured by the name 'Tribal Collection'.

They were right to count on it. Habitat thrived in those years, and after a short period in the wilderness between its 2011 liquidation and its recent relaunch, is once again a go-to place for modern kilims. But the firm had not simply accurately read the shifting winds of fashion. Attitudes to carpets closely follow turns in the kaleidoscope of history.

The 1960s had been a period of anxiety for the West. There were unresolved memories of the Second World War, nuclear threat from the Cold War, and escalation of European and North American military involvement in Asia. Awareness was dawning of the ecological problems caused by modernity. Women, gay people and people of colour fought for their civil liberties, their struggles intersecting and their efforts in many cases strengthening one another. Visionary leaders were assassinated across the world, from the Kennedy brothers to Malcolm X, Martin Luther King to Patrice Lumumba. A generation of middle-class youth in Europe and North America became disillusioned with Western values and their consequences and turned to non-Western culture for enlightenment and inspiration.

They not only read, talked, wrote and protested, but travelled.

Long-distance coach routes opened within Europe and Asia in the 1960s, and the so-called magic bus – a route rather than an individual vehicle – took Western seekers through Turkey, Iran, Afghanistan and India, delivering them as far as Kathmandu in Nepal. Sharif Gemie and Brian Ireland, historians of the hippie movement, estimate that several million young Western travellers were on the move in the 1960s.[2] A heady mix of role models like the Beatles and Jack Kerouac and the ready availability of drugs along the route of the magic bus added to the seductions of the trip. But these Western seekers were not simply sybarites looking for sensual escape. They sought more profound satisfactions. Buddhism, for example, had become familiar as a Tibetan diaspora arrived in Europe and North America from 1950 onwards, in flight from Chinese control and repression. Young travellers from Europe and North America looked for spiritual and political alternatives in pre-colonial Eastern religions and values.

As they made their way, tired, thirsty and often sick, along the route of the magic bus, young Western pilgrims had an encounter with local cultures and their artefacts so intense it was almost hallucinatory, even if they weren't already high. Joss Graham, one of these adventurers, who later became a famed supplier of textiles to private collections and museums, remembers his first trip to India in 1970:

> I had spent the day at Ajanta, the Buddhist caves. I had become immersed in the visual splendour of the extraordinary frescoes. When I came down I jumped on a bus back to the railway station. There were a couple of young Banjara men on the seat opposite me wearing a long scarf around both their heads, singing antiphonally. They were peeling oranges and shooting the juice from the peel up their noses and singing. It was like watching a Fellini movie and I was in it![3]

Among the memorabilia they brought home were cheap and transportable rugs, the flatwoven dhurries of India, the village kilims of Anatolia, the Caucasus, Afghanistan and Iran and of nomadic groups who wandered the borders of those geographies. Many now-famous names in the carpet world began their relationship with carpets in this phantasmagorical way.[4]

Kilims powerfully symbolised the qualities the Western counterculture desired. They were not associated with what were perceived as the destructive aspirations of empire and capitalism, but with a pastoralist way of life in harmony with nature, self-sufficient and communally and spiritually rich. They were also part of a new celebration of nomadism. When Kerouac encouraged his readers to become dharma bums, dispossessed and free to pursue the path of goodness, he also proposed to them that being on the road was itself the path to enlightenment.[5] In the eyes of these young free thinkers, nomadism was no longer an antiquated way of life, culturally inferior and potentially threatening to settled communities, but an aspiration. The North American and European counterculture's joy in kilims came from their association with the ancient, the remote, the exotic, the traditional. They were Orientalist objects par excellence. Their Western enthusiasts celebrated them but at the same time used them to invent an imagined nomadic Asian Other. If in the 1960s and 1970s a kilim lay on your stripped and varnished pine floorboards in a Western town, you declared your affiliation with these values. The proportion of university-educated people on the magic bus was higher than that of the average population at the time, 30 per cent rather than 8 per cent.[6] The hippie trail was a middle-class phenomenon.

Over the subsequent decades kilims embedded themselves more broadly in the culture of the developed world. As young hippies became young professionals, architects, designers, teachers, academics, publishers, bankers and lawyers, their hippy treasures began to define a consumer style, troublingly described as 'bohemian', 'ethnic' or 'tribal'. A European and North American encounter with kilims which had begun in adventure, exploration of the spiritual and artistic recognition became, as evidenced by Habitat's 1992 ad, a form of shopping.

Thirty years later, in 2022, I drove across an early-spring landscape to an old US Air Force base in the UK. Bunkers interlinked by a maze of roads were surrounded by a double perimeter fence and barbed wire. During the latter part of the Cold War in the 1980s, these bunkers were the home of US F-111 planes carrying nuclear missiles aimed at the USSR. The barbed wire had protected the base from a Peace Camp, where anti-nuclear protestors and their families lived. The 2019 TV series *Good Omens* used such an airbase as the location for Armageddon.[7] But in a modern version of forging swords into ploughshares, one of the bunkers had that day become an examination site for a collection of Turkish kilims, some dating back to the eighteenth century, unusually old for these artefacts.

As I unrolled a commanding, twelve-foot rug, the dingy concrete floor came alive with the penetrating blue of indigo and the intense true red of madder, enduringly vivacious thanks to the staying power of natural dyes and the skills of the dye-mistress. The four broad bands which formed the kilim's main design structure could be read as a series of large medallions or a series of smaller pyramids depending on the viewer's focus, mathematical imagination translated into the geometry of the loom. Interspersed were narrow bands of enigmatic smaller symbols which urgently insisted that they meant something, even though we couldn't read them. This product of a rural weaver and her sisters was about to enter Oxford's University Museum, the Ashmolean, as an example of one of the carpet world's great art forms: the Anatolian kilim.

Not long ago, such a description of their status would have been contested by all but a few far-sighted collectors.[8] Museums saw them as anthropological evidence rather than art objects. As contemporary carpet scholar Walter Denny observes, writing about an exhibition of kilims at the Textile Museum, Washington in 2018, 'There was a time in the past century when the words "kilim" and "museum exhibition" were almost never to be found in the same sentence.'[9] From the late 1960s, the institutional ice had begun to melt, and a breakthrough moment came in 1977 with a show titled *The Undiscovered Kilim* at London's prestigious Whitechapel Gallery of Modern Art.[10] In 1977 the kilim was undiscovered, but by 1992 it could be relied upon to sell Habitat's mass-market interior design, and in 2023 a kilim collection was bought for the nation by the UK government and placed in a national museum.

In the 1970s, a contemporary gallery like the Whitechapel was not an obvious setting for a celebration of an ancient, female, communal craft. Artists exhibited there in the late 1960s and early 1970s included David Hockney, John Hoyland and Joseph Beuys, all now regarded as geniuses of modern art. Nicholas Serota, the gallery's visionary young director, was not a carpet specialist nor was he particularly interested in their symbolism, weaving technique or the weavers' ways of life. What attracted him was the modernity of the kilims' imagery; their handling of colour and geometry, which seemed to foreshadow the preoccupations of twentieth-century painting. His show brought kilims into the mainstream as high-status participants in the international hierarchy of contemporary art, redefined as something distinct from the world of their making and slotted instead into the modernism and abstraction which had come to dominate aesthetics in the twentieth-century developed world.*

The team working with Serota – the exhibition's curators, catalogue editors and lenders – were all kilim enthusiasts. They included now-famous names in the world of carpets: writers Jon Thompson and Yanni Petsopoulos, dealers Oliver Hoare, David Black and Clive Loveless. Of the fifty kilims depicted in the

---

* This was an early example of the prescience which led to Serota's ascent in the art world. He became Sir Nicholas Serota, chair of the Arts Council of Great Britain, holder of the purse strings for government funding of all the arts in the UK.

catalogue's colour plates, ten belonged to the architect Georgie Wolton. It was the Wolton collection that had made its way to the bunker on the airbase, en route to the Ashmolean Museum, and Georgie Wolton's kilim that exploded into colourful life as I unrolled it on to the military concrete.

Daughters of a wealthy family, both Georgie and her sister Wendy became modernist architects. Together with Richard Rogers and Norman Foster, they established the innovative design practice Team4 in 1960s London, a standout success in that decade of creative ferment. Rogers and Foster went on to become global figures in the notoriously male world of architecture, but the famous firm was only able to open in the first place because Georgie, alone among them, had completed her training and had a licence to practise.[11] Georgie's sister Wendy married Foster, whose reputation would eclipse hers, but the free-spirited Georgie soon left Team4 and its aggressive modernism to work independently and follow her own vision. In her obituary, the critic Jonathan Meades described her as the greatest female modernist architect until Zaha Hadid.[12]

Modernism had its roots in politics as well as design. By the end of the nineteenth century the intelligentsia of Europe and North America had developed a profound anxiety about industrialisation, urbanisation and globalisation. They believed that gimcrack industrial products, the debased lives of industrial workers who were forced to produce them, and the overblown and ornate design choices of industrialising nations caused cultural and moral decay. Artistic movements as apparently distinct as William Morris's Arts and Crafts group and Walter Gropius's Bauhaus School of modernism grappled with this problem.[13]

Modernists set out to provide both an aesthetic and a social solution. They believed that buildings and products using stripped-down design and modern materials like concrete, steel, industrial glass and plastics would improve the well-being of the whole of society. Yet modernism had ambiguities at its core. Truth to materials, the effacing of the individual touch, and an almost spiritual purity of design derived from enduring principles of form and mathematics sat uncomfortably with sleek, mass-produced consumer goods and performative buildings heavily branded for their designers: Le Corbusier, Mies van der Rohe, Charles and Ray Eames.

Many people trace modernism's first salvo to Vienna in 1910, when the architect Adolf Loos gave a lecture provokingly titled 'Ornament and Crime'.[14] Decorative elements were to be expunged from architecture and design. And if ornament was crime, there was apparently no room in modernist interiors for the ornate pile carpets so beloved by both the nineteenth-century wealthy of Europe and North America and their bourgeois imitators.

In this set-to between decorative patterned carpets and the principles of modernist design, carpets won. Consumers continued to buy and use them. Rugs even rolled back into the modernist home. By 1925, modernist innovator Le Corbusier included Beni Ouarain carpets made by North African Berber women in his Villa La Roche in Paris. These were far from the workshop precision, intricate designs and rich dye palette of the 'Turkey rugs' and 'Persian carpets' of the Victorian parlour. Instead, they were monochrome, with abstract black lines on a shaggy white pile, their design condensed to a few evocative gestures. From the 1930s, Beni Ouarain carpets became part of the aesthetic vocabulary of modernism, used in architect-designed homes as far apart as Alvar Aalto's Villa Mairea in Finland and Frank Lloyd Wright's iconic Fallingwater in Pennsylvania.

Georgie Wolton was an independent thinker. Just as she had established, then moved on from, Team4's brand of modernism, she also moved on from the narrow taste for North African carpets of earlier modernist architects. Retaining their preference for the geometric and abstract, she also embraced colour and intricacy of design. Describing her first encounter with a kilim, Georgie recalled:

It was in a house in Regents Park. I was an architecture student very much under the influence of the Bauhaus [. . .] But to me this dusty but quietly glowing Caucasian kilim was as

stimulating as a Klee and more exciting than a Mondrian [. . .]
To begin with I was attracted to Caucasian and Kurdish pieces
with bold eye-catching geometric designs against a simple
background. Then I got crazy about Sehna kilims from North
West Persia with their small, intricate and very complicated
patterns. Lately I'm gravitating back to geometric designs, but
more complex than at the beginning [. . .] I am always looking
for something which is free, not tight, controlled or rigid.[15]

Georgie had a holistic approach to the spaces she designed, creating not only buildings but also their interiors and gardens. Plants
and kilims were at the heart of her sensibility, as well as concrete,
steel and glass. The fusion came together most completely in the
modernist houses she designed for herself. Of her London house
and garden she said: 'I found a site which cried out for a sin-
gle-storey house. I was able to plan walls with rooflights to bring
out the natural colours of the kilims. I made one room fourteen
feet high to take the big vertical pieces. I concentrate my rugs in
rooms I walk through, not where I'm sitting. This way I keep the
impressions fresh.'[16] Georgie was twenty-six as the 1960s began.
She bought her first kilim in 1965. Although she travelled widely,
her wealth allowed her to begin collecting not along the hippie
trail but from respected dealers and at auction. She recalled that
'Those first few weeks were an Alice in Wonderland experience.'[17]

When I unrolled her kilim at the airbase, it was not the first
time I had met it. Some months earlier, in the January cold, I had
visited her London house to look at her collection. She had died in
2021 at the age of eighty-seven, and the house was empty and un-
heated. The boundary between outside and inside was dissolving,
as creepers broke through a conservatory into the main house and
rain came in. A gardener who practised landscape design alongside architecture, Georgie may well have been happy with this. She
didn't insist on the dominance of the settled built environment
in her work, but instead sought to integrate ecology and the craft
objects of wandering tribes and remote villages into the homes she
created. Unusually placed windows opened unexpected views of

landscapes and gardens, walls soared high to give space for spectacular Anatolian kilims. Among the vaulting spaces, the views
of ancient trees and the huge old rugs, minimalist and strictly
functional furniture and fittings were dwarfed. Her daughter Suke
ruefully remembers the extreme simplicity of Georgie's kitchens.[18]
In her hands, kilims had found their place in the elite environment
of architect-designed houses where their vibrant, boldly geometric
designs had taken on the identity of works of abstract art. They
had become modern.

But what if they were in fact very ancient indeed?

In 1958, a young Dutch-British archaeologist, James Mellaart,
was excavating near Konya, on Turkey's Anatolian plain. He did
not have high hopes, describing his belief (shared by the archaeological community of the time) that Anatolia was a 'Neolithic
backwater', with only a 'few miserable huts of poverty-stricken
farming communities'.[19] The unhealthy marshy conditions had
discouraged other researchers, but Mellaart was young and keen
and had a career to make. At Çatalhöyük he began excavating a
mound more than sixty feet high and a third of a mile long.[20]

The thrill of discovering something exceptional came after only
three days of excavation, when he uncovered a wall painting. While
archaeologists had found prehistoric cave paintings, no paintings
had previously been found on the walls of prehistoric buildings.
Mellaart soon found further evidence of the religion, art and trade
of a complex and successful culture. Established sometime in the
eighth millennium BCE, and with a population of between five
and eight thousand people, this settlement at Çatalhöyük was
older and more populous than Eridu in Mesopotamia. Mellaart's
discovery of the previously unknown site revolutionised thinking
about the Neolithic city, taking it further back in time, and further
north and west in space.

Mellaart described a community at Çatalhöyük that lived
a settled life in a prosperous high-density city, where people

comfortably crowded in upon each other. The Çatalhöyük wall paintings showed domestic events, scenes of trading, manufacture and building, animals and the hunt, but also appeared to include religious symbols, particularly cults of the bull and the mother goddess. A squat, heavily breasted figurine the team named the Çatalhöyük goddess became the symbol of the dig and its findings. Mellaart became convinced that Çatalhöyük was a matriarchal society, where men played a largely functional role, which was organised around the worship of the Great Mother and her realm of fertility, sexuality, healing and collaboration. He had a special message for carpet enthusiasts: 'In Turkey today there are still echoes of life in Çatalhöyük 8,000 years ago. The wall-paintings provide a key to understanding Anatolian kilim motifs. Among themes from Çatalhöyük identifiable on modern kilims are *bucrania*, or bulls' heads, and goddesses with vultures, giving birth and flanked by felines, frequently shown in mirror image.'[21]

He suggested that the wall paintings were in fact copies of weavings: that now-lost kilims were the source of Neolithic designs. By way of supporting evidence, he claimed that holes in the plaster walls at the site were in fact originally pegs on which to hang large, heavy textiles. To demonstrate the close relationship between past and present, he published his excavation drawings of the Çatalhöyük wall paintings alongside sketches of motifs from recent Anatolian kilims, both showing the same iconography.[22]

Space was made by Mellaart's interpretation of his findings for a particular vision of the weavers of Çatalhöyük: as women whose prestige was enhanced in an already female-dominated society by their skills in a major religious art form, the weaving of large wall hangings, and their knowledge of the sacred symbols of the Great Mother. In Mellaart's version of Çatalhöyük, weavers were matriarchs in a society that focused on well-being, harmony and the spiritual. They could not have been better matched to the zeitgeist of the late twentieth century.

Mellaart had tapped into the persistent belief among twentieth-century carpet enthusiasts – be they meditating hippies, artists and architects looking for inspiration, or consumers adding panache to their interiors – that rug designs are expressions of religious symbolism. Many of us respond to the aesthetic and material presence of carpets so strongly that we need to believe that they are also powerful spiritual objects. It's useless for anthropologists like Brian Spooner who have lived among carpet-weaving communities to tell us that tribal women are not working out their religious problems in their daily weaving.[23] Many of us remain profoundly convinced that they are. The market reinforces this. A carpet-dealer today would explain that they belong to a timeless tradition, drawing on ancient religious symbolism, among remote peoples untouched by the modern world. Successful dealers are empaths. They understand the deeper needs we try to fulfil when we buy a kilim, and they are happy to sell us our dreams.

An important part of Mellaart's story was the presence of what he identified as the 'goddess' motif. This design is made from two triangles, one inverted, so that they balance on each other to create a narrow 'waist', sometimes with hook shapes at each side which can be read as arms. Mellaart believed that the geometrical motif's knob-like residual head, narrow waist and wide hips were a symbol of fertility going back to the Neolithic cult of the Great Mother, which he proposed was the dominant religion of the earliest settled peoples. He found the motif in the wall paintings at Çatalhöyük and in more recent kilims. Both the rug in the 1992 Habitat ad and the eighteenth-century Wolton kilim I unrolled in the bunker use this foundational design.

The Habitat designers might have known about its special status as the 'goddess' motif, but the weavers of the Wolton carpet drew from their own pattern repertoire. Unlike Mellaart, when local weavers and dealers named a motif they tended to choose something quotidian and jokey, such as *egrice*, 'slightly bent', for the small hooks which often surround a larger motif, or a reflection of parts of the weaver's life experience, like the chilling *gelin Çatlatan*, 'bride-cracker', a complex combination of triangles, diamonds and hooks in intricate repeats. The colloquial phrase evokes the stressful difficulty of a young bride's early weavings, but also carries a suggestion of the loss of her virginity.[24] Much local terminology evoked the weaver's aching, work-worn body: the main motifs in the Wolton kilim, for example, are fringed by shapes called in the Turkish of the weavers *parmakli*, 'white fingers', and the top and bottom bands are made up of *elebelinde*, 'hands-on-hips' motifs.[25] This local vocabulary reminds us of the intense physicality of weaving, and while it probably also carried vestiges of the community's own esoteric beliefs, reminds us of the largely workaday, pragmatic nature of the relationship between weavers and their rugs. Mellaart eliminated the individuality and authenticity of this local experience when he renamed the weavers' hands-on-hips *elebelinde* as the 'goddess' motif, to support his framing of Neolithic culture and religion.

Mellaart developed his theories throughout the 1960s and 1970s, finally publishing the four volumes of his long-awaited *Goddess from Anatolia* in 1989. The impact on carpet-thinking and on the market for kilims was dramatic. The leading carpet magazine *Hali* described the work as revolutionary, saying his hypothesis had a 'brilliant inevitability'.[26] Kilims began to be sold at auction with the marketing strapline 'archaic kilim motifs of possible Neolithic origin', and are reported to have reached prices as high as $75,000 (around £57,000).[27] (Only in recent times have prices for Anatolian kilims again achieved such heights, driven by a booming market in old carpets – in 2022 a new benchmark was set at $187,500, around £140,000.)[28] Romantic idealism had once again transformed itself into a commercial opportunity.

But Mellaart's story was never innocent. He was repeatedly involved in archaeological and art controversies. A scandal had blown up in the late 1950s over the so-called Dorak Treasure, artefacts which the Turkish authorities suspected were connected with the black market in antiquities. Mellaart confessed to knowledge of them, claiming to have seen them at the home of one Anne Papastrati, whom he had met on a train and who had adjured him to secrecy. When the Turkish authorities investigated her there were no records of such a person, and correspondence from Papastrati to Mellaart appeared to have been typed on Mrs Mellaart's typewriter.[29] The Turkish government finally ran out of patience with the buccaneering archaeologist and in 1965 expelled him, removing his licence to carry out fieldwork in Turkey.

This is just one of the many murky areas in his research. While the transformation he inspired in thinking about the temporal and geographical limits of the Neolithic is still accepted, and it is agreed that Çatalhöyük places Anatolia in the vanguard of the cultural achievements of the earliest human city-dwellers, what Mellaart said about its kilims seems to have been false – and not simply a mistaken academic hypothesis, but actively fraudulent.

After Mellaart's expulsion from Turkey the Çatalhöyük excavations were abandoned for almost thirty years. When they reopened in 1993, the British archaeologist Ian Hodder was not able to substantiate Mellaart's claims about goddess worship.[30] The remains Hodder and his team found suggested an early Neolithic religion focused on animals rather than on either men or women, and still in transition from the beliefs of hunter-gatherers to agricultural fertility rites. Indeed, archaeologists continue to be sceptical about Neolithic goddess worship across West Asia in general. Instead they tend to see a range of cults that, very far from celebrating a benign fertility and balance with nature, are often filled with fear and danger and a preoccupation with placating ferocious natural and divine threats. As was the case for the Iron Age Scythians, the artistic focus was on the predatory nature of existence and the savagery of the strong towards the weak. The archaeologist Steven Mithen has described these religions as a 'Neolithic hell': 'Every aspect of their lives had become ritualised, any independence of thought and behaviour crushed out of them by an oppressive ideology manifest in bulls, breasts, skulls and vultures.'[31]

And what of the wall paintings that Mellaart claimed showed goddess kilim motifs? They have not been found. There were no photographs of them in the excavation records. No fragments of kilim-like weavings turned up, nor indeed any pegs to fix them to walls. The only evidence was drawings made by Mellaart himself, which were becoming increasingly suspect. As the archaeological evidence for goddess worship at Çatalhöyük collapsed, so did the claim for a Neolithic source of kilim design. We can only speculate on the reasons why Mellaart committed so fully and with such reputational risk to his kilim theories. The suspicions the Dorak affair raised about his associations with the black market for antiquities suggest he was interested in money, and he might have been talking up kilims for commercial reasons. But it is equally possible that he too was a hippie, longing for the Great Mother and her faithful weavers.

Despite the increasing scepticism in the archaeological community towards Mellaart's ideas about goddess worship in Neolithic Anatolia, his theory had already lit many fires. It inspired scholars to search out examples across Eurasia in support of a matriarchal interpretation of Eurasian prehistory.[32] It fed into the questioning cultural ethos of the 1960s, with its interest in social, sexual and religious experiment. It came to the attention of feminists in the late 1970s as an example of an alternative to patriarchal societies. Seekers from across the world still make annual pilgrimages to celebrate the divine feminine at Çatalhöyük. Despite the debunking of some of Mellaart's theories, Ian Hodder, the site's lead archaeologist between 1993 and 2018, recognised the strength of feeling they evoked. He somewhat equivocally welcomed the diverse groups drawn by it, be they, in his words, 'amateur vulture specialists, carpet dealers interested in the origin of kilim carpets, eco-feminists, Gaia theorists or Mother Goddess worshippers'.[33]

In the late twentieth century kilims took on multi-layered meanings in the service of modern identities. They became primordial expressions of goddess worship, or representatives of a way of life free from capitalism and its discontents, or modernist art objects, or consumer goods reflecting an aspirational bohemian taste. This was a significant departure from the status they'd held from the nineteenth century, when they were dismissed as generically inferior to patterned pile carpets.

A quirk of the human–carpet relationship rested on that fluffy surface. A cult of pile carpets had developed during the nineteenth century in Europe and North America, where they were associated with the peaks of past imperial cultures. Mamluk, Ottoman, Mughal and – first among equals – Iranian Safavid carpets had come to be seen as some of the greatest representatives of what was beginning to be called 'Islamic' art.[34]

Kilims, the flatwoven carpets of nomadic and peasant peoples, did not share this sanctified aura. They weren't collected by great nineteenth-century museums like the V&A in London or the Musée des Arts Decoratifs in Paris, and they didn't become part of the scholarly Western story of Asian carpets. They were the products of the poor. Stunning artefacts like the Ashmolean's Wolton carpet often came into Europe as wrapping materials, dust sheets for more valued goods. Even today they can take second place. Two kilim fragments dating back to the fourth century BCE found in the Pazyryk mounds by Sergei Rudenko in the late 1940s have slipped out of a narrative which regards the pile carpet found in the same dig as one of the world's pre-eminent textile objects. (While they show the hook design still found on kilims, there is no evidence on the Pazyryk fragments of Mellaart's goddess motif.)[35]

The Wolton rug was made in Anatolia, now the Asian part of modern Turkey, east of the straits of the Bosphorus, during the six-hundred-year rule of the Ottoman Empire. The kilim specialist Belkis Balpinar gives us an even tighter fix, suggesting that it was made at the end of the eighteenth or the beginning of the nineteenth centuries, which would make it old for such textiles, with their vulnerable yarns and often hard lives as domestic objects. Balpinar suggests that it was woven by a community based around the Anatolian settlement of Haymana, about forty miles from the current Turkish capital of Ankara.[36] Its makers would have been women in an extended family group of pastoral nomads. The Haymana families did not farm but moved between Anatolia's Mediterranean regions and the mountains which fringed them, seeking temperate weather, new grass for their animals and supplementary food supplies for themselves. Their largely self-sufficient way of life was ancient. They travelled along old, fixed routes, living by a remembered calendar of weather, resources and dangers in their ecology, telling time by the sun. The phases of their lives were governed by tribal customs.[37]

We don't need to live in the dreamworld of late-twentieth-century visions of the kilim-makers. We actually know a good deal about kilim-weaving and what the life of weavers is like. Anatolian communities still do it and remember how it was done in the past, and anthropologists and photographers report back to the curious.[38] It's a tradition that has repeatedly come under pressure but has hung on unbroken, at least to the fifth century BCE. Those hardy few who seek them out in remote places still find weavers who, like the makers of the Wolton kilim, manage the practical difficulties of weaving a carpet twelve feet long while unpacking and repacking belongings for the next journey, building shelters, finding and cooking food, raising children, maintaining family relationships, caring for animals and all the other almost overwhelmingly demanding tasks undertaken by nomadic and semi-nomadic women. In the past and today, looms had to be assembled and taken apart, dyestuffs found in the fields and hedgerows on the route, and time found to carry out the meticulous process of weaving itself. We can imagine them singing as they worked, sometimes chanting instructions for other weavers alongside them, as contemporary handweavers still do. We don't know how Anatolian women were nourished and cared for to endure this arduous and exacting life. The anthropologist Richard Tapper, working with Iranian nomads in the late twentieth century, has suggested that the diet of nomadic women impacted their fertility.[39] Continuous pregnancy and carpet-weaving is a difficult combination.

To these practical and human difficulties were added great technical, intellectual and aesthetic challenges. Rugs didn't happen through mindless obedience to traditional rules or through muscle memory. The weaver of the Wolton kilim I unrolled in the bunker understood her technology and the aesthetic history of her carpet, just as Georgie Wolton understood the technology and aesthetics of her buildings. But, unlike Georgie's house, the work of the nomadic woman who wove the kilim that Georgie bought and displayed is still intact after two hundred and fifty years.

It has a dramatic palette, with strong reds and blues, but at the same time there is subtlety, with tender reds and pinks, paler blues, and evocative colours like leaf-green and delicate turquoise. The palette of a kilim is partly defined by local tradition, partly by the creative impulse of the weaver, and partly by the availability of dyestuffs. Apart from indigo-dyeing, a tricky process which was sometimes carried out by a professional indigo-dyer, the weavers of the community dyed their own wool. The Wolton kilim's weaver was first of all a botanist, identifying and foraging the hedgerow madder that made the reds and pinks, the weld which provided yellow, and which when overdyed on indigo would produce green and turquoise. She was a chemist, understanding the active ingredients of familiar materials such as alum, tannin from oak galls, iron and urine, and how they could be used to fix different dyes to give precise shades and durability. The dramatic and sophisticated palette of the Wolton kilim was the work of a gifted eighteenth-century dye-mistress, who in the mountains and pastures of Anatolia, through experiment and observation, identified and controlled the chemical and aesthetic interaction of plant infusions and fibres. This was science in the hands of illiterate Asian women.

The experimental and observational scientific method extended to the carpet's fibres. The weaver was exceptionally close to her wool. The tribe's sheep had to some extent been selectively bred for qualities in their fleece. In Anatolia, the aspiration was not a luxurious soft fineness like the fine-goat-hair pashmina of northern India and the Himalayas, but a tough wiriness. This makes the carpet hard-wearing, but also has an aesthetic impact. Wiry Anatolian wool gains a slight polish as it wears, adding depth to the colour.[40] Our weaver had the specialist's eye, touch and nose for the best wool for the job. She had participated in carding and spinning it and knew her community's sheep well. She could identify a promising fleece.

She was not a unique specialist in the tribe. Carding, spinning, knotting, weaving and twisting took up a large part of nomadic people's lives, and had done since at least between 8,500 and 7,500 BCE when we have the first archaeological hints of weaving and knotting. Even in settled communities in West Asia, there was an intimacy with fibre that transcended social class until very recent times.[41] Everyone participated, particularly in spinning. Sixteenth- and seventeenth-century book paintings suggest that Shahs and Sultans were spinsters. Even now, cut off as we are from the sources of our textiles, we retain this ancient ability to discriminate between different types of wool, our cashmere and merino sweaters, an ability which has been part of human life ever since people began herding sheep.

Kilims are often described as flatwoven or tapestry-woven. They do not have the velvety surface we find in a pile carpet, where a knot, a short piece of wool, is looped round the lengthways warp threads and secured in place by the widthways weft threads. Knots are not part of the structure of a carpet, and a pile rug would not fall apart if the knots were not there. They exist only to create pattern and velvety texture. If there are mistakes in the design the weaver can take the knots out, or correct the error in the next row. Weaving with knots is a forgiving technology. But a kilim has no knots, and so the complex geometry of the design, the balance of the colour palette and the strong, smooth structure of the textile must be created together and at the same time. Every change of colour at the edge of a motif compromises the strength of the rug, creating a slit in the carpet as the weaver turns back on her previous row of weaving to complete a single-coloured shape. Mistakes emerge slowly.

The cognitive challenge of this is huge. The kilim-weaver is a mathematician thinking about geometry, an engineer thinking about tension and strength, and an artist thinking about palette and design. And as she thinks she also feels, noting changes in tension, adjusting physically to the creative process. She holds all this in her head and body as she works inch by inch while the wind blows, children cry, and food and water supplies run down.

In the 1980s, a member of the nomadic Sarıkeçili of Anatolia described her experience of weaving a particularly difficult motif to an anthropologist, saying: 'I would rather drive the flocks as I weep than weave a *heykel*.'[42]

We do not know why nomadic women set themselves this extraordinary challenge, and we do not fully know how eighteenth-century Anatolian nomads used kilims like this. Until the beginning of the nineteenth century they were not woven for trade, although they were sometimes sold. They had and still have functional roles as furnishings and bedding, as part of the structure of their tents, as storage bags and animal trappings. The great length of kilims, it is suggested, makes them particularly suitable as camel blankets. On the other hand, it is easy to imagine how these textiles might have given comfort and pleasure to wandering tribes with few possessions living in austere ecologies.

But the question remains of why Anatolian nomads chose to fulfil those needs in this particularly challenging way. Apart from a few tribal leaders, a characteristic of nomadic life is that there is little excess. They take from nature what they need, and tread lightly on the earth. The huge physical and intellectual investment of nomadic groups in kilims could absorb the entire surplus of a nomadic family or tribe, everything they had spare. Writers who have spent time with modern weaving tribes record that they often struggle to pull together the necessary materials for a carpet, yet they persist.[43] There are many quicker and less resource-intensive ways of producing textiles: lighter woollen and linen weaves, undecorated fabrics, sizes which are easier to handle.

Understanding why nomadic women set themselves this challenge requires us to question easy assumptions about what stimulates creativity. The twentieth-century archaeologists we met in Chapter One struggled to understand who could have made the ancient Pazyryk pile carpet, and under what circumstances. They were befuddled by an assumption that great art could only be produced by literate settled societies, not wandering illiterate nomads. But an alternative story is that nomadic weavers made their rugs because, like all artists, they were driven to create, regardless of economics, empires, written histories and laws, and regardless of later Western fantasies of what their artefacts represented.

Which isn't to say that empires aren't interested in weavers. Haymana lies at the heart of a historic Eurasian superpower, the mighty Ottoman Empire. As the sisters, cousins, daughters and grandmothers began work on the Wolton kilim, the Ottomans accelerated their policy of settling nomads. An ancient way of life was under threat.

The Ottomans were descended from the pastoralist Osmanli tribe, and as their empire expanded into Europe, North Africa and across the Middle East they maintained a strong relationship with nomads in their territories. This was not a ragtag population scattered in the deserts, mountains and marshes of Ottoman territories in Egypt, Arabia, Mesopotamia and the Balkans. Historians estimate that in the sixteenth and seventeenth centuries, 30 to 60 per cent of the population of the Ottoman Empire was nomadic. A single federation of nomadic families could number forty thousand individuals, moving together with several hundred thousand sheep.[44]

Nomadic tribal chieftains administered Ottoman law in areas unreachable by formal Ottoman infrastructure and carried messages across vast tracts of the empire as they migrated. They contributed to international trade and provided seasonal labour, as well as military muscle. Their culture permeated settled Ottoman life. In return for alliance with the Ottomans, nomadic routes and privileges were protected for the so-called *yoruk* and written into legislation in the Yoruk Code of 1608. A particularly attractive privilege was that they were exempt from most taxes.

Taxation, however, is always a great motivator for sedentary imperialists to settle nomads. From the late seventeenth century Ottomans began encouraging nomads to move into permanent farming villages, where they were given plots of land on which they could be taxed. Meanwhile, the previously unstoppable

Ottoman military came under pressure after the failure of the final Ottoman attempt to take Vienna in 1683. They were decisively defeated, their territories came under threat, and their previously indomitable confidence was shaken. More than ever, the empire needed armies to defend its unwieldy geographies. Nomadic men would become soldiers, and the elders, children and women of the tribe would become farmers. No longer autonomous and free, one way or another they were transformed into registered servants of the state.

Meanwhile, nomadism had begun to cast a psychological shadow over the Ottomans. The fourteenth-century Islamic historian Ibn Khaldun had argued that there was an inevitable cycle of confrontation between settled and nomadic peoples, in which sedentary empires matured, grew senile, then were destined to be overwhelmed by more virile nomadic peoples with expansionist ambitions.⁴⁵ Ibn Khaldun was translated into Turkish in the eighteenth century, and the sophisticated, cosmopolitan Ottoman elite living in their great cities found themselves haunted by his vision.⁴⁶ Their own history had followed his model precisely. They resolved that no virile new nomadic threat should come from within their empire.

From the beginning of the eighteenth century, increasingly intrusive efforts were made to settle what the Ottomans began to call tribes, *asiret*, differentiating them from other peoples of the empire. The very vocabulary of imperial power had turned against our weaver's community. In a propaganda trick borrowed from European colonialists, nomadic tribes were described as barbaric and savage, in need of a civilising mission.⁴⁷ Although there was a good deal of resistance, nomads were increasingly compelled (by force, if necessary) to live on what were in effect reservations, just as Native Americans were. The loss and grief of the Anatolian nomad forced into a sedentary life is communicated in interviews conducted in the 1980s with members of the Sarıkeçili. Looking back, an elder said: 'We would spend the summers where we wanted, wintering along the Mediterranean . . . We are left with no autumnal pastures, no ancestral home.'⁴⁸

This forced settlement programme bequeathed the Ottoman Empire a set of administrative and military tools for the large-scale movement of peoples. It also created a mindset which saw coerced migrations as a legitimate political strategy and violence as a form of governance. Among the bitter fruits of this process was the forced population exchange in 1923 of Anatolian Greeks and Turks settled in Greece, and the disaster of the Armenian death marches between 1913 and 1915.

And yet, one day in the late eighteenth or early nineteenth centuries, a weaver settled down with her family to select wool, agree on dyes and designs and began to weave what I probably should not call the Wolton kilim. She worked on the carpet with other women from her tribe, possibly for months, as their migratory routes turned into farms and villages around her, the community's men were sent off to Ottoman wars, and their way of life and traditions came under pressure from one of Eurasia's most powerful empires. Eventually their kilim made its way to the West. It might have been used as wrapping for more highly regarded pile carpets as they crossed continents to feed the European and North American appetite for 'Oriental' decor. It could have spent time hung as a curtain in Vienna or Berlin, where there was a brief trend for using kilims in this way.[49] Finally, it made its way to a new generation of consumers in the tribal carpet boom of the late twentieth century, and then to Georgie Wolton's modernist house in London, the endurance and creative discipline of its makers subsumed into the agenda of another place and time.

The reinvention of the kilim continues. I do it myself. Georgie Wolton is only one of a number of Western women who were drawn to Anatolia and its weavings, making important contributions to our understanding of kilims along the way. I cannot rid myself of the sentimental belief that kilims are a particularly unmediated act of communication between women, and that they attract women to them. When I look at a beautiful and accomplished knotted-pile carpet from the court of an Asian emperor, I am inspired to think of the patron who bought or commissioned it and his imperial aspirations, the role the carpet played in his performance of power and status. I imagine the complex supply chain for its materials, and the equally complex way in which its design and production were organised, its routes of travel to wherever it now lies, and its place in the market for great carpets. But when I look at a flatwoven kilim I think about the maker and her sisters, the sun on her bowed head, the children and chickens in the dirt around her, the to-do list ticking through her mind. It doesn't seem to me at all surprising that kilims play a part in how people think about the female; be it carpet enthusiasts clinging to Mellaart's discredited account of Neolithic goddess cults, the perceptive image-making of Anatolian weavers by photographers like Josephine Powell and Ulla Johansen, the fieldwork carried out alongside Anatolian women by May Beattie, or Georgie Wolton's feminising of architectural modernism. [50] My companion on the day we first unrolled what are now the Ashmolean's kilims was the museum's textile conservator Sue Stanton. She was so haunted by them that she created pottery boxes with their images on the lids. Her work was a transformation across media, time, culture and geography, but very much woman-to-woman. We were both participants in the archaeology of the perception of kilims.

Meanwhile, the precedent set by Mellaart has not stopped Westerners trying to interpret individual motifs. Theories abound. Are they expressions of animist religions or abstractions of natural phenomena? Are they apotropaic, with the power to ward off evil and bad luck? Could they be echoes of the geometries found in other Islamic media such as tiles or reed tent-screens, or insignia of particular tribes? Or are they, as Marina Warner suggests in a discussion of Sigmund Freud's carpets, archetypes drawn from the deep well of the human unconscious?[51] Questions of symbolism continue to attract a disproportionate amount of attention from commentators, all of it reflecting the interests of the writers rather than those of the weavers, and some of them, as in the case of Mellaart, outright conspiracies.

But when all the tales are told, the story of the work of an individual irreducible woman is the most heroic, memorable and moving. Despite being buffeted by the day-to-day difficulties of her life, the extreme challenge of the ecologies she roamed and the turn of history against her, she produced the Wolton kilim. She chose its explosive colour and energetic design, fully resolved like a well-constructed piece of music, and made its solid and consistent structure, undamaged by time. The Wolton kilim is more than a bibelot for another age. It is not the work of a victim, or a misery memoir mourning a declining world, but rather a creative affirmation of a woman and her tribe. It was a blaze of defiance in the face of Ottoman pressures on her way of life, a celebration of what she knew and what she could do.

Chapter 8
Hegemon

KNOTTED-PILE CARPET, NINETEENTH CENTURY CE, CAUCASUS OR IRAN

On a February afternoon in 1945, Joseph Stalin, Franklin Delano Roosevelt and Winston Churchill sat together on a palace terrace among stunted oleanders and cypresses. The wall behind them had lost parts of its plaster. They were seated on what look like dining chairs, hastily assembled in a row facing outwards towards a cameraman. Churchill and Stalin flanked Roosevelt, all at ease. People strolled in the background under the arches of the palace. Churchill smoked a cigar, and Roosevelt a cigarette. Stalin looked ahead, calm and assured. It's an oddly casual photo, considering the stakes of the meeting. The Second World War was almost over and these were the three victors, settling down to divide the spoils at Yalta, in Crimea.

The staging for this summit may have been organised in haste, but somebody made sure to add a crucial detail. As they sat together to agree upon the future of the world, the three leaders rested their feet on decorative handwoven carpets.[1] The photo shows three rugs draped across the terrace: two small carpets with the predominantly red palette associated with Eurasian weaving and a large, pale one with rich designs of foliage and blossom. Only this pale carpet is clearly visible. All three men have their highly polished footwear firmly planted on its velvety surface, Churchill in particular appearing to have twisted his legs so as to claim his place within the borders of this little dominion. Immortalised in a photograph, the pale carpet seems to stand for the world they now controlled.

From 1941, as the world descended into in chaos, more than fourteen summit meetings were held among the most senior members of the Allied governments. Alongside Churchill, Stalin and FDR at these tense assemblies – Churchill famously described their discussions as jaw-to-jaw* – were China's General Chiang Kai-Shek, Sheikh Abdul-Aziz Ibn Saud of Saudi Arabia, King Farouk of Egypt and Emperor Haile Selassie of Ethiopia. France's General de Gaulle was notably absent, cold-shouldered after what was perceived as a too-easy defeat by the Germans in 1940 and limited involvement in the final fightback.[2] But by 1945 only three voices really mattered: those of Roosevelt, Churchill and Stalin.

The philosopher Antonio Gramsci, imprisoned by the Italian fascist government from 1926, had theorised about how a dominant group or nation is able to control others.[3] Force, politics and economics were part of it, but Gramsci argued that norms and ideas that come to seem commonsensical when backed by hard power are one of the most powerful tools of dominance. He called this potent combination of coercion and consent 'hegemony', and the controlling individuals or states 'hegemons'. Stalin agreed. 'This war is not as in the past,' he stated. 'Whoever occupies a territory also imposes his own system as far as his army can reach. It cannot be otherwise.'[4] By 1945, with the war almost over, a summit conference was needed to define the changed world. A new hegemony would have to be forged by the victors.

---

* The International Churchill Society points out that the more famous 'jaw-jaw is better than war-war' was Harold Macmillan's misquotation of Churchill's 'jaw-to-jaw discussions are better than going to war'.

From the start, there were mind games. Roosevelt favoured meeting in Taormina in Sicily, with other locations in Malta and Cyprus also suggested. Stalin, however, insisted on a Black Sea setting, citing his ill-health. Not everyone was convinced; in a telegram to Roosevelt during the wrangling about the conference location, US ambassador to the Soviet Union Averell Harriman remarked dryly that 'Stalin appeared well'.[5]

Roosevelt, on the other hand, had been seriously ill for some time, as Stalin well knew. They had met in Tehran at the end of 1943, when the president's poor health first became publicly clear.[6] By pushing for a Black Sea location, Stalin may have been counting on the difficult journey to weaken Roosevelt's resolve in negotiations. He would face a trip of seven thousand miles, including a flight over Axis territory armed with anti-aircraft artillery. The closest airport to the Black Sea coast was almost a hundred miles away at Saki, leaving Roosevelt to endure a final arduous overland journey through the winter mountains. As staff officers checked all the details before the arrival of the delegates, one reported to Churchill: 'Two attempts made by American General Hill resulted in failure to pass mountain track in blizzard. Personally accompanied General on 1st attempt and endured most terrifying experience.'[7] The ailing president would then have to make his way the seven thousand miles back home.

In the end, Stalin won. The Second World War's peace conference would be held at Yalta on the Black Sea coast.[8] With its pleasant beach, warm sub-tropical climate and backdrop of snowy mountains, Yalta had long been a spa resort for the Russian elite. The Romanov tsars had built palatial summer dachas there. After the revolution in 1917, Lenin gave orders for Yalta to become a holiday and medical resort for Soviet workers. But its restorative airs could do nothing for Roosevelt, who had to take to his bed during the conference. Two months later, he was dead.

The choice of Yalta was not only tactical but symbolic. Empires have fought for centuries to control the Crimean peninsula. A strategically valuable land bridge between eastern Europe and West Asia, it was part of the Russian Empire from 1783 up until the pro-monarchy, anti-Bolshevik White Russian Army made its last stand there in 1921. The Red Army defeated the monarchists, and Crimea became an autonomous Soviet republic. In 1942 the Germans invaded, but Stalin took it back in 1944. In short, the Allied hegemons were meeting on Stalin's territory, on land won from the Russian and Nazi Empires, in the heart of the USSR.

Stalin choreographed Roosevelt's journey through war-blasted Russian territory to ensure the greatest possible impact on his body and mind. It paid off: Roosevelt's translator described the voyage through the devastated countryside and towns of Crimea to Yalta as a psychological turning point for the president. Roosevelt had seen the reality of the Russian struggle against the Nazis, and his attitude towards the post-war treatment of the defeated Germans hardened.[9]

The president and his staff were shocked by the state Crimea had been left in by the destructive Nazi campaign. US soldiers were strictly forbidden from taking spoons or ashtrays as mementos from the conference site as 'supply in Russia is very short' and should not expect to buy souvenirs as 'no worthwhile purchases can be made'.[10] Major-General John R. Deane, working in Moscow with Stalin's team, warned against the burden placed on the ruined Soviet state by the ballooning scale of the US demand for accommodation at Yalta. He saw the devastation of Russia on a daily basis, and tried to alert his colleagues to the pressure they were putting on Soviet resources, a pressure Stalin was unlikely to acknowledge himself, but which Deane believed might erode goodwill between the Soviet Union and the US.[11]

Churchill, who had lived through the German destruction and deprivation of British cities, didn't need the shock treatment Stalin meted out to Roosevelt. He did, however, grumble characteristically about the arrangements, saying: 'If we had spent ten years on research we could not have found a worse place in the world than

Yalta.' In his view it was only 'good for typhus and deadly lice'.[12]

Having insisted on the unpopular location, Stalin turned Yalta into a theatre in which to test his influence on the victorious allies. There were more mind games. The three national teams were housed in Yalta's grandest dachas; houses with deep historical symbolism, as Stalin was keenly aware. Stalin himself stayed at the Yusupov Palace, seized at the revolution from Princess Zinaida Yusupova, the richest heiress in pre-revolutionary Russia, and mother of Rasputin's assassin, its story an emblem of Soviet domination over the previous Russian regime. Yusupov later became Stalin's favourite Black Sea dacha, its lovely gardens backed by rugged mountain peaks.

Meanwhile, Churchill stayed at the Vorontsov Palace. The architect who put together this fantastic pastiche of Gothic Revival, Scottish Baronial and Islamic architecture on the Black Sea's Crimean peninsula was Edward Blore, who had also completed Buckingham Palace. Perhaps Stalin was playing an ironic game, suggesting that Churchill was possessed by a *folie de grandeur* which might feel at home in a version of the official residence of King George VI.

Roosevelt, the official host of the critical meeting, stayed at the Livadia Palace and the conference itself was held there. On a promontory above the Black Sea with gardens running down to the pebbly shore, Livadia had been a summer residence of the Romanov tsars since the 1860s. It had been luxuriously redeveloped by the last tsar, Nicholas II, only six years before the Bolshevik Revolution. It was to Livadia that Dowager Empress Maria Feodorovna, Nicholas's mother, fled the revolutionaries and the hunting down of the Romanov royal family. When Stalin chose to house the US president in the former home of tsars, he offered a deferential acknowledgement of Roosevelt's decisive role in the war effort and his power in the post-war dispensation. But at the same time, the Livadia Palace was haunted by the fate of the Romanovs at the hands of the Bolsheviks, a constant reminder of the fragility of an existing hegemon to the rise of the new.

The three leaders agreed that there should be no press or commercial photographers at Yalta. Instead, each delegation would bring their own. Stalin and Churchill in particular wanted control of the timing and content of any mass communications about the conference. On 9 February 1945, as the talks neared their end, a soldier from the US Signal Corps took the now-legendary photograph of the 'Big Three' on the terrace of Livadia Palace.[13]

A further black-and-white image taken a few moments after the formal, coloured photograph shows a relaxed and joshing group of colleagues, letting off steam. Even the stern-faced Viscount Alanbrooke, the most senior officer in the Allied forces, whose troops were still fighting and dying, permits a smile as he stands behind the seated leaders. A colleague catching sight of the image unawares as we drank coffee spontaneously suggested to me that in the second, more candid image the new hegemony resembled 'a gang of old reprobates'.[14]

In both the black-and-white candid shot and the formal, colour image the pale rug beneath the leaders' feet is distinctive. Its background is ivory, and its motifs a warm orangey-red, with a sparing use of indigo for contrast. We can see large, stylised floral palmettes, and behind them a tracery of leaves and small blossoms. The foliage may be part of the stem and branches of what carpet specialists describe as the tree of life design, growing the length of a rug, with its symbolism of fruitfulness and interconnection. Meanwhile, the corners of the main field are filled with a quarter-circle of contrasting motifs. Such corners are often quadrants of a large, intricate medallion motif found at the centre of the carpet. We can't see the pale rug's centre because it is in the shadow of Roosevelt's legs, so we don't know whether the design resolved itself into a medallion or a tree of life. The carpet has multiple borders, narrow interspersed with wide, containing blossoms and the spearhead motifs known as lancets. Medallions, palmettes, floral tracery, lancets and tree of life motifs are all found in Iranian carpets (though we don't know if Iran was the original source), but were also adapted and bricolaged by weavers from the Caucasus to India. So far as we can tell from the image, the pile surface of the rug looks fresh, and its fringes relatively undamaged.

Before the war, imported carpets would have been common in Yalta. The Black Sea is criss-crossed by maritime trading routes linking Crimea to some of the world's great carpet-making cultures: Anatolia, the Caucasus and the South Balkans. But the Nazis had looted and pillaged, leaving it empty and desolate. Oriental carpets presumably weren't lying around ready for use at impromptu photoshoots for world leaders. It seems likely that the carpet reached its destination by more circuitous routes.

After the 1917 revolution, the Livadia Palace was stripped of Nicholas II's possessions and became a sanatorium, in some accounts for patients with tuberculosis, in others for those with psychological illnesses. We don't know if this ambiguity was a deliberate cover-up, and it is possible that Stalin housed Roosevelt in what had been a lunatic asylum. During Crimea's two years of Nazi occupation, the Germans had taken what was left in the sanatorium 'down to the plumbing fixtures, doorknobs and locks',[15] leaving only vermin behind.

In 1945, the palace did not offer the comforts that might have been expected for the world's most powerful men. Roosevelt's translator noted ruefully that the US president had the only private bathroom in the palace.[16] The staff officers of the three hegemons had to figure out a way of transforming the grand but comfortless and barely functioning Livadia, Vorontsov and Yusupov Palaces into environments suitable for a diplomatic meeting of historic significance. The solution found was that teams from three Moscow hotels, supported by hard-pressed Crimean labourers, both men and women, would create suites of rooms for the leaders and their entourages.[17] The works were supervised by the Soviet

Security Services, the NKVD, to whom Stalin often turned when he needed to be sure his orders would be carried out to the letter.

After the 1917 Bolshevik Revolution many of Russia's grand hotels were closed, but some were nationalised. What is today the five-star Metropol Hotel on Red Square, an early-twentieth-century Art Deco palace, became the home of the leaders of the revolution when they moved their headquarters from Leningrad to Moscow in 1918.[18] It was renamed the Second House of the Soviets, but by the time of the Yalta Conference was operating again as a hotel. The Metropol was one of the hotels whose staff were seconded to Yalta, bringing the necessary equipment and furnishings with them from Moscow by train.[19] These nationalised hotels had inherited the contents of their dispossessed previous owners, including their carpets. It is possible that the pale blossoming carpet came to Yalta with the chattels from one of these Moscow hotels.

Another possibility is that it arrived from Moscow on Stalin's personal train. The train is now part of the Stalin Museum in Gori, his birthplace in Georgia. The museum is hagiographic, described by one of its own former guides as 'the worst museum in the world'.[20] Among its tools for the glorification of the Soviet leader is its collection of portrait rugs of Stalin, made by the weavers of the USSR's Caucasian and Central Asian territories. Carpets also lie in the carriages and corridors of Stalin's personal train. In a gallery mocked up as Stalin's study there is a white-ground rug with floral decoration and a central medallion beneath the handsome desk. It is not the Yalta carpet, but a cousin of it. The displays in the Gori museum raise the tantalising possibility that Stalin ordered a favourite carpet brought from his train to the Livadia Palace for the photoshoot, reinforcing the sense that although Roosevelt was the formal host, Stalin was the householder, and the person who called the shots.

One eighty-year-old tinted photograph is not a good source for working out where, when and by whom a carpet is made.

Nevertheless, history gives us some clues. Throughout the nine-teenth century the Russian Empire expanded into the Caucasus, north-west Persia and Central Asia, triggering an intense imagi-native encounter with its half-known and mysterious conquests. Pushkin, Lermontov and Gogol helped create a vision of the new imperial territories as lands where life was more free and lived more authentically.[21] Tolstoy, who had been a soldier in the imperial wars, first published an account of the Caucasus in *The Cossacks* of 1863, and was still writing about it in his last novel, *Hadji Murat*, in 1904.[22] He has one of his heroes, Olenin, compare his life in Moscow with his new life as a soldier on the steppe: 'The people live as nature lives, they die, are born, unite and more are born – they fight, eat and drink, rejoice and die, without any restrictions but those that nature imposes on sun and grass, on animal and tree. They have no other laws. Therefore, these people, compared to himself, appeared to him beautiful, strong and free'.[23]

The Caucasus, north-west Persia and Central Asia were all great carpet-weaving societies. As they fought their way south, Russian soldiers bought or pillaged rugs and brought them home, tokens of their time spent among the mountains and on the remote steppe. When peace returned the international carpet trade boomed, feeding the blaze of interest in St Petersburg, Moscow and other fashionable Russian cities for dark, moody rugs with repeated ele-phant's foot motifs woven by the Turkmen tribes of Central Asia or Afghanistan; for the vivid geometric carpets of Caucasian villages; and for curvilinear and floral styles with a nuanced palette often called 'Persian', although not necessarily made in Iran.[24] It was one of these last that found its way to the conference at Yalta.

In the early nineteenth century, carpet-weaving was still a domestic industry in the Caucasus, but with Russian support it became a major source of exports to the empire and its trading partners. It is estimated that by 1911, as many as 200,000 women were employed at Caucasian looms.[25] One of the centres of this effort was Shusha in what is now known as Nagorno-Karabagh, an Armenian-Azeri enclave within Caucasian Azerbaijan.

Nagorno-Karabagh has been a disputed territory for centuries.[26]

From 1991, for instance, it was the self-declared Armenian Republic of Artsakh, before it was retaken in 2023 by Azerbaijan, leading
to an exodus of Armenians. Both Armenian and Azeri communities are famously accomplished weavers. If the Yalta carpet was
made in late-nineteenth- or early-twentieth-century Shusha or its
environs, it could have been woven by either an Azeri Muslim
woman or an Armenian Christian woman, living in different
faith communities but sharing a weaving culture. An authoritative commentator observed of Susha carpets, 'The patterns were
curvilinear and altogether in the Persian manner'. [27]

There was an alternative possible source for the rug: Iran itself.
The centre of trade between tsarist Russia and Persia was the far
north-western city of Tabriz, in a disputed Iranian province also
called Azerbaijan. Iranian and Caucasian Azerbaijan were and
still are separated by a nation-state border. On the eve of the First
World War, Tabriz was Iran's biggest and richest city.[28] Closer to
Europe than other major Iranian cities, it had become a commercial hub for trade between Asia and the West, and modernised
early. It was not solely an entrepot, but had its own major textiles
industry. It was a great carpet centre, credited with reviving the
Iranian carpet industry in the nineteenth century and turning it
into an export business. Its merchants were canny and its weavers skilled. It responded early and successfully to the 'Oriental
Carpet Boom', the intense interest in Asian rugs which developed
in Europe, North America and Russia in the second half of the
nineteenth century.[29] Like Shusha, Tabriz and the villages around
it were also home to floral and curvilinear styles, and carpets with
pale backgrounds.

Tabriz is only three hundred miles from Shusha. In 1948 a
British commentator in Tabriz observed: 'its people are not Persians, but a mixed race, mainly Turkish, and indistinguishable
from their kinsmen across the border'.[30] As for its people, so for
its carpets, with their shared designs and techniques. Tabriz carpets often used the symmetrical 'Turkish' knots associated with
Anatolia and the Caucasus, rather than the asymmetrical 'Persian'
knots associated with Iran. Shusha carpets, meanwhile, often used

the floral and medallion idioms associated with Iran, rather than the abstract and geometric designs found elsewhere across the Caucasus.

Attempts to attribute a particular carpet to one community rather than another are highly contentious. The debate over where individual historic carpets of the region were made, and indeed where carpet-making originated, is entangled with religious and national identity. In 2010, Azerbaijan successfully lobbied UNESCO to include Azeri carpet-weaving on the Representative List of the Intangible Cultural Heritage of Humanity. This was represented in the Azeri press as an ideological victory over both Iran and Armenia.[31] Iranian, Armenian and Azeri scholars and museums tell divergent stories about carpet heritage, each centring their own national tradition.[32] This is sometimes expressed with a degree of vitriol, as this broadside from an exhibition review in an Azeri news outlet shows:

> Armenians, who are constantly trying to falsify and misap-propriate the cultural heritage of Azerbaijan, intend to openly demonstrate another product of their aggression – carpets stolen from Azerbaijan's Shusha City, which they have been holding under occupation for almost 30 years [. . .] The carpets to be showcased at the exhibition are samples of the national heritage, woven by Azerbaijani carpet-weavers of the region – an integral part of Azerbaijan.[33]

Given the fusions and pluralism of these weaving communities, probably the most we can safely say about the carpet glimpsed under the feet of Churchill, Roosevelt and Stalin at Yalta is that it was woven by skilled Armenian, Azerbaijani or north-west Iranian women.

Wherever it was made, the Yalta carpet does not seem to me to have the aesthetic and craft refinement of an old carpet made in

One woman inspires another. As she worked on the Wolton Collection, the Ashmolean's textile conservator, Sue Stanton, was moved to recreate their designs on pottery boxes.

The author and a colleague unroll an Anatolian kilim from the collection of Georgie Wolton, now in the Ashmolean Museum, University of Oxford.

The victors of the Second World War celebrate their division of the spoils, their feet planted on a white ground Persianate carpet laid over the soil of the Livadia Palace gardens, Yalta.

The style of carpet may have been a favourite of Stalin, influencing its choice for the iconic Yalta image. The recreation of his study at the Stalin Museum in Gori uses a similar rug.

Jail labour in colonial India gave the British the opportunity to re-invent the idea of the Indian carpet. This rug is in the V&A, London.

The British re-invention turned to Persianate styles, rather than to India's own Mughal tradition, like the whole plant style shown here. This example is in the Metropolitan Museum of Art, New York.

The weavers of jail carpets have no voice in history, but images can give an insight into their experience, Karachi Jail, 1873.

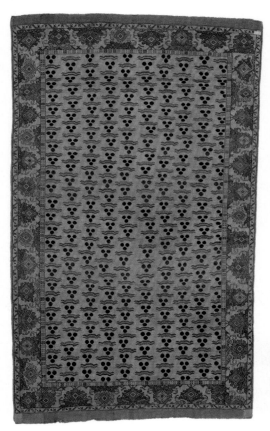

Highly skilled and knowledgeable forgers waged war against the expertise of museum curators, dealers and collectors. This rug is now attributed to the twentieth-century workshop of Teodor Tuduc but was sold to the V&A as the famous seventeenth-century Schwarzenberg carpet. It can still be found in the V&A.

A clue to a forgery is sometimes that it is too perfect, Tuduc's weavers tidied up the corners of the Schwarzenberg original. The original Schwarzenberg carpet shown here is in the collection of the Prague National Museum.

The 'Bokhara' carpet has become a global commodity, sold at modest prices by international retailers. This carpet was made recently in Peshawar, Pakistan.

Modern Bokhara rugs are based on the weaving tradition of the Turkmen nomadic tribes of Central Asia and Iran. The medium of knotted pile textiles was used by the Turkmen to make domestic objects they needed, like this woven tent band, the equivalent of a modern builders' strap used to brace the structure of a yurt. Everyday objects show great artistry. This example is in the Textile Museum, Washington.

Modern Bokhara rugs borrow the guls, or abstract floral motifs, found in Turkmen weaving. Tribes each have their own traditional guls. The weaver of this old rug used that of the Tekke tribe. It may have been woven by a bride-to-be and her mother-in-law. This is a treasured rug from the author's collection.

This carpet was destroyed in RAF attacks on
Berlin in 1945. It inspired the work of the father of
carpet studies, Wilhelm Bode, and was Inventory
No 1.1 in the famous Islamic Art Collection in
Berlin. When it burned, the work of a team
of great artist-weavers was lost, along with a
foundation-stone of carpet scholarship.

Like the Ardabil, the Bode Animal Carpet was one of a pair.
The surviving rug, which can be found at the Los Angeles County
Museum of Art, allows us to conjure up the lost carpet.

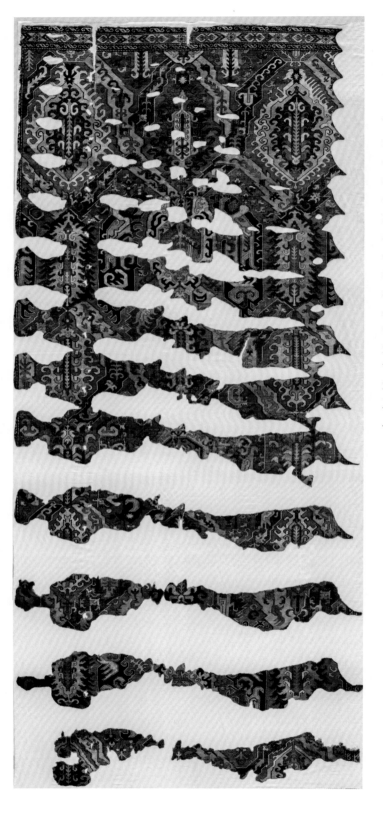

The 1945 Berlin Mir fire stimulated the development of the art and technique of conservation in Germany. This seventeenth-century Dragon rug smouldered in the attack but did not completely burn. Conservators have now brought it bach to numinous life an it is on display at th Museum of Islamic Art in Berlin.

an elite atelier. Nor do I recognise in it the vibrancy and close presence of the maker, her choices and mistakes, found in a tribal or a village rug. Rather, it looks to me like a commercial product woven in a quality-controlled workshop or factory as a desirable consumer object by specialised craftspeople using the most advanced design and weaving technologies available to them.[34]

If the rug dates from before the 1917 Bolshevik Revolution it may have come from commercial factories in Tabriz or Shusha, weaving for an international export market. If it dates from after 1917 it may have been woven in a Soviet factory in the Caucasus, as part of the Soviet planned economy, producing rugs for export across the USSR.[35] Workshops and factories in both free-market and collectivised systems had a focus on costs, production targets and supervision. In both economic structures, factory weavers lost the autonomy of village and tribal weavers. They no longer chose their designs and dyes, selected their wool or husbanded their sheep. Instead, they served a master and a market.

It is easy to assume that both their carpets and their lives were diminished by this. Ultimately, we have to make the assessment case by case. But industrial modernity could raise weaving standards through improved resources and quality control, and factory weaving could bring greater freedom than a cottage industry, particularly to young women. Even if they had to tip up their wages to their families, the money gave them some leverage in family politics. If they worked at the factory itself, rather than weaving at home, they met a broader range of people and had a broader range of experiences. Mrs. Gaskell captures this in her account of nineteenth-century factory hands: 'They came rushing along, with bold, fearless faces and loud laughs and jests, particularly aimed at all those who appeared to be above them in rank or station [. . .] The girls, with their rough but not unfriendly freedom, would comment on her dress; even touch her shawl or gown to ascertain the exact material.'[36]

The hegemons at Yalta were at work negotiating the ideological faultiness of the post-war world, as well as dividing up territory and populations. Whatever the differences in their belief systems,

all three were driving the world towards a future of industrialisation. The carpet under their feet at Yalta was a product and
symbol of this modernity.

It so happens that Crimea itself had a carpet-making community
among its Muslim Turkic-speaking population, sometimes called
Tatars. Their carpets were flat-woven kilims rather than knotted-pile carpets with a velvety finish. They were decorated with
Ornek, a system of motifs used across Crimean artefacts. Although
Ornek has many commonalities with the motifs of Anatolia and
the Caucasus, it is unusual in that its symbols have specific meanings which are used to build stories, rather than carrying shadowy,
half-forgotten connotations.* So, a rose represents a married woman, a tulip a young man and a carnation the wisdom of maturity,
and the story they tell could be of a wife and mother who takes
a younger lover and regrets it in old age. *Ornek* has long had a
powerful association with Tatar national identity. It was highly
unlikely that an *Ornek*-decorated Tatar carpet would have been
chosen by Stalin to dress his performance of power at Yalta. In
the summer of 1944, only six months before the Yalta Conference,
Stalin had purged Crimea of its Tatars.

This was a recurring experience in the history of the peninsula.
When Catherine the Great colonised Crimea in 1783, renaming it
Taurida after the ancient Greek name for the territory, the vast
majority of its population comprised Muslim Turkic speakers,
the Crimean Tatars. The Russian empress planned to make it a
'New Russia', implanting Russians aristocrats and Ukrainian
serfs.[37] By the beginning of the twentieth century, Tatar numbers
had reduced to only 35 per cent of the population, alongside 33
per cent Russian and 11 per cent Ukrainian.[38] In the early 1920s
Crimea was the last holdout of the anti-Bolshevik White Russians,

---

* In 2021 the practice of *Ornek* was inscribed in the UNESCO List of Intangible Cultural Heritage.

becoming part of the Soviet Union only after their defeat by the Red Army.

Nazi Germany invaded Crimea in 1941. Its main civilian targets were Russians and Jews. The Germans protected the interests of the Crimean Tatars as part of their effort to maintain good relations with their traditional ally Turkey, also a Muslim Turkic community. Turkey remained neutral for much of the Second World War, and Germany did not wish to drive it into the arms of the Allies. Meanwhile, some Crimean Tatars worked with the Germans against the Soviet Union's interests, having no desire for a return to Russian domination. Unluckily for them, the Red Army drove the Germans out of Crimea in early February 1944, and three months later Stalin issued a decree to expropriate and deport all Crimean Tatars on the grounds of collaboration. He sent 200,000 Crimean Turkic Muslims to join what he regarded as a fellow subordinate 'Asiatic' race in the Uzbek Autonomous Soviet Socialist Republic three thousand miles east. The decree states:

> All Tatars are to be banished from the territory of the Crimea and resettled permanently as special settlers in the regions of the Uzbek SSR. The resettlement will be assigned to the Soviet NKVD. The Soviet NKVD (comrade Beria) is to complete the resettlement by 1 June 1944.[39]

The expulsion was to take three weeks. Comrade Beria and his NKVD were feared and ferocious – Stalin could rely on them to make it happen. The decree itemises railway cars, fuel for the journey and precise instructions about what the refugees were to take with them, for instance 500kg of food per family. Stalin's expulsion was wholesale; no Tatars were recorded in Crimea in the 1959 or 1979 censuses.

The expulsion of the Crimean Tatars in 1944 was a foretaste of the great movements of peoples after the Second World War ended, numbering many tens of millions. Historian Mark Mazower comments: 'Wars invariably displace populations. But this war had been waged specifically to establish a New Order through extermination, incarceration, deportation and transfer [. . .] people were now being moved to consolidate political boundaries.'[40]

The power grabs and capitulations of Yalta laid the groundwork for huge and often forced migration of peoples like the one conducted by Stalin against the Crimean Tatars. Only months after expelling them, Stalin was seated on the white-ground carpet at Yalta with Roosevelt and Churchill, dividing up Europe and establishing global 'spheres of influence' where the hegemons gave themselves permission to do what they liked, regardless of the wishes of the communities and governments within those spheres. The absence in the famous Yalta photograph of a carpet made by Crimean Tatars is an augury of the consequences of this kind of power. The Tatars, their culture and their rugs had ceased to exist, because Stalin willed it so.

Perhaps the single most significant political decision associated with the Yalta Conference was that the three 'old reprobates' seated on the pale Persianate rug should be the ones to decide the peace. There were no invitees from defeated European nations, even if they had fought bravely in Allied armies or in the resistance. France and Poland, for instance, had no voice. Chinese leader General Chiang Kai-Shek was presented with a series of decisions about the extension of Soviet influence in Manchuria three months after the conference. It was the first he'd heard of it.[41] North Africa and the Middle East, crucial theatres of war and of support for the Allies, were not represented. Roosevelt and Churchill went on in the following weeks to hold unilateral meetings with Sheikh Adul-Aziz Ibn Saud, King Farouk and Emperor Haile Selassie, where post-war arrangements favourable to the US and UK were negotiated against the background of the Yalta fait accompli. The world was to become a US-Russia-UK hegemony.

Despite holding the cards, the three leaders struggled to reconcile their divergent ambitions and values. Stalin wanted to protect the Soviet system by extending its sphere of influence and ensuring that Russia's significant wartime sacrifices were rewarded with territory in Europe and Asia. Churchill wanted to preserve the British Empire and create an enduring peace in Europe without too much Russian influence in central and eastern Europe and the Balkans. While everyone was confident that the Germans would be defeated, it was by no means a given that the US could win the war with Japan in East Asia. The Yalta meeting was held five months before the successful test of the US Atom Bomb at Los Alamos, and in February 1945 Roosevelt had no concrete evidence that the Japanese could be defeated without the aid of Russia. Stalin had the upper hand.

The decisions made at the conference affected innumerable nations, but it is the fate of Poland which illuminates who was really in control and what the Big Three meant to do with their new hegemony. Throughout the early twentieth century, Poland's borders were contested by European Germany to the west and Russian, then Soviet territories to the east. Germany's invasion of Poland had been the reason why Britain and France had declared war in 1939. The Poles had fought with great courage in Allied armies and in the Polish resistance, and the suffering of Poland's Jews was among the most intense in Europe. The freedom of Poland was at the emotional core of the war effort. But influence in Poland was a non-negotiable requirement for Stalin, who said: 'Throughout history, Poland has been a corridor for attack on Russia [. . .] Poland is not only a question of honour, but a question of life and death for the Soviet State.'⁴² Thus it became the sacrificial victim to heal the fractures in the new hegemony, and to keep Stalin onside to ensure the support of the Red Army against the Japanese.

Stalin bargained hard and succeeded in consolidating the control of the USSR over the eastern part of Poland, including what is now Lithuania, Belarus and part of Ukraine. Meanwhile, the loose wording in Yalta's 'Declaration of Liberated Europe', encouraging 'free elections' without defining what that meant or how they would be monitored, gave Stalin space to intervene in Polish politics. The declaration was breached by Stalin within mere weeks of the conference when, in a sign of things to come, he imposed a communist-dominated government on Romania. Yalta continues to be seen by many as delivering not only the Poles, but much of eastern and central Europe and the Balkans out of the hands of Hitler into those of Stalin. This was the price of his participation in the war against the Japanese.

The treaty was severely criticised in the US, with its large immigrant populations from central and eastern Europe, the Balkans and the Baltic states, many of whom had fled from earlier persecutions. Roosevelt could only respond that it was the best he could do at the time. Meanwhile, Churchill attempted to persuade a House of Commons which had been spurred by Hitler's invasion of Poland to vote for war in Europe that it was not a problem now to give Polish territory to Stalin. His address was combative: 'I decline absolutely to embark here on a discussion about Russian good faith . . . It seems to me that this talk of cutting Poland in half is very misleading.'[43] With a rhetorical flourish he described the Polish territory given to Stalin as 'the enormous dismal region of the Pripet marshes [. . .] which [Poland] exchanges for more fruitful and developed land in the West'.[44]

The speech met widespread criticism, and indeed ministerial resignations. In truth, Churchill could hardly have chosen a worse example to play down the scale of Poland's loss. In 1941, the Pripyat Marshes had been the site of what historians now regard as one of the first planned Nazi mass murders of Jewish civilians. On 1 August 1941, Himmler wrote to the SS military commander in the region that not enough Jews had been killed in the first wave of murders. All Jewish males over fourteen were to be shot, and women and children were to be drowned in the marshes, presumably to save ammunition. The water proved too shallow, so they were shot also; 23,700 Polish Jews are thought to have died in the Pripyat Marshes.[45] John Colville, Churchill's private secretary, wrote in his diary: 'He is trying to persuade himself that all is well, but in his heart I think he is worried about Poland and not convinced of the strength of our moral position.'[46]

History's judgement is less sympathetic than that of Churchill's private secretary. 1985 saw the fortieth anniversary of the Yalta Conference. The UK Foreign and Commonwealth Office produced briefing papers suggesting the public position Margaret Thatcher's government should take. The potato was so hot that the decision was taken by senior civil servants not even to circulate the briefing papers: 'Mr Thomas agrees that there is no, repeat, no, difficulty about making the background papers available to a small selection of posts and departments for information only. His only concern is that any suggestion of stimulating debate about the issues should be avoided.'[47]

It is hard to avoid the conclusion that part of the motive was to protect the reputation of a previous Conservative Party prime minister, Sir Winston Churchill. The president of the US, Ronald Reagan, simply blamed Stalin.

> Since that time, Yalta has had a double meaning. It recalls an episode of co-operation between the Soviet Union and free nations, in a great common cause. But it also recalls the reasons that this co-operation could not continue – the Soviet promises that were not kept, the elections that were not held, the two halves of Europe that have remained apart.[48]

As the conference came to a close back in Yalta, Stalin's mood was unsurprisingly buoyant. He had many victories to celebrate, sitting on the terrace of the Livadia Palace with his military boots firmly planted on the white-ground carpet.

Within weeks, Roosevelt was dead and Churchill's confidence about Yalta had disappeared. He sounded the alarm to the new US president, Harry S. Truman, copying in King George VI and the British foreign secretary:

> I am profoundly concerned about the European situation [. . .] What is to happen about Russia? [. . .] I feel deep anxiety because of their misinterpretation of the Yalta decisions, their

attitude towards Poland, and their overwhelming influence in the Balkans [. . .]An iron curtain is drawn down upon their front. We do not know what is going on behind it.[49]

Yalta's woollen carpet was replaced by a curtain of suspicion, secrecy and mutual threat which was not to be raised for almost fifty years.

In 2005, the Georgian-Russian sculptor Zurab Tsereteli created a statue commemorating the sixtieth anniversary of the Yalta Conference, as a gift to the Russian nation. Tsereteli, the People's Artist of Russia and President of the Russian Academy of Arts, forged a version in bronze of the photograph taken in the gardens of the Livadia Palace in 1945. The press dubbed it the 'Big Troika', and noted that while Churchill and Roosevelt measured ten feet in height, Stalin measured ten feet four. The white-ground carpet was represented as a piece of rumpled metal. The statue was offered free to Crimea.

After the fall of the Soviet Union in 1991, Crimea became a semi-autonomous province of an independent Ukraine. The Tatars began to return, and their *Mejlis*, the assembly of the Muslim Tur-kic-speaking minority, became part of the governance of Crimea. When the statue of the Big Troika was offered to Crimea the Tatars and their Mejlis protested, and the Ukrainian government supported them. For these Crimean Tatars, Stalin was not the cunning negotiator of Yalta who won supremacy for the USSR in eastern and central Europe, but the racist dictator who, after the expulsion of the Nazis from Crimea in 1944, had ordered the ethnic cleansing of their community. They had no desire to see him celebrated in Yalta. After their resistance, the statue of the Big Two and the Bigger Stalin found it difficult to find a home.[50]

In 2014, Russia annexed Crimea from Ukraine and Crimea's political reality was transformed. The Tatar Mejlis was first re-stricted then proscribed by Russia as an extremist organisation.

In 2015, on the seventieth anniversary of the Yalta Conference, Tsereteli's sculpture was moved to Yalta and unveiled in the gardens of the Livadia Palace. The unveiling ceremony was led by the speaker of Russia's State Duma, Sergei Naryshkin, to the sound of the Russian national anthem.

The sculpture in the gardens of the Livadia Palace was a blunt and brutal reminder that Russia had reconfigured Europe to its advantage, and could do so again. But the symbolism of the carpet under the Troika's feet at Yalta was more ambiguous. It was part of the remaking of Russia and Europe after 1945, but also carried with it histories of Iran, Armenia, Azerbaijan and of its weavers, driven headlong towards industrialisation and modernity. Even when they are appropriated as props by the great and powerful, carpets find ways to tell their individual stories, which sometimes subvert and always complicate received histories.

Chapter 9
Sahib

KNOTTED-PILE CARPET, NINETEENTH CENTURY CE, INDIA

In 1877 Queen Victoria was created Empress of India by Benjamin Disraeli's government at Westminster. To mark the event her viceroy, Lord Lytton, organised a lavish celebration in Delhi attended by nearly seventy thousand people, including Indian princes and the ruling caste of the British establishment in India. At the Delhi Durbar, among elephants, blazing jewels, brazen horns and tents made from exquisite textiles, they jointly acknowledged Victoria as their *Qaisar-i-Hind*. Celebratory events rippled out through British India. In Punjab, in the north-west, preparations were made for an imperial exhibition celebrating the province, the last part of India to be conquered by the British East India Company in 1849. The Punjab exhibition was masterminded by Baden Henry Baden-Powell (1841–1901), an eminent and respected *sahib* who went on to become a British commissioner in Lahore.[1]

Baden-Powell had shown an interest in India's carpets since his arrival there in 1860, using the official reports he wrote as a government surveyor to suggest ways of improving skills and to express design preferences.[2] As the preparations for the 1881 imperial Punjab exhibition began, he sent out a memorandum of government guidance to Punjabi carpet-makers:

> During the last few years there has been a great revival of public taste, in the course of which it has become universally

recognized as a principle, that all truly national and indigenous forms of art are valuable in themselves and worth preserving [. . .] No prize will be given to any carpet not purely Oriental or original in design or not copied from a good Oriental original. [. . .] Special efforts should be made to borrow old Kabul, Persian, Herat and other rugs and carpets to serve as examples for guidance.[3]

His instructions demanded that their designs should be at once 'national and indigenous' to India, which had a distinguished tradition of Mughal carpet-making, yet at the same time Persian. He threw in Herat on the border between Iran and Afghanistan, and Kabul in eastern Afghanistan for good measure, and collapsed them into the single term 'Oriental', as if all the carpets of the vast area and multiple cultures of Asia were one. But as it turned out, the judging committees of the exhibition, along with the British colonial establishment in India and Baden-Powell himself, wanted not 'indigenous' rugs but those modelled on the intricate floral carpets of urban Persia, with their nuanced palette of soft colours and the standardised craftsmanship demanded by a quality-controlled workshop.

One of the rugs in the exhibition, woven in response to Baden-Powell's assertion of the principles of carpet design, was bought in 1882 for the South Kensington Museum. It is a knotted-pile carpet eight feet wide by ten feet long, with a design of stylised blossoms and leaves covering its entire central space, organised into a trellis of interlocking octagons. The pink, yellow and white blossoming octagons and black ground have little contrast and the overall effect is muted. The red border is similarly subdued. It would fit comfortably as a tasteful hint of the old and exotic in a modern interior. It was born from Britain's imperial convictions about the 'Oriental' rug tradition and the empire's duty to safeguard and promote it in India.

Baden-Powell came from a highly capable family of eminent Victorians. His father, Baden Powell, was Savilian Professor of Geometry at Oxford and an early supporter of Darwinism; his brother Robert Baden-Powell was a general in the British Army and founder of the Scout movement. His sister Agnes founded the Girl Guides. His brother Frank was an artist and Royal Academician, and Henry himself was an accomplished watercolourist. His early life was spent in the robust intellectual atmosphere of Oxford, where his family lived in New College Lane. In 1860, fresh from St Paul's School in London, he passed the newly established competitive examination for the Indian Civil Service, whose upper age limit for entry was twenty-three. At nineteen, he set sail on the arduous three-month journey round the Cape of Good Hope to India.

The Suez Canal was not to open for another decade, so his passage through the stormy Atlantic under sail was the same difficult route taken by Vasco da Gama almost four hundred years earlier, and with similar privations. When he arrived, the schoolboy faced further threats to his health from the cholera, malaria and syphilis which contributed to the high death rate among Europeans in India.[4]

These were not the only challenges awaiting him. He joined a British community under severe pressure. For more than a century, the British East India Company had rapaciously exploited India's resources and people in the interests of the British establishment, enforcing its authority through ferocious military action.[5] After a major uprising against the East India Company in 1857 – known variously as the First Indian War of Independence, the Sepoy Revolt or the Indian Mutiny, depending on the political viewpoint of the speaker – the British took direct control of much of India.[6]

As one of the first wave of British government officials in India after the uprising, Baden-Powell lived through the intense early decades of the extraordinary experiment in government carried out by the British in its aftermath. For the next ninety years the Parliament in Westminster made decisions for a country four thousand miles away and over ten times bigger than itself, dictating the terms on which two hundred million people of many different faiths lived. The nineteen-year-old Baden-Powell took his place among those deciding the future of India, its peoples, its resources, its art and manufacturing.

Not only were the new rulers of India often young, but they were few and relatively unprotected. In 1860, as Baden-Powell arrived in India, the numbers of British fighting men and administrators were small compared to the size of the population and the scale of the territory. The new Indian Civil Service set up after the 1857 uprising was ultimately to be around twelve hundred-strong but had not reached that target yet.[7] It was backed up by an army inherited from the East India Company in 1858, in which fifty thousand British officers supervised three hundred thousand largely Indian recruits.[8] But their precarious hold did not daunt their ambition. Clever young men like Henry Baden-Powell and other bright but poor second sons of upper-middle-class and aristocratic British families set out to bring India under close British control.

Baden-Powell had the perfect hinterland for a colonial ruler, and his star began to rise. He was sent to Punjab to impose the will of Westminster. Punjab's population was nineteen million, half that of the entire UK at the time, and at a hundred and forty thousand square miles was a third larger than Britain. Baden-Powell worked his way through the junior ranks of the Indian Civil Service and by 1873 held the formal title of Surveyor of Punjab's Forests, although his responsibilities in the huge province were wider. In the years to come he became British commissioner in Punjab, its chief justice and vice-chancellor of its university, controlling Punjab's government, law and education.

In the short decades after their arrival, Baden-Powell and his small number of British colleagues in the Indian Civil Service established the Punjab System, described by historian Kim Wagner as government by 'despotic paternalism'.[9] Born out of a mixture of anxious memories of the 1857 uprising, the strong British sense of entitlement to India's resources and a phenomenal will to power, the Punjab System rested on the assumption that Britain knew best and that Punjabis should do as they were told. It relied on an efficient chain of command, up from the British colonial officers on the ground in the subdivisions of Punjab set up by the British to the British lieutenant-governor of Punjab and his civil service secretariat. They in their turn had absolute legal, military and executive powers over Punjab. Nothing would escape British scrutiny and direction, from Punjab's people and languages, its flora and fauna, mines and factories to its arts and crafts, including its carpets.

The imperial Punjab exhibition Baden-Powell oversaw in 1881 was organised as a series of competitions in different media – woodwork, metalwork, ceramics, textiles and rugs. Baden-Powell and his team set targets for the numbers and types of objects to be submitted by British district officers, some working in remote corners of the province, and by the workshops, factories, schools and jails of Punjab. Most achieved their targets, an indication of the strength of the hold of the small band of British officials over the vast territory, and the excuses of those who couldn't are poignant. The district officer for the Punjabi area of Amritsar wrote apologising to the exhibition organising committee that he might miss his target for goods because of an outbreak of typhoid.[10]

The 1881 exhibition was not primarily a historical review, but a survey of current manufacture intended to influence future production. India was a commercial engine for Britain and needed to be finely tuned. While memos like the one Baden-Powell issued were framed as aesthetic judgements, they also had the effect of encouraging styles of products which would sell well in Europe, North America and British colonies elsewhere in the world, where tastes were assumed to be similar to those of the British. These two ambitions could coexist comfortably because the British in India had come to believe that their taste was in fact an expression of absolute aesthetic quality rather than a product of time, place and fashion.[11] Having used their directives to set the standard for Punjabi artists and craftspeople, the British then organised competitions like the 1881 exhibition in order to judge them.

There was a sense of jeopardy around the carpet submissions to the exhibition. When Baden-Powell asserted that 'During the last few years there has been a great revival of public taste, in the course of which it has become universally recognized as a principle, that all truly national and indigenous forms of art are valuable in themselves and worth preserving',[12] he described not just a change in taste but a growing anxiety. The British arts establishment in Britain and India had begun to develop a conviction that India risked losing its own craft traditions in the face of industrialisation and global trade, among them its rich history of carpet-making.[13]

British merchant-princes of the East India Company had collected fine Mughal rugs and exported them to Britain from the first establishment of the East India Company in the seventeenth century.[14] But from 1851, a much wider UK public was exposed to Indian carpets. That year saw the Great Exhibition at London's Crystal Palace, which inaugurated almost a century of international exhibitions across the developed world. The exhibition of Indian carpets in 1851 became the standard against which Western commentators began judging more recent production as the nineteenth century progressed. Vincent Robinson, whose eponymous dealership had sold the repaired Ardabil carpet to the South Kensington Museum, grieved the loss since 1851 'of an Art centuries' old', which had 'perished under our very gaze', in the service of 'trade instincts and interests'.[15] By the end of the century concerns had solidified into accepted fact. J.K. Mumford, an opinion former in the American market for Indian carpets, whose textbook on rugs was required reading in liberal arts courses in some leading US universities,[16] wrote in 1900: 'Indian carpets sold today are wholly modern creations. The industrial development of India under English rule dissipated the old methods so rapidly that within twenty-five years after the first public exhibition of these fabrics in London, in 1851, the carpet product had become entirely altered in character.'[17] British and British-Indian intelligentsia and opinion formers in export markets had come to a consensus view that a crisis in Indian carpet-making existed, and that the crisis arose from British intervention in India's industry.

Indian pile carpet-weaving had always taken place in factories, where it was mostly carried out by men and boys. India did not have the tradition of women weaving in cottages and tents that was common across Anatolia and Iran. What changed in the second half of the nineteenth century was that Indian manufacturers took advantage of the growing market for Indian carpets, producing and exporting them in greater numbers from their factories. This contributed to a growth in the bottom end of the market, where cheap synthetic dyes and less skilled labour were often used. Cost pressures on local carpet-making firms were intensified by low production costs in British institutions like regimental and military schools, art colleges and jails, where carpet-weavers were paid lower than market rates. Meanwhile, British and North American dealers and contractors intervened in local design traditions, encouraging the production of certain designs over others in carpets made for export.[18] The problems at the cheaper end of the market led to complaints from rival Indian producers of higher-quality carpets. As late as the Indian Industrial Commission of 1916–18, carpet-manufacturer Shaik Gulam Sadik was still making this case in his evidence to a British government industrial commission.[19]

As the volume of noise grew about the decline in Indian carpets, the British set out to solve the problem they themselves had helped create, and the solution they found was yet more British intervention.

By the 1800s, Punjab had been a traditional Mughal territory for centuries. The court of the first Mughal emperor, Babur, was established there around 1526. Babur was descended from both Mongol and Timurid emperors and had spent time as a young man at the Iranian court. His court and those of his descendants Akbar, Jahan and Jahangir became international cultural powerhouses in their own right.

The Mughals had an exceptional carpet-making heritage.[20] They were semi-nomadic like their tribal forebears and carpets were central to their way of life. As their sumptuous tents moved between imperial centres to the hunt or to battle, so did their carpets, providing comfort, aesthetic pleasure, the means to practise their religion and markers of status among the world's great empires.

India's diversity of dyestuffs and fine local wools like pashmina meant that the materials available to Mughal weavers were arguably better than those of other great weaving centres like Anatolia or Iran. The fineness of the fibres and the skill of the knotters permitted counts of thousands of knots per square inch, compared to the three hundred and fifty of the V&A's Ardabil (which is often offered as the gold standard of carpet-weaving). These characteristics created an extraordinarily lifelike vivacity. Wild animals like cheetahs and bears have flashing eyes and bloodstained chops. We're told that Emperor Jahangir commissioned carpets with flowers so lifelike that they allowed him to walk constantly in the 'garden of eternal spring' which he had encountered on a visit to the valleys of Kashmir in 1620. Yet this tradition was not the one prioritised by Baden-Powell and the British establishment. Instead, manufacturers were encouraged to look further west to Persian styles.

There was a push and pull at work. The emergent empires of nineteenth-century Europe liked to associate themselves with previous successful empires, such as Iran's. The material culture of Persia's sixteenth- and seventeenth-century Safavid dynasty was held in Europe and North America to be 'the pre-eminent branch of Muhammedan Art', its carpets seen as outstanding representatives of that success.[21] Mughal India, however, was a much more challenging imperial model for the British. British rule in India was the direct consequence of the 1857 uprising against the East India Company, an uprising whose figurehead was the last Mughal emperor, the aged and scholarly Bahadur Shah.[22] The Mughals were all but a spent political and military force by the time of the uprising, but 1857 proved that enduring allegiance to the Mughal Empire was enough to mobilise dissent in India, and there was no desire among the British to reawaken it. The focus in Baden-Powell's memo on Persianate carpets may have been influenced by political caution.

The carpet-manufacturers and dealers of Punjab went to work preparing for the exhibition.

People in the Global North who love Asian rugs like to think of them as the products of ancient traditions, using designs with symbolic meanings which date back centuries. They hope that rugs are made from only natural and local materials, foraged plant, insect and animal dyes, local wool. They, and I am one of them, have vivid mental images of weavers sitting in villages or tent encampments against a backdrop of snow-capped peaks, or in small urban workshops alongside old mosques covered in dazzling skins of multi-coloured tiles. Perhaps the weavers, who we usually imagine as women, are singing knotting instructions to each other or teaching their daughters and nieces their ancient, creatively fulfilling craft.

The rug bought for the South Kensington Museum from the 1881 Punjab exhibition, made under Baden-Powell's guidance, challenges every aspect of this version of rug-making.

The first break with the dream is the Persian model which was used to weave it. The 1881 exhibition catalogue explains that the rug was based on a Persian carpet sold by the Maison de Louvre, a Parisian department store.[23] There was an international trade in paper copies of designs for such fashionable carpets, which were exported from the consuming nations in Europe to carpet-weaving territories like India. The weavers of the rug seem to have followed such a paper design, which may also have included a row-by-row knot plan specifying colours – for example, five black knots followed by two red knots followed by one yellow. The design of the V&A carpet did not flow from a traditional fountainhead: it was repeatedly mediated, first by a British idea of how Oriental carpets made in India should look, and then by the tastes of nine-teenth-century Paris.

The warps, loops and securing horizontal wefts of the V&A carpet are all made from animal fibre. While sheep's wool, camel hair and pashmina were all used for traditional carpet-making in Punjab, we only find sheep's wool in the V&A rug. This may have come from local flocks of sheep, but it is entirely possible that it was made from soft merino wool imported from Australia or New Zealand; imperial free-trade rules introduced in the middle of the nineteenth century encouraged such trade between Britain's colonies.[24] And then there are the dyes. India has a distinguished history of making dyes distilled from plants and insects. However, some dyes in the V&A carpet have faded to grey, suggesting they were produced in Western laboratories. These 'synthetic' dyes first became available after W.H. Perkin synthesised aniline purple in 1838 and were notoriously unstable in the early years of their production.[25] By the 1880s they had become an international com-modity, with Germany their leading producer.

As well as its origin in a Parisian department store, its import-ed materials and its partly synthetic dyes, the V&A carpet differs from the romantic view of carpet-making in a final, crucial aspect. It was not the product of local craftswomen with an enduring tradition of artisanship. It was made by Indian men imprisoned by the British state, weaving under duress in the Central Jail at Lahore, the home of Punjab's British government. What they produced in the prison workshop was a Persian-British-Parisian-German-Pacific-Rim co-production, a cultural Frankenstein's monster brought to life through the brutal force of Britain's colo-nial infrastructure and its commercial drive.

Throughout the colonial period between 1858 and 1947, the British ran an extensive jail system in India. Indian prisoners, both male and female, were incarcerated in British jails for defying British expectations of behaviour. Their transgressions were not always obvious crimes; they merely had to be a divergence from British values and ways of life that shocked the Raj. The British did not seek agreement that what was being punished was a crime in the eyes of both parties. This was not rule by consent.

As the effort to reform and reshape Indians as subjects of the British Empire intensified, prison numbers grew and so did their costs. India was intended by the British as a source of revenue, so jail workshops and convict labour gangs were set up to defray the costs of prison upkeep. Workers were paid 'a few coins' for their labour – they were not slaves in the technical sense – but there was rarely an attempt to build skills, and the products of these workshops and labour gangs were not intended to be commercial. The exception to this was jail carpets.[26]

Jail carpets were woven in India from as early as 1860, and by end of the century there were several Indian jails well known for carpet manufacture: Lahore and Amritsar in Punjab, and Agra, Yerawada, Jaipur, Gwalior and Bikaner across British India. These imperial reimaginings of the Indian carpet became a commercial success in Europe and North America, playing a part in the 'Oriental Carpet Boom' of the later nineteenth century.[27] Baden-Powell's colleague in the government of Punjab, William Coldstream, claimed:

'It is not too much to say that it is the Lahore Central Jail manufacture of these carpets which has kept it alive and even extended it in the Province. Had the Lahore Central Jail not taken up the orders for carpets of Messrs Watson and Bontor's of Bond Street, London, they would not have been executed.'[28]

Despite their export success, they did not sell well among Indian consumers. British government trade records show that the number of carpets exported from Punjabi jails to Europe, North America and settler colonies like South Africa and Australia far outstripped the number traded within India itself.[29] An export value of carpets of four thousand rupees (equivalent to around £35,000 or $45,000 in 2024) was recorded in each of the years 1903 to 1907, although the British government report remarks that 'it was considerably larger a decade or so ago'. Sales within India

were a tenth of that amount in those years.[30] The British government tried to encourage the Indian middle class to use what they
saw as traditional crafts in their homes, but prosperous Indians
shopping for decor had already begun to prefer a forward-look-
ing, cosmopolitan aesthetic to the garbled Orientalism of British
jail carpets.[31] They had set off on a path that over a few decades
resulted in Art Deco flats in middle-class Indian areas of cities
like Mumbai, decorated with suites of Austrian steel furniture that
were regarded as more suitable for the climate than the traditional
wood, and floors made from modern, easy-clean materials.[32]

Jail carpets diverged widely in quality. The V&A has in its collection a poignant example of the work of an unskilled jail weaver,
very coarse in its execution. The carpet includes an inscription in
English provided by the British overseer indicating the jail where
it was made, but the illiterate or non-Anglophone weaver wove
the inscription reversed and inverted, and it is unreadable. More
is communicated about the lives of these weavers by this mistake
and the humble artefact that bears it than by more elaborate and
polished productions. At the opposite end of the spectrum is
perhaps the most famous Indian jail carpet, now in the Waterloo
Chamber at Windsor Castle. Made in Agra jail as a gift for Queen
Victoria in 1893, the enormous 23-by-12-metre-carpet was woven
to a fashionable design and palette by highly skilled weavers as a
tribute to India's empress.

It has been suggested that the men who wove in British jails
were long-term political prisoners whom the British government
was willing to train, and who had time to develop their craft.[33]
If this is true, some of the weavers of early Punjabi jail carpets
may have been participants in that very 1857 rebellion which
brought about direct rule of India from Westminster in the first
place. While the Sikh military in Punjab collaborated with the
British in suppressing the uprising, there was Punjabi support for
the rebellion outside Sikh military ranks.[34] Some jail weavers may
have been not felons but political activists.

Meanwhile, among the jail carpets in the 1881 Punjab exhibition
was one woven in Lahore's Female Penitentiary, which in the late

nineteenth century contained up to two hundred women. More than 90 per cent of these women were married and had their children living in jail with them.[35] A population of female vagrants, petty thieves and prostitutes moved in and out of Punjabi jails, but these short-term prisoners were not trained up as weavers.[36] The long-term female prison population was largely composed of women who had aided or attempted the religious practice of *suttee*, the self-immolation of a wife on her husband's funeral pyre, or committed murder, particularly female infanticide, which Indian village customs sometimes tolerated. These traditional practices had become a major focus of what historian Satadru Sen describes as British 'sanitising colonialism', the desire to bring Indian traditional behaviour into line with British norms.[37] The carpet from Lahore Female Penitentiary in the 1881 Punjab exhibition was likely woven by one of these women. We can only imagine their confusion and pain as they wove under coercion and punitive discipline in British jails, imprisoned for what did not seem to them a crime.

Weavers' voices are always difficult to uncover, but they can sometimes be heard indirectly in British government reports. C.H. Brierley, a British prison official, recorded that male prisoners preferred to break rocks and build roads than to weave, and often requested transfers.[38] British data gathered on the effects of prison shows that male and female prisoners rarely took up weaving as their trade after their release. It seems that their experiences in jail were enough for them to turn away from a potentially profitable living as a skilled artisan.

We can also draw on images of jail weavers. In the early 1870s the British government in India commissioned a series of photographs of Indian crafts from British photographers Michie and Company. They were intended for display in the 1873 Universal Exhibition in Vienna, where central European visitors would encounter the British vision of India and its material culture. Among the images, now in the British Library, are jail weavers. A man at work in Karachi jail stares full into the camera, forcing the viewer to encounter him as an individual, but his expression is so guarded

that we cannot know anything about his experience. John Lockwood Kipling, father of Rudyard, made a series of drawings now
in the V&A of the Amritsar jail weaving workshop, also in Punjab.
They focus exclusively on the equipment and materials, which are
rendered in detail and colour, rather than on the prisoners, who
are mostly drawn from behind, only one being given a sketchy
face, and all of them shrouded in generic clothing. We cannot
even see the point of contact between their human hands and the
materials they work. Kipling's jail weavers are of less interest and
value to him than the equipment and materials they used.

Perhaps the most shocking manifestation of this dehumanising
attitude is found in the display of a group of thirty-four prisoners
from Agra jail, including carpet-weavers, in the 1886 Colonial and
Indian Exhibition at the South Kensington Museum in London.
Under the supervision of Dr J.W. Tyler, the superintendent of Agra
jail, they were displayed as traditional Indian artisans at work in
an Indian marketplace. The London *Saturday Review* observed:
'Here are the carpet weavers, four in number, mingling work and
song, their chant barbaric and not without fascination.'[39] Very unusually, we have a comment from one of the prison artisans, who
'quietly told me that he did not quite like the very audible remarks
of some visitors, who seem to look upon them as animals'[40].

When Baden-Powell set to work 'saving' the Indian carpet, he was
playing a small part in a much larger imperial project, one that,
perhaps surprisingly, had its home in a suburb of London.

Once eighty acres of market gardens producing fruit and vege-
tables for London's kitchens, from around 1850 South Kensington
became home to a string of cultural institutions that continue to
draw visitors in their millions. These included the South Kensington V&A Museum, the Natural History and Science Museums,
the Royal Albert Hall, Imperial College, the Royal Colleges of Art
and Music and the Royal Geographical Society. This intellectual
powerhouse for an empire with aspirations for global dominance

was the vision of Queen Victoria's consort, Prince Albert. Described satirically by journalists as 'Albertopolis', it was initially mocked as the effort of a vainglorious German princeling to find a role for himself beyond that of Queen Victoria's husband.[41] It was as if the current Queen-Consort, Camilla, set about developing a large intellectual and technological hub intended to transform the UK economy and its global standing on a large chunk of one of London's leafy suburbs. But Albertopolis outlived its doubters, becoming and remaining one of the world's great cultural and scientific centres, and Prince Albert looks down on it to this day from his gilded memorial in Kensington Gardens.

The centre of operations for this great ideas incubator was the well-funded British government Department of Science and Art, at its offices in the South Kensington Museum. The department was the hub of Prince Albert's vision of a Britain which would lead the world in industrial design, art, science, manufacturing and trade. Established in 1853, it not only controlled the institutions of Albertopolis but had direct and autocratic control of design and technical education across the whole of the UK.[42] The syllabus, books and teachers were selected centrally by the department. Many of the art and technical colleges it established or sponsored continue to be famous names today: the Royal College of Art, the Glasgow School of Art, the Edinburgh School of Art. Fashions have changed, but there is still a strong emphasis in these schools on the relationship between design and technology, and on commercial impact, although the old insistence on training by copying and the obsession with patterns which are not naturalistic and use no perspective have gone. The department, its new education system and the institutions of Albertopolis locked together like a set of gears, one element amplifying the next in the interests of British imperial power and global economic supremacy. Those gears have come to be known as the South Kensington System.

The Department of Science and Art aimed to 'reform' arts, crafts and manufacture not only in Britain but also across the British Empire. Exhibitions like that held in 1881 in Punjab were part of the department's ambition to roll out the South Kensington

System in India. Exhibition entries which met British standards were rewarded with prizes and published in British-controlled publications. Prize-winning artefacts went back into the Indian community of entrepreneurs and artisans as the British-approved direction of Indian manufactures. The tightly centralised control of design and technical education that the Department of Science and Art had set up in Britain was replicated in India. British art, regimental and mission schools trained Indian artisans in British expectations, and museums displayed British-approved collections.[43] There were few local Indian voices in this self-reinforcing system. When Baden-Powell wrote to the carpet-makers of Punjab about the 'recent great revival of public taste' and its underlying 'principles' of design, both the revival and its principles had been engineered and articulated from South Kensington.[44] Carpet-weaving in British jails is one of the clearest examples of the South Kensington System at work, a board of trade masquerading as scholarly protectors of cultural standards.

The South Kensington System was primarily controlled by a coterie of close colleagues, scholars, artists, writers, designers and architects. Among them were the founding head of the department, Henry Cole (1808–82), polymath, critic of art and music, inventor and force of nature; designer Owen Jones (1809–74), author of the taste handbook of the period, *The Grammar of Ornament*;[45] and Caspar Purdon Clarke (1846–1911), future director of the V&A. During the second half of the century these men transformed their personal taste into a wing of the government of an empire on which the sun never set.

As Baden-Powell's imperial Punjab exhibition opened to the public in September 1881, South Kensington's Caspar Purdon Clarke was on a shopping trip in India with the modern equivalent of £500,000 (around $660,000) of the Department of Science and Art's money in his pocket. Purdon Clarke epitomises the Victorian mixture of scholar and man of action, aesthete and administrator.

He was in his thirties when he undertook his year-long Indian trip, already a successful architect, writer and lecturer. He had acted as representative of and buyer for the South Kensington Museum in important cultural locations from Paris to Tehran. He ultimately became director of the South Kensington Museum, and subsequently of the new Metropolitan Museum of Art in New York.[46]

In 1879, the South Kensington Museum contained around 19,000 objects from the India Museum, home of the collection of the East India Company, which had finally been dissolved in 1874. Much of the East India Company collection was the result of warfare, plunder and looting, but the grandees of South Kensington were more concerned by its ad hoc and unscientific nature. Purdon Clarke's instructions from the Department of Science and Art as he left for India were to fill gaps in the South Kensington Museum's new Indian collection.

One of those gaps was carpets. There was a major British domestic industry in carpets, but the quality of their design elicited mockery in South Kensington and made them difficult to export. The sophisticated suburbs of Paris, Berlin and Vienna showed little desire to decorate their homes with out-of-proportion woollen swans floating along deep-perspective woollen rivers.[47] This problem was to be solved by exposing British designers, manufacturers and exporters to great examples of traditional Indian carpet-making, but only those filtered through the South Kensington System and mediated by judicious British officials like its wingman Purdon Clarke.

Purdon Clarke travelled the length and breadth of India in 1882 meeting Indian princes.[48] (With typical South Kensington precision he was given a fifth-class civil service uniform, the lowest rank of court dress worn by officials in the British Empire, its gold embroidery a modest three-eighths of an inch wide compared to the five inches of a first-class uniform.) With his excellent letters of introduction he was able to take advantage of the hospitality of British colonial officials, their airy bungalows, solicitous servants

and often glamorous social lives, and with the department's warrant was able to travel everywhere first-class. Nevertheless, much
of his time was spent in arduous expeditions on what Rudyard
Kipling in *Kim* describes as 'that great river of humanity', the Grand
Trunk Road from the south of India to Afghanistan, through both
the sweltering humidity of the monsoon and the dust and heat of
the dry season.[49] He was slowly gathering the three thousand four
hundred objects that would ultimately fill three hundred crates on
a ship bound for London's recently opened Victoria and Albert
Docks and the South Kensington Museum. It must have been a
relief when he reached the pleasant cool of Punjab in early 1882, in
time to see the exhibition of Punjabi arts, crafts and manufactures
which was running in the state's capital. Maybe he was weary as he
reviewed the exhibition, but there is a sour note of imperial racism
in a remark recorded by Baden-Powell and attributed to Purdon
Clarke: 'A traveller in India, who did us the honour to visit our
Punjab exhibition in 1882, remarked jokingly that it seemed the
only way to get native workmen to do anything was to shut them
up in a jail!'[50]

The Persian-Parisian-British-German-Pacific Rim rug made
in Lahore Central Jail by political prisoners had won a prize in
the jail carpets section of the 1881 Punjab exhibition. This was
unsurprising given that the terms of its making had been defined
by the very same British administrators who now came to judge its
quality. The government report written on the exhibition praised
it warmly, saying: 'This is an exceptionally beautiful carpet; the
design is very handsome, the colouring good, and the workman-
ship perfect.'[51] Equally unsurprising was its purchase by Caspar
Purdon Clarke, visiting Punjab as the agent of the Department of
Science and Art. The price he paid communicates the high regard
in which he held it. At the modern equivalent of £1,200 (around
$1,600) it was seven or eight times the price of Purdon Clarke's
average purchase in India.[52] Caspar Purdon Clarke sent the rug
back to Britain, where it was funnelled into the home end of the
South Kensington System.

After the carpet arrived in East London's docks with the rest of Purdon Clarke's haul of Indian crafts in 1883, it was initially displayed at the South Kensington Museum. Then, in common with many objects at the museum, it was loaned out to manufacturers and art colleges across the UK as a choice model of Indian carpet-making whose example would improve the quality of British manufacturing and increase sales and exports.

We don't know which industrialist the Department of Science and Art sent the Lahore jail carpet to, but the rich archive of Templeton's Carpet Manufacturing Company in Glasgow shows us what often happened to Asian rugs lent out to improve British industrial design. One of the world's leading carpet-manufacturers during the late nineteenth and early twentieth centuries, Templeton's had developed technologies for making versions of the handwoven pile rugs of Asia by machine. The South Kensington Museum lent them many carpets to use as inspiration. The firm's designers drew or photographed the rugs, then analysed the designs to produce meticulously hand-painted knot plans as the basis for recreating the rugs on a machine. Templeton's large design studio was populated by former and current students of the Department of Science and Art's Glasgow School of Art.[53] The designers who would have mediated between the Lahore jail carpet and the mechanised loom were themselves part of the South Kensington System. Templeton's produced versions of these confected British-Indian rugs for sale in the UK and for export to colonial Canada, New Zealand, Australia, Africa, Malaysia, Europe and the Americas.

In the South Kensington System, a carpet was woven under coercion by Indian prisoners in Lahore Central Jail, following British government preferences for Persian styles and mediated by Parisian tastes. It was made from Australian or New Zealand merino wool and German synthetic dyes, and finally purchased with British government funds for the South Kensington Museum as an

exemplary Indian carpet. Sent out to Britain's cities as a model of
excellent Indian design, it was reproduced by a British industrial
carpet-manufacturer. From there it was sold for homes in the UK
and for the parlours and lounges of European settler populations
across the globe. Unaware of its origins, those global consumers
learned from such rugs what an Indian carpet should look like. It
was from this circularity that the South Kensington System gained
its power.

In 2016 I was at work in the V&A's archives, which at the time
were housed in a nineteenth-century Post Office Savings Bank in
London, a touchstone of Victorian financial probity and security.
In this high Victorian fortress, an eerie building of clanking old
lifts and long, echoing tiled corridors, I was chasing the idea of
mapping the changing tastes of the curators who assembled the
V&A's carpet collection in its formative years.[54]

As so often in research, what I found was something else. A
yellowed and fragile document in copperplate handwriting listed
purchases including a carpet from Lahore Central Jail. It was one
of those rare moments when the past unexpectedly reaches out
to the researcher, and the hairs on the back of my neck stirred.
Neither V&A curator Avalon Fotheringham nor I had ever seen
this mysterious rug, despite spending a good deal of our dust-
covered lives amid the textile collection. The carpet had come back
from its tour of duty in the service of Britain's manufacturers and
exporters but had then disappeared into the museum's stores,
unphotographed, undocumented and lost to history for more than
a century. This document provided the only clue to its continuing
existence.

We set about finding the carpet in a decoding exercise which
linked the numbers on the nineteenth-century list through generations of museum numbering systems to its present-day reference:
IS-797-1883. The document I had looked at by chance was the
inventory of objects sent back from Caspar Purdon Clarke's

shopping trip to India in 1882 on behalf of the Department of Science and Art.[55]

We retrieved the Lahore jail carpet from the V&A's offsite stores, passing shrouded objects whose purpose we could not guess at. It was bigger than we expected, and duller in colour, but it did not need to be beautiful to thrill us. It was a historical treasure, an artefact telling a lost story. We photographed and documented it, but visitors can only encounter it in the V&A's catalogue; it is not on display.[56] The museum contains one of the world's great historic collections of carpets, including rugs woven for the fifteenth-century Ottoman Sultan Mehmet, the conqueror of Constantinople, and the sixteenth-century Iranian Safavid Shah Tahmasp. The carpet from Punjab is not one of these iconic objects. Unlike the high art of the great court carpets displayed in the V&A's Islamic gallery, with their radiant dyes, luxuriant wools and silks and their designs which communicate drama, spirituality and exceptional creativity, the Punjabi carpet is simply a pleasant commercial object. The casual observer would not guess the role it played in Britain's struggle for the soul of Indian carpet-making.

Yet at the same time the carpet is a highly conflicted object. It is a response to imperial demands for commercial products with readily understandable and broadly appealing cultural brands, for example 'Oriental rugs'. But it is also an attempt to place the Indian rug on a higher cultural footing, as a representative of an ancient and elevated artistic tradition of which the most powerful nineteenth-century indicator for the British was 'Persian'. These British commercial and cultural efforts separated Indian carpets from the lived experience of carpet-making in India, replacing it with a miscellany of emotional, spiritual and aesthetic triggers which were important to Britain, not India.

But this does not make the Lahore jail carpet worthless. The whole history of carpets is made up of appropriations and re-contextualisations, of traditions adapting to change, be it the turn of mind of the individual weaver, ecological change affecting sheep and dyes, or the agendas of interventionist empires. The taste-makers of South Kensington may have seen themselves as guardians of absolute standards, but they were just another set of agents in the long history of carpet-weaving, pressing their transitory imperial agenda. Modern tastes may find the V&A's Lahore carpet rather muddy in design and palette, lacking the graphic drama and vivid colours of abstract Anatolian or Caucasian carpets, or the graceful intricacy and subtlety of colour range of Persian and Mughal carpets. Equally, modern sensibilities may be affronted by the history of jail carpets. Nevertheless, the V&A carpet can be seen as survivors' art. Its imprisoned weavers left their mark, both through the expertise of their disciplined execution of its complex composition and through their occasional mistakes, their minds straying during the long hours in the prison weaving shed, distorting a leaf or a blossom. We know they existed.

Chapter 10
Trickster

KNOTTED-PILE CARPET, TWENTIETH CENTURY CE, ROMANIA

On the morning of 7 November 1933, a Viennese art-dealer named Paul Perlefter left his lodgings in the luxurious Park Lane Hotel, London with a rolled-up carpet under his arm. At around 117 inches (three metres) long and 75 inches (two metres) wide when unfurled, it made a compact package. Perlefter was on his way to the V&A Museum to see its curator of textiles, Cecil Tattersall.

What Perlefter showed Tattersall excited the curator so much that he wrote that same afternoon to the V&A's Deputy Keeper of Textiles, A.B. Wace, urging the museum to buy the carpet. Within two days the request had made it to the desk of the V&A's director, Eric Maclagan. As soon as he viewed the item, Maclagan approved the purchase. Whereas most acquisitions were ponderous affairs, this one took little more than a week from beginning to end.

The V&A paid Perlefter £310, the equivalent today of £8,000, just over $10,000. This was 25 per cent of the V&A's entire acquisition budget for that year. In their correspondence, Wace and Maclagan acknowledged the V&A's 'depleted funds' – the Great Depression had put it under severe pressure – but asserted their conviction that the cost was justified even 'in the present state of affairs'.[1]

The carpet galvanised them for many reasons. There was nothing else like it in the museum's collections, and filling gaps is always of interest to curators. It wasn't too big, so could be displayed readily. It was well preserved and beautiful. What's more, it had an impressive provenance. Perlefter claimed that it came from the collection of the Schwarzenberg princes, an aristocratic German-Czech family that had fought and traded with the Ottomans for centuries, forming a famously fabulous carpet collection along the way. The rug had been illustrated in the two most important carpet exhibitions of the era, one curated by Alois Riegl in Vienna in 1891 and the other by Friedrich Sarre in Munich in 1910.[2]

This highly desired carpet was ivory, with a distinctive repeated pattern of three circles organised into a pyramid and underscored by two wavy lines, forming regular rows marching across the entire field of the carpet. The motifs and borders were knotted in red, blue, black and other shades of cream or natural wool. Carpets of this type are believed to have originated in western Anatolia in the sixteenth century. Contemporaneous Ottoman price registers record similar white-ground carpets with spots and stripes as 'Selendi' type, suggesting that they may have originated in the village of that name, west of the great carpet-making centre of Ushak.[3]

To those with a taste for the esoteric, they have much to recommend them. Only around thirty are still in existence, and it is likely they were always a small-scale specialised production.[4] Aesthetically, they are completely unlike the richly coloured and busy designs of other carpets from Anatolia, offering instead a serene, pale minimalism. Their signature three-circle motif floating on a pale sea invites questions and provokes fantasies. Speculation on the history and meaning of the motif offered what has been described as 'a boon for rug dealers and authors on the lookout for a lurid sales pitch'.[5]

These spots and stripes were a favoured motif of Ottoman makers and merchants, with objects bearing the design traded across the empire's growing territory throughout the sixteenth century. It

can be found on tiles from the peak of Ottoman ceramic production in İznik and woven into velvet and brocade for splendid royal
kaftans. Theories abound. Some modern commentators suggest
that the circles represent the triple role of Ottoman sultans as
chieftain, warrior and emperor.[6] Others see the three circles and
two wavy lines as a symbol of the three continents and two seas
ruled by the sultans – Europe, Asia and Africa, and the Mediterranean and the Black Seas.[7]

But the symbol had been in use across Asia for centuries before
the white-ground rugs from Anatolia were woven, and indeed long
before the Ottoman Empire itself. In 1902, the scholar Wilhelm
Bode suggested that it derived from an older Buddhist symbol
of three jewels surrounded by fire.[8] Bode interpreted the three
circles as the Buddhist magic gems which can fulfil all material
and spiritual desires, and the two wavy lines as a stylised version
of the flames. He gave the motif a Sanskrit name: *tschintamani*,
wish-fulfilling jewels. Carpets which bear it are known as *chintamani* to this day.

Other scholars looked to Iranian and Central Asian folklore for
the meaning of the motifs, proposing that the spots and stripes
might be intended to evoke the leopard and tiger skins worn by
ancient warriors in those cultures.[9] Rustam, the hero of the elev-
enth-century Iranian epic *Shanama: The Book of Kings*, famously
wore a tiger-skin jerkin. The gigantic red-haired warrior fought
the seven-headed White Div to save his shah, Kay Kāvus, who
had been captured and blinded by the demon chieftain. Rustam
needed to cut out the Div's liver so that he could burn it and smear
the ashes on Kay Kāvus's eyes to restore his sight. In the many glo-
riously illustrated versions of this episode of the *Shanama*, Rustam
is shown wearing his tiger-skin jerkin, sometimes complete with
its claws.[10]

By the time Tattersall and Wace set about making their case
for acquisition in 1933, a wealth of intriguing stories were available
about the meaning of the motifs in the carpet. And yet the two
curators did not evoke Buddhist monks, legendary Persian heroes

or even mighty Ottoman emperors to ignite the imagination of the V&A's budget-holders. Instead they turned to Central Asia.

The Turco-Mongol emperor Timur Leng, known to the West as Tamerlane, was a monumentally successful nomadic leader, renowned and feared in late-medieval Europe. Said to be descended from Mongol emperor Chinggis (Genghis) Khan, Timur forged a vast empire across Asia in the fourteenth century. The *chintamani* motif has been found on coins minted in his name, and Ruy González de Clavijo, who met Timur as Henry III of Castile's ambassador to Samarkand, believed it to symbolise the ruler's three territories: Persia, Central Asia and India. It is said that Timur celebrated the 1366 conquest of Samarkand by dipping his fingers into the blood of an enemy corpse and printing three red circles on the door of a mosque.[11]

Here was a seductive pitch for Perlefter's carpet. Tattersall and Wace immediately began describing it as a carpet bearing the 'badge of Tamburlaine' in their correspondence with V&A director Maclagan,[12] despite believing that it was made in sixteenth-century Anatolia, three hundred years after Timur, two thousand miles from Samarkand and under a different empire. The curators were of course mindful that the motif had also been used by the Ottomans, but this was manifestly not an Ottoman court carpet – and so Timur offered a useful imperial alternative. Furthermore, the Central Asian heartlands that Timur had once ruled were a very present concern in 1930s Britain. British India faced Soviet Central Asia across the Wakhan Corridor, a strip of Afghanistan only eleven miles wide at its narrowest points, which in 1893 had been designated the buffer zone between the Russian and British Empires.[13] The fathers and grandfathers of the curators of Britain's leading museums had spent the previous century anxiously watching the Afghan frontier as imperial Russia expanded into what had long ago been Timurid territory. There were Maclagans in the British government in Punjab in the late nineteenth and early twentieth centuries.[14]

For thirty years, Perlefter's carpet hung peacefully on the wall in the museum, delighting visitors with its beauty, its unusual palette, enigmatic motifs and its echoes of four empires.

And then, one day in March 1962, George Wingfield Digby, Keeper of Textiles at the V&A, received a letter from one Nessim Cohen. An art-dealer and carpet specialist in the US, Mr Cohen believed that, far from being centuries old, the V&A's Schwarzenberg *chintamani* had in fact been woven mere decades ago. Curators often receive information from the public suggesting alternative histories for objects in a museum's care, and at first Mr Cohen was rebuffed as just another amateur enthusiast.[15] But he refused to let the matter go, continuing to write to the museum every six months for two years. 'I am a little puzzled', Digby wrote, 'at Mr Cohen's extraordinary persistence.'[16]

At length, worn down by Cohen's determination, Digby consulted a number of well-known dealers (including some suggested by Cohen). Alas, no consensus could be reached. Even the two Bernardout brothers, highly respected rug specialists of the period, could not agree: in what might have been a scene from a farce, one brother thought the carpet was genuine while the other brother believed it to be a fake.[17]

At a loss, Digby turned to (who else) May Beattie. Her suspicions were alerted from the start. Her analysis sheet notes that among the 'yellow/camel' wool of the lengthwise warp (the yarns which are strung on the loom as the first step of constructing a carpet), there were three stripes of red. This looked to Beattie 'like aniline' – the family of synthetic dyes that had only entered large-scale carpet production in the second half of the nineteenth century.[18]

When the red warp dye was chemically analysed in 1964, it was found to be a mixture of purpurin, first produced in 1867, and chrysophenine, first synthesised in 1885.[19] The aniline-dyed threads were part of the foundational structure of the carpet; there was no possibility of them having been added as part of a repair. The carpet had to have been made after 1885 rather than in the sixteenth century. Beattie amended her analysis sheet to record this, unusually for her, in red ink. The carpet was quietly withdrawn from the gallery and placed in storage.

That the carpet was a forgery may have come as a shock to Mr Digby, but other dealers had long suspected Perlefter of dealing in fakes. He had even boasted to C. John, a London dealer so respectable that he sold carpets to the British royal family, about his successful deception of the V&A. But carpet-dealers, even reputable ones, were hardly going to publicly volunteer information that would destabilise their market, and Digby would only hear of Perlefter's boasts when it was too late.

Badly stung, it wasn't long before Digby's ire extended to the messenger who first alerted him to Perlefter's deception: Nessim Cohen. As he faced down embarrassing publicity in the international press, Digby wrote to a fellow V&A official in a barely legible scrawl of angst, 'This is clever advertising for the dealer and "expert" Nessim Cohen! [. . .] I wonder if he doesn't know too much about this and other of Perlefter's carpets.'[20]

His suspicions about Cohen were not ungrounded. In 1969, five years after the confirmation that the V&A rug was a fake, Professor Dr Klaus Brisch, the director of the Museum of Islamic Art in Berlin, tested the dyes in a sixteenth-century *chintamani* carpet in the Berlin collection. Some of the dyes turned out to be nineteenth-century synthetics. The carpet had been bought for the museum sometime before 1945 by the great Kurt Erdmann – Tattersall was not alone in his mistake. Knowing of their recent similar experience a few years earlier, Brisch wrote to the V&A's textile curators with the results.[21] He was able to fill in gaps in the story of the V&A's *chintamani*, explaining that there were indications that carpets produced in the Balkans in the early twentieth century were sent to Cairo to be artificially aged, and that Nessim Cohen, the implacable pursuer of V&A keeper George Wingfield

Digby, had been a dealer in Cairo. Brisch suggested that Cohen knew more about the deception than he acknowledged and may have been involved with the carpet in Cairo before it returned to Europe. If this were true, it wasn't Cohen's connoisseurship that had turned up the forgery but his prior knowledge.

As with all good conspiracy theories, the story of Perlefter and Cohen would soon become associated with other nefarious activities. On 2 January 1964, Digby was contacted by Labour Member of Parliament Tom Driberg, later Baron Bradwell.[22] Driberg had long been suspected, without confirmation, of being part of the Soviet spy ring that included Kim Philby and Guy Burgess. He had louche tastes. As a young man he had been a close friend of necromancer Aleister Crowley, and in the early 1960s included in his social circle both the Rolling Stones and the East End gangsters the Kray twins.[23] He was also connected to Nessim Cohen, and had learned of the scandal of the faked carpet through that connection. In early 1964 he sought more information from Digby, for now lost and unknown purposes. He was an inveterate collector of gossip, so maybe it was just lust to know secrets; but, given his connections with the criminal underworld, perhaps he was checking that he himself wasn't somehow exposed in the story.

Demand for luxury objects exploded in the late nineteenth and early twentieth centuries, driven by private collectors who had amassed huge wealth in the Industrial Revolution and by public museums established to celebrate and preserve the spoils of empire. As prices soared, scammers and fraudsters got in on the action.

The trick that caught out Tattersall and Wace was neat. Where conmen had previously attempted the extremely difficult task of passing off a single recently woven carpet as the rare product of a super-elite sixteenth-century atelier, they now switched to marketing *many* copies of commercial carpets from the 1500s, 1600s and 1700s. Each one made a smaller individual profit than the jackpot offered by an atelier carpet, but there was a much lower chance of detection and a higher likelihood of a sale. The most dangerous moment in the fight against forgery is when the scammers suddenly change tactics.[24] The early decades of the twentieth century were one such moment. Faced with examples of a larger population of commercial rugs with many small variations, the carpet specialist Kurt Erdmann wrote: 'detection based on design was no longer possible'.[25]

What's more, the V&A's curators may have been distracted by the prospect of a bargain. Tattersall observed that a similar carpet from Wilhelm Bode's personal collection had sold in 1930 for £2,000 – more than six times Perlefter's price, which, as Wace declared, was 'almost absurdly cheap'.[26] No alarm bells rang because scammers were not then known to pass off carpets of this type. The experts were blindsided.

Congratulating themselves on spotting the opportunity, the grandees of the V&A Textile Department grew more and more committed to the scam over the course of the week it took to effect the purchase. There was an increasing sense of urgency, and an inflation in the praise it received. For curator Tattersall the rug was 'very pleasing'; for deputy keeper Wace 'very attractive'; and by the time V&A director Maclagan gave his verdict the rug was 'extraordinarily beautiful'. Its state of preservation, meanwhile, kept getting better, from Tattersall's 'practically unrepaired', to Wace's 'practically perfect condition', to Maclagan's 'apparently in perfect condition'. Wace asserted that on its arrival with them it would immediately become one of the finest examples of the Turkish carpets in the V&A's already world-leading collection. In short, they worked themselves up.

They should have known better. Tattersall was familiar to the point of overconfidence with the Schwarzenberg *chintamani*. He had described it and recorded its history in his 1922 survey *Hand-Woven Carpets: Oriental and European*, co-authored with fellow V&A curator A.F. Kendrick.[27] Historical textual records proved that it was in the Schwarzenberg collection in 1724, then displayed in Vienna in 1891 and Munich in 1910. It is not clear whether Tattersall attempted to investigate the route by which it entered Perlefter's hands. Herr Perlefter of Vienna told him that it was the familiar *chintamani* named for the princely German-Czech family, and Tattersall took him at his word.

Tattersall may have been reassured that the rug looked identical to the photographs he had consulted in his earlier research. Knowing now that the V&A and Schwarzenberg *chintamani* are different carpets, it is possible to see that the designs in the borders of the sixteenth-century rug are more angular than those in the 1920s version. But the image in Kendrick and Tattersall's *Hand-Woven Carpets* was black and white and partial, and it is understandable that Tattersall missed the difference, particularly in a state of gathering excitement.

As it happens, the rug that Tattersall, Wace and Maclagan thought they were buying would have made a very decent investment. In 2012, a sixteenth-century white-ground *chintamani* from western Anatolia sold at Christie's for almost a quarter of a million pounds ($370,000).[28] Indeed, even if the V&A chose to sell its early-twentieth-century imitation now it would still recoup the initial investment. A rug from the same producer sold at Christie's the same year for £8,000 (around $10,500),[29] the equivalent of the £310 the V&A paid for it in 1933. Even the fakes have become collector's pieces, as they deserve to be. They are often beautiful and charismatic objects, alongside their attractive history of mischief.

Carpet conmen had won the battle in the early twentieth century, and it took decades for institutional knowledge to catch up and wrestle back authority. Meanwhile Herr Perlefter slipped out of history with the V&A's money in his pocket.

In 1914, a man called Stelian Kehayoglou Senior moved his family from Kayseri in Anatolia to Bucharest in Romania. The Ottoman Empire was at the time increasing its persecution of its long-settled non-Muslim populations – Armenians, Assyrians and Greeks like Stelian – and many people were choosing to leave before they were expelled. By the 1920s he owned two rug shops.[30] From Kayseri he had brought his expertise in Anatolian rugs, and his new workshops could draw on a rich pool of manufacturing talent: Romania itself had excellent weavers,[31] but Kehayoglou also employed a number of skilled Armenians who had likewise fled to central Europe from Ottoman persecution.[32]

Sometime in the early 1920s, a young man in search of work walked into Kehayoglou's shop in Bucharest. Teodor Tuduc (1888–1939) was a Romanian Orthodox Christian. He had been educated in the Hungarian capital, Budapest, where he had trained in basic textile restoration in the workshops of émigré Armenians. Kehayoglou recognised a spark of skill and carpet insight in the young Romanian. He helped him develop his craft, introduced him to a network of weavers and designers, and supported him in setting up his own rug-dealing and restoration business. Tuduc travelled widely in carpet-producing countries, learning, buying and building up an international clientele. By 1924 he employed fourteen people at his own Bucharest workshop. By 1931, two years before Perlefter turned up at the V&A, Tuduc's success justified the opening of a second workshop. But Tuduc was not simply an excellent rug-dealer and restorer, with all that this implies about his showmanship, knowledge, connections and so on. He was also a forger of genius.

'To art critics, the forger is a mediocre artist seeking revenge; to the media, a conman interested only in money; to the apologist, he is the equal of the masters he forged; to the public he is often a folk hero.'[33] The response to master forgers is a complex mixture of outrage and attraction, and the forger's motives seem equally mixed. They are described as narcissists greedy for attention and motivated by a certainty of their superiority, provocateurs deliberately unsettling hierarchies and bypassing gatekeepers, and charming but compulsive liars.[34]

Tuduc seems to have possessed some of these characteristics.

After he sold three carpets to Erich Maria Remarque, author of *All Quiet on the Western Front*, Tuduc had to face Remarque's rage at discovering they were not authentic. The conversation was initially heated, but after 'an evening of rug talk, and a bottle or two of wine' Remarque was so pacified by the silver-tongued deceiver that he bought two further rugs.[35] Meanwhile, leading Tuduc scholars Alberto Boralevi and Stefano Ionescu regard him as highly venal, a self-serving manipulator who, when he wasn't faking, was exporting choice originals out of the country. They are equally critical of his work to salvage old carpets: 'His restorations are always acts of imitative reconstruction in the style of the time, essentially lacking any ethical basis or any respect for the surviving fragments of the original rug.'[36] The censorious tone of these judgements suggests the degree of disturbance Tuduc created among the gatekeepers of the carpet world.

Tuduc steadfastly claimed that he never told his clients that his carpets were old.[37] In at least a part of his mind, he saw his work as a modern iteration of an old creative impulse. The deliberate and misleading slippage his sophisticated marketing created in the minds of his clients between early rugs and his modern versions seems to have existed in a separate compartment of Tuduc's consciousness. There may also have been deeper impulses at work. In a suggestive naming, Tuduc called his rugs *meine Kinder*.[38] He seems to have seen his carpets as his creative offspring and his legacy to the future. Indeed, there is something playful and childlike about Tuduc himself. Photos of him in old age show a lover of life, a puckish and merry individual. There is just a suggestion in them that he is laughing at a remembered prank.

Tuduc had a speciality: he liked to make copies of Anatolian village carpets from the sixteenth, seventeenth and eighteenth centuries. He seems to have first encountered the beauty, historical resonance and sensuousness of the originals at a Budapest exhibition in 1914, when he was just twenty-six. At that time these

Anatolian rugs were described as Transylvanian, which may have intrigued him and appealed to his love for his home country. As is often the case with early passions, that first encounter seems to have permanently shaped him.

The so-called Transylvanian carpets Tuduc encountered in 1914 were the rugs which had been collected from the sixteenth century onwards in the Lutheran churches of Saxon Siebenbürgen by early converts to Protestantism. During the early decades of the twentieth century these largely unknown carpets emerged from the Transylvanian darkness in which they had lain hidden for centuries.[39] Their first appearance in Budapest in 1914 was at the Hungarian Museum of Applied Arts – one of the many responses by European museums to the growing interest in carpets in the late nineteenth and early twentieth centuries. In 1925 the exhibition's long-delayed catalogue of thirty representative items appeared.[40]

Tuduc had everything he needed to become a successful forger of Transylvanian rugs; physical carpets in nearby churches, photographs of rugs from the Budapest exhibition, his skills and those of his weavers, his workshops and his reputation with a network of clients. It is surely no coincidence that when he expanded his business in 1931 he located his second workshop in a village near Brașov, home of the Lutheran Black Church and its now world-famous collection of early Anatolian carpets, imitations of which were at the heart of his business.

Such was the craze for these Anatolian commercial rugs of the sixteenth, seventeenth and eighteenth centuries that there are reports of dealers attempting to bribe church officials to steal carpets on their behalf. Such dealers might not be too particular about how a carpet came to be available at an attractive price, once initial supply had dried up.[41] But the wealthy and prestigious clients that Tuduc had in his sights were not so easily convinced. These collectors were highly sensitive about the authenticity of their purchases. The publication of a carpet in a scholarly text or catalogue of an esteemed exhibition or collection was the primary source sophisticated buyers turned to in order to validate a rug. Tuduc used images of carpets in such publications as models for his forgeries, allowing a careful buyer to track them down. In the case of the V&A rug, the Schwarzenberg *chintamani* had been published in Riegl's revered catalogue of the 1891 Vienna exhibition, Sarre's almost equally respected catalogue of the 1910 Munich Exhibition, and in Tattersall's own 1922 *Survey*.

But Tuduc could only sell a fake Schwarzenberg once. If his business was to grow, he had to move beyond a small group of named rugs traceable through published scholarship. In a stroke of criminal brilliance, he decided to make his own fake catalogue in which his modern Romanian carpets could be depicted as old Anatolian ones.

In 1933 Professor Dr Emile Schmutzler published *Altorientalische Teppiche in Siebenbürgen* ('Old Oriental Carpets in Siebenbürgen', that is, in the seven cities whose Lutheran churches had amassed rugs), and for eighty years it remained the most authoritative account of carpets in Transylvanian collections. Soon after Schmutzler's book appeared, one Professor Dr Otto Ernst – a Tuduc invention – published *Antike OrientTeppiche aus Siebenbürgen* ('Antique Oriental Carpets from Siebenbürgen'). The catalogue was purportedly issued by the Black Church in Braşov, which later insisted that it played no part in the enterprise.[42] The differences between the two books' titles were minute, *aus* instead of *in*, *Antike* instead of *Alt*, enough to discourage suggestions of misrepresentation but not enough to destroy the impression that Ernst's publication was a close relative of Schmutzler's authoritative book. The type, paper and design of the Ernst catalogue were all impeccably drab and scholarly. Tuduc was a master of both the materiality and the psychology of fakes.

The contents of the invented Professor Dr Ernst's catalogue were a mix of authentic early Anatolian rugs and modern replicas from the Tuduc workshops. Tuduc's sales agents across Europe and the Americas used the Ernst catalogue in discussions with buyers, who were reassured by the proof of provenance it seemed to offer. One of Tuduc's *chintamani* is now in Sibiu's Brukenthal Museum in the heart of the Transylvanian Siebenbürgen. It originally belonged to none other than Emil Schmutzler, the renowned authority on

Transylvanian carpets who wrote the 1933 survey on which Tuduc based his fake catalogue. Tuduc sold straight into the lion's den.

Anatolian carpet specialists and Tuduc experts alike agree that the V&A's Schwarzenberg *chintamani* came from his workshop. May Beattie, who was acquainted with his work and had analysed many of his carpets, first pointed to him as the likely source following her 1963 examination.[43] Tuduc himself claimed to have proof that he made it, perhaps proud of his skill in fooling the V&A, although he is not the most reliable witness.[44] But if some of the great Western connoisseurs of the early twentieth century were taken in, how sure can we be now?

When there is a chink of light in the darkness, other details begin to emerge from the gloom. Once chemical analysis redesignated a group of museum-quality sixteenth-century *chintamani* as late-nineteenth or early-twentieth-century production, a number of similarities of material, technique and design could be observed between the modern carpets that were not shared with the old ones. Connoisseurs and scholars now take these as warning signs.

First of all, Tuduc workshop wool is not Anatolian, and his rugs are often described as rough, dry or hard. The dyes are clearly different from their Anatolian inspiration; the experienced eye of a May Beattie can spot that they are sometimes modern aniline. White-ground carpets favour the forger because there is less skill needed in the management of pigments,[45] but some of Tuduc's *chintamani* fakes used only one colour for their spots, whereas the old weavers used a variety. Perhaps Tuduc's simplifications helped save time, and hence money, or maybe his weavers were working from black-and-white photos so didn't catch the multicoloured detail. Tuduc's rugs were aged artificially, abraded with stones and metal objects and vigorously cleaned, practices which leave signatures of their own. Tattersall noted that the pattern of wear on the V&A *chintamani* was what he expected, but with the wisdom of hindsight it is now seen as too even.

Some of the tells have a strange pathos. In his early production Tuduc didn't pick up on an idiosyncratic practical technique of Anatolian village weavers. They often sit two or three to a loom, knotting part of the way across the rug then turning back on themselves when they meet the boundary with their neighbour. Even a single weaver will sometimes weave only as far as she can reach, then move along the bench later to catch up on a whole section. These reversals are visible as seams on the back of the rug: the technical term is 'lazy lines'. Tuduc rugs generally don't have these lines, and when his workshop tried to replicate them they looked different. Meanwhile, the designs of early Anatolian village rugs were rarely perfect and contained much variation. Corners especially are rarely 'resolved' – in other words, they can be a bit messy. It's very hard for village weavers to manage the tension of warp and weft and the geometry of the loom so that the design fully works at the far end of the carpet. But Tuduc weavers and designers were, ironically, too good, and Tuduc rugs have perfect designs. Commentators now describe their regularity as mechanical and use it as a clue in detection. This judgement once again rests on an imagined vision of 'authentic' production, this time on the idea that variations and errors are evidence of the autonomy and creativity of the weaver.

In carpet workshops the world over and through time, there is a continuum that stretches from repairs and restoration of old rugs through to the weaving of new versions of traditional styles. These reworkings are part of normal weaving practice. Rugs are fragile and must be maintained; Tuduc himself began as a restorer. And in a sense, all carpet-weaving is borrowing and *bricolage*. Designs pass from generation to generation or are shared with other communities. Tuduc's designers were trained within a traditional craft. New rugs must be woven if the craft is not to disappear. A problem only arises if these modern repairs or versions are misrepresented as something else – older, or in original pristine condition, or made in a different place – to inflate their prices.[46]

Even then, the lines between legitimate and corrupt practice are not clear. How many repairs must be done to an old carpet before it can no longer be described by its original place and time of making? If dealers exaggerate the antiquity of their rugs, which they have done for as long as there have been rug-sellers, how many years' exaggeration is acceptable? It is a traditional part of carpet production to wash carpets, leave them in the street to be trodden on by people, camels and horses, and expose them to harsh sun to give them the patina of age. Are these makers forgers, or simply adapting their practices to meet the taste of their customers, just as they might choose certain colours over others?[47] Authenticity, date and place of making are grey areas which are constantly renegotiated in the carpet world. If Tuduc had never attached that false trail to his rugs, they would no doubt have been seen as intrinsically beautiful artefacts in their own right, made by skilled craftspeople connected to a distinguished and historically resonant tradition.

The upheaval of the early twentieth century was the perfect smokescreen for a skilled carpet conman. Craftspeople were on the move across Europe, intermingling their weaving traditions. Curators in colonial centres were competing fiercely with each other for prestige objects with which to invigorate their maturing museum collections. Old Persian carpets, the darlings of the nineteenth century, were by now both familiar and very expensive. The appearance in the early twentieth century of an unfamiliar and substantial group of old Anatolian carpets in the church collections of Romania created a new market. Like iron filings attracted to a magnet, the attention of collectors turned to the apparently unlikely location of Transylvania, where Tuduc and his fellow forgers stood ready to respond.

A 2012 catalogue illustrated eight known Tuduc *chintamani* in elite collections, including both Tattersall's V&A and Erdmann's Berlin Museum purchases, and the hunt has since continued for more.[48] But from only eight copies of this one carpet, Tuduc would have earned the modern equivalent of more than £50,000 (around $65,600), if each sold for the price paid by the V&A. The financial impact of two workshops weaving many different carpets for twenty-five years can only be guessed at.

Tuduc closed his workshops in 1948. After the Second World War Romania aligned with the Soviet Union, and Hungary fell unwillingly under Soviet economic controls. The game was up. Later, he became something of a celebrity in the world of carpet enthusiasts and had a successful career as a legitimate carpet-dealer and rug-restorer.[49] He gave up his scam – or so it seems.

We now know that the Schwarzenberg *chintamani* carpet that the V&A thought it was buying eventually found its way to the collection of the National Gallery in Prague. After it was displayed in the 1910 Munich exhibition *Masterpieces of Muhammadan Art*, it disappeared from the spotlight for almost a century. Then, in 2008, the National Gallery loaned it to an exhibition of *The Most Beautiful Oriental Carpets from Bohemian and Moravian Collections* at Špilberk Castle, Brno, Czechia. A new image of it was published for the exhibition, and its reappearance caused a small stir in the world of rug specialists and dealers. Visitors can now gaze at the storied carpet at Hluboká Castle in confidence that they are connecting with the work of a Muslim woman who lived near the village of Selendi in Ottoman Anatolia at the sixteenth-century peak of the Ottoman Empire. But its forged twin is rolled in the darkness of the V&A's stores, where only a few rare visitors can encounter the work of a Christian or Muslim woman living in Romania in the early twentieth century as empires collapsed and re-formed around her.

The imperial museums that sprang up from the mid-nineteenth century onwards used the credibility of their collections to bolster that of the world view of the states they represented. The Berlin Museums, the Louvre in Paris, the Metropolitan Museum of Art in New York, the V&A: their authority rested on the authenticity of their objects. That authority, and with it that of the hegemonies they served, was undermined if someone deceived them. Such a

deception carried more weight than embarrassment and an un-
wise investment. Tattersall, Wace and Maclagan continued their
illustrious careers despite their error, but the V&A continues to
hide the carpet in its stores, a shaming triumph of the forces of
anarchy and mischief. But the Tuduc carpet also reminds us that
mischief and anarchy can be powerfully seductive.

Chapter 11
Migrant

KNOTTED-PILE CARPET, TWENTY-FIRST CENTURY CE, PAKISTAN

Persian rugs have a special status and historical resonance. We are attracted to their floral intricacy and soft, glowing colours, and however little specialist knowledge we have, we know that Persian carpets will give our interiors, and by association ourselves, sophistication and élan.[1] But Persian rugs have a close competitor when middle-class consumers go shopping for interior decor. Carpet Vista, a major international online retailer (they claim to be the largest in the world), estimates that 90 per cent of the non-Iranian styles they sell are carpets from a single group.[2] They are sold across the developed world as Bokhara rugs, named after an ancient Silk Roads city in Uzbekistan.

I did not have to go far to look at a Bokhara rug, coming across one recently in the Edinburgh branch of a UK department store, proudly displayed between the soft furnishings and the bedlinen. Woven from lustrous merino wool, it had a minimalist palette of red and black with some paler highlights and a repeated design of octagonal motifs suggesting highly stylised blossoms. Often called *guls*, these abstract floral motifs are also described by retailers as 'the timeless elephant's foot design', evoking the animal's central pad with its circle of toes imprinted at watering holes in far-off and exotic places.

Bokhara carpets are now an international mass-market commodity. You can get one for a few hundred pounds or dollars.

While replica Persian carpets promise to lend an interior a sense of urban sophistication, a Bokhara provides its buyer with a ready-made 'tribal' aesthetic, imbuing the living room or bedroom with the mystique of ancient nomadism. They offer us two very different shortcuts to an interesting home.

The modern Bokhara rug is indeed a reinvention of a much older tradition, but it has little to do with the city that shares its name. Located in the Uzbek desert, Bokhara was for over a thousand years one of the great trading posts on the Silk Roads. Now, sixteenth-century bazaars and caravanserai coexist with a grey Soviet-era city, while shopping malls and tourist hotels spread into the immense space of the desert. Tourists can still buy handicrafts in small shops, but modern Bukhara is no longer a place that great carpets pass through and was never the place where they were made. The name is a fiction: a branding exercise which can be traced back to the late nineteenth century, dreamed up from a ragbag of Arabian Nights fantasies.

For the tradition that genuinely underlies the Bokhara style we must look instead to a powerful tribal federation that inhabited the wide expanse of the Eurasian steppe.

The Turkmen have their roots in the westward spread of nomadic tribes from the eastern steppe that began early in the Common Era. We sometimes think of tribespeople as small groups wandering wild places, but they had strong affiliations, and together tribal federations could number many thousands of people. It's also easy to think that empires are synonymous with settled peoples, but great tribal federations could become the dominant political power in their region. Between the twelfth and the sixteenth century CE, nomadic empires not only conquered huge tranches of Asia but brought with them the art, thought and political creativity which formed medieval and early modern states in the Caucasus, Anatolia, Iran, Afghanistan and the steppe. Some of these nomadic empires are familiar: the Seljuks, Mongols, Timurids

and Ottomans. Less often remembered is that between the end
of the fourteenth century and the beginning of the sixteenth, a
period as long as the British Empire, the White Sheep and Black
Sheep dynasties of the Turkmen ruled the southern Caucasus,
eastern Anatolia and west and central Persia, fighting between
themselves for dominance. Their capital at Tabriz in modern north-
western Iran became an Islamic cultural centre under White Sheep
Sultan Yakub (r. 1478–90).[3] Their dynastic names remind us that
the wellspring of Turkmen life and society remained nomadic,
herding sheep and horses. Even during their periods of imperial
dominance, they were always on the move.

The Black Sheep Turkmen were decisively defeated by the
White in 1467, and the White Sheep Turkmen were themselves
defeated by the new Safavid dynasty in Iran between 1501 and
1503. Their power was broken and their people initially scattered,
but the Turkmen federation did not become a sleepy society that
time had forgotten. They maintained their culture of storytelling,
metalwork, jewellery and carpet-weaving well into the nineteenth
century. They continued to breed their famous bloodline of
Akhal-Teke horses, highly prized across Eurasia for their speed
and endurance and the beauty of their elegant frames and shimmering coats. They were able to mobilise large military forces and
use sophisticated strategic skills when circumstances required it.

At the heart of their way of life was their nomadic pastoralism.
A Turkmen clan judged how much sustenance a piece of land
could safely yield and, when they had taken its contribution,
moved on, allowing it to regenerate until they returned with the
turn of the seasons. Over time, some Turkmen chose to settle
on more fertile land and become farmers, but within the tribal
federation the nomads, or *charwa*, retained a higher status than
the *chomur*, their settled brethren.[4]

Turkmen wasted nothing, including their own creative imagination, which they poured into artefacts both practical and
beautiful. It wasn't just floor coverings. With great ingenuity,
Turkmen craftspeople replaced the wood, metal and leather used
by settled peoples with the products of their way of life. Camels,

goats and sheep provided wool. Berries, leaves, wood and insects provided dyes. Minerals found in different soils provided mordants to fix colours. Belongings were stored in carpet bags rather than in boxes or furniture. Animal trappings were knotted-pile weavings. Doors were constructed from rugs. Circular Turkmen tents, made from felt over a wooden frame, were stabilised by multiple narrow woven textiles that held them rigid. These tent bands might be less than a foot wide but were as long as the circumference of the tent; examples in museums reach forty-five feet.[5]

All these woven surfaces were opportunities for Turkmen craftspeople to express their creativity. The most everyday object, for example a tiny salt bag, was adorned with the stylised floral guls which were the emblems of the tribe. As well as being functional building materials, tent bands were themselves extremely long and thin patterned pile rugs. The Turkmen equivalent of a tough builder's strap, made now from polyester or flexible metal, was an aesthetically satisfying carpet. One example from the early nineteenth century depicts foals and camel calves sheltering under their protective mothers, just as the Turkman family would shelter within the tent.[6]

I have a small nineteenth-century Turkmen carpet, one metre square. It bears the gul of the Tekke Turkman tribe, marching in rows across a softly glowing dark-pink field, its tessellated borders shimmering and precise. It was likely made by a bride-to-be with her future mother-in-law as part of her dowry. The bride and mother-in-law would become a weaving team when the bride moved from her family's tent to that of her husband, and the carpet enacts that future relationship. At the same time, the rug gave the mother-in-law the opportunity to observe the bride-to-be's skills. Perhaps confidence in her weaving led to confidence in her as a mother and wife.

It is part of the interaction between people and beautiful artefacts that we project our fantasies on them. I have critiqued many such projections of meaning on carpets, some misleading and distorting, all meeting a personal need of the commentator. But of course, I do it myself. This small, square carpet has come to represent for me a dream of family: nomadic clans working together for the common good, but at the same time negotiating profound emotions and life changes. I very much hope that the identification of my rug as a bridal carpet is correct, otherwise for the last twenty tears I too have been dreaming over it misguidedly.[7]

There is a good deal of curiosity in the West about what old Turkmen carpets mean.[8] Although there are some pictographic examples, like the tent band with its camel calves described earlier, most Turkmen rugs are severely abstract, bearing a narrow range of forms in rhythmic and disciplined repetition. Something about these designs causes Western observers to read them as a kind of secret language. Special weavings were clearly made for ritual occasions that were important to the tribe, like my wedding carpet. But many commentators seek a more complete spiritual account of these designs, rooted in the Turkmen religious fusion of Islam and Animism, the nature-worship of the steppe. The anthropologist Brian Spooner, who lived with a Turkmen community at the end of the twentieth century, is sceptical: 'We have no good reason to believe that there ever was a Golden Age when Turkmen culture was an integrated systemic whole, within which noble tribeswomen conscientiously worked out their religious problems in their daily craft.'[9]

The fundamental abstract motif of these rugs is the *gul*. Different tribes are associated with different versions of it, and indeed these different versions have themselves changed over time. This offers endless material for the puzzle-solving appetite of international carpet connoisseurship. Decoding Turkmen *guls*, their derivation and their meaning is a perennial pastime, which a mystified female colleague at the V&A hazarded is 'a boy thing'. In the seminal 1980 volume *Turkmen: Tribal Carpets and Traditions*, the leading carpet scholar Jon Thompson illustrated a complete genealogy of Turkmen *guls* from what he believed was their origin – wispy octagonal Chinese motifs known as cloud collars.[10] The family tree he devised showed his interpretation of the connections between the motifs of different tribes. But on top of every decoding effort like this comes another one. Learned periodicals like *The Textile Museum Journal, Washington*, and more popular publications like *Hali* both play the game, and social media is alive with debates.

Whether or not she was weaving a secret code which could be cracked (even if we haven't yet managed to), there is agreement among carpet specialists that a traditional Turkmen weaver created mesmerising variations on her themes, minute and entrancing modulations of the minimalist design of the vocabulary of *guls* and tessellated borders. She played the same intellectual and artistic game we hear in a Bach variation. Perhaps the constraints of her designs freed up some of the weaver's creativity for the perfection of her technical craft, rather like Jane Austen's description of her equally boundaried work as painting with a fine brush on two inches of ivory. Certainly, traditional Turkmen weavers are widely regarded as technically among the best in the Eurasian rug-weaving belt. I evoke Bach and Jane Austen deliberately: the Turkmen have long been among the great artists of nomadic weaving.

They made these artefacts for their own use. Sure enough, there was some exchange and sale on the unusual occasions when the Turkmen couldn't provide for themselves in some way, but the entry of old Turkmen rugs as a commodity in the global marketplace began only as their world fragmented. The presence of both antique and modern Turkmen rugs in our homes of brick, glass, steel and concrete is not a celebration of their way of life but a sign of its collapse.

For centuries after the fall of the Black Sheep and White Sheep Empires, the Turkmen continued to ride their proud golden horses along their traditional steppe and mountain migration routes, hunting, herding, foraging and weaving. They sang their tribal histories over fires in remote encampments, occasionally mobilising to see off interference from the Safavid, Ottoman and Mughal gunpowder empires which spread across West and Central Asia from the sixteenth century, or striking canny deals with them. Nomads who wandered across borders could be useful sources of intelligence and helpful imperial messengers. The flow of nomadic peoples across the steppe continued even as empires rose and fell in its settled centres.

But in the nineteenth century, Russia began expanding southwards in a land grab that sought to contain and control the entire region. At first, nomadic resistance succeeded where the khans and emirs of Khiva, Bokhara, Tashkent and Ferghana failed, facing down Russian troops to protect their traditional routes. Late-nineteenth-century images show Turkmen warriors in their battle dress, wielding weapons that could have belonged to Scythian warriors of the fifth century BCE. Not only did they equip themselves like Scythians, but they also fought like them – on horses, using surprise attacks, deceptive retreats, speed and mobility – with the guileful courage so admired by Herodotus. Alas, it wasn't equal to the rockets, mines and artillery of the Russian Imperial Army.

The most formidable and successful resistance was mounted by the powerful Tekke tribe. In 1879, Russian imperial forces attacked its stronghold of Geok Tepe in modern Turkmenistan, a strategically valuable oasis in the desert between Russia's new Central Asian colonies to the north, Iran to the south-west and Afghanistan to the south. The Tekke Turkmen held their oasis. Two thousand tribespeople died defending it, but so did two hundred Russians. The tsar wanted revenge. He launched a second attack in 1881 and this time the Russians defeated the Turkmen in their mud fortress, chasing them into the desert and killing an estimated fourteen and a half thousand tribespeople, including elders, babies and pregnant women. The episode is recorded by both Asian and Western historians as an atrocity.[11] General Skobelev, who led the attack, was unabashed, telling a British journalist: 'I hold it as a principle that in Asia the duration of the peace is in direct proportion to the slaughter you inflict.'[12] After Geok Tepe, the Turkmen resistance fragmented into intertribal rivalries. The Russian Empire took control of their traditional routes and most of Central Asia. What had for more than a thousand years been an autonomous collective of nomads began to transform into a group of refugees and migrants harried by a settled empire.

As Russian troops colonised the steppe, steppe nomads surged into the Russian imagination. In 1880 the composer Alexander Borodin wrote *In the Steppes of Central Asia*, in celebration of the silver jubilee of Romanov Tsar Alexander II. At the very moment when General Skobelev was mustering his army to drive the Tekke tribespeople into the desert *pour encourager les autres*, Borodin wrote in the preface to his score:

> In the sandy steppes of Central Asia, the melody of a peaceful Russian song first resounds. The approaching clatter of horses and camels and the plaintive tones of an oriental song are then heard. A native caravan passes across the endless desert, guarded by Russian troops. Confident and unafraid, it follows its distant journey protected by Russian military might. The caravan moves further and further into the distance. The peaceful melodies of the Russians and the native people blend into one overall harmony, echoes of which linger over the steppes before finally fading away in the distance.[13]

It is difficult to find any trace of this 'harmony' in the Imperial Army's treatment of defeated tribes. Russia imposed punitive indemnities, forcing tribespeople to sell their possessions in order to make good on their debt. The Chodor Turkmen tribe of Iran, for instance, was required to pay three hundred thousand roubles in reparation, something like £3.8 million ($5 million) in today's money, after the Russians crushed their resistance in 1873.[14] They sold their tribal treasures to pay it, and so survived.

After the final defeat of the Tekke Turkmen by the Russian Empire at Geok Tepe in 1881, fire sales by tribespeople accelerated. Russian buyers were seduced by their heavy sculptural jewellery, wrought from silver and unpolished gemstones, and their dramatic sombre carpets. Before long, they – along with alert European and North American dealers – found they could snap up Tekke carpets that had never before been traded, in Central Asian bazaars in the Silk Roads cities of Khiva, Samarkand and Bokhara.

Taking the name from the city in whose markets they were most often found, dealers began calling these new additions to the family of Oriental carpets 'Royal Bukhara', for the finest-quality carpets, and 'Princess Bukhara' for lesser rugs. The name has stuck.[15] Modern Bokhara rugs inherit the name given to Tekke rugs by nineteenth-century dealers (they also borrow a simplified form of Tekke *guls* as their principal design motif).

Once on the market, they moved quickly. A Turkmen carpet brought back as loot by a Russian soldier might end up displayed in a St Petersburg salon, part of an ensemble of jewellery, kaftans and armour celebrating the new Russian Empire in Central Asia – another example of conquerors fetishising the cultures of the vanquished.[16] A Tekke rug sold for the first time by a defeated clan to a dealer in Bokhara might find its way to a US collector, priced out of the market for classical Persian carpets by the likes of Rockefeller and Frick. Consulting engineer Arthur Irwin, for example, attempted to turn his New York flat into a Turkmen tent, with carpets on the walls and floors, chairs upholstered with rugs, and camel trappings adorning the fireplace, where they float uneasily.[17] A rug taken from fleeing Turkmen by a British administrator as he monitored Britain's Afghan borders against incursions might end up in the lounge of a suburban villa in Surrey.[18] As their international popularity grew, the demand for Turkmen rugs soon outstripped the number of plundered and fire-sale carpets available. Impoverished by their wars with the Russian Empire, Turkmen began weaving for the commercial market.

In the modern-day market for old carpets, many dealers and buyers turn up their noses at post-1881 Turkmen rugs. It has become an accepted fact that the defeat of the Tekke and the transition to commercial weaving led to a deterioration in the spiritual and aesthetic qualities of Turkmen carpets. This (largely Western) nostalgia confuses the tragedies of Turkmen history with a decay in their weaving abilities.[19] The story blames the Turkmen for any degradation in their culture, rather than their aggressors. Meanwhile great carpets woven in the mountains and desert sands continue to appear for sale in auction houses and are donated to museums. They cannot be accurately dated before or after the perceived breakpoint of 1881 – we just don't have the technology to do it.

By 1911, at the height of Russian imperial domination of Central Asia, it is estimated that three hundred and fifty thousand Turkmen, some still nomadic, some now settled, remained in their traditional territories, tending their flocks, breeding horses, supplementing their stores by some scratch agriculture and weaving.[20] That we even know this number says a lot about the degree to which they had become part of the early-twentieth-century world of states and censuses. There were repeated efforts to settle the remaining nomads throughout the later nineteenth and early twentieth centuries, but it was not an easy job.[21] Ultimately, it was achieved in Central Asia as a consequence of Soviet collectivisation.

When Stalin came to power after Lenin's death in 1924, he divided Russia's Central Asian territories into what he saw as distinct nations – the Autonomous Soviet Socialist Republics of Turkmenistan, Tajikistan, Kyrgyzstan, Uzbekistan and Kazakhstan – each stan named after what was supposed to be its dominant ethnic group. The new borders were of course bitterly contentious and arbitrary, but it wasn't actually Stalin's intention to settle the nomads. Much more significant in his programme was the collectivisation of agriculture.[22]

Russia had often suffered from food shortages – shortage of bread contributed to the 1917 revolution. The civil war between the Bolsheviks and monarchist White Russians further disrupted food supplies in the fledgling USSR, and there was severe famine in the early 1920s. It was a pressing problem for Stalin. He had come to believe that agriculture managed collectively through a central agency and plan would be more productive than agriculture managed by individuals. From 1928 the state organised land and labour into huge collective farms, plantations and forests, each required to make a fixed contribution defined by the Communist Party's Five-Year Plan. From the level of the farm these targets were aggregated into goals for entire republics. Soviet republics were then required to send their target volumes of produce elsewhere, for redistribution as the central authorities saw fit. The policy was enforced with violence – executions of protestors and deportations enforced at gunpoint – and not only on settled communities.

From 1928 onwards, a Central Asian nomad's fate was decided by what the Soviet Five-Year Plan requisitioned from the territory they roamed; cotton on the one hand, or meat and grain on the other.[23]

Northern Kazakhstan had to contribute meat and grain. Nomadic livestock was collectivised. In 1930–31, 80 per cent of Kazakh meat went to Moscow and Leningrad.[24] Traditional nomadic pastures were ploughed and turned over to grain. Nomads were forced to feed the animals they still possessed on grain, rather than move them around grassy steppe pastures they had husbanded for centuries. They began to sell their starving animals, and when that became impossible they slaughtered them.[25] As historian of Central Asia, Adeeb Khalid, describes the predicament: 'Nomads could neither eat nor move [. . .] In their utter destitution, many families abandoned their starving children and inevitably there were cases of cannibalism.'[26]

Southern Turkmenistan and Uzbekistan were required to contribute cotton. Although the death rate was not so high as in famine- and disease-struck Kazakhstan, the nomadic way of life was nevertheless severely damaged. Pastoral nomadism and small-scale farming were replaced by destructive forms of high-intensity cultivation that still persist, particularly in Uzbekistan. Contemporary aerial images of the Aral Sea show it heavily polluted and shrunken almost to nothing, its inflowing rivers the Amu Darya and Syr Darya, the Oxus and Jaxartes of classical Greece, diverted for irrigation of farmland and cotton production. It is easy to become sentimental about the harmony between nomads and nature. Much has been written recently about the calamities, extinctions and ecological collapses caused by humanity before industrialisation and globalisation, even at its most arcadian. But clearly, something had begun to go badly wrong. The symbiosis of nomads and the Central Asian steppe had broken down.

Many Turkmen nomads were forced into factories in Soviet Central Asia to serve the Five-Year Plan. Contemporary records reveal the impact of this move on every stage of the carpet-making process.[27] Local wool was collected from the steppe and distributed within the empire, while wool from elsewhere of a different type and quality was allotted to Central Asian factories. This broke the link between the weaver and her sheep. Chemical dyes were specified and provided centrally, replacing those made from plants and insects, leaving weavers to struggle with this strange new palette. Nomadic weavers were forced to work daily for a set number of hours in workshops and factories, delivering a product defined by Soviet central planners. They told Russian anthropologist V.G. Moshkova, who worked among them for twenty-five years before her death in 1954, that what they had loved they came to hate.[28]

The Central Asian Soviets of Uzbekistan, Tajikistan and Turkmenistan all bordered Afghanistan. Turkmenistan also bordered Iran. Neither Iran nor Afghanistan were under Soviet control in the 1920s and 1930s. Turkmen began to flee south into these geographies. By the mid-twentieth century an estimated two hundred thousand Turkmen had found their way to Afghanistan, in the hope of escaping rising ethnic prejudice and the privations of collectivisation.[29] But Afghanistan was not the safe haven they had hoped for. In the 1930s, Nadir Shah, the modernising leader of

258 THREADS OF EMPIRE

Afghanistan, sent his armies to subdue the refugee Turkmen nomads arriving from the Soviet Union. By the 1960s, the Turkmen
were taking part in elections and other aspects of Afghan national
life.[30] They might still move short distances between summer and
winter bases and grazing, but by the second half of the twentieth
century they were effectively sedentary.

And things got worse. In 1979 Soviet armies invaded Afghanistan in support of its failing communist regime, an important
Cold War chess piece. Afghan Islamist Mujahideen guerrillas
resisted the Soviets, forcing their humiliating withdrawal after ten
years of war. This miscalculation accelerated the collapse of the
entire USSR, but for Afghanistan the result was that Islamic fundamentalists took power. In 2001, waging a quixotic 'war on terror'
in the wake of 9/11, the US and its allies invaded with the goal
of dethroning the 'medieval' Taliban and didn't leave for twenty
years. During this long period of destruction, the former nomads
found themselves driven still further from their traditional routes
in Central Asia and Iran.

From 1979, Turkmen refugees began streaming across the Afghan border into Pakistan. Huge camps were set up to house them,
and Pakistani entrepreneurs spotted the opportunity for cheap
skilled labour. Turkmen weaving became part of the mainstream
supply chain for Pakistan's international carpet industry. Through
a twist of history, the loss of the Turkmen refuge in Afghanistan
and yet another forced migration transformed their rugs from
the vestiges of an ancient craft tradition into a mass-produced
consumer object.

Pakistan itself had an eventful journey through the late twentieth
century. The nation only came into being in 1947, when Britain
passed the Indian Independence Act and dissolved the Raj. The
British instigated Partition, a mass resettlement programme
separating Muslim Indians from Indians of other religions, a
tool Stalin would have recognised. The new border between West

Pakistan and India ran through the state of Punjab, which under both the Mughal and British Empires had been a great centre of carpet-weaving. In 1947, Indian Punjab's Muslim weavers moved to Pakistani Punjab, where their skills helped to build the economic base of the new state.

On their present-day websites and social media pages, three of the largest companies exporting from Pakistan – PAK Persian Rugs, the Lahore Carpet Company and the Multan Oriental Handmade Carpet Company – claim that they were established in 1947: their origin stories are that of Pakistan itself.

The weaving industry recovered slowly after Partition and became a focus for state intervention. Between 1956 and 1977 the government set up over a hundred weaving schools, furnishing them with two thousand carpet looms, to train over three thousand skilled craftsmen each year.[31] The goal was to boost exports, and tax subsidies gave carpets up to 40 per cent relief on export duty. [32] In 2005–06 the industry hit a peak of production: 2.83 million square metres of carpet, an astonishing expanse of woven and dyed textile valued at over £131 million (around $171 million). Ninety-nine per cent of this production flew and sailed away to locations distant from Pakistan in a developed world hungry for magic carpets.[33]

This was not an industry of independent weavers following their creative impulses or upholding the traditions of their forebears. Central to Pakistan's export-focused model was the role of the contractor. In 2015 more than 90 per cent of Pakistani hand-woven carpets were woven for contractors, who provided design and colour specifications and materials, carried out quality control and acted as intermediaries with the major export houses. Only 10 per cent were sold independently and locally.[34] The supply chain was designed to meet the demands of global retailers.

The structure of the Pakistani carpet industry obscures the reality of working conditions. It is estimated that 60 per cent of carpet-making businesses in Pakistan still employ fewer than twenty people and that they are mostly outside cities.[35] But these are still very tough industrial environments controlled by powerful intermediaries, not a network of cosy family-run businesses. Scandals about child labour are commonplace, and refugee labour is part of its lifeblood.

Fully integrated into global trade as it is, the Pakistani industry often uses imported rather than local wool. Local pashmina and silk are sometimes used, but their scarcity means there is a heavy reliance on imported merino, with its deep, soft pile. From these materials weavers make three broad groups of carpet. There are versions of well-loved carpet types from across the Eurasian weaving belt, for example hundreds of variations on the theme of the Ardabil carpet. There are modern reworkings of the structure and motifs of traditional carpets, which play strikingly with scale and colour.

The third group is the carpets Western retailers describe as 'Bokhara'.

In 1989, the anthropologist and carpet entrepreneur Chris Walter described the Sawabi refugee camp in Pakistan's Kyber Pakhtunkhwa: 'Six hundred thousand people live in this amorphous, infinitely expandable Central Asian village sitting on the Panjabi plain. [. . .] Everyone continues doing what they have been doing for the last five or eight years, which for the Turkomans is primarily weaving carpets.'[36] He describes the carpets they wove as Bokharas, not Turkmen rugs; not tribal products but commodities for a global market. The presence of vast numbers of Turkmen in Pakistani refugee camps brought 'a blast of knowledge for us', said Shahed Hassan of the Lahore Carpet Company.[37] But he and other canny contractors and export houses quickly went on to standardise the Turkmen design vocabulary and leverage Turkmen technical skills to produce the simplified Bokhara which took sitting rooms in the Global North by storm.

When Turkmen refugees began returning to Afghanistan in the early decades of the twenty-first century, the Pakistan State Bank identified it as a risk to the carpet industry.[38] Indeed, exports of Pakistani carpets halved between 2014 and 2017.[39] Ever adaptive, carpet intermediaries began importing carpets from Afghanistan to be finished in Pakistan, sometimes smuggling them across borders and breaking international sanctions. Bokharas described in retail stores today as made in Pakistan may have been washed and cropped there but woven by Turkmen refugees who have returned to an Afghanistan that is again closed.

The 'nomadic' rugs we can now buy so easily online and in stores across the developed world are often the products of weary refugees in makeshift encampments, in an industry organised for an international trade. In Pakistan, Turkmen rugs once again lost their link with their environment and ecology. Their designs were reduced to essentials and individual creativity was marginalised. They became a subsistence product made for export by a demoralised ethnic group.

Perhaps unsurprisingly, Bokhara rugs are often seen by carpet specialists as objects of little aesthetic and cultural worth – the bastardised commercial offspring of a great but broken tradition. But we can choose to see modern Bokhara rugs as offering a genuine connection with a profound experience: the stoicism and persistence of Turkmen tribespeople in the face of all odds. I don't own one myself, but every time I see one I pay mental homage to the weavers who used it as a ticket to survival. The Bokhara carpet gives us purchase on a lifestyle we admire but don't understand. If we understood it more we might yearn for it less.

Chapter 12
Lost

KNOTTED-PILE CARPET, SIXTEENTH CENTURY CE, IRAN

In 1891, Italy's economy was under pressure, its colonial exploits had failed, and its government was corrupt.[1] And so the wealthy German art-historian Wilhelm Bode came to Genoa to shop. He wasn't looking for commonplace souvenirs, though. He wanted museum-quality artefacts: carpets, in particular. Bode visited the Jewish synagogue by the Malapaga walls, the site of the city's old debtor's prison, where he snapped up a Persian rug.[2] It was a white-ground animal rug representing the paradise gardens found across Iranian culture from Safavid times, made for an aristocratic patron in sixteenth-century Persia.[3]

Later, Bode would write of his trip that in Italy, at that time, beautiful historic carpets 'lay practically in the streets and could be had for a song.'[4] His follower Kurt Erdmann claimed that Bode's entire collection 'was acquired originally for not more than the cost today of one of its more ordinary pieces'. Bode is now famous for the unscrupulousness of his Italian dealings, but scholars still hide behind euphemism out of deference to the great scholar. 'To avoid spoiling the market,' Erdmann continued diplomatically, 'these transactions were obviously not advertised.'[5] Genoa's rabbi was likely unaware of the carpet's value and Bode did nothing to enlighten him. The rabbi could not have anticipated the consequences of the deal he had made.

Soon after his return, Bode was inspired by his new acquisition to write an essay that would later become the book *Antique Rugs from the Near East* – without the rug we would not have this foundation stone of modern carpet studies. But the purchase also set off a chain of events that ended in calamity. Within sixty years, the centuries-old artefact would be destroyed.

Like the legendary Ardabil, Bode's carpet had a twin, the Coronation Carpet, which is in the Los Angeles County Museum of Art. The twin rugs may have been made in the same workshop or by the same creative team as it moved from patron to patron. A lifelike bestiary of lions, panthers, bulls, stags, jackals, hares and dogs was woven into the two rugs, alongside the phoenix, flaming deer and dragons of Asian legends. Trees are filled with apes and songbirds. Cranes strut across the rugs' large red central medallions.[6] The composition is complex, but there is order to it. Nature's fecundity is balanced by a spiritual tranquillity. It evokes the joy, beauty and repose of a park in paradise.

The two carpets are identical in all but one aspect. The winged figures that gaze out from the corners of the Coronation Carpet have been excised from Bode's version, which at some point had almost sixteen inches removed from its top and bottom borders. The figures have disappeared entirely from two corners, and in the remaining two the excision has decapitated them and dismembered their wings.

These figures are often called angels, but they are more properly described as *houri*, an Islamic religious motif representing beautiful and pure beings who inhabit paradise, offering rewards to the righteous and pious. Some Islamic theologians view them as allegorical figures embodying the spiritual rewards and pleasures of paradise. Modern fundamentalists have sometimes interpreted them literally as the virgins awaiting jihadis in heaven. They are powerful and contentious symbols, and at some point someone, perhaps a Genoan rabbi, decided to remove them.

Bode was already a well-known historian of Renaissance and Dutch art when he visited Italy in 1891. His father was a judge, and both his father and grandfather had been administrators for the Duke of Braunschweig, an imperial connection which served Bode well throughout his career. As curator of the Gemäldegalerie, the home of Berlin's main collection of paintings, he had brought that collection up to the level of those in Munich and Dresden, which had begun collecting earlier under influential patrons at a time when Berlin was focused on industrial development. By 1887 he had moved on to a bigger task: establishing the new Kaiser-Friedrich-Museum. Built like the prow of a boat on Museum Island in central Berlin, it opened in 1904, and Bode had a fittingly adventurous vision for how to fill it. He believed that painting and sculpture should be shown in their full historical context, alongside contemporaneous applied arts and crafts such as carpets. He also wanted dedicated galleries for both Islamic and East Asian Art, rather than an exclusive focus on the European tradition. Such was his enthusiasm for the project that he was prepared to give his personal collection of twenty-one carpets to the museum.[7]

Richard Schoene, the general director of the Prussian Royal Museums, refused the donation.[8] Bode was a highly respected scholar and a formidable administrator – his colleagues nicknamed him the 'Bismarck of Museums' – but this fascination with carpets was deemed eccentric.[9] An Islamic and Eastern Arts department was one thing, but putting rugs on display was a step too far for his more traditional colleagues. Yet by December 1905 Schoene had retired and Bode had taken his place. His Islamic department was set up. In 1954 it was renamed the Berlin Museum of Islamic Art, and the collection is now famous across the world.

With nobody to stand in his way, Bode was finally able to instal his rugs as objects of artistic value equal to the other artefacts in the museum. Indeed, the Persian animal carpet he had bought in

Genoa was given the inventory number I.1, the first and primary object in the department's milestone collection. Bode went on to become Germany's most famous museum curator, and what was the Kaiser-Friedrich-Museum now bears his name.

When the Second World War broke out the Berlin Museums closed, and work began to ensure the safety of the collections. It fell to Kurt Erdmann, met earlier in these pages, to protect Bode's carpets. Unlike Bode, Erdmann had not come from wealth or received the patronage of the German aristocracy.[10] As a young scholar he often lived hand to mouth, on a tight budget, hopping from one short-term contract to another, sometimes taking pay cuts or volunteering without pay. By 1939 he had been in a steady post at the Department of Islamic Art for seven years, building his career while carefully navigating the political environment of the Third Reich (while not a member of the Nazi Party itself, he attended Nazi meetings and training courses in this period).

The department was housed in the Pergamon Museum on Museum Island, which not only looked like a fortress but was at first assumed to be strong enough to withstand direct hits from Allied bombers, and so the Islamic art collection went into its cellars.[11] As the war intensified, however, keeping all these treasures in one place came to seem like less of a good idea. Berlin was still believed to be well defended from air attack, and so the Islamic art was distributed to multiple city locations, where it was to be protected by the deep cellars of the Berlin Mint and the anti-aircraft towers of the city zoo.

It is estimated that by the end of the Second World War, a fifth of Europe's art was in Nazi hands.[12] In 1940, Hermann Göring had issued an order giving instructions for the seizure, redistribution and 'safeguarding' of Jewish art.[13] Art was also seized from other persecuted groups, and major collections in its occupied territories were ransacked. Jan Van Eyck's *Altar Piece* was stolen from the cathedral in Ghent and Michelangelo's *Madonna and Child* was stolen from a church in Bruges after the defeat of Belgium.[14] Many objects disappeared into the homes and collections of powerful Nazi officials, and others were sold to finance Nazi projects. Thousands of objects were earmarked for a planned Führer Museum in Linz, Austria, near Hitler's birthplace.[15] The plunder went on even as the war ended. Many artefacts were stolen as German soldiers retreated.

For safekeeping, objects were evacuated to remote country estates and to salt mines where the salt's absorption of air moisture offered a stable low humidity. In 1945, as the war ended, the US Army's 'Monuments Men', a military unit dedicated to the recovery of art looted by the Nazis, retrieved more than six thousand paintings, more than a thousand prints and drawings, 137 pieces of sculpture, 122 tapestries and over six hundred boxes of books and archives from just a single mine in Altaussee, near Austria's border with Bavaria.[16]

As part of Nazi Germany's attempt to protect its art treasures, Erdmann in 1944 visited a group of salt mines to assess their suitability as storage for the Berlin collection of Islamic Art. At Kaiseroda in Thuringia and Grasleben in Saxony he identified the necessary dry and cool conditions at levels of three to four hundred metres below ground. The collection would be transported in mining tubs down narrow, poorly maintained tunnels into the depths of the mines. With his boss Ernst Kühnel, Bode's collaborator and now director of the Museum of Islamic Art, Erdmann made a fateful decision. He records: 'Rolls three metres in length cannot be transported in mining tubs, and neither Kühnel nor I had the courage to fold fragile antique carpets to make them into bales.'[17] Smaller carpets might go to Kaiseroda or Grasleben, but large carpets like the museum's Iranian court carpets would remain at the Mint.

On the night of 9 March 1945, ninety-two RAF Mosquito bombers attacked Berlin.[18] Erdmann would later write that 'when the fire was discovered, it was too late to extinguish it, and for days, it was impossible to open the armoured doors and drench the smouldering remains of the carpets. It was one of the bitterest moments of my life, when up to the knees in water, I fished about with a pole for what remained of them. I did not find much.'[19]

Most of the Oriental prints from the Art Library, fine porcelain from the Museum of Decorative Arts, most of the East Asian collection and the entire collection of the Ethnographic Museum were lost.[20] In the confusion it was hard to establish exactly how many carpets were affected. Kurt Erdmann listed twenty carpets as destroyed or damaged, and the current curator of the Berlin carpet collection, Anna Beselin, estimates that more than seventeen carpets were completely destroyed in the fire.[21] Among the greatest casualties was the animal carpet, the original inspiration for Bode's scholarship.[22] A US eyewitness described the distress of the museum staff at the annihilation of their professional achievements:

> The old men watched their life's work sink into chaos, chaos of fire, rubble, dirt, water and the unutterable messiness of destruction. They grew accustomed to it, and puttered and muttered in their ruined offices, wrapped in all the clothing they owned [. . .] Thirteen department heads died 'natural' deaths in two or three years. Five were killed in action. Three are missing and several more committed suicide. This doesn't count the little fellows, the guards, workmen and general help, who didn't hold resounding titles.[23]

The survival chances of carpets significantly worsen during times of conflict, when fire is used as a weapon. The bitter loss that Erdmann describes could have happened to any guardian of rugs at any point in the long history of human warfare and carpet-weaving. But he was not describing a thirteenth-century Mongol siege or a seventeenth-century battle between the Ottomans and the Hapsburgs. He was reliving the days following attacks on Berlin by the British RAF under a bomber's moon in mid-March 1945. It is not only the good guys in a conflict who treasure their artefacts and genuinely mourn their loss.

Throughout history, as power is violently disrupted in war, carpets are taken as booty, vandalised as proxies for their defeated owners, or simply destroyed by mistake. Sometimes, as was the case with Bode's animal carpet, they are lost in the very attempt to protect them. The disappearance of precious objects leaves us with only stories and questions. If the Kaiser-Friedrich-Museum had stuck to its original decision not to accept Bode's donation the animal rug may have been sold into private hands in the late 1920s and early 1930s, along with the rest of Bode's collection, and made its way out of Germany. If Erdmann and Kühnel had sent it to the salt mines rather than the Berlin Mint, it might not have burned.

Then again, if the carpet had survived its journey to Kaiseroda, its fate, like that of all the artefacts stored in Germany's mines or country houses or remaining in its museums, would have been decided by whichever victor controlled the place where it washed up. At the war's end, Germany was divided between a US zone in the south, a British zone in the north-west, a French zone in the south-west and a Russian zone in the east. Berlin lay in the Russian zone and was itself subdivided between the Allied powers. Kaiseroda was in the US zone; had Bode and Kühnel decided to send the collection there, it would have been taken to a US depot in Wiesbaden. The US and UK abided by the 1907 Hague Commission, which forbade a victorious state from seizing the cultural property of its defeated enemy.[24] By 1956, objects found in their zones were safely housed in the newly established Islamic Collection in West Berlin.[25]

What if Bode's carpet had stayed in its original location and somehow survived? Museum Island, home to the Kaiser-Friedrich and Pergamon Museums, was in the Russian zone, and the Soviets had a score to settle. During their invasion of Russia, German troops had not simply seized Russia's treasure but had set about systematically annihilating the Slavic culture the Nazis deemed to be racially inferior. An estimated 427 Russian museums were destroyed and 110 million books in four thousand libraries burned. Orthodox churches were put to the torch. Stalin couldn't recover what was lost, so he sought 'equivalent replacements'.[26] As well as Museum Island, after the war the Russians gained the ancient cultural centres of Dresden and Leipzig. The Soviet Restitution Committee used their Red Army Trophy Brigades to expropriate an estimated £4.9 billion ($6.4 billion) of artefacts from their new territory in today's money.[27] Had the Mint not burned, Bode's white-ground animal carpet would likely have been one of them.

For forty years, most people believed that these disappeared objects had been destroyed. It was only with Gorbachev's glasnost reforms that Russian investigators were able to start uncovering the story of the Soviet Trophy Brigades. When the work of Konstantin Akinsha and Grigorii Kozlov was published in 1991, it began a landslide.[28] In 1995 a high-level conference was held in New York; it was billed as 'The Spoils of War, World War II and its Aftermath: The Loss, Reappearance and Recovery of Cultural Property'.[29] A second conference was held in Washington in 1998 to focus on specifically Jewish losses.[30] The conferences resulted in new UN guidelines about looting and restitution and a shift in the practices of museums, which became more vigilant about the sources of their objects and more (although still not completely) prepared to return them to owners who had been victims of conflict.[31]

As the international climate of opinion about war trophies changed around them in the mid-1990s, Gorbachev and glasnost fell out of favour, and Russia's new rulers were less sympathetic to Western values. In 1995 and 1996, the Pushkin and Hermitage Museums held exhibitions of some of the Red Army's Second World War trophies, most of which had not been seen since leaving Germany. The exhibitions were partly to celebrate the fiftieth anniversary of the victory over Germany in what Russians call the Great Patriotic War, but also to assert a public claim to the artefacts. In 1998, as the world was waking up to the fate of cultural property taken during the war, the Russian government passed the Federal Law on Cultural Valuables, stating that the Soviet Trophy Brigades had acted perfectly legally in claiming German art as compensation for Russian losses. The following year, Vladimir Putin came to power. With his dreams of Greater Russia and Slavic cultural supremacy, he had about as little appetite for returning artefacts as he did for ceding territory.

But even if Bode's carpet been found after all in Russia, and its restitution agreed, it might then have been disputed by multiple owners, as other famous objects were. War deeply unsettles assumptions about who owns what. Alongside Berlin, where it had an institutional home for forty years, claims on the rug could be made by Iran, the home of its makers, or the Jewish community of Italy from whom Bode bought it. It most likely would never have come back to Germany.

The story of the carpet's twin follows a very different arc. It first came to public attention in August 1902 at the coronation of King Edward VII, from which it takes its name, when it was included among the carpets Joseph Duveen had been asked to select for the altar at Westminster Abbey.[32] Duveen was one of twentieth-century carpet history's most colourful characters, 'A titan amongst dealers.'[33] Captured in a popular painting by Edwin Austen Abbey, Duveen's Coronation Carpet exudes the imperial grandeur that Safavid carpets had come to represent.

Duveen benefited twice from the coronation publicity. In 1902 he sold the carpet to a US utilities and transportation magnate called Marsden J. Perry. Having bought it back from Perry in the merry-go-round of purchase and sale that collectors ride with their dealers,[34] a few years later Duveen sold it to another wealthy

American: Clarence Mackay, a financier and infrastructure entrepreneur.[35] After Mackay's death in 1938 the carpet was bought by J. Paul Getty, who in 1949 donated it to the Los Angeles County Museum of Art. As it turned out, a white-ground Persian animal carpet was safer with an East Coast industrialist or a Californian oilman than it was in a museum in Europe.

The wall separating East and West Berlin fell in 1989 and by 1991 the Soviet Union had been dissolved. Reunification began of Germany's two post-war republics: the Soviet-influenced German Democratic Republic in the East and the Federal Republic of Germany in the West. In 2001 the Pergamon Museum on Museum Island reopened and once again became the home of Germany's collections of Islamic art. A new conservation laboratory was established alongside it in 2012, and at that point all Berlin's carpets and fragments were reunited.[36]

In 2018 its galleries were redesigned for the first time since 2001. Previously the carpets had been displayed in a white space, without context, following a twentieth-century museum fashion for treating carpets as art comparable to paintings.[37] By 2018, however, there was a strong drive to contextualise them. They were hung alongside exhibits of weavers and weaving techniques, illuminating the skill and complexity of their making. There were explanations of their role in the formation of the museum as part of Bode's donation, and accounts of the burning of the collection and its separation into two parts in 1945–46.[38] The new, permanent exhibition was called *Traum und Trauma*: Dream and Trauma. Drawing on the healing power of storytelling and of physical repair, it brought together the creative achievements of weavers, Bode's original vision for the museum, and the circumstances of the carpets' destruction.[39]

It helped that there had been some recent breakthroughs in textile conservation, themselves stimulated by the Berlin Museums' need to rescue the damaged carpets and protect those that had

survived. In 1948 the elderly Mizzi Donner, the needlework teacher of the Austrian empress and author of a popular handicrafts
book,[40] had attempted a reconstruction of what Anna Beselin calls
the 'pitiful remains' of the Bode animal carpet. She writes ruefully
that 'Donner restored the famous animal carpet to the best of her
knowledge and conscience [. . .] cranes, panthers, hoofed animals,
trees and flowers from the preserved scraps of fabric were sewn
together, stuffed and patched, both in mirror image, upside down,
turned by 90 degrees, and also from back to front.'[41]

A black-and-white image in the archives of the Berlin Museums
shows a photograph of the original carpet lying on the carpet's
burned fragments. Mitzi Donner is there, looking uneasy at the
task in hand. She works on the rug in the cold and deprived
Germany of the post-war period, one of many museum staff who
laboured 'wrapped in all the clothing they owned'.[42] The crazy
patchwork of her efforts only underlines what was lost with the
original.

If Bode's carpet endured a suboptimal restoration, another carpet
burned in the Berlin Mint in March 1945 stands as an example
of everything conservation can now achieve. Also displayed in
the Pergamon's *Traum und Trauma* galleries, it is a rug from the
Caucasus, made by village or workshop weavers around 1600.
Acquired by Bode in 1881, its abstract and stylised forms suggest
dragons to some observers, and carpet specialists have given them
that name, although the figurative and symbolic meanings of the
motifs are lost. The restored dragon carpet is an example not just
of the art of carpets but of the art of conservation.

The dragon carpet had been rolled from the top end, meaning
that the bottom edge ended up on the outside, and when the Mint
burned it smouldered from the outside in, without ever quite going up in flames. A wide horizontal band remained substantially
intact, from which more severely damaged remnants hung in
narrowing ribbons. The astonishing restoration has revived more

than eight feet (572 centimetres) of those parallel ribbons. Like the huge, discarded skin of a serpent, each strip reveals part of the weaver's vision. Our understanding of her design is sharpened now that its visual unity is broken. We can see enough to reconstruct the carpet in our minds, but we can also feel the way in which the fire slowly ate through it. It commands the wall it hangs on in Berlin, dominating the entire gallery.

The *Traum und Trauma* galleries offer a final visceral shock. In a small glass box lies a burned scrap of carpet from the 1945 Mint fire, displayed as if thrown down and abandoned. When a lever is pressed the box releases the smell from the fragment, of 'sulphur, incendiary powder, naphthalene, scorched wool, and other toxic residues'.[43] The carpet fragment brings the long-ago war directly to our modern senses, a shadow of horror.

The two wounded carpets are a reminder of the forces humanity can let loose, and of all the carpets lost to us over time – those which came too close to the heat of empires and those worn away in more humble and domestic lives. But they also remind us of the fightback against loss, the conservator's patient efforts, the community's investment in museums and education, the individual owner's care for a precious object (I have just taken advantage of fine weather to beat my carpets in the fresh air, releasing them from a year's dust). Above all the burned carpets are evidence of the enduring relationship between humankind and its rugs.

Epilogue

THE INVISIBLE WEAVER

Until quite recently in the long sweep of history, a majority of people, male or female, prince or pauper, spent part of their life spinning, weaving, knotting. Textiles were a universal occupation. An emperor was in some ways only as good as his carpets, and his carpets were only as good as the weavers who made them.

If we were able to record interviews with the weavers of the carpets in this book, they would be able to tell us what it was like to weave in an Iron Age workshop with super-exacting standards, preparing carpets for great chieftains, or to be moved forcibly around the Ottoman Empire, or to have woven under duress in a jail in British colonial India. But we can't. The best we can do is to look at their carpets with an openness and respect for all the histories that are woven into them and listen to the voices of weavers who are our contemporaries. Weavers don't live in a textile dreamtime, but in their own time.

Between 1998 and 1999, the Iranian film-maker Ghasem Salimi made video recordings with weavers in Kamo village in central Iran.[1] The women specialised in weaving *sofreh*, small, patterned flatwoven rugs which are used in the baking of bread. Dough is kneaded on them, and the yeasty remains are wrapped up with the rug, ready for the next round of baking. They are a special gift for a new bride, who has a lifetime of bread-baking and nurturing ahead of her.

The young women of the villages had mainly moved away or not taken up sofreh-weaving, so the practice was in its last generation. The remaining weavers had the startling lack of reserve of some elderly women. They were casual about their skills and aesthetic impulses, though one insisted that a sofreh she was shown couldn't be hers because the central design wasn't one she used regularly, despite a video that showed her making it. The weavers were equally offhand about the meaning and symbolism of designs. Questioned about the name and meaning of a motif, one said dismissively, 'this is the pine motif, but it has about sixteen other names'.

The stories they wanted to tell were not about traditional craft skills and creativity, or the cultural importance of rugs and their making, or motifs and their meanings, but about economics. Major figures in their lives were the intermediaries who bought their carpets, either as gifts for brides in other villages or for the growing international market for 'tribal' rugs. Two told stories of taking up sofreh-weaving to survive after being orphaned. One specified that she lost her parents and began weaving professionally at twelve years of age.

They talked a great deal about what they were paid. One elderly woman, looking back to her youth, waved at the camera the beater she was using to pack down the wefts of the sofreh. Pointing to the beater, she said with palpable outrage and remembered despair: 'I worked all day and night to finish the first one, and this is what they paid me with.' They all had clear memories of the very slow increase in the amount they were paid for a carpet over the decades: one *toman*, two *toman*, six *toman*.

One elderly woman, now so crippled with arthritis that she couldn't light a fire, told Salimi with greater irony than sorrow: 'Now you're willing to pay a good price for sofreh, I can't weave them.'

But another replied 'They consumed our time, but it was our life they consumed.'

Endnotes

Preface

1 Marina Warner has written extensively on the mythography of carpets, for instance *Stranger Magic: Charmed States and the Arabian Nights* (London: Chatto and Windus, 2011); 'Freud's Couch: A Case History', *Raritan*, vol. 31, no. 2, 2011, pp. 146–63.

Introduction

1 Lucy Knight, 'Why we need the Women's Prize for Non-Fiction', the *Guardian*, 10 February 2023.
2 Quoted by James Butler in 'Review of Italo Calvino's *The Written World and the Unwritten World*' (London: Penguin, 2023), *London Review of Books*, 45, no. 12, 15 June 2023, pp. 9–14.

Chapter 1: Chieftain

1 Jennifer Wagelie, 'X-ray Style in Arnhem Land Rock Art', *Heilbrunn Timeline of Art History* (New York: Metropolitan Museum of Art, 2000), https://www.metmuseum.org/toah/hd/xray/hd_xray.htm
2 Ludmila Barkova, 'The Pazyryk Fifty Years On', *Hali*, no. 107, 1999, p. 64.
3 https://www.dangerousroads.org/eastern-europe/russia/5118-katu-yaryk-pass.html
4 M.W. Thompson, Preface, in S.I Rudenko, *The Frozen Tombs of Siberia: The Pazyryk Burials of Iron Age Horsemen*, M.W. Thompson trans. and ed. (Oakland: University of California Press, 1970), pp. xvii–xix.
5 For summary descriptions of the Rudenko excavations see St John Simpson and Svetlana Pankova (eds), *Scythians: Warriors of Ancient Siberia* (London and St Petersburg: Thames and Hudson, British Museum and Hermitage Museum, 2017), pp. 14–15, 98–9.

6   Thompson, Preface, Rudenko, *Frozen Tombs*, p. xxii.

7   Rudenko, *Frozen Tombs*, p. 5.

8   Ibid., p. 3.

9   For details of barrow congelation see ibid., pp. 7–12.

10 For the history of Soviet archaeology see A.L. Mongait, *Archaeology in the USSR*, M.W. Thompson trans. and ed. (London: Penguin, 1961), pp. 25–31 (translator's Preface), pp. 40–48; Leo S. Klejn, *Soviet Archaeology: Trends, Schools and History*, Rosh Ireland and Kevin Windle trans. (Oxford University Press, 2012), pp. 12–49.

11 Simpson and Pankova, *Scythians*, p. 13.

12 For Rudenko's own detailed account of these famous excavations see *The Frozen Tombs of Siberia*.

13 Klejn, *Soviet Archaeology*, pp. 28–9.

14 Simpson and Pankova, *Scythians*, pp. 14–15.

15 Klejn, *Soviet Archaeology*, pp. 285–8, 314–17.

16 Ibid., pp. 285–8, 314–17.

17 Ibid., pp. 33, 318.

18 Ibid., pp. 285–8, 314–17.

19 Ibid., p. 288.

20 Thomas J. Farnham, 'From Lessing to Ettinghausen: The First Century of Safavid Carpet Studies', *Hali*, issue 154, p. 90.

21 Rudenko, *Frozen Tombs*, pp. 295–304.

22 Simpson and Pankova, *Scythians*, p. 72.

23 For a discussion of this transformation see Steven Mithen, *After the Ice: A Global Human History 20,000–5000 BCE* (London: Weidenfeld & Nicolson, 2003).

24 Cecil Parham, 'How Altaic/Nomadic Is the Pazyryk Carpet?', *Oriental Rug Review*, vol. 13, no. 5, 1993; Robert Pinner, 'The Earliest Carpets', *Hali*, vol. 5, no. 2, 1982; Jon Thompson and Harald Bohmer, 'The Pazyryk Carpet', *Notes in the History of Art*, vol. 10, no. 4, 1991.

25 Barkova, 'The Pazyryk Fifty Years On', p. 67.

26 Ibid., p. 68.

27 https://www.hermitagemuseum.org/wps/portal/hermitage/digital collection/25.+archaeological+artifacts/879870

28 Bevis Longstreth, 'The Riddle of the Pazyryk', *Hali*, issue 137, 2004; Longstreth, *The Spindle and the Bow* (London: Hali Publications, 2005).

29 Michael Ryder, 'A Note on the Wool Type in Carpet Yarns from the Pazyryk', *Oriental Carpet and Textile Studies*, 3, 1987, pp. 20–21.

30 M.C. Whiting, 'A Report on the Dyes of the Pazyryk Carpet', *Oriental Carpet and Textile Studies*, 1, 1985, pp. 18–23; Jon Thompson and Harald

Boehmer, 'Dyes in the Pazyryk Carpet', *Source*, vol. 10, no. 4, 1991, pp. 30–36.

31 Barkova, 'The Pazyryk Fifty Years On', p. 69.
32 For a description of barrow five and its contents see ibid., pp. 13–44.
33 Rudenko, *Frozen Tombs of Siberia*, pp. 110–14; E.V. Stepanova and S.V. Pankova 'Personal Adornment' in *Scythians*, Simpson and Pankova (eds.), p. 97.
34 Stepanova and Pankova, *Scythians*, pp. 96–7.
35 For a discussion of 'Physical Type of the Population' see Rudenko, ibid., pp. 45–53.
36 For example, Vasily Ivanovich Abaev, *The Ossettian Epic Tales of the Narts* (Princeton University Press, 2016).
37 Thompson, 'Preface', Rudenko, *Frozen Tombs*, p. xxi.
38 Rudenko, ibid., p. 217.
39 Ibid., p. xxiii.
40 Herodotus, *The Histories*, Tom Holland trans. (London: Penguin, 2013), Book Four, p. 286.
41 Ibid., p. 96.
42 Abaev, *The Ossettian Epic Tales of the Narts*.
43 Eugene Halton, *From the Axial Age to the Moral Revolution: Karl Jaspers, John-Stuart Glennie and a New Understanding of the Idea* (New York: Palgrave Pivot, 2014).
44 Naoíse Mac Sweeney, *The West: A New History of an Old Idea* (London: W.H. Allen, 2023), pp. 13–37.
45 Kimball Armayor, 'Did Herodotus Ever Go to the Black Sea?', *Harvard Studies in Classical Philology*, vol. 82, 1978, pp. 45–62, 62.
46 Herodotus, *Histories*, pp. 284–9.
47 Ibid., p. 263.
48 Ibid., p. 289.
49 Ibid., pp. 289–90.
50 Stepanova and Pankova, *Scythians*, pp. 90–98.
51 François Hartog, *The Mirror of Herodotus: The Representation of the Other in the Writing of History*, Janet Lloyd trans. (Oakland: University of California Press, 1988), p. 11.
52 Aleksander Blok, *The Scythians*, Alex Miller trans. (Moscow: Progress Press, 1981).
53 Victor A. Shnirelman, 'Archaeology, Nationalism and "The Arctic Homeland"', in *Selective Remembrances: Archaeology in the Construction, Commemoration and Consecration of National Pasts*, Philip L. Kohl, Maria Kozelski, Nachman Ben-Yehuda (eds.) (University of Chicago Press, 2007), pp. 31–71.
54 Ibid.

55 'Arzhan: The Golden Burial of a Scythian King', *World Archaeology*, 24 January 2019 (WorldArchaology.Com); 'Swiss Archaeologist discovers the Earliest tomb of a Scythian Prince', *Science Daily* (Science Daily.com).

56 Shnirelman, 'Archaeology, Nationalism and "The Arctic Homeland"', pp. 31–71.

57 The *Guardian*, 26 April 2023, https://www.theguardian.com/world/live/2023/apr/26/russia-ukraine-war-live-lavrov-blames-west-for-deadlock-over-grain-deal-two-killed-in-kharkiv-museum-attack

Chapter 2: Sultan

1 Conservation Record Card, 9–67, Burrell Collection Archives, Glasgow Museums.

2 Ibid.

3 Moya Carey, *Persian Art: Collecting the Arts of Iran for the V&A* (London: V&A Publishing, 2017), p. 180.

4 Jennifer Wearden, 'The V&A Ardabil: The Early Repairs', *Hali*, issue 80, 1995, pp. 102–8.

5 *Grace's Guide to British Industry*, http://www.gracesguide.co.uk

6 Victor Behar, *History of Eastern Carpetmaking* (Glasgow: privately printed, n.d.) Glasgow School of Art Special Collections (held off-site at The Whisky Bond) ('World Cultures' BEH). I am grateful to Jonathan Cleaver for drawing my attention to this little-known source.

7 Ronald Grigor Suny, 'The Hamidian Massacres, 1894–1897', *Études Arméniennes Contemporains*, vol. 11, 2018, pp. 125–34.

8 Malcolm Gladwell, *Dragon Psychology 101*, Revisionist History series 5, episode 1, Pushkin, https://www.pushkin.fm/podcasts/revisionist-history/dragon-psychology-101, p. 1.

9 9-67 Object File, Burrell Collection Archives, Glasgow Museums.

10 Martin Bellamy and Isobel MacDonald, *William Burrell: A Collector's Life* (Edinburgh: Glasgow Museums Publishing and Birlinn, 2022), pp. 45–7.

11 Kenneth Clark, 'Sir William Burrell – A Personal Reminiscence', *The Scottish Review*, vol. 2, no. 6, Spring 1977, p. 140.

12 Richard Marks, *Sir William Burrell 1861–1958* (Glasgow Museums and Art Galleries, 1985), pp. 8–11; Bellamy and MacDonald, *William Burrell* for shipping business 1885–99 see pp. 25–8 and pp. 36–42; for 1889–1919 see pp. 74–93

13 See William Dalrymple, *The Anarchy: The Relentless Rise of the East India Company* (London: Bloomsbury, 2019).

14 Marks, *Sir William Burrell*, p. 17.

15 Correspondence of Robert Lorimer, friend of Sir William Burrell, January 1902, quoted in ibid., p. 6.

16 Ibid., pp. 8–11; Bellamy and MacDonald, *William Burrell*, pp. 25–8 and pp. 36–42, 74–93.

17 Bellamy and MacDonald, *William Burrell*, pp. 50–51.

18 John Julius Norwich, Barry Gasson et al., *The Burrell Collection* (Glasgow Museums, 2001), p. 11.

19 9-67 Object File, Burrell Collection Archives.

20 Bellamy and MacDonald, *William Burrell*, p. 167.

21 Wilhelm von Bode and Ernst Kühnel, Charles Grant Ellis trans., *Antique Rugs from the Near East* (Berlin: Klikhardt and Biermann, 1958), p. 83. In this later edition of Bode and Kuhnel's 1901 original, it is made clear that such motifs might indicate only that the carpets were made for the Knights of St John, rather than manufactured in a local industry in Rhodes.

22 Michael Franses and Robert Pinner, 'East Mediterranean Carpets in the V&A', *Hali*, vol. 4, no. 1, 1981, p. 51.

23 'Armenians to hold exhibition of carpets stolen from Azerbaijan's Shusha: UNESCO is silent', *Azer Focus*, 17 February 2021; Volkmar Gantzhorn, *The Oriental Carpet*, previously *The Christian Oriental Carpet* (Cologne: Taschen, 1998).

24 Attributed to Kühnel in Franses and Pinner, 'East Mediterranean Carpets', p. 51.

25 Noorah Al-Gailani, *Introducing Islamic Carpets: The Burrell Collection* (Glasgow Museums Publishing, 2022), pp. 76–7.

26 See for example Dan Hicks, *The Brutish Museums: The Benin Bronzes, Colonial Violence and Cultural Restitution* (London: Pluto, 2020).

27 These included the South Kensington Museum in London (1852/7), the Musée des Arts Decoratifs in Paris (1905), the Kunstgeberwemuseum in Berlin (1868), the Handels-Museum (1887) and the K.K. Österreichisches Museum für Kunst und Industrie (1863), both in Vienna, the Metropolitan Museum of Art, New York (1870) and the Chicago Art Institute (1879).

28 Kurt Erdmann, *Seven Hundred Years of Oriental Carpets*, Hannah Erdmann and May Beattie (eds.) (London: Faber and Faber, 1970), p. 36.

29 For a seminal discussion of the process of constructing the East through European structures of knowledge see Edward Said, *Orientalism* (New York: Pantheon, 1978).

30 Bode and Kühnel, *Antique Rugs from the Near East*, pp. 70,75.

31 Ibid. In the fourth edition (1958) Kühnel updates the original chapter on Mamluk carpets, tracing the history of the German School's interpretations.

32 Louisa Bellinger and Ernst Kühnel, *Cairene Rugs and Others Technically Related, 15th–17th Centuries* (Textile Museum, Washington, 1957), p. 5.

33 Kurt Erdmann, 'Carpets from Cairo', *Ars Islamica*, 5, 1938, pp. 179–206; 7, 1940, pp. 55–70.
34 Erdmann, *Seven Hundred Years of Oriental Carpets*, p. 154.
35 9-67 Object File, Burrell Collection Archives.
36 For a general history of the crusades see Jonathan Riley-Smith, *The Crusades: A Short History* (New Haven and London: Yale University Press, 1987).
37 Carole Hillenbrand, 'The Evolution of the Saladin Legend in the West', *Islam and the Crusades* (Edinburgh University Press, 2022), Chapter 10. The process continues in, for example, Ridley Scott's 2005 movie *Kingdom of Heaven* and Tariq Ali's 1998 novel *The Book of Saladin*.
38 James Waterson, *The Knights of Islam: The Wars of the Mamluks* (London: Greenhill Books, 2007).
39 Robert Hillenbrand, 'The Great Mongol Shanameh', lecture, Nomad's Tent, Edinburgh, Saturday, 11 March 2023.
40 Carl F. Petry, *The Mamluk Sultanate: A History* (Cambridge University Press, 2022), pp. 53–80.
41 Doris Behrens-Abouseif (ed.), *The Arts of the Mamluks in Egypt and Syria: Evolution and Impact* (Bonn University Press, 2012), pp. 13–21.
42 Esin Atil, *Renaissance of Islam: Art of the Mamluks* (Washington: Smithsonian Institution Press, 1981).
43 Behrens-Abouseif, *The Arts of the Mamluks*, pp. 13–21.
44 Eliyahu Ashtor, *Levant Trade in the Later Middle Ages* (Princeton University Press, 1983); for a summary see Sean Gough, 'The Mamluk Sultanate', *Hali*, vol. 4, issue 1, 1981, pp. 33–5.
45 Waterson, *The Knights of Islam*, Chapter 11.
46 Behrens-Abouseif, *The Arts of the Mamluks*, pp. 13–21.
47 For the role and impact of childhood textile fragments see D.W. Winnicott, 'Transitional Objects and Transitional Phenomena: A Study of the First Not-Me Possession', *International Journal of Psychoanalysis*, vol. 34, 1953, pp. 89–97.
48 Denny, 'Turkmen Rugs and Early Rug Weaving in the Western Islamic World', *Hali*, vol.4 no. 4, pp. 329-338, p. 335.
49 Erdmann, *Seven Hundred Years of Oriental Carpets*, p. 114.
50 Janet L. Abu Lughod, *Cairo: 1001 Years of the City Victorious* (Princeton University Press, 1971).
51 Wladyslaw B. Kubiak, *Al-Fustat: Its Foundation and Early Development* (The American University of Cairo Press, 1987).
52 Bellinger and Kühnel, *Cairene Rugs*, pp. 79–80.
53 Gough, 'The Mamluk Sultanate', pp. 33–5.
54 Bellinger and Kühnel, *Cairene Rugs*, p. 81; Denny, 'Turkmen Rugs', p. 355.

55 See for instance Jon Thompson, 'Late Mamluk Carpets', *The Arts of the Mamluks*, Behrens-Abouseif (ed.), pp. 115–41; Louise Mackie, 'Woven Status: Mamluk Silks and Carpets', *The Muslim World*, 1983, pp. 253–61.

56 Denny, 'Turkmen Rugs', pp. 331–5.

57 Jon Thompson, *Milestones in the History of Carpets* (Milan: Moshe Tabibnia, 2006), pp. 160–75; Thompson, 'Late Mamluk Carpets', pp. 115–41.

58 Reşat Kasaba, *A Moveable Empire: Ottoman Nomads, Migrants and Refugees* (University of Washington Press, 2007), pp. 14–15.

59 See Halil Inalcik, *The Ottoman Empire: The Classical Age 1300–1600* (London: Weidenfeld & Nicolson, 1973).

60 Walter Denny and Sumru Belger Krody, *The Classical Tradition in Anatolian Carpets* (Textile Museum, Washington, 2003), pp. 14–55.

61 Julius Lessing, *Ancient Oriental Carpet Patterns after Pictures and Originals of the Fifteenth and Sixteenth Centuries* (Berlin: 1877, London: 1879); Donald King and David Sylvester (eds.), *The Eastern Carpet in the Western World: From the 15th to the 17th Century* (London: Arts Council of Great Britain, 1983).

62 Walter Denny, 'The Origin and Development of Ottoman Court Carpets', *Oriental Carpet and Textile Studies*, vol. 2, 1986, pp. 243–61; Julian Raby, 'Court and Export: Part 1. Market Demands in Ottoman Carpets 1450–1550', *Oriental Carpet and Textile Studies*, vol. 2, 1986, pp. 29–39; Raby 'Court and Export: Part 2. The Ushak Carpets', ibid., pp. 177–88

63 Denny, 'Origin and Development', pp. 243–61.

64 Ibid.

65 Thompson, *Milestones*, p. 172.

66 Alberto Boralevi, 'The Cairene Carpets of the Medici', *Hali*, vol. 5, no. 3, 1983; Rosamond E. Mack, *Bazaar to Piazza: Islamic Trade and Italian Art, 1300–1600* (Oakland: University of California Press, 2002), pp. 88–90.

67 See Peter Jackson, *The Mongols and the Islamic World: From Conquest to Conversion* (New Haven and London: Yale University Press, 2017).

68 For an analysis of possible provenience see Friedrich Spuhler, 'Chessboard Rugs', *Oriental Carpet and Textile Studies*, vol. 2, 1986, pp. 261–9.

69 Anna Beselin, *Knots, Art and History: The Berlin Carpet Collection* (Milan: Skira Editore, 2018), p. 118, inventory no. 1.14.

Chapter 3: Shahenshah

1 Telman Ibrahimov, *Medallion Carpets: Origin, Symbolism and Transformation of Definitions*, https://issuu.com/yandex3765/docs/medalion_carpets._the_origin___symb#google_vignette

2   Robert Hillenbrand, *Islamic Art and Architecture* (London: Thames and Hudson, 1996), p. 248.

3   For V&A Ardabil catalogue entry see https://collections.vam.ac.uk/item/ O54307/the-ardabil-carpet-carpet-unknown/

4   *The Art Newspaper*, 1 July 2006.

5   Arthur Gobineau, *An Essay of the Inequality of Races* (Paris: 1853–55), *Histoire des Perses* (Paris: 1869); Marcel Dieulafoy, *L'Art Antique de la Perse* (Paris: 1884–89); Yuka Kadoi and Ivan Szanto, Introduction, in Kadoi and Szanto (eds.), *The Shaping of Persian Art* (Newcastle Upon Tyne: Cambridge Scholars Publishing, 2013).

6   Jon Thompson, 'Early Safavid Carpets and Textiles', in Jon Thompson and Sheila R. Canby (eds.), *Hunt for Paradise: Court Arts of Safavid Iran 1501–1576* (Milan: Skira Editore, 2003), pp. 271–317.

7   For a survey of the background to 'scientific racism' see Charles King, *The Reinvention of Humanity* (London: Bodley Head, 2019).

8   Ibid.

9   Suzanne Marchand, *German Orientalism in the Age of Empire: Religion, Race and Scholarship* (Cambridge University Press, 2009) pp. 21–8, 125–31.

10 Gobineau, *An Essay of the Inequality of Races, Histoire des Perses*; Dieulafoy, *L'Art Antique de la Perse*; Kadoi and Szanto, Introduction, *The Shaping of Persian Art*.

11 William Jones, *A Grammar of the Persian Language* (Oxford: Clarendon Press, 1771).

12 Carey, *Persian Art*, pp. 21–5.

13 Arthur Upham Pope and Phyllis Ackermann (eds.), *A New Survey of Persian Art* (Oxford University Press, 1939), vol. 11, pp. 2258–9.

14 William Morris, 'The History of Pattern Designing', *Lectures on Art*, 1879, https://www.marxists.org/archive/morris/works/1879/pattern.htm

15 Eva Marie Troelenberg, 'The Most Important Branch of Muhammedan Art', in Kadoi and Szanto, *The Shaping of Persian Art*.

16 This discrepancy persists; see for example the sale of the estate of the painter Howard Hodgkin, sothebys.com/en/auctions/2017/howard-hodgkin-portrait-artist-l17120

17 Leonard Helfgott, *The Ties That Bind: A Social History of the Iranian Carpet* (Washington: Smithsonian Institute, 1994).

18 William Dalrymple, *The Last Mughal: The Fall of a Dynasty, Delhi, 1857* (London: Bloomsbury, 2006).

19 Pope and Ackermann, *A New Survey of Persian Art*, vol. 11, pp. 2258–9.

20 The V&A catalogue can be found online at *V&A: Explore the Collections*. The Qing throne is at https://collections.vam.ac.uk/item/O18895/ throne-unknown/

21 David Roxburgh, 'Au Bonheur des Amateurs', in Linda Komaroff (ed.),
    'Exhibiting the Middle East: Collections and Perceptions of Islamic Art',
    Ars Orientalis, 30 (2000).

22 V&A Archives, MA/1/R1314/1, Report by Caspar Purdon Clarke, 31 July
    1880.

23 Nélia Dias, 'Le musée d'ethnographie du Trocadéro (1878–1908)', *Anthro-
    pologie et Muséologie en France*, CNRS, 1991.

24 For nineteenth-century collecting practices see Stephen Vernoit and Doris
    Behrens Abouseif (eds.), *Discovering Islamic Art: Scholars, Collecting and
    Collections 1850–1950* (London: I.B. Tauris, 2000).

25 For the history of carpet acquisition at the V&A see Moya Carey, 'The
    Palmy Days of Persian Design', *Hali*, issue 221, October 2024, pp. 65–71;
    Carey, *Persian* Art, pp. 174–82; Jennifer Wearden, 'Acquisition of Persian
    and Turkish Carpets by the South Kensington Museum', in Vernoit and
    Behrens Abouseif, *Discovering Islamic Art*.

26 Carey, *Persian Art*, p. 211.

27 Ibid., p. 176.

28 Minute Paper, Department of Science and Art (11 January 1893), MA 1/1/
    R1314, V&A Archives.

29 *The Times*, 26 May 1892.

30 Edward Stebbing, *The Holy Carpet of the Mosque at Ardebil: A Mono-
    graph* (London: Robinson and Company, 1892).

31 Ibid., pp. 3–7.

32 V&A Ardabil catalogue entry, https://collections.vam.ac.uk/item/O54307/
    the-ardabil-carpet-carpet-unknown/

33 William Morris to Thomas Armstrong, 13 March 1893. MA/1/R1314, V&A
    Archives.

34 'An Extraordinary Carpet', *The Times*, 26 May 1892.

35 William Morris to Thomas Armstrong, 13 March 1893. MA/1/R1314, V&A
    Archives.

36 Rexford Stead, *The Ardabil Carpets*, (Malibu: The J. Paul Getty Museum,
    1974)

37 Wearden, 'The V&A Ardabil: The Early Repairs'.

38 J.K. Mumford, *The Yerkes Collection of Rugs and Carpets* (New York: The
    Knapp Company, 1910), catalogue note p. 228.

39 Erdmann, *Seven Hundred Years of Oriental Carpets*, p. 32.

40 A.F. Kendrick to Edward Stebbing, 4 June 1914. MA/1/R/1314, V&A
    Archives.

41 May Beattie, 'The Ardabil Carpet', *Encyclopaedia Iranica* (15 December
    1986), pp. 365–8, iranicaonline.org/articles/ardabil-carpet-persian-car-
    pet-acquired-by-the-victoria-and-albert-museum-in-1893

42 Carey, *Persian Art*, pp. 179–80; Stead, *The Ardabil Carpets*, pp. 22–5; Wearden, 'The V&A Ardabil: The Early Repairs', pp. 102–10.

43 Patrick Brantlinger, *Rule of Darkness: British Literature and Imperialism, 1830–1914* (Ithaca and London: Cornell University Press, 1990).

44 For a discussion of such archetypes see Partha Mitter, *Much Maligned Monsters: A History of European Reactions to Indian Art* (Chicago University Press, 1992), and Partha Mitter and Craig Clunas, 'The Empire of Things: The Engagement with the Orient', in Malcolm Baker and Brenda Richardson (eds.), *A Grand Design: The Art of the Victoria and Albert Museum* (London: Victoria and Albert Museum, 1997), pp. 221–34.

45 Sheila Blair, 'Proclaiming Sovereignty: the Ardabil carpets', in Sheila Blair (ed.), *Text and Image in Medieval Persian Art* (Edinburgh University Press, 2014); Kishwar Rizvi, *The Safavid Dynastic Shrine: Architecture, Religion and Power in Early Modern Iran* (London: I.B. Tauris, 2011).

46 Mehdi Keyvani, *Artisans and Guild Life in the Later Safavid Period* (Berlin: Klaus Schwarz Verlag, 1982).

47 Thompson 'Early Safavid Carpets', in Thompson and Canby, *Hunt for Paradise*, pp. 271–317.

48 See for example Pope and Ackermann, *A New Survey of Persian Art*, vol. 11; Erdmann, *Seven Hundred Years of Oriental Carpets*.

49 Thompson, 'Early Safavid Carpets'.

50 For example, Sir John Chardin, *Voyages du Chevalier Chardin en Perse* (Amsterdam: 1711); P.Fr. Florencio del Nino-Jesus, *En Persia 1608–1624* (Pamplona: Biblioteca Carmelitano-Teresiana de Misiones); Johann Baptiste Tavernier, *Les Six Voyages de J.B. Tavernier en Turquie en Perse et aux Indes* (Paris: 1676).

51 May Beattie, 'On the Making of Carpets', in King and Sylvester, *The Eastern Carpet in the Western World*, pp. 106–9. Also published in David Sylvester (ed.), *Islamic Carpets from the Collection of Joseph V. McMullan* (London: Arts Council of Great Britain, 1972).

52 Donald King 'The Carpets in the Exhibition', in King and Sylvester, *The Eastern Carpet in the Western World*, p. 25.

53 For this debate see Glenn Adamson, *The Invention of Craft* (London: Bloomsbury, 2013); Larry Shiner, *The Invention of Art: A Cultural History* (University of Chicago Press, 2003).

54 For a discussion of the preference for reproductions over originals see Judy Attfield, *Wild Things* (Oxford: Berg, 2000), pp. 99–120. For a discussion of the aura of originals see Walter Benjamin, 'The Work of Art in the Age of Mechanical Reproduction', in Hannah Arendt (ed.), *Illuminations*, (London: Pimlico, 1999).

55 Avinoam Shalem, 'Multivalent Paradigms of Interpretation and the Aura

or Anima of the Object', in Benoit Junod, Georges Khalil, Stefan Weber and Gerhard Wolf (eds.), *Islamic Art and the Museum: Approaches to Art and Archaeology of the Muslim World in the 21st Century* (London: Saqi Books, 2012), p. 111.

Chapter 4: Samurai

1   Stephen Turnbull, *Toyotomi Hideyoshi: Leadership, Strategy, Conflict* (Oxford: Osprey Publishing, 2010), pp. 43–63.
2   L. John Anderson, Sachiko Hori, Morihiro Ogawa, *Samurai Armour from the Ann and Gabriel Barbier-Mueller Collection* (New Haven and London: Yale University Press, 2011). The collection includes a set of Hideyoshi's armour.
3   Valerie Foley, 'The Jinbaori: Oneupmanship on the Battlefield', *Textile Society of America Symposium Proceedings*, 1992, pp. 91–8; Aki Yamakawa, 'Japanese Warriors' Surcoats (Jinbaori) in the Age of Exploration', *ICOM Costume Committee Proceedings*, Kyoto, 2019.
4   Mary Elizabeth Berry, *Hideyoshi* (Cambridge MA: Harvard University Press, 2008), p. 9.
5   Ibid., p. 245 n.4.
6   For a detailed analysis of the sixteenth- and seventeenth-century craft landscape in Japan see Christine Guth, *Craft Culture in Early Modern Japan: Materials, Makers, and Mastery* (Oakland: University of California Press, 2022).
7   Foley, 'The Jinbaori', pp. 91–8.
8   For a review of the field see Halle O'Neal (ed.), 'Reuse, Recycle, Repurpose: The Afterlives of Japanese Material Culture', *Ars Orientalis*, 52, 2022.
9   Yumiko Kamada, 'The Use of Imported Persian and Indian Textiles in Early Modern Japan', *Textile Society of America Symposium Proceedings*, September 2012, pp. 4–8.
10 Susan Westhafer Furukawa, *The Afterlife of Toyotomi Hideyoshi; Historical Fiction and Popular Culture in Japan* (Cambridge MA: Harvard University Asia Center, 2022), pp. 46–83.
11 Ibid., p. 23.
12 Utagawa Yoshitora, *Funny Warriors – Our Rulers' New Year's Rice Cakes*, 1849. Satiric ukiyo-e woodblock print.
13 Guth, *Craft Culture in Early Modern Japan*, pp. 31–5.
14 Christine Guth, 'Textiles', in Money L. Hickman (ed.), *Japan's Golden Age: Momoyama* (New Haven and London: Yale University Press, 1996), p. 276.

15 For biographical details see Berry, *Hideyoshi*.

16 Robert Treat Paine and Alexander Soper, *Art and Architecture of Japan* (New Haven and London: Yale University Press, 1981), p. 415.

17 Berry, *Hideyoshi*, pp. 176–206.

18 For contemporaneous tea-diary records see Bibliography, Louise Allison Cort, 'The Grand Kitano Tea Gathering', *Chanoyu Quarterly*, no. 31, 1982.

19 Guth, 'Textiles', pp. 275–7.

20 May Beattie, March 1974, Beattie Archive, Ashmolean Museum, Oxford, Ref. 46, 84.

21 Announced via press release by Akirhiro Watanabe of the Nara National Research Institute for Cultural Properties, October 2016. For press example, https://scienceinfo.net/persians-who-taught-mathematics-in-japan-more-than-a-thousand-years-ago.html

22 Hiroyuki Honda, *The 16th-Century Silver Rush in East Asia, and the Unification of Japan* (Tokyo: Yoshikawa Kobunkan, 2015). For summary see https://www.hiroshima-u.ac.jp/en/HU_research/honda

23 Janet Abu Lughod, 'The World System in the Thirteenth Century: Dead End or Precursor?', in Michael Adas (ed.), *Islamic and European Expansion: The Forging of a Global Order* (Philadelphia: Temple University Press, 1993), pp. 82–5.

24 Edward Dreyer, *Zeng He: China and the Oceans in the Early Ming Dynasty 1405–1433* (New York: Pearson Longman, 2007); Jung-Pang Lo, *Empire in the Western Ocean: Sea Power and the Early Ming Navy 1355–1449* (Chinese University of Hong Kong Press, 2023).

25 Abu Lughod, 'The World System', p. 90.

26 Peter Frankopan, *The Silk Roads: A New History of the World* (London: Bloomsbury, 2015), pp. 508–23; 'Special Report: China is making substantial investment in ports and pipelines worldwide', *The Economist*, 6 February 2020.

27 Abu Lughod, 'The World System', pp. 75–100.

28 Abu Lughod, 'The World System', p. 90.

29 K.N. Chaudhuri, *Trade and Civilisation in the Indian Ocean: An Economic History from the Rise of Islam to 1750* (Cambridge University Press, 1985), pp. 75–9; For contrasting North Atlantic and Asian perspectives on Portuguese imperialism see Charles Boxer, *The Portuguese Seaborne Empire, 1415–1825* (London: Hutchinson, 1969) and Sanjay Subrahmanyam, *The Portuguese Empire in Asia 1500–1700: A Political and Economic History* (Oxford: Wiley-Blackwell, 2012).

30 Ghoncheh Tazmini, 'The Persian-Portuguese Encounter in Hormuz: Orientalism Reconsidered', *Iranian Studies*, vol. 50, no. 2, 2017, pp. 1–22.

31 Rui Manuel Loureiro, 'The Macau–Nagasaki Route (1570–1640)', in Richard W. Unger (ed.), *Shipping and Economic Growth 1350–1850* (Leiden:

Brill, 2011), pp. 189–206.

32 Hickman, Introduction, *Japan's Golden Age*, p. 24.

33 May Beattie, *The Thyssen Bornemisza Collection of Oriental Rugs* (Ticino: The Thyssen Bornemisza Collection, 1972), p. 31; *Carpets of Central Persia*, (London: World of Islam Festival Publishing Company, 1976), pp. 44–5; Arthur Upham Pope and Phyllis Ackerman, *A New Survey of Persian Art* (Oxford University Press, 1939), vol. 12, p. 2404, pl. 1268A; Friedrich Spuhler, *Carpets and Textiles: The Thyssen Bornemisza Collection* (London: Philip Wilson Publishers, 2003), pp. 84–7.

34 Dorothy Armstrong, 'Technocracy and Persophilia: Carpets in the World of Islam Festival, 1976', *Journal of Art Historiography*, 28, 2023.

35 Willem Floor, *The Persian Textile Industry in Historical Perspective, 1500–1925* (Paris: L'Harmattan, 1999).

36 Foley, 'The Jinbaori', p. 95. Foley attributes this suggestion to Ohta Ezio.

37 Janet Abu Lughod, Introduction and Epilogue, *Before European Hegemony: The World System 1250–1350* (Oxford University Press, 1989).

38 For example, L.M. Cullen, *A History of Japan 1582–1941: Japan's Internal and External Worlds* (Cambridge University Press, 2003), pp. 1–18; Ronald P. Toby, *State and Diplomacy in Modern Japan: Asia in the Development of the Tokugawa Bakufu* (Stanford University Press, 1991).

39 Daniel Walker, 'Rugs in the Gion Matsuri Preservation Associations', in Nobuko Kajitani and Kōjirō Yoshida (eds.), *A Survey of the Gion Festival Float Hangings: Imported Textiles Section* (Kyoto: Gion Matsuri Yama Hoko Rengokai, 1992).

40 Beattie, *The Thyssen Bornemisza Collection*, p. 31; Beattie, *Carpets of Central Persia*, pp. 44–5; Pope and Ackerman, *A New Survey of Persian Art*, vol. 12, p. 2404, pl. 1268A; Spuhler, *Carpets and Textiles*, pp. 84–7.

Chapter 5: Priest

1 Agnes Ziegler and Frank-Thomas Ziegler, *In Honour of God, for Adornment and Use by the Honourable Guild* (Braşov: privately printed, 2019).

2 For alternative datings of this Braşov rug see Stefano Ionescu, *Antique Ottoman Rugs in Transylvania* (Rome: Verduci Editore, 2005) catalogue no.11; Ionescu, 'Anatolian Rugs in Transylvanian Churches', *Aliev*, January 2017, table, pp. 15–16.

3 Julian Raby, 'Court and Export. Part 2: The Ushak Carpets', *Oriental Carpet and Textile Studies*, vol. 2 pp. 177–89, 180; see also Raby, 'Court and Export: Part 1', *Oriental Carpet and Textile Studies*, vol. 2, pp. 29–39.

4 Rozsika Parker, *The Subversive Stitch: Embroidery and the Making of the Feminine* (London: Women's Press, 1984); Elizabeth Wayland Barber,

Women's Work: The First 20,000 Years: Women, Cloth and Society in Early Times (New York: Norton, 1995).

5 Ionescu, *Antique Ottoman Rugs in Transylvania*, 2005, catalogue no. 11.

6 Zsolt G. Torok, 'Rennaissance Cartography in East Central Europe', in D. Woodward (ed.), *The History of Cartography* (Chicago University Press, 2015), vol. 3, part 2, 1806–51, 1828–33.

7 Ioan-Gheorge Rotaru, 'Johannes Honterus', *Jurnal Teologic*, vol. 17, no. 9, 2018, pp. 161–84.

8 Andrei Kertesz in Ionescu, *Ottoman Rugs in Transylvania*, 2005, p. 19.

9 Radu Sageata, Mircea Buza, Traian Cracea, 'The Germans in Romania with special regard to the Transylvanian Saxons', *Journal of the Austrian Geographical Society*, 2017, pp. 297–322.

10 Kertesz in Ionescu, *Antique Ottoman Rugs in Transylvania*, 2005, p.19, 35–40.

11 Maria Pakucs-Willcocks, 'Transylvania and its International Trade 1525–1575', *Annales Universitatis Apulensis*, Series Historica, 16/11 (2012), pp. 173–82, 173.

12 Albert Eichorn, 'Kronstadt und der orientalische Teppich', *Forschungen zur Volks- und Landeskunde*, vol. 11, no. 1, 1968, pp. 72–84.

13 Pakucs-Willcocks, 'Transylvania and its International Trade 1525–1575', p. 178; Mack, *Bazaar to Piazza*, pp. 73–95.

14 Pakucs-Willcocks, 'Transylvania and its International Trade 1525–1575', pp. 180–81.

15 Eichorn, 'Kronstadt und der orientalische Teppich', p. 73.

16 Emil Schmutzler, *Old Oriental Carpets in Siebenbürgen* (Leipzig: Hiersemann, 1933).

17 Ionescu, *Antique Ottoman Rugs in Transylvania*, 2005, p. 7.

18 Marino and Clara Dall'Oglio, Preface to new edition of Gyula Vegh and Karoly Layer's 1925 *Turkish Rugs in Transylvania* (Fishguard: The Crosby Press, 1977), p. 12.

19 Ionescu, *Antique Ottoman Rugs in Transylvania*, 2005, inventory no. 189.

20 Charles Grant Ellis, 'Ellis in Holbeinland', in Robert Pinner and Walter Denny (eds.), *Oriental Carpet and Textile Studies*, 1, 1985, pp. 55–75.

21 Ionescu, *Antique Ottoman Rugs in Transylvania*, 2005, p. 75.

22 Ibid., pp. 10–11.

23 Naoíse Mac Sweeney, *The West: A New History of an Old Idea*, pp. 152–63.

24 Bram Stoker, *Dracula* (New York: Vintage, 2019), p. 2.

25 May Beattie, Tuesday, 28 July 1964, MBA Doc.18, p. 334, May Beattie Archive, Ashmolean Museum, Oxford.

26 Stoker, *Dracula*, p. 18.

27 Patricia Furstenberg, *Dreamland: 100 Stories of Folklore and History, Banat, Crisana, Maramures, Transylvania* (Waterloo, IL: Alluring Creations, 2022).

28 John Mills, 'The Coming of the Carpet to the West', in King and Sylvester, *The Eastern Carpet in the Western World*, pp. 11–24.

29 Lessing, *Ancient Oriental Carpet Patterns*.

30 Ellis, 'Ellis in Holbeinland'.

31 Master of St Giles, *Mass of St Giles*, National Portrait Gallery, London, https://www.nationalgallery.org.uk/paintings/master-of-saint-giles-the-mass-of-saint-giles; Sarah Bowden, *Charlemagne's Unspeakable Sin*, June 2019, https://tvof.ac.uk/blog/charlemagnes-unspeakable-sin

32 Lorenzo Lotto, *The Alms of St Anthony*, Chiesa di Santi Giovanni e Paulo Venice, https://omeka.warburg.sas.ac.uk/document/64#?c=0&m=0&s=0&cv=0

33 Workshop of Hans Holbein the Younger, *Portrait of Henry VIII*, Walker Art Gallery, Liverpool, https://www.liverpoolmuseums.org.uk/artifact/henry-viii

34 Denny and Belger Krody, *The Classical Tradition in Anatolian Carpets*.

35 Ibid., p. 35.

36 Ibid., pp. 31, 58.

37 Lessing, *Ancient Oriental Carpet Patterns*.

38 Elizabeth Gill, 'From Turkey to Transylvania', *Hali*, 86, May 1996, pp. 71–86.

39 Beattie, MBA Doc.18, p. 343.

40 For example, for alternative datings of the Braşov 'Tintoretto' double-niche rug see Ionescu, *Antique Ottoman Rugs in Transylvania*, 2005, catalogue no. 11; Ionescu, 'Anatolian Rugs in Transylvanian Churches', 2017, table, pp. 15–16.

41 Schmutzler, *Old Oriental Carpets in Siebenbürgen*, p. 54.

42 Beattie, MBA Doc.18, p. 350.

Chapter 6: Tycoon

1 John Paul Getty's manuscript diaries are digitised and available through The Getty Research Institute's Institutional Archives, Los Angeles. Getty's memoirs include E. Le Vane and J.P Getty, *Collector's Choice: The Chronicle of an Artistic Odyssey through Europe* (London: W.H. Allen, 1955); J.P. Getty, *My Life and Fortunes* (New York: Duell, Sloan and Pearce, 1963); *How to Be Rich* (Chicago: The Playboy Press, 1966); *The Joys of Collecting* (London: Country Life Publications, 1966); *The Golden Age* (New York: Trident Press, 1968); *As I See It* (London: W.H. Allen, 1976). Biographies

of John Paul Getty include R. Hewins, *The Richest American* (London: Sidgwick & Jackson, 1960); R. Lenzer, *The Great Getty* (New York: Signet, 1985); R. Miller, *The House of Getty* (London: Michael Joseph, 1985).

2   J. Paul Getty, Diary, 14 April 1970, Institutional Archives, Getty Research Institute.

3   Alois Riegl, *Problems of Style*, Evelyn Kane trans. (Princeton University Press, 1992). Originally published as Riegl, *Stilfragen* (Berlin: G. Siemens, 1893).

4   Louise Mackie, 'May Beattie: Biographical Note and Bibliography', *Oriental Carpet and Textile Studies*, 3, 1987, pp. 6–11.

5   A. Clarke and B.I. Duerden, 'Obituary: Colin Panton Beattie', *Journal of Medical Microbiology*, vol. 25, 188, pp. 75–6.

6   May Beattie, Diary, MBA Ref. 52, 30–112, May Beattie Archive, Ashmolean Museum, Oxford.

7   Mackie, 'May Beattie', pp. 6–11.

8   Suny, 'The Hamidian Massacres, 1894–1897', pp. 125–34; Alyson Wharton-Dugaryan, '"I have the honour to inform you that I have just arrived from Constantinople": Migration, Identity and Property Disavowal in the Formation of the Islamic Art Collection at the V&A', *Museum and Society*, July 2020.

9   Oleg Grabar, 'The Implications of Collecting Islamic Art', in Vernoit and Behrens Abouseif, *Discovering Islamic Art*, p. 194.

10 Yelena Rakic, 'Hagop Kevorkian', *Encyclopaedia Iranica Online*, 2020, Trustees of Columbia University in the City of New York, http://dx.doi.org/10.1163/2330-4804_EIRO_COM_12372

11 Beattie Archive, Ashmolean Museum, Oxford, Folder MBA Ref. 18, 279–329.

12 Getty's will has been subject to much popular writing. The Getty Institutional Archives at the Getty Research Institute contain the relevant original papers, Getty.edu/about/getty/pdfs/gia_getty_comp_will.pdf

13 The correspondence referenced in this chapter between John Paul Getty and May Beattie via Getty Museum curator Burton B. Fredericksen can be found in the Beattie Archive, Ashmolean Museum, Oxford, Folder MBA Ref. 18, 279–329.

14 Burton B. Fredericksen, *The Burdens of Wealth: Paul Getty and his Museum* (Bloomington IN: Archway Publications, 2015), p. 276, n.80.

15 May Beatty to Fredericksen, Getty et al., 21 March 1970, Folder MBA Ref. 18, Beattie Archive, Ashmolean Museum, Oxford.

16 May Beattie, *The Thyssen Bornemisza Collection of Oriental Rugs* (Ticino: The Thyssen Bornemisza Collection, 1972).

17 Abu'l Fazl, *Akbarnama* (late sixteenth century), Henry Blochman, H.S.

Jarrett, D.C. Phillott trans. (Bengal: Royal Asiatic Society, 1977). For an assessment of the accuracy of this account of the development of Indian carpet-weaving see Stephen Cohen, 'Indian and Kashmiri Carpets before Akhbar', *Oriental Carpets and Textile Studies*, 3, part 1, 1987, pp. 119–26.

18 Glasgow, University of Glasgow Special Collections, Stoddard Templeton Archive, Archives Hub, GB O248 STOD/201.

19 R. Lubar, 'The Odd Mr Getty', *Fortune Magazine*, 17 March 1986.

20 For details of Getty's early years and early collecting see Getty, *Joys of Collecting*; Lenzer, *The Great Getty*.

21 Getty, *As I See It*, p. 280.

22 Getty, *Joys of Collecting*, p. 40.

23 Getty, 9 April 1939, Diary, Getty Institutional Archives.

24 Getty, 27 October 1938, Diary, Getty Institutional Archives.

25 Getty, *Joys of Collecting*, p. 36.

26 For example, Stead, *The Ardabil Carpets*, p. 36.

27 Carey, *Persian Art*, pp. 174–80.

28 Getty, *Joys of Collecting*, p. 35.

29 Fredericksen, *Burdens of Wealth*, Kindle location 2337

30 Daniel Walker, *Flowers Under Foot: Indian Carpets of the Mughal Era* (London: Thames and Hudson, 1998), p. 6.

31 J.K. Mumford, *Oriental Carpets* (New York: Charles Scribner's Sons, 1903), pp. 257–8.

32 V.I Lenin, *Sochineniya*, 3:381, quoted in Charles Issawi (ed.), *The Economic History of Iran 1800–1914* (University of Chicago Press, 1971), p. 298.

Chapter 7: Goddess

1 Pennina Barnett, 'Rugs R Us (*And* Them)', *Third Text: Third World Perspectives on Contemporary Art and Culture*, no. 30, Spring 1995.

2 Sharif Gemie and Brian Ireland, *The Hippie Trail: A History* (Manchester University Press, 2017), pp. 1–32.

3 Sheila Fruman, *Pull of the Thread: Textile Travels of a Generation* (London: Hali Publications, 2023), p. 21.

4 Ibid.

5 Jack Kerouac, *The Dharma Bums* (New York: Viking, 1958).

6 Gemie and Ireland, *The Hippie Trail*, p. 3.

7 *Good Omens*, series 1, Amazon, 2019.

8 Walter Denny, 'Kilims and the History of Art', in Sumru Belger Krody (ed.), *A Nomad's Art: Kilims of Anatolia* (Textile Museum, Washington, 2018), pp. 23–40.

9 Ibid., p. 23.

10 David Black and Clive Loveless, *The Undiscovered Kilim*, is the catalogue of this exhibition; see also Clive Loveless, 'The Discovered Kilim', *Hali*, issue 154, Winter 2007, pp. 61–2.

11 For Georgie Wolton's life as an architect see Rowan Moore, 'Britain's Most Influential Modern Architect? In Praise of the Lost Buildings of Georgie Wolton', The *Observer*, 8 October 2023.

12 Jonathan Meades, *Museum Without Walls* (London: Unbound, 2013), pp. 395–6.

13 Christine Poulson (ed.), *William Morris on Art and Design* (Sheffield University Press, 1996); Walter Gropius, I. Gropius, H. Bayer (eds.), *Bauhaus 1919–28* (London: Secker and Warburg, 1975).

14 Adolf Loos, 'Ornament and Crime', *Les Cahiers d'Aujourd'hui*, 1913.

15 'James Moore talks to Georgie Wolton', Black and Loveless, *The Undiscovered Kilim*, p. 14.

16 Quoted in 'Kilims in the Home', *Hali*, vol. 4, issue 1, 1981, pp. 1–6.

17 Black and Loveless, *The Undiscovered Kilim*, p. 14.

18 Conversation with Suke Wolton, 2022.

19 James Mellaart, 'Under the Volcano', *Cornucopia: Turkey for Connoisseurs*, vol. 4, issue 19, 1999, pp. 76–99.

20 For all things Çatalhöyük see the website of its head of excavations between 1993 and 2018, Ian Hodder of Cambridge then Stamford Universities, at http://www.ian-hodder.com, and https://catalhoyuk.ku.edu.tr

21 Mellaart, 'Under the Volcano', p. 96.

22 James Mellaart, 'Çatalhöyük and Anatolian Kilims', in *The Goddess from Anatolia*, vol. 2 (Milan: Eskenazi, 1989).

23 Brian Spooner 'Weavers and Dealers: The Authenticity of an Oriental carpet', in Arjun Appadurai (ed.), *The Social Life of Things* (Cambridge University Press, 1988) pp. 195–235.

24 Hilmi Dulkadir, 'The Sarıkeçili Tribe and their Flatweaves', *Oriental Carpet and Textile Studies*, 3, no. 2, 1987, pp. 188–99, 194.

25 Yanni Petsopolous and Belkis Balpinar, *100 Kilims: Masterpieces from Turkey* (London: Laurence King Publications, 1991), pp. 33–43.

26 Bennett, Ian, 'The Mistress of All Life', *Hali*, 50, April 1990, pp. 97–9.

27 Z.G. Burnett, 'Material Culture Rolls Out Fine Carpets Record', *Antiques and Arts Weekly*, 12 July 2022.

28 Marla Mallet, 'The Goddess from Anatolia, an updated view of the Çatalhöyük Controversy', *Oriental Rug Review*, 1993, pp. 1–19, 15.

29 Eberhard Zangger, 'Facts, Fantasies and Forgeries: Discussing James Mellaart', *Talanta: Proceedings of the Dutch Archaeological and Historical Society*, vol. 50, 2018, pp. 125–82.

30 Ian Hodder, 'Women and Men at Çatalhöyük', *Scientific American*, vol. 290, no. 1, 2004.

31 Stephen Mithin, 'Heaven and Hell at Çatalhöyük', in *After the Ice*, pp. 88–97, 94.

32 Marija Gimbutas, *The Civilisation of the Goddess: The World of Old Europe* (New York: Harper and Row, 1991).

33 Ian Hodder, quoted in Kathryn Rountree, 'Archaeologists and Goddess Feminists at Çatalhöyük: An Experiment in Multivocality', *Journal of Feminist Studies in Religion*, vol. 23, no. 2, Fall 2007.

34 Leonard Helfgott, *The Ties That Bind: A Social History of the Iranian Carpet* (Washington: Smithsonian Institute, 1994).

35 Rudenko, *The Frozen Tombs of Siberia*, p. 205 and fig. 157.

36 Petsopoulis and Balpinar, *100 Kilims*. The commentaries for catalogue nos 36 and 37 have been reversed. The relevant image is catalogue no. 37, and the relevant commentary catalogue no. 36.

37 Halil Inalcik, 'The Yuruks: Their Origins, Expansion and Economic Role, *Oriental Carpet and Textile Studies*, 2, 1986, pp. 39–66.

38 For example, Serife Altihan, 'The Anatolian Kilim-Weaving Tradition Today', in Krody, *A Nomad's Art*, pp. 135–54; Harald Bohmer, Josephine Powell and Serife Atlihan, *Nomads in Anatolia: Their Life and their Textiles: Encounters with a Vanishing Culture* (Ganderkesee: Remhob Verlag, 2008).

39 Richard Tapper, 'The Nomads of Iran', in Richard Tapper and Jon Thompson (eds.), *The Nomadic Peoples of Iran* (London: Azimuth, 2002), pp. 10–40.

40 Jon Thompson, in Black and Loveless, *The Undiscovered Kilim*, pp. 18–21.

41 Willem Floor, *The Persian Textile Industry in Historical Perspective, 1500–1925* (Paris: L'Harmattan, 1999).

42 Dulkadir, 'The Sarıkeçili Tribe', pp. 188–99.

43 Anna Badkhen, *The World Is a Carpet: Four Seasons in an Afghan Village* (New York: Riverhead Books, 2013).

44 For the history and settlement of Anatolian nomads see Reşat Kasaba, 'Nomads and Tribes in the Ottoman Empire', in Christine Woodhead (ed.), *The Ottoman World* (Abingdon: Taylor and Francis, 2011); Kasaba, *A Moveable Empire*.

45 Ibn Khaldun, *The Muqaddimah: An Introduction to History* (Princeton University Press, 1969), N.J.Dawood (ed.).

46 N.J. Dawood, Preface, ibid.

47 Selim Deringil, '"They Live in a State of Nomadism and Savagery": The Late Ottoman Empire and the Post-Colonial Debate', *Journal for the Comparative Study of Society and History*, 2003; Nora Elizabeth Barakat, 'Making "Tribes" in the Late Ottoman Empire', *International Journal of Middle East Studies*, 53, 2021.

48 Dulkadir, 'The Sarıkeçili Tribe', p. 189.
49 I am grateful to Markus Voigt, contributing editor to *Hali*, for pointing this out.
50 Kimberley Hart (ed.), *What Josephine Saw: Twentieth Century Photographic Visions of Rural Anatolia* (Istanbul: Koc University Press, 2012); May Beattie's photographs and archive are held in the Ashmolean Museum, Oxford.
51 Warner, 'Freud's Couch: A Case History'.

Chapter 8: Hegemon

1 For an analysis of the use of a carpet in earlier diplomacy between Hitler and Italy see Costanza Carrafa and Avinoam Shalem, '"Hitler's Carpet": A Tale of One City', *Mitteilungen des Kunsthistorischen Institutes in Florenz* (2013), pp. 119–45.
2 For a candid description of these views and de Gaulle's response see Robert Hopkins, *Witness to History: Recollections of a World War II Photographer* (Washington: Castle Pacific Publishing, 2002), pp. 130–32.
3 Antonio Gramsci, *Selections from the Prison Notebooks*, Quinton Hoare (ed.) (London: Lawrence and Wishart, 1999).
4 M. Djilas, *Conversations with Stalin* (New York: Harcourt and Brace, 1962), p. 114.
5 Averell Harriman to Franklin Delano Roosevelt, 15 December 1944, NCR 3975, 'Argonaut' Files, Box 21, Folder 1, Map Room, Roosevelt Library and Archives, Hyde Park, New York.
6 Eti Muharremi and Gentian Vyshka, 'The Ill-fated Triad: Roosevelt, Stalin and Churchill, Post-Yalta Strokes', *Journal of Medical Ethics and History of Medicine*, vol. 16, no. 9, 2023.
7 Churchill to Roosevelt, 26 January 1945, 'Argonaut', Box 21, Folder 2, Map Room, Roosevelt Library.
8 A collection of Pathé newsreels of the Yalta Conference can be found on YouTube. For a detailed bibliography of archives, memoirs and secondary sources on the Yalta Conference see Diana Preston, *Eight Days at Yalta: How Churchill, Roosevelt and Stalin Shaped the Post-War World* (London: Picador, 2019), pp. 370–79.
9 Charles E. Bohlen, *Witness to History: 1929–1969* (New York: W.W. Norton, 1973), p. 155.
10 General Information Bulletin no. 1, 'Argonaut', Box 21, Folder 2, Map Room, Roosevelt Library.
11 General Deane to Joint Chiefs of Staff, US Military Mission, Moscow, Minute no. M22363, Box 21, Folder 2, Map Room, Roosevelt Library.

12 Log of the Trip: Conferences of Malta and Yalta, February 1945, Foreign Relations of the United States, White House Papers, US Office of the Historian.

13 Bohlen, *Witness to History*, p. 159.

14 Andrew Haughton, proprietor of Edinburgh's sublime Nomad's Tent.

15 Bohlen, *Witness to History*, p. 155.

16 Ibid.

17 Ibid.

18 Amor Towles, *A Brief History of the Metropol*, AmorTowles.com.

19 Preston, *Eight Days at Yalta*, p. 99.

20 Hans Gutbrod, 'The Ethics of Political Commemoration: The Stalin Museum and Thorny Legacies in the Post-Soviet Space', Policy Memo, *PONARS Eurasia*, 23 March 2022.

21 Alexander Pushkin, *The Gypsies*, 1827; Nikolai Gogol, *Taras Bulba*, 1835; Mikhail Lermontov, *Ishmael Bey*, 1843.

22 Leo Tolstoy, *Cossacks*, 1863, *Hadji Murad*, 1904.

23 Tolstoy, *Cossacks* (online: OPU 2018) Kindle location 1811.

24 Oleg Semenov, 'Oriental Carpets and the Russian Interior in the 19th Century', *Oriental Carpet and Textile Studies* 1, 1985, pp.153–66.

25 Richard E. Wright, *Caucasian Carpets*, Carpets 15, *Encyclopaedia Iranica*, vol. 5/1, pp. 1–5.

26 M. Hakan Yuvuz and Michael Gunter (eds.), *The Nagorno–Karabagh Conflict: Historical and Political Perspectives* (London: Routledge, 2022).

27 Wright, *Caucasian Carpets*, pp. 1-5

28 A. Cecil Edwards, *The Persian Carpet: A Survey of the Carpet-Weaving Industry of Persia* (London: Gerald Duckworth, 1960), p. 54.

29 Helfgott, *The Ties That Bind*.

30 Edwards, *The Persian Carpet*, p. 52.

31 'Art of Azerbaijani carpet-weaving inscribed into UNESCO Intangible Heritage List', *Azertac* (Azerbaijani State News Agency), 25 November 2010.

32 For Iran–Azerbaijan divergences see Roya Taghiyeva, 'The Art of Azerbaijani Carpet Weaving in the Context of Intercivilisational Dialogue', *Geo-Culture*, vol. 3, no. 2–3 (2009). For Armenia–Azerbaijan divergences see Ali Mozzaffari and James Barry, 'Heritage and Territorial Disputes in the Armenia–Azerbaijan Conflict: A Comparative Analysis of the Carpet Museums of Baku and Shusha', *International Journal of Heritage Studies*, vol. 28, no. 3, 2022. For the case for Armenia as *fons et origo* see Gantzhorn, *The Oriental Carpet*. For the case for Azerbaijan see Liatif Kerimov, Nonna Stepanian, Tatyana Grigoliya and David Tsitsishvili, *Rugs and Carpets from the Caucasus: The Russian Collections* (Leningrad:

Aurora Publishers and London: Penguin Books, 1984).

33 'Armenians to hold exhibition of carpets stolen from Azerbaijan's Shusha: UNESCO is silent', *Azer Focus*, 17 February 2021.

34 Jon Thompson, *Carpets from the Tents, Cottages and Workshops of Asia* (London: Barrie & Jenkins,1988), pp. 131–47.

35 Carole Bier, 'Carpets for Commerce: Rug Weaving in the Caucasus', *Textile Society of America Symposium Proceedings*, 1990, pp. 166–77.

36 Elizabeth Gaskell, *North and South* (1854) (London: Leopold Classic Library facsimile of 1898 edition), p. 54.

37 Kelly Anne O'Neill, *Claiming Crimea: A History of Catherine the Great's Southern Empire* (New Haven and London: Yale University Press, 2015).

38 *The First General Census of the Russian Empire of 1897: Taurida Governate*, demoscope.ru.

39 Josef Stalin, State Defence Committee Decree no. 5859ss, Kremlin, Moscow. US Library of Congress.

40 Mark Mazower, *Dark Continent: Europe's Twentieth Century* (London: Penguin, 1998), p. 217.

41 Bohlen, *Witness to History*, pp. 180–82.

42 Minute of meeting between Churchill, Roosevelt and Stalin, 6 February 1945, 4 p.m., Yalta. Foreign Relations of the Unites States, Diplomatic Papers, Conferences at Malta and Yalta, 1945, Document 354, US Office of the Historian.

43 Winston Churchill to House of Commons, 27 February 1945, *Hansard*, 1944–5, no. 408, 5th series, 1274–85 (London: His Majesty's Stationery Office).

44 Ibid.

45 Henning Pieper, *Fegelein's Horsemen and Genocidal Warfare: The SS Cavalry Brigade in the Soviet Union* (Basingstoke: Palgrave Macmillan, 2015).

46 John Colville, *The Fringes of Power: Downing Street Diaries 1939–1955* (London: Phoenix, 2005), p. 565.

47 FCO 33/8016, The National Archives, Kew.

48 Ibid.

49 Winston Churchill to President Truman, Official Telegram no. 44, serial no. T895/5, 12 May 1945, Churchill Archives, CHAR 20/2018/109–10.

50 'Monument to Big Three Allied Leaders Installed in Yalta', *TASS Russian News Agency*, 5 February 2015.

Chapter 9: Sahib

1 For Baden-Powell's biography see the records of St Sepulchre's Church,

Oxford, http://www.stsepulchres.org.uk/burials/baden_powell_baden.
html

2 Baden Henry Baden-Powell, *Handbook of the Manufactures and Arts of
Punjab* (Lahore: Punjab Printing Company, 1873).

3 Baden-Powell, 'Memorandum to Contributors', *Report on the Punjab
Exhibition 1881–2* (Lahore: Punjab Secretariat Press, 1883), pp. 6–7.

4 *The Medical History of British India*, National Library of Scotland, https://
digital.nls.uk/indiapapers/

5 William Dalrymple, *The Anarchy: The Relentless Rise of the East India
Company* (London: Bloomsbury, 2019).

6 Kim A. Wagner, *Amritsar: An Empire of Fear and the Making of a
Massacre* (New Haven and London: Yale University Press, 2019), pp. 1–17.

7 Anthony Kirk-Greene, *Britain's Imperial Administrators, 1858–1966*
(London: Palgrave Macmillan, 2000), pp. 87–124.

8 Rob Johnson, *The British Indian Army: Virtue and Necessity* (Newcastle
upon Tyne: Cambridge Scholars Publishing, 2014), pp. 1–15.

9 Wagner, *Amritsar*, p. 24.

10 *Report on the Punjab Exhibition 1881–2*, Appendix.

11 See Jules Lubbock, *The Tyranny of Taste: The Politics of Architecture and
Design in Britain 1550–1960* (New Haven and London: Yale University
Press, 1995), pp. 243–97; Arindam Dutta, *The Bureaucracy of Beauty:
Design in the Age of its Global Reproducibility* (New York: Routledge,
2006).

12 Baden-Powell, 'Memorandum to Contributors', pp. 6–7.

13 For a summary of the position see George Birdwood, *Industrial Arts
of India* (London: Chapman and Hall, 1880), vol. 1, pp. 285–300 and
Tirthanker Roy, *Traditional Industry in the Economy of Colonial India*
(Cambridge University Press, 1999), pp. 197–231.

14 Two fine examples are the V&A's Fremlin Carpet and the Girdler's Livery
Company Carpet, London.

15 Vincent Robinson, 'Indian Carpets', in *Oriental Carpets*, Caspar Purdon
Clarke (ed.) (Vienna, 1892), p. 6.

16 Olive Olmstead Fester, *Fine Arts, Including Folly: A History of the Hajji
Baba Club 1932–1960* (New York: Hajji Baba Publications, 1966), p. 12.

17 Mumford, *Oriental Carpets*, p. 252.

18 Roy, *Traditional Industry*, pp. 197–230.

19 *Indian Industrial Commission* (Calcutta, 1916–18), vol. 5.

20 See Walker, *Flowers Under Foot*.

21 Troelenberg, 'The Most Important Branch of Muhammedan Art', pp.
237–54.

22 See Dalrymple, *The Last Mughal*.

23 'Catalogue, Jail Carpets Section', *Report on the Punjab Exhibition 1881–2*. I am grateful to Laure de Gramont and Dr Theodora Zemek for their help in identifying Les Grands Magasins de Louvre in the nineteenth-century Palais Royal, Paris.

24 Martin Lynn, *British Policy, Trade and Informal Empire in the Mid-19th Century* (Oxford University Press, 1999), pp. 101–21; William Beinart and Lotte Hughes, *Environment and Empire* (Oxford University Press, 2007), pp. 93–100.

25 See A.S. Travis, *The Rainbow Makers: The Origins of the Synthetic Dye-stuffs Industry in the West* (London and Toronto: Associated Universities Press, 1993).

26 Abigail McGowan '"All that is Rare, Characteristic or Beautiful": Design and the Defence of Tradition in Colonial India, 1851–1903', *Journal of Material Culture*, vol. 10, no. 3 (2005), pp. 263–86; McGowan, 'Convict Carpets: Jails and the Revival of Historic Carpet Design in Colonial India', *The Journal of Asian Studies*, vol. 72, no. 2, May 2013, pp. 391–416.

27 Helfgott, *The Ties That Bind*.

28 W. Coldstream, *Report on the Punjab Exhibition 1881–2*, p. 61.

29 Cecil Latimer, 'Carpet-Making in the Punjab', *Journal of Indian Art and Industry*, vol. 17, no. 131 (1916), pp. 15–26; Latimer, *Monograph on Carpet-Making in the Punjab, 1905–6* (Lahore: 1907).

30 Latimer, *Monograph on Carpet-Making in the Punjab*, p. 7.

31 McGowan, 'Convict Carpets', pp. 391–416.

32 Abigail McGowan, 'Domestic Modern: Redecorating Homes in Bombay in the 1930s', *Journal of the Society of Architectural Historians*, vol. 75, no. 4, pp. 424–46.

33 Roy attributes this assertion to Sir George Birdwood in *Traditional Industry*, pp. 199, 206 n.33; *Report on the Punjab Exhibition 1881–2*, p. 57 states that the 'longest serving prisoners are most skilled'.

34 See Ganda Singh, *The Indian Mutiny of 1857: The Sikhs* (Delhi: Sikh Student Federation, 1969).

35 Satadru Sen, *Disciplined Natives, Race, Freedom and Confinement in Colonial India* (Delhi: Primus Books, 2012), pp. 222, 234.

36 Ibid., p. 220.

37 Ibid., pp. 87, 189–216, 222–38.

38 McGowan, 'Convict Carpets', pp. 397–8.

39 'Colonial and Indian', *Saturday Review*, 22 May 1886, p. 707.

40 Frank Banfield, 'The Colonial and Indian Exhibition', *Time*, June 1886, pp. 662–72; see also Saloni Mathur, 'Living Ethnological Exhibits: The Case of 1886', *Cultural Anthropology*, vol. 15, no. 4, November 2000, pp. 492–520.

41 For Prince Albert's own account of his plan for Albertopolis, its history

and an analysis of reactions to it see Andrew Cusworth, 'Royal Commission for the Exhibition of 1851', https://royalcommission1851.org/uploads/publications/104911851-A5-16pp-Booklet_web.pdf

42 The V&A Archives, 'Précis of Board Minutes of the Science and Art Department 1852 Onwards' in the sequence ED 83/34, ED 84/35 etc.

43 John Lockwood Kipling, 'The Functions of the Art Schools in India', *Journal of the Royal Society of Arts*, 57, no. 2952, 18 June 1909.

44 Baden-Powell 'Memorandum to Contributors', *Report on the Punjab Exhibition 1881–2*, pp. 6–7.

45 Owen Jones, *The Grammar of Ornament* (London: Day and Sons, 1856).

46 P.G. Konody and Tessa Murdoch, 'Caspar Purdon Clarke', *Oxford Dictionary of National Biography* (Oxford University Press, 2004).

47 Suga Yasuko, 'Designing the Morality of Consumption: "Chamber of Horrors" at the Museum of Ornamental Art, 1852–53', *Design Issues*, vol. 20, no. 4, Autumn 2004, pp. 43–56.

48 Ekta Raheja, 'Caspar Purdon Clarke: Collecting India in the 19th Century', lecture, Royal Museums Greenwich, 28 February 2023.

49 Rudyard Kipling, *Kim* (London: Macmillan, 1901).

50 Baden-Powell, 'On Some Difficulties of Art Manufactures', *Journal of Indian Art*, vol. 1, no. 5, 1886, p. 37; attributed to Purdon Clarke by Dutta, *Bureaucracy of Beauty*, p. 226.

51 A.M. Dallas, *Report on the Punjab Exhibition 1881–2*, p. 59.

52 'Mr. C. Purdon Clarke's Visit to and Purchases in India, 1883', V&A Archives, MA/2/1/1-3.

53 Helena Britt (ed.), *Interwoven Connections: The Stoddard-Templeton Design Studio and Design Library, 1843–2005* (Glasgow School of Art, 2013); Fred H. Young, *A Century of Carpet-Making 1839–1939* (Glasgow: Collins, 1943).

54 This task has now been executed brilliantly by Moya Carey in *Persian Art: Collecting the Arts of Iran for the V&A*.

55 For a complete list of the V&A's India files see 'Guide to the Records in the V&A Archives Relating to the India Museum and Indian Objects', vam.ac.uk

56 V&A catalogue entry https://collections.vam.ac.uk/item/O472054/carpet/

Chapter 10: Trickster

1 A.F. Kendrick and C.E.C. Tattersall, *Handwoven Carpets: Oriental and European* (London: Benn Brothers, 1922).

2 Alois Riegl et al., *Katalog der Ausstellung Orientalischer Teppiche im K. K. Handels-Museum* (Vienna: Verlag des K. K. Österr.

Handels-Museum,1891; Friedrich Sarre and Robert Martin, *Die Ausstellung von Meisterwerken* (Munich: Bruckmann, 1912).

3 Inalcik, 'The Yuruks', Oriental Carpets and Textile Studies, 2, 1986, p. 58.
4 Marino Dall'Oglio, 'White Ground Anatolian Carpets', *Oriental Carpet and Textile Studies*, 2, 1986, pp. 189–94. This number was suggested in 1986. The pursuit continues.
5 RugTracker.com, 'Selendi Cintamani'.
6 Patricia Baker, *Islamic Textiles* (London: British Museum, 1995), pp. 88–9.
7 J.M. Rogers, *Islamic Art and Design 1500–1700* (London: British Museum, 1983), p. 95.
8 Bode and Kühnel, *Antique Rugs from the Near East*, p. 53, fig. 64.
9 Ibid., 4th edition (Berlin: Klinkhardt and Biermann, 1955), pp. 52–3, 173. Kühnel revised his and Bode's earlier conclusions after Bode's death, moving the interpretation from Buddhist symbols to animal skins.
10 Abul Qasem Ferdowsi, *Shahnama*, composed between 977 and 1010 CE. Epic poem of Iranian history and mythology, foundational to Iranian identity through to modern times.
11 John Train, *Oriental Carpet Symbols: Their Origins and Meaning from the Middle East to China* (London: Philip Wilson, 2001), p. 85.
12 Perlefter Nominal File, MA/1/P945, V&A Archives.
13 For the Wakhan Corridor's controversial Durand Line, which became the de facto border between the Russian and British empires, see Hasan Kakar, *A Political and Diplomatic History of Afghanistan, 1863–1901* (Leiden: Brill, 2006), pp. 159–92.
14 Latimer, *Carpet-Making in the Punjab 1905–6*, Preface E. Maclagan.
15 'Art Notes', *New York Times*, 15 March 1964, Section X.
16 George Wingfield Digby to V&A director Sir George Trenchard Cox, 10 January 1964, V&A Asia Department Records, Files transferred from former Furniture, Textiles and Fashion Department (carpets) II (Acquisitions) 1909 onwards, under T.130–1933.
17 Ibid.
18 MBA_1_1_21_407, Beattie Archive, Ashmolean Museum, Oxford.
19 Dye analysis was carried out by a Dr Skelly at the CIBA Clayton near Manchester. Digby to Cox, 10 January 1964.
20 George Wingfield Digby to V&A official Charles Gibbs-Smith, 17 February 1964, T.130–1933, V&A Asia Department Records, see above.
21 Klaus Brisch, director of the Museum of Islamic Art, Berlin, to Natalie Rothstein, V&A textiles curator, 17 March 1969, V&A Asia Department Records as above. Natalie Rothschild summarises this story in her catalogue entry for the V&A *chintamani* in Mark Jones (ed.), *Fake? The Art of Deception* (Berkeley: California University Press, 1990), p. 227.

22 Digby to Cox, 10 January 1964, V&A Asia Department Records as above.
23 Francis Wheen, *The Soul of Indiscretion: Tom Driberg, Poet, Philanderer, Legislator and Outlaw* (London: HarperCollins, 2001).
24 Erdmann, *Seven Hundred Years of Oriental Carpets*, pp. 81–5.
25 Ibid., p. 82.
26 The carpet was sold at Bode's death and is now in the collection of the Textile Museum, Washington. Its dyes have been tested and contain no post-1856 synthetics. For full discussion of the Bode *chintamani* see Louise Mackie, 'A Turkish Carpet with Spots and Stripes', *Textile Museum Journal*, vol. 4, no. 3, 1976, pp. 4–20; Tattersall, Wace and Maclagan, 17–13 November 1933, Perlefter Nominal File, V&A.
27 Kendrick and Tattersall, *Handwoven Carpets*, p. 46a.
28 Christie's Lot 5548483.
29 Christie's Lot 5598024.
30 For a biography of Tuduc and the history of the Kehayoglou family see Alberto Boralevi and Stefano Ionescu, 'Teodor Tuduc (1888–1983)', in Stefano Ionescu (ed.), *Handbook of Fakes by Tuduc* (Rome: Verduci Editore, 2012), pp. 7–16, and Stefano Ionescu, 'Stelian Kehayoglou (b.1924)', in ibid., pp. 17–19.
31 Romanian and nearby Bessarabian weavers traditionally made exceptional kilims and began weaving pile carpets in the early twentieth century.
32 There is an extensive historiography of the expulsions of Armenians from the Ottoman Empire from the late nineteenth century onwards. For an overview of Ottoman diasporas, with an international perspective, see Isa Blumi, *Ottoman Refugees 1878–1939: Migration in a Post-Imperial World* (London: Bloomsbury, 2015).
33 Frank Wynne, *I Was Vermeer: The Forger Who Swindled the Nazis* (London: Bloomsbury, 2007), p. ix.
34 Anna Altmann, 'Masterpiece Theatre', *The Atavist Magazine*, no. 94.
35 Ionescu, *Antique Ottoman Rugs*, pp. 202–3.
36 Ibid., p. 203.
37 Ibid., p. 204.
38 Ibid., p. 202.
39 See Chapter 5, 'Priest', for a discussion of these collections.
40 Marino and Clara Dall'Oglio, Preface to new edition of Vegh and Layer's *Turkish Rugs in Transylvania*; for a discussion of the 1914 Budapest exhibition see Emese Pasztor, *'Transylvanian' Turkish Rugs: Tracing the Ottoman Rugs from the 1914 Budapest Exhibition* (Budapest Museum of Applied Arts, 2020).
41 Schmutzler, *Old Oriental Carpets in Siebenbürgen*, p. 54.
42 Ionescu, *Handbook*, p. 9.

43 Recorded in May Beattie's analysis sheets, prefix MBA_1_1 and identifiers 3_102; 4_200; 7_65; 8_52; 12_184; 21_98; 21_124; 21_406; 21_407, May Beattie Archive, Ashmolean Museum, Oxford.

44 Clara Dall'Oglio in conversation with Stefano Ionescu, Ionescu, *Handbook*, p. 57.

45 Franses and Pinner, 'Turkish Carpets in the Victoria and Albert Museum', p. 380, fn.100, *Hali*, vol 6, no. 4, 1984.

46 There is an extensive historiography of forgeries, replicas and versions. See for example Jones, *Fake?*; Oliver Watson, 'Authentic Forgeries', in *Creating Authenticity: Authentication Processes in Ethnographic Museums*, Alexander Geurds and Laura van Broekhoven (eds.) (Leiden: Sidestone Press, 2013), pp. 59–71; Hillel Schwartz, *The Culture of the Copy: Striking Likenesses, Unreasonable Facsimiles* (Cambridge MA: MIT Press, 1998).

47 Myriem Naji, 'A Falsification of Temporality: Carpet Distressing in Morocco', in *Surface Tensions*, Glenn Adamson and Victoria Kelley (eds.) (Manchester University Press, 2013), pp. 60–72.

48 Clara Dall'Oglio in Ionescu, *Handbook*, pp. 56–9.

49 Ibid.

Chapter 11: Migrant

1 For the idea of cultural capital see Pierre Bourdieu, *Distinction*, Richard Nice trans. (Abingdon: Routledge, 2010).

2 Figures from Carpet Vista, online Swedish carpet-dealer, carpetencyclopedia.com/styles-origin/pakistani-carpets

3 Louise Mackie and Jon Thompson (eds.), *Turkmen: Tribal Carpets and Traditions* (Textile Museum, Washington, 1980), pp. 16–17.

4 Ibid., p. 287.

5 In 1851 Gottfried Semper had controversially suggested that all architecture derived from carpets. *The Four Elements of Architecture* (1851), Harry Francis Mallgrave and Wolfgang Hermann trans. (Cambridge University Press, 2011).

6 Turkmen tent band, wool, pile carpet, 13.8m. x 21.5cm, 45ft 4ins x 8ins, Tekke tribe, Central Asia, first half of the nineteenth century, Textile Museum, Washington, R 37.12.4.

7 I am optimistic, as I was told this by Turkmen expert Jon Thompson.

8 Siawosch Azadi, *Turcoman Carpets and the Ethnographic Significance of their Ornament*, Robert Pinner trans. (Fishguard: Crosby Press, 1975).

9 Spooner, 'Weavers and Dealers', pp. 195–235.

10 Mackie and Thompson, *Turkmen*, p. 63, fig. 34.

11 Adeeb Khalid, *Central Asia: A New History from the Imperial Conquests*

to the Present (Princeton University Press, 2021), pp. 83–5; Alexander Morrison, *The Russian Conquest of Central Asia: A Study in Imperial Expansion 1814–1914* (Cambridge University Press, 2020), pp. 405–10; Mehmet Saray, *The Turkmens in the Age of Imperialism: A Study of the Turkmen People and Their Incorporation into the Russian Empire* (Ankara: Turkish Historical Society, 1989).

12 Morrison, *The Russian Conquest of Central Asia*, p. 409.

13 Alexander Borodin, Preface to *'Polovtsian Dances' and 'In the Steppes of Central Asia' in Full Score* (London: Dover Publications, 1997).

14 Tapper and Thompson, *The Nomadic Peoples of Iran*, p. 290.

15 Ibid., p. 291.

16 Semenov, 'Oriental Carpets and the Russian Interior', Oriental Carpets and Textile Studies, 1, 1985, pp. 153–66; for a contemporaneous Russian view of Turkmen carpets and early collections see Andrei Bogolyubov, *Carpets of Central Asia*, J.M.A Thompson trans. and ed. (Ransdell: Crosby Press, 1973) first published 1908–9.

17 Thomas J. Farnham, *Rugs in the City*, <hajjibaba.org/rugs-in-the-city>

18 A vivid account of the stand-off between Russia and Britain in Afghanistan is given in Arthur Campbell Yate, *England and Russia Face to Face in Asia: Travels with the Afghan Boundary Commission* (Edinburgh: Blackwell, 1887).

19 Johannes Fabian, *Time and the Other: How Anthropology Makes its Object* (New York: Columbia University Press, 2014).

20 *Turanians and Pan-Turanianism* (London: Naval Staff Intelligence Department, November 1918).

21 For the settling of nomads in the Ottoman Empire see Kasaba, *A Moveable Empire*; in Iran under the Qajar dynasty see Eckart Ehlers, 'Nomadism', *Encyclopaedia Iranica* online, 2011; for Turkmen see Thompson, 'From Nomads to Farmers', in Tapper and Thompson, *The Nomadic Peoples of Iran*.

22 Khalid, *Central Asia*, pp. 223–9.

23 Marianne Kamp and Niccolo Pianciola, 'Collectivisation, Sedentarisation and Famine in Central Asia', *Routledge Handbook of Central Asia*, Rico Isaacs and Erica Marat (eds.) (Abingdon: Routledge, 2021), pp. 41–55.

24 Khalid, *Central Asia*, p. 227.

25 For an account of twentieth-century Kazakh history from the perspective of one village and its inhabitants see Anna Odland Portisch, *A Magpie's Tale: Ethnographic and Historical Perspectives on the Kazakh of Western Mongolia* (New York and London: Berghahn, 2023).

26 Khalid, *Central Asia*, pp. 228–9.

27 V.G. Moshkova, *Carpets of the People of Central Asia*, George W. O'Bannon ed. (Tucson: privately printed, 1996), pp. 5–27.

28 George W. O'Bannon 'Preface and Introduction', Moshkova, *Carpets of the People.*

29 *US Library of Congress Country Studies: Turkmen* (1991).

30 'Turkmen in Afghanistan', *Central Asian Cultural Intelligence for Military Operations*, Marine Corps Intelligence Association, undated, 6–9, https:// info.publicintelligence.net/MCIA-AfghanCultures/Turkmen.pdf

31 Feliccia Yacopino, *Threadlines Pakistan* (Karachi: Ministry of Industries, Government of Pakistan and United Nations Development Programme, 1977), pp. 122–4.

32 *Handmade Carpet Manufacturing* (Karachi: State Bank of Pakistan, 2015)18–21. The State Bank is Pakistan's Central Bank.

33 Trade Development Authority of Pakistan, *Carpet Industry* (Karachi: Trade Development Authority of Pakistan, 2006).

34 State Bank, *Handmade Carpet Manufacturing*, p. 24.

35 Ibid., p. 23.

36 Chris Walter, 'Turkomans in Exile', *Oriental Rug Review*, vol. 9, no. 5, June/July 1989, pp. 28–31. For a project to revive less commercial Turkmen weaving see Chris Walter, 10 March 2010, https://www.culturalsurvival. org/publications/cultural-survival-quarterly/weaving-project-afghan-turkmen

37 Emmett Eiland, 'The Afghan Dilemma', *Hali*, issue 131, November/ December 2003, pp. 153–5.

38 State Bank, *Handmade Carpet Manufacturing*, p. 13.

39 Ceicdata.com/en/pakistan/trade-statistics-by-economic-categories-and-commodity-group-annual/exports-annual-value-carpets—rugs.

Chapter 12: Lost

1 John A. Davis, *Italy in the Nineteenth Century* (Oxford University Press, 2000), pp. 154–78.

2 Beselin, *Knots, Art and History*, p. 20; Linda Komaroff, 'The Coronation Carpet', *Hali*, issue 162, Winter 2009, pp. 46–7. Komaroff, curator at LACMA, suggests that Bode bought the rug in Venice. I have followed the more recent reading of the archives by Beselin, current curator of Bode's collection.

3 Komaroff, 'The Coronation Carpet', pp. 46–7; Thomas Farnham, 'A Tangled Tale', *Hali*, issue 164, Summer 2010, pp. 48–9. A second white-ground animal carpet from slightly later in the sixteenth century, inventory no. KGM73,1195, was also destroyed in the Berlin fire.

4 Bode's memoirs quoted in Erdmann, *Seven Hundred Years of Oriental Carpets*, p. 27.

5 Ibid., p. 28.
6 For an analysis of design see von Bode and Kühnel, *Antique Rugs from the Near East*, pp. 101–2, Erdmann, *Oriental Carpets*, p. 126, fig. 151.
7 Beselin, *Knots*, p. 19.
8 Volkmar Enderlein, 'Wilhelm von Bode and the Berlin Carpet Collection', *Hali*, vol. 69, June/July 1993, pp. 84–95.
9 Lee Sorensen, 'Bode, Wilhelm' *Dictionary of Art Historians*, https://arthistorians.info/bodew/.
10 For Erdmann's biography see Jens Kroeger, 'Kurt Erdmann (1901–1964)', *Journal of Art Historiography*, issue 28, June 2023, pp. 1–26.
11 Erdmann, *Oriental Carpets*, pp. 125–42.
12 Jessica Loudis, 'Haul of Shame: The Trophy Art Taken from Germany by the Red Army', *Apollo*, 6 January 2020.
13 Robert M. Edsel and Bret Witter, *Monuments Men: Allied Heroes, Nazi Thieves and the Greatest Treasure Hunt in History* (London: Arrow Books, 2010), p. 31.
14 Ibid., pp. 97–120.
15 For the Führer Museum and Hitler's history with the arts see Frederick Spotts, *Hitler and the Power of Aesthetics* (London: Hutchison 2002).
16 Edsel and Witter, *Monuments Men*, pp. 382–7.
17 Erdmann, *Oriental Carpets*, p. 125.
18 Pablo Lopez Ruiz, 'Raids', *Berlin Luft Terror*, https://www.berlinluftterror.com/raids
19 Erdmann, *Oriental Carpets*, p. 125.
20 Konstantin Akinsha and Gregorii Kozlov, *Beautiful Loot: The Soviet Plunder of Europe's Art Treasures* (New York: Random House, 1995), p. 54.
21 Beselin, *Knots*, p. 19; Erdmann, *Oriental Carpets*, pp. 125–37.
22 Wilhelm von Bode, 'Ein Altpersischer Teppich im Besitz der Koeniglichen Museen zu Berlin, Studien zur Geschichte der Westasiatische Knupftteppiche' ('An Old Persian Carpet in the Royal Museums in Berlin, Studies on the History of the West Asian Knotted Carpet'), *Jahrbuch der Kgl. Preuszischen Kunstsammlunger*, 13, 1892, pp. 26–49, 108–37. This article formed the basis of the still-influential Bode and Kühnel, *Antique Rugs from the Near East*.
23 Richard Howard, unpublished memoir, quoted in Konstantin Akinsha and Grigorii Kozlov, 'Spoils of War: The Soviet Union's Hidden Art Treasures', *Art News*, April 1991, pp. 54–5.
24 Loudis, 'Haul of Shame'.
25 Beselin, *Knots*, p. 24.
26 Loudis, 'Haul of Shame'.
27 Ibid.

28 Akinsha and Kozlov, 'Spoils of War'.

29 Elizabeth Simpson (ed.), *The Spoils of War, World War II and its Aftermath: The Loss, Reappearance and Recovery of Cultural Property, Conference Proceedings* (New York: Harry N. Abrams and Bard Graduate Center, 1997).

30 J.D. Bindenagel (ed.), *Proceedings of the Washington Conference on Holocaust-Era Assets* (US Department of State and US Holocaust Memorial Museum, 1999).

31 Accounts of personal efforts to track items stolen from European Jews include Anne-Marie O'Connor, *The Lady in Gold* (New York: Knopf, 2015); Edmund de Waal, *The Hare with the Amber Eyes* (New York: Farrar, Strauss and Giroux, 2010). For a bibliography of restitution cases see Victoria Reed, 'Art Restitution', *Oxford Bibliographies*, 2023, https://www.oxfordbibliographies.com/display/document/obo-9780199920105

32 Komaroff, 'The Coronation Carpet', pp. 46–7.

33 See Chapter 6, 'Tycoon' and J. Paul Getty, 27 October 1938, Diary, Getty Institutional Archives, Getty Research Institute.

34 Elizabeth Pegram, 'Provenance as Pedigree: The Marketing of British Portraits in Gilded Age America', in G. Feigenbaum and I. Reist (eds.), *Provenance: An Alternate History of Art* (Los Angeles: Getty Publications, 2012), pp. 105–22.

35 Thomas Farnham, 'A Tangled Tale', *Hali*, issue 164, Summer 2010, pp. 48–9.

36 Beselin, *Knots*, pp. 24–5.

37 Benoit Junod, Georges Khalil, Stefan Weber and Gerhard Wolf (eds.), *Islamic Art and the Museum: Approaches to Art and Archaeology of the Muslim World in the 21st Century* (London: Saqi Books, 2012).

38 *Carpet Exhibition, Research and Conservation in the Museum for Islamic Art, Berlin* (State Museums of Berlin, 2018), https://islamicart.smb.museum/wpcontent/uploads/2021/12/Web_Bro_Carpet.pdf

39 Isabelle Hore-Thornburn, 'Traum und Trauma at the Berlin Museum of Islamic Art', *BerlinArtLink*, 23 November 2018.

40 Mizzi Donner and Carl Schnebel, *I Can Do Handcrafts* (Berlin: Verlag Ullstein, 1922).

41 Beselin, *Knots*, pp. 20–21.

42 Richard Howard, unpublished memoir, quoted in Akinsha and Kozlov, 'Spoils of War', pp. 54–5.

43 *Carpet Exhibition, Research and Conservation*, p. 6.

Epilogue: The Invisible Weaver

1   Ghasem Salimi, *The Sofreh of Kamo* (1998–9). Recent UK showing at *Iconic Iran*, Nomad's Tent, Edinburgh, March 2023.

Bibliography

Vasily Ivanovich Abaev, *The Ossettian Epic Tales of the Narts* (Princeton University Press, 2016)

A Brief History of the Trinitarias Carpet (Glasgow: James Templeton and Company, 1959)

Glenn Adamson, *The Invention of Craft* (London: Bloomsbury, 2013)

Michael Adas (ed.), *Islamic and European Expansion: The Forging of a Global Order* (Philadelphia: Temple University Press, 1993)

Konstantin Akinsha and Grigorii Kozlov, 'Spoils of War: The Soviet Union's Hidden Art Treasures', *Art News*, April 1991

—*Beautiful Loot: The Soviet Plunder of Europe's Art Treasures* (New York: Random House, 1995)

Joseph W. Angell, *Historical Analysis of the 14–15 February 1945 Bombings of Dresden* (Maxwell, Alabama: USAF Historical Division Research Institute, 1953)

Arjun Appadurai (ed.), *The Social Life of Things* (Cambridge University Press, 1988)

Kimball Armayor, 'Did Herodotus Ever Go to the Black Sea?', *Harvard Studies in Classical Philology*, vol. 82, 1978

Felipe Fernandez Armesto, *1492: The Year Our World Began* (London: Bloomsbury, 2010)

Dorothy Armstrong, 'Inventing the Ardabil Carpet: The Appropriation and Transformation of a Persian Artifact', *Iran: The Journal of the British Institute of Persian Studies*, November 2018

—'Wandering Designs: The Repossession of the Oriental Carpet and its Imaginary', in *Rhapsodic Objects: Art, Agency and*

Materiality, Yaelle Biro and Noemie Etienne (eds.) (Boston: De Gruyter, 2021)

—'Technocracy and Persophilia: Carpets in the World of Islam Festival, 1976', *Journal of Art Historiography*, 28, 2023

—'Networks of Coloniality and Capitalism: Two Carpets made in Punjab, 1880–1900', *Journal of the Textile Museum, Washington*, vol. 51, November 2024

Eliyahu Ashtor, *A Social and Economic History of the Near East in the Middle Ages* (London: Collins, 1976)

—*Levant Trade in the Later Middle Ages* (Princeton University Press, 1983)

Esin Atil, *Renaissance of Islam: Art of the Mamluks* (Washington DC: Smithsonian Institution Press, 1981)

Judy Attfield, *Wild Things: The Material Culture of Everyday Life* (Oxford: Berg, 2000)

Siawosch Azadi, *Turcoman Carpets and the Ethnographic Significance of their Ornament*, Robert Pinner trans. (Fishguard: Crosby Press, 1975)

Anna Badkhen, *The World Is a Carpet: Four Seasons in an Afghan Village* (New York: Riverhead Books, 2013)

Martin Bailey, 'British Museum to Finally Display Treasures of Troy', *The Art Newspaper*, 18 June 2019

Malcolm Baker and Brenda Richardson (eds.), *A Grand Design: The Art of the Victoria and Albert Museum* (London: Victoria and Albert Museum, 1997)

Patricia Baker, *Islamic Textiles* (London: British Museum Press, 1985)

Simon Baker, 'A Romanov Coronation Rug', *Hali: The International Journal of Oriental Carpets and Textiles*, issue 95, November 1997

Belkis Balpinar, 'Anatolian Kilims Past and Present', in James Mellaart, Udo Hirsch, Belkis Balpinar, *The Goddess from Anatolia*, vol. 4, (Milan: Eskenazi, 1989)

Nora Elizabeth Barakat, 'Making "Tribes" in the Late Ottoman Empire', *International Journal of Middle East Studies*, 53, 2021

Ludmila Barkova, 'The Pazyryk Fifty Years On', *Hali*, issue 107, 1999

Pennina Barnett, 'Rugs R Us (*And* Them)', *Third Text: Third World Perspectives on Contemporary Art and Culture*, no. 30, Spring 1995

May Beattie, 'The Burrell Collection of Oriental Rugs', *Oriental Art*, vol. 7, no. 4, 1961

—*The Thyssen Bornemisza Collection of Oriental Rugs* (Ticino: The Thyssen Bornemisza Collection, 1972)

—*Carpets of Central Persia* (London: World of Islam Festival Publishing Company, 1976)

—'The Ardabil Carpet', *Encyclopaedia Iranica*, 15 December 1986

Doris Behrens-Abouseif (ed.), *The Arts of the Mamluks in Egypt and Syria: Evolution and Impact* (Bonn University Press, 2012)

William Beinart and Lotte Hughes, *Environment and Empire* (Oxford University Press, 2007)

Martin Bellamy and Isobel MacDonald, *William Burrell: A Collector's Life* (Glasgow Museums Publishing and Birlinn, 2022)

Louisa Bellinger and Ernst Kühnel, *Cairene Rugs and Others Technically Related, 15th–17th Centuries* (Washington DC: Textile Museum, 1957)

Walter Benjamin, 'Paris, Capital of the Nineteenth Century', *The Arcades Project*, Rolf Tiedemann trans. (Cambridge MA: Harvard University Press, 1999)

—'The Work of Art in the Age of Mechanical Reproduction', in Hannah Arendt (ed.), *Illuminations* (London: Pimlico, 1999)

Ian Bennett, 'The Mistress of All Life', *Hali*, issue 50, April 1990

V.M. Berezhkov, *At Stalin's Side – His Interpreter's Memoirs* (New York: Carol Publishing Company, 1994)

Mary Elizabeth Berry, *Hideyoshi* (Cambridge MA: Harvard University Press, 2008)

Anna Beselin, *Knots, Art and History: The Berlin Carpet Collection* (Milan: Skira Editore, 2018)

Carole Bier, 'Carpets for Commerce: Rug Weaving in the Caucasus', *Textile Society of America Symposium Proceedings*, 1990

J.D. Bindenagel (ed.), *Proceedings of the Washington Conference on Holocaust-Era Assets* (Washington DC: US Department of State and US Holocaust Memorial Museum, 1999)

George Birdwood, *Industrial Arts of India* (London: Chapman and Hall, 1880)

David Black and Clive Loveless, *The Undiscovered Kilim* (London: David Black Carpets and Whitechapel Gallery, 1977)

Sheila Blair (ed.), *Text and Image in Medieval Persian Art* (Edinburgh University Press, 2014)

Aleksander Blok, *The Scythians*, trans. Alex Miller (Moscow: Progress Press, 1986)

Isa Blumi, *Ottoman Refugees 1878–1939: Migration in a Post-Imperial World* (London: Bloomsbury, 2015)

Wilhelm von Bode and Ernst Kühnel, *Antique Rugs from the Near East*, trans. Charles Grant Ellis (Berlin: Klinkhardt and Biermann, 1958)

Wilhelm von Bode, 'An Old Persian Carpet in the possession of the Royal Museums in Berlin, Studies on the History of the West Asian Knotted Carpet', *Jahrbuch der Kgl. Preuszischen Kunstsammlunger*, 13, 1892

Andrei Bogolyubov, *Carpets of Central Asia*, J. M. Thompson trans. and ed. (Fishguard: Crosby Press, 1973)

Charles E. Bohlen, *Witness to History: 1929–1969* (New York: W.W. Norton, 1973)

Harald Bohmer, Josephine Powell and Serife Atlihan, *Nomads in Anatolia: Their Life and their Textiles: Encounters with a Vanishing Culture* (Ganderkesee: Remhob Verlag, 2008)

Alberto Boralevi, 'The Cairene Carpets of the Medici', *Hali*, vol. 5, no. 3, 1983

—'A Mamluk Carpet Unveiled', *Hali*, issue 200, 2019

Alexander Borodin, 'Polovtsian Dances' and 'In the Steppes of Central Asia' in Full Score (New York: Dover Publications, 1997)

Pierre Bourdieu, *Distinction*, Richard Nice trans. (London: Routledge, 2010)

Charles Boxer, *The Portuguese Seaborne Empire, 1415–1825* (London: Hutchinson, 1969)

Fernand Braudel, *Wheels of Commerce: Civilisation and Capitalism,*

15th to 18th Centuries (Berkeley: University of California Press, 1983)

Helena Britt (ed.), *Interwoven Connections: The Stoddard-Templeton Design Studio and Design Library, 1843–2005* (Glasgow School of Art, 2013)

Julius Bryant and Susan Weber (eds.), *John Lockwood Kipling: Arts and Crafts in the Punjab and London* (New Haven and London: Yale University Press, 2017)

Hans Burger, Arnold Huijgen and Eric Peels (eds.), *Sola Scriptura: Biblical and Theological Perspectives on Scripture, Authority and Hermeneutics* (Leiden: Brill, 2017)

The Burrell Collection (Harper Collins and Glasgow Museums, 1983)

Filiz Cagman, Nazan Olcer and David J. Roxburgh (eds.), *Turks: A Journey of 1,000 Years 600–1600* (London: Royal Academy of Arts, 2005)

Moya Carey, *Persian Art: Collecting the Arts of Iran for the V&A* (London: V&A Publishing, 2017)

Carpet Exhibition, Research and Conservation in the Museum for Islamic Art, Berlin (State Museums of Berlin, 2018), https://islamicart.smb.museum/wpcontent/uploads/2021/12/Web_Bro_Carpet.pdf

Costanza Carrafa and Avinoam Shalem, '"Hitler's Carpet": A Tale of One City', *Mitteilungen des Kunsthistorischen Institutes in Florenz* 2013

Angelo Cattaneo, 'Geographical Curiosities and Transformative Exchange in the Nanban Century', *Études Epistémes*, 26, 2014

Sir John Chardin, *Voyages du Chevalier Chardin en Perse* (Amsterdam, 1711)

Caspar Purdon Clarke (trans and ed.), *Oriental Carpets: The Catalogue of the 1891 Exhibition at the Handels-Museum, Vienna* (London: South Kensington Museum, 1892)

Ruy Gonzales de Clavijo, *Embassy to Tamerlane 1403–1406*, trans. Clements Robert Markham (London: 1859)

John Colville, *The Fringes of Power: Downing Street Diaries 1939–1955* (London: Phoenix, 2005)

Robert Conquest, *The Great Terror: A Reassessment* (London: Pimlico Press, 2008)

Joseph Conrad, *Heart of Darkness* (Edinburgh: William Blackwood, 1899)

—*Lord Jim* (Edinburgh: William Blackwood, 1901)

Michael Cooper SJ, *They Came to Japan: An Anthology of European Reports on Japan 1543–1640* (London: Thames and Hudson, 1965)

Anthony H. Cordesman, *A Graphic Comparison of the United States, Russia, China and Other Selected Countries* (Washington DC: Center for Strategic and International Studies, 2022)

Louise Allison Cort, 'The Grand Kitano Tea Gathering', *Chanoyu Quarterly*, no. 31, 1982

L.M. Cullen, *A History of Japan 1582–1941: Japan's Internal and External Worlds* (Cambridge University Press, 2003)

Adam Curtis, *Traumazone: Russia 1985–1999* (London: BBC, 2022)

Andrew Cusworth, 'Royal Commission for the Exhibition of 1851' https://royalcommission1851.org/uploads/publications/1049 11851-A5-16pp-Booklet_web.pdf

William Dalrymple, *The Last Mughal: The Fall of a Dynasty, Delhi, 1857* (London: Bloomsbury, 2006)

—*The Anarchy: The Relentless Rise of the East India Company* (London: Bloomsbury, 2019)

Norman Davies, *God's Playground: A History of Poland, vol. 2: 1795 to the Present* (Oxford University Press, 2003)

Peter Davies, *The Tribal Eye: Antique Kilims of Anatolia* (New York: Rizzoli, 1993)

Walter B. Denny, 'Introduction: Carpets and Flat-weaves', *Oxford Islamic Art Online*, 6, 4

—'Turkmen Rugs and Early Rug Weaving in the Western World', *Hali*, vol. 4, no 4, 1982

—'The Origin and Development of Ottoman Court Carpets', *Oriental Carpet and Textile Studies*, vol. 2, 1986

—'The Trinitarias Carpet: Early Masterpiece or Modern Reproduction?', *Art Journal*, 51, 1992

—and Sumru Belger Krody, *The Classical Tradition in Anatolian Carpets* (Washington DC: Textile Museum, 2003)

Selim Deringil, '"They Live in a State of Nomadism and Savagery":
The Late Ottoman Empire and the Post-Colonial Debate',
Journal for the Comparative Study of Society and History, 2003

Nélia Dias, 'Le musée d'ethnographie du Trocadéro (1878–1908)',
Anthropologie et Muséologie en France, CNRS, 1991

Marcel Dieulafoy, *L'Art Antique de la Perse* (Paris: 1884–89)

Maurice Dimand, 'A Loan of Two XVI Century Persian Rugs',
Bulletin of the Metropolitan Museum of Art, 1940

M. Djilas, *Conversations With Stalin* (New York: Harcourt and
Brace, 1962)

Mizzi Donner and Carl Schnebel, *I Can Do Handcrafts* (Berlin:
Verlag Ullstein, 1922)

'The Dothraki and the Scythians: Game of Clones?', British
Museum.org, July 2017

Edward Dreyer, *Zeng He: China and the Oceans in the Early Ming
Dynasty 1405–1433* (New York: Pearson Longman, 2007)

Hilmi Dulkadir, 'The Sarıkeçili Tribe and their Flatweaves',
Oriental Carpet and Textile Studies, 3, no. 2, 1987

Mary Dusenbury, *Colour in Ancient and Medieval East Asia* (New
Haven: Spencer Museum of Art, University of Kansas and Yale
University Press, 2015)

Arindam Dutta, *The Bureaucracy of Beauty: Design in the Age of
its Global Reproducibility* (New York: Routledge, 2006)

Economist, 'Special Report: China Is Making Substantial Investment in Ports and Pipelines Worldwide', 6 February 2020

Robert M. Edsel and Bret Witter, *Monuments Men: Allied Heroes,
Nazi Thieves and the Greatest Treasure Hunt in History* (London:
Arrow Books, 2010)

A. Cecil Edwards, *The Persian Carpet: A Survey of the Carpet-
Weaving Industry of Persia* (London: Gerald Duckworth, 1960)

Albert Eichorn, 'Kronstadt und der orientalische Teppich',
Forschungen zur Volks- und Landeskunde, vol. 11, no. 1, 1968

Charles Grant Ellis, 'The Mystery of the Misplaced Mamluks',
Journal of the Textile Museum, Washington, vol. 2, no. 2, 1967

Kurt Erdmann, 'Carpets from Cairo', *Ars Islamica*, 5, 1938, pp.
179–206; 7, 1940, pp. 55–70

—*Oriental Carpets: An Account of their History*, Charles Grant Ellis trans. (New York: A. Zwemmer, 1960)

—*Europa und der Orientteppich* (Mainz: Florian Kupferberg, 1962)

—*Seven Hundred Years of Oriental Carpets*, Hannah Erdmann and May Beattie (eds.) (London: Faber and Faber, 1970)

Johannes Fabian, *Time and the Other: How Anthropology Makes its Object* (New York: Columbia University Press, 2014)

Thomas Farnham, 'A Tangled Tale', *Hali*, issue 164, Summer 2010

'Fateful Night in the Vault of the Old Mint: The End of the Important Bode Collection', *Hali*, issue 176, June 2013

Abu'l Fazl, *Akbarnama*, Henry Blochman, H.S. Jarrett, D.C. Phillott trans. (Bengal: Royal Asiatic Society, 1977)

G. Feigenbaum and I. Reist (eds.), *Provenance: An Alternate History of Art* (Los Angeles: Getty Research Institute, 2012)

Abul Qasem Ferdowsi, *Shahnama*, 977–1010 CE. For translations see https://www.iranicaonline.org/articles/sah-nama-translations-iii-English

Orlando Figes, *A People's Tragedy: The Russian Revolution, 1891–1924* (London: Bodley Head, 2017)

F. Scott Fitzgerald, *The Great Gatsby* (New York: Charles Scribner's Sons, 1925)

Sheila Fitzpatrick, *The Russian Revolution* (Oxford University Press, 2017)

Willem Floor, *The Persian Textile Industry in Historical Perspective, 1500–1925* (Paris: L'Harmattan, 1999)

Valerie Foley, 'The *Jinbaori*: Oneupmanship on the Battlefield', *Textile Society of America Symposium Proceedings*, 1992

Michel Foucault, *Discipline and Punish: The Birth of the Prison*, Alan Sheridan trans. (London: Penguin, 1991)

Peter Frankopan, *The Silk Roads: A New History of the* World (London: Bloomsbury, 2015)

Michael Franses and Robert Pinner (eds.), 'East Mediterranean Carpets in the V&A', *Hali*, vol. 4, no. 1, 1981

— 'Mamluk: Special Edition', *Hali*, vol. 4, no. 1, 1984

—'Turkish Carpets in the Victoria and Albert Museum', *Hali*, vol. 6, no. 4, 1984

W. Hamish Fraser and Irene Maver (eds.), *Glasgow: 1830–1912* (Manchester University Press, 1997)

Burton B. Fredericksen, *The Burdens of Wealth: Paul Getty and his Museum* (Bloomington IN: Archway Publications, 2015)

Sheila Fruman, *Pull of the Thread: Textile Travels of a Generation* (London: Hali Publications, 2023)

Susan Westhafer Furukawa, *The Afterlife of Toyotomi Hideyoshi: Historical Fiction and Popular Culture in Japan* (Cambridge MA: Harvard University Asia Center, 2022)

Noorah Al-Gailani, *Introducing Islamic Carpets: The Burrell Collection* (Glasgow Museums Publishing, 2022)

Volkmar Gantzhorn, *The Oriental Carpet*, previously *The Christian Oriental Carpet* (Cologne: Taschen, 1998)

Sharif Gemie and Brian Ireland, *The Hippie Trail: A History* (Manchester University Press, 2017)

John Paul Getty, Diaries, Institutional Archives, Getty Research Institute, Malibu

—*My Life and Fortunes* (New York: Duell Sloan and Pearce, 1963)

—*How to Be Rich* (Chicago: The Playboy Press, 1966)

—*The Joys of Collecting* (London: Country Life Press, 1966)

—*The Golden Age* (New York: Trident Press 1968)

—*As I See It* (London: W.H. Allen, 1976)

Elizabeth Gill, 'From Turkey to Transylvania', *Hali*, 86, May 1996

Marija Gimbutas, *The Civilisation of the Goddess: The World of Old Europe* (New York: Harper and Row, 1991)

Arthur Gobineau, *An Essay of the Inequality of Races* (Paris, 1853–55)

—*Histoire des Perses* (Paris, 1869)

Sean Gough, 'The Mamluk Sultanate', *Hali*, vol. 4, issue 1, 1981

Antonio Gramsci: *Pre-Prison Writings*, Richard Bellamy ed., Virginia Cox trans. (Cambridge University Press, 1994)

—*Selections from the Prison Notebooks*, Quinton Hoare ed. (London: Lawrence and Wishart, 1999)

Walter Gropius, I. Gropius and H. Bayer (eds.), *Bauhaus 1919–28* (London: Secker and Warburg, 1975)

Hans Gutbrod, 'The Ethics of Political Commemoration: The

Stalin Museum and Thorny Legacies in the Post-Soviet Space',
Policy Memo, *PONARS Eurasia*, 23 March 2022

Christine Guth, *Craft Culture in Early Modern Japan: Materials,
Makers, and Mastery* (Oakland: University of California Press,
2022)

S. Hales and J. Paul (eds.), *Pompeii in the Public Imagination from
Its Rediscovery to Today* (Oxford University Press, 2011)

Jessica Hallet and Teresa Pacheco Pereira (eds.), *The Oriental
Carpet in Portugal* (Lisbon: Museu Nacional de Arte Antiga,
2007)

Eugene Halton, *From the Axial Age to the Moral Revolution: Karl
Jaspers, John-Stuart Glennie and a New Understanding of the
Idea* (Basingstoke: Palgrave Macmillan, 2014)

Yuval Noah Harari, *Sapiens* (London: Vintage, 2015)

Christopher Harding, *The Japanese: A History in 22 Lives* (London:
Penguin, 2022)

Kimberley Hart (ed.), *What Josephine Saw: Twentieth Century
Photographic Visions of Rural Anatolia* (Istanbul: Koç University
Press, 2012)

François Hartog, *The Mirror of Herodotus: The Representation of
the Other in the Writing of History*, trans. Janet Lloyd (Berkeley:
University of California Press, 1988)

Leonard Helfgott, *The Ties That Bind: A Social History of the
Iranian Carpet* (Washington DC: Smithsonian Institute, 1994)

Herodotus, *The Histories*, Book Four, trans. Tom Holland (London:
Penguin, 2013)

R. Hewins, *The Richest American* (London: Sidgwick & Jackson,
1960)

Money L. Hickman (ed.), *Japan's Golden Age: Momoyama* (New
Haven and London: Yale University Press, 1996)

Dan Hicks, *The Brutish Museums: The Benin Bronzes, Colonial
Violence and Cultural Restitution* (London: Pluto, 2020)

Carole Hillenbrand, *Islam and the Crusades* (Edinburgh University
Press, 2022)

Robert Hillenbrand, *Islamic Art and Architecture* (London: Thames
and Hudson, 1996)

Eric Hobsbawm, *Age of Empire: 1875–1914* (London: Abacus, 1989)

Ian Hodder, 'Women and Men at Çatalhöyük', *Scientific American*, vol. 290, no. 1, 2004

W.R. Holmes, *Sketches on the Shores of the Caspian* (London: Richard Bentley, 1845)

Hiroyuki Honda, *The 16th-Century Silver Rush in East Asia, and the Unification of Japan* (Tokyo: Yoshikawa Kobunkan, 2015)

Robert Hopkins, *Witness to History: Recollections of a World War II Photographer* (Seattle: Castle Pacific Publishing, 2002)

Peter Hopkirk, *The Great Game: On Secret Service in High Asia* (London: John Murray, 1990)

Isabelle Hore-Thornburn, '*Traum und Trauma* at the Berlin Museum of Islamic Art', *BerlinArtLink*, 23 November 2018

Vicki Howard, *From Main Street to Mall* (Philadelphia: University of Pennsylvania Press, 2016)

Tristram Hunt, *Ten Cities that Made an Empire* (London: Penguin, 2015)

Halil Inalcik, *The Ottoman Empire: The Classical Age 1300–1600* (London: Weidenfeld & Nicolson, 1973)

—'The Yuruks: Their Origins, Expansion and Economic Role', *Oriental Carpet and Textile Studies*, 2, 1986

—and Donald Quaetart, *An Economic and Social History of the Ottoman Empire* (Cambridge University Press, 1994)

Stefano Ionescu, *Antique Ottoman Rugs in Transylvania* (Rome: Verduci Editore, 2005)

—(ed.), *Handbook of Fakes by Tuduc* (Rome: Verduci Editore, 2012)

—*The Transylvanian Heritage: A New Perspective (on Transylvanian Rugs circa 1450–1700)*, expected publication date 2024

Rico Isaacs and Erica Marat (eds.), *Routledge Handbook of Central Asia* (London: Routledge, 2021)

Charles Issawi (ed.), *The Economic History of Iran 1800–1914* (University of Chicago Press, 1971)

Peter Jackson, *The Mongols and the Islamic World: From Conquest to Conversion* (New Haven and London: Yale University Press, 2017)

Mark Jones (ed.), *Fake? The Art of Deception* (Berkeley: California University Press, 1990)

Owen Jones, *The Grammar of Ornament* (London: Day and Sons, 1856)

Matthew Josephson, *The Robber Barons: The Great American Capitalists 1861–1901* (New York: Harcourt Brace International, 1962)

Benoit Junod, Georges Khalil, Stefan Weber and Gerhard Wolf (eds.), *Islamic Art and the Museum: Approaches to Art and Archaeology of the Muslim World in the 21st Century* (London: Saqi Books, 2012)

Rana Kabanni, *Imperial Fictions: Europe's Myths of the Orient* (London: Saqi books, 1986)

Yuka Kadoi, 'Cintamani: Notes on the Formation of the Turco-Iranian Style', *Persica*, 21, 2006–07

—and Ivan Szanto (eds.), *The Shaping of Persian Art* (Newcastle Upon Tyne: Cambridge Scholars Publishing, 2013)

Nobuko Kajitani and Kōjirō Yoshida (eds.), *A Survey of the Gion Festival Float Hangings: Imported Textiles Section* (Kyoto: Gion Matsuri Yama Hoko Rengokai, 1992)

Hasan Kakar, *A Political and Diplomatic History of Afghanistan, 1863–1901* (Leiden: Brill, 2006)

Yumiko Kamada, 'The Use of Imported Persian and Indian Textiles in Early Modern Japan', *Textile Society of America Symposium Proceedings*, September 2012

Reşat Kasaba, *A Moveable Empire: Ottoman Nomads, Migrants and Refugees* (University of Washington Press, 2007)

—'Nomads and Tribes in the Ottoman Empire', in Christine Woodhead (ed.), *The Ottoman World* (Abingdon: Taylor and Francis, 2011)

Nikki Keddie and Rudi Mathee (eds.), *Iran and the Surrounding World: Interactions in Culture and Cultural Politics* (University of Washington Press, 2002)

A.F. Kendrick and C.E.C. Tattersall, *Handwoven Carpets: Oriental and European* (London: Benn Brothers, 1922)

Liatif Kerimov, Nonna Stepanian, Tatyana Grigoliya and David Tsitsishvili, *Rugs and Carpets from the Caucasus: The Russian Collections* (Leningrad: Aurora Publishers and London: Penguin Books, 1984)

Jack Kerouac, *The Dharma Bums* (New York: Viking, 1958)

Mehdi Keyvani, *Artisans and Guild Life in the Later Safavid Period* (Berlin: Klaus Schwarz Verlag, 1982)

Ibn Khaldun, *The Muqaddimah: An Introduction to History*, N.J. Dawood ed. (Princeton University Press, 1969)

Adeeb Khalid, *Central Asia: A New History from the Imperial Conquests to the Present* (Princeton University Press, 2021)

Yasmin Khan, *The Great Partition* (New Haven and London: Yale University Press, 2007)

Charles King, *The Reinvention of Humanity* (London: Bodley Head, 2019)

Donald King and David Sylvester (eds.), *The Eastern Carpet in The Western World: From the 15th to the 17th Century* (London: Arts Council of Great Britain, 1983)

Rudyard Kipling, *Kim* (Macmillan, 1901)

Leo S. Klejn, *Soviet Archaeology: Trends, Schools and History*, Rosh Ireland and Kevin Windle trans. (Oxford University Press, 2012)

Linda Komaroff (ed.), 'Exhibiting the Middle East: Collections and Perceptions of Islamic Art', *Ars Orientalis*, 30, 2000

—'The Coronation Carpet', *Hali*, issue 162, Winter 2009

P.G. Konody and Tessa Murdoch, 'Caspar Purdon Clarke', *Oxford Dictionary of National Biography* (Oxford University Press, 2004)

Sumru Belger Krody, *A Nomad's Art: Kilims of Anatolia* (Washington DC: Textile Museum, 2018)

Jens Kroeger, 'Kurt Erdmann (1901–1964)', *Journal of Art Historiography*, issue 28, June 2023

Wladyslaw B. Kubiak, *Al-Fustat: Its Foundation and Early Development* (The American University of Cairo Press, 1987)

Olli Lagerspetz, *A Philosophy of Dirt* (London: Reaktion Books, 2018)

C. Latimer, *Monograph on Carpet-Making in the Punjab, 1905–6* (Lahore, 1907)

—'Carpet-Making in the Punjab', *Journal of Indian Art and Industry*, vol. 17, no. 131, 1916

Robert Lenzer, *The Great Getty* (New York: Signet, 1985)

Julius Lessing, *Ancient Oriental Carpet Patterns after Pictures and Originals of the Fifteenth and Sixteenth Centuries* (Berlin: 1877, London: 1879)

Jung-Pang Lo, *Empire in the Western Ocean: Sea Power and the Early Ming Navy 1355–1449* (Chinese University of Hong Kong Press, 2023)

Bevis Longstreth, 'The Riddle of the Pazyryk', *Hali*, issue 137, 2004

—*The Spindle and the Bow* (London: Hali Publications, 2005)

Adolf Loos, 'Ornament and Crime', *Les Cahiers d'Aujourd'hui*, 1913

Jessica Loudis, 'Haul of Shame: The Trophy Art Taken from Germany by the Red Army', *Apollo*, 6 January 2020

Clive Loveless, 'The Discovered Kilim', *Hali*, issue 154, Winter 2007

Janet Abu-Lughod, *Before European Hegemony: The World System 1250–1350* (Oxford University Press, 1989)

Janet L. Abu-Lughod, *Cairo: 1001 Years of the City Victorious* (Princeton University Press, 1971)

Martin Lynn, *British Policy, Trade and Informal Empire in the Mid-19th Century* (Oxford University Press, 1999)

Roy Macey, 'Romanian Carpets: A Modern Industry', *Hali*, vol. 2, no. 1, 1979

James MacGregor Burns, *Roosevelt: Soldier of Freedom* (New York: Harcourt Brace Jovanovich, 1970)

Rosamond E. Mack, *Bazaar to Piazza: Islamic Trade and Italian Art*, 1300–1600 (Berkeley: University of California Press, 2002)

John M. MacKenzie and Tom Devine (eds.), *Scotland and the British Empire* (Oxford University Press, 2011)

Louise Mackie, 'Woven Status: Mamluk Silks and Carpets', *The Muslim World*, 1983

Louise Mackie and Jon Thompson (eds.), *Turkmen: Tribal Carpets and Traditions* (Washington DC: Textile Museum, 1980)

—'May Beattie: Biographical Note and Bibliography', *Oriental Carpet and Textile Studies*, 3, 1987

Naoise MacSweeney, *The West: A New History of an Old Idea* (London: W.H. Allen, 2023)

Marla Mallet, 'A Weaver's View of the Çatalhöyük Controversy', *Oriental Rug Review*, 1990

—'The Goddess from Anatolia, an updated view of the Çatalhöyük Controversy', *Oriental Rug Review*, 1993

Suzanne Marchand, *German Orientalism in the Age of Empire: Religion, Race and Scholarship* (Cambridge University Press, 2009)

Richard Marks, *Sir William Burrell 1861–1958* (Glasgow Museums and Art Galleries, 1985)

A.H. de Oliviera Marques, *A History of Portugal* (New York: Columbia University Press, 1972)

Saloni Mathur, 'Living Ethnological Exhibits: The Case of 1886', *Cultural Anthropology*, vol. 15, no. 4, November 2000

Mark Mazower, *Dark Continent: Europe's Twentieth Century* (London: Penguin, 1998)

Abigail McGowan '"All that is Rare, Characteristic or Beautiful": Design and the Defence of Tradition in Colonial India, 1851–1903', *Journal of Material Culture*, vol. 10, no. 3, 2005

—'Convict Carpets: Jails and the Revival of Historic Carpet Design in Colonial India', *The Journal of Asian Studies*, vol. 72, no. 2, May 2013

Jonathan Meades, *Museum Without Walls* (London: Unbound, 2013)

James Mellaart, 'Some notes on the pre-history of Anatolian kilims', in *Early Turkish Tapestries*, Bertram Frauenknecht (ed), (B. Frauenknecht, 1984)

—'Çatalhöyük and Anatolian Kilims', in Mellaart, Hirsch, Balpinar, *The Goddess from Anatolia*, vol. 2 (Milan: Eskenazi, 1989)

— 'Under the Volcano', *Cornucopia: Turkey for Connoisseurs*, vol. 4, issue 19, 1999

Russell Miller, *The House of Getty* (New York: Henry Holt, 1986)

Steven Mithen, *After the Ice: A Global Human History 20,000–5000 BCE* (London: Weidenfeld & Nicolson, 2003)

Partha Mitter, *Much Maligned Monsters: A History of European*

Reactions to Indian Art (Chicago University Press, 1992)

A.L. Mongait, *Archaeology in the USSR*, M.W. Thompson trans. and ed. (London: Penguin, 1961)

Rowan Moore, 'Britain's Most Influential Modern Architect? In Praise of the Lost Buildings of Georgie Wolton', the *Observer*, 8 October 2023

Alexander Morrison, *The Russian Conquest of Central Asia: A Study in Imperial Expansion 1814–1914* (Cambridge University Press, 2020)

V.G. Moshkova, *Carpets of the People of Central Asia*, George W. O'Bannon trans. and ed. (Tucson: Printed privately, 1996)

Ali Mozzaffari and James Barry, 'Heritage and Territorial Disputes in the Armenia–Azerbaijan Conflict: A Comparative Analysis of the Carpet Museums of Baku and Shusha', *International Journal of Heritage Studies*, vol. 28 no. 3, 2022

J.K. Mumford, *Oriental Carpets* (New York: Charles Scribner's Sons, 1903)

—*The Yerkes Collection of Rugs and Carpets* (New York: The Knapp Company, 1910)

Myriem Naji, 'A Falsification of Temporality: Carpet Distressing in Morocco', in *Surface Tensions*, Glenn Adamson and Victoria Kelley (eds.) (Manchester University Press, 2013)

Thomas Nelson, 'Slavery in Medieval Japan', *Monumenta Nipponica*, 59, 2004

R. Neugebauer and Siegfried Troll, *Oriental Carpet Science* (Leipzig: Hiersemann, 1923)

P.Fr. Florencio del Nino-Jesus, *En Persia 1608–1624* (Pamplona: Ramon Bergeray, Biblioteca Carmelitano-Teresiana de Misiones, 1929-30)

Anne-Marie O'Connor, *The Lady in Gold* (New York: Knopf, 2015)

Marino Dall'Oglio, 'White Ground Anatolian Carpets', in *Oriental Carpet and Textile Studies*, 2, 1986

Marino and Clara Dall'Oglio (eds.), *Turkish Rugs from Transylvania*, The Crosby Press, 1977

Halle O'Neal (ed.), 'Reuse, Recycle, Repurpose: The Afterlives of Japanese Material Culture', *Ars Orientalis*, 52, 2022

Kelly Anne O'Neill, *Claiming Crimea: A History of Catherine the Great's Southern Empire* (New Haven and London: Yale University Press, 2015)

R.J. Overy, *The Nazi Economic Recovery 1932–38* (Cambridge University Press, 1992)

Robert Treat Paine and Alexander Soper, *Art and Architecture of Japan* (New Haven and London: Yale University Press, 1981)

Maria Pakucs-Willcocks, 'Transylvania and its International Trade 1525–1575', *Annales Universitatis Apulensis*, Series Historica, 16/11, 2012

Cecil Parham, 'How Altaic/Nomadic Is the Pazyryk Carpet?', *Oriental Rug Review*, vol. 13, no. 5, 1993

R.D. Parsons, *The Carpets of Afghanistan* (Woodbridge: Antique Collectors Club, 1983)

Emese Pasztor, *'Transylvanian' Turkish Rugs: Tracing the Ottoman Rugs from the 1914 Budapest Exhibition* (Budapest: Museum of Applied Arts, 2020)

Elizabeth Pegram, 'Provenance as Pedigree: The Marketing of British Portraits in Gilded Age America', in G. Feigenbaum and I. Reist (eds.), *Provenance: An Alternate History of Art* (Los Angeles: Getty Publications, 2012)

John Perkins, 'Coins for Conflict: Nickel and the Axis, 1933–1945', *The Historian*, vol. 55, no. 1, Autumn 1992

Carl F. Petry, *The Mamluk Sultanate: A History* (Cambridge University Press, 2022)

Yanni Petsopoulis and Belkis Balpinar (eds.), *100 Kilims: Masterpieces from Anatolia* (London: Laurence King Publishing, 1991)

Henning Pieper, *Fegelein's Horsemen and Genocidal Warfare: The SS Cavalry Brigade in the Soviet Union* (Basingstoke: Palgrave Macmillan, 2015)

Robert Pinner, 'The Earliest Carpets', *Hali:*, vol. 5, no. 2, 1982

—and Walter Denny (eds.), 'Carpets of the Mediterranean Countries: 1400 – 1600', *Oriental Carpet and Textile Studies*, 2, 1986

Plutarch, 'On the Malice of Herodotus', *Moralia*, Lionel Pearson trans. (Loeb Classical Library: W. Heinemann and Harvard University, 1965)

Arthur Upham Pope and Phyllis Ackermann (eds.), *A New Survey of Persian Art* (Oxford University Press, 1938)

Anna Odland Portisch, *A Magpie's Tale: Ethnographic and Historical Perspectives on the Kazhak of Western Mongolia* (New York and London: Berghahn, 2023)

Christine Poulson (ed), *William Morris on Art and Design* (Sheffield University Press, 1996)

Diana Preston, *Eight Days at Yalta: How Churchill, Roosevelt and Stalin Shaped the Post-War World* (London: Picador, 2019)

Kavita Puri, *Partition Voices* (London: Bloomsbury, 2019)

Magtymguly Pyragi, *Magtymguly: Poems from Turkmenistan*, Paul Taylor trans. (Washington DC: Smithsonian Institute in association with the National Institute of Manuscripts, Turkmenistan Academy of Sciences, 2014)

Julian Raby, 'Court and Export: Part 1. Market Demands in Ottoman Carpets 1450–1550'; 'Court and Export: Part 2. The Ushak Carpets', *Oriental Carpet and Textile Studies*, vol. 2, 1986

Victoria Reed, 'Art Restitution', *Oxford Bibliographies*, 2023, https://www.oxfordbibliographies.com/display/document/obo-9780199920105

Report on the Punjab Exhibition 1881–2: Selections from the Records of the Government of the Punjab and its Dependencies, new series no. 22 (Lahore: Punjab Government Secretariat Press, 1883)

Alois Riegl et al., *Katalog der Ausstellung Orientalischer Teppiche im K. K. Handels-Museum* (Vienne: Verlag des K. K. Österr. Handels-Museum, 1891)

Jonathan Riley-Smith, *The Crusades: A Short History* (New Haven and London: Yale University Press, 1987)

Kishwar Rizvi, *The Safavid Dynastic Shrine: Architecture, Religion and Power in Early Modern Iran* (London: I.B. Tauris, 2011)

J.M. Rogers, *Islamic Art and Design 1500–1700* (London: British Museum, 1983)

Ioan-Gheorge Rotaru, 'Johannes Honterus', *Jurnal Teologic*, vol. 17, no. 9, 2018

Kathryn Rountree, 'Archaeologists and Goddess Feminists at Çatalhöyük: An Experiment in Multivocality', *Journal of Feminist Studies in Religion*, vol. 23, no. 2, Fall 2007

Tirthanker Roy, *Traditional Industry in the Economy of Colonial India* (Cambridge University Press, 1999)

S.I. Rudenko, *The Frozen Tombs of Siberia: The Pazyryk Burials of Iron Age Horsemen*, M.W. Thompson trans. and ed. (Berkeley: University of California Press, 1970)

Vincenzo Ruggiero, *Dirty Money: On Financial Delinquency* (Oxford University Press, 2015)

Pablo Lopez Ruiz, 'Raids', *Berlin Luft Terror*, https://www.berlin luftterror.com/raids

Michael Ryder, 'A Note on the Wool Type in Carpet Yarns from the Pazyryk', *Oriental Carpet and Textile Studies*, 3, 1987

Edward Said, *Orientalism* (New York: Pantheon, 1978)

Mehmet Saray, *The Turkmens in the Age of Imperialism: A Study of the Turkmen People and Their Incorporation into the Russian Empire* (Ankara: Turkish Historical Society, 1989)

Friedrich Sarre and Robert Martin, *Die Ausstellung von Meisterwerken* (Munich: Bruckmann, 1912)

Friedrich Sarre and Hermann Trenkwald, *Old Oriental Carpets* (Vienna: Schroll and Herzmann, 1926)

Jennifer Scarce, 'The Burrell Collection of Oriental Carpets', *Arts of Asia*, vol. 20, no. 3, May–June 1990

Emil Schmutzler, *Old Oriental Carpets in Siebenbürgen* (Leipzig: Hiersemann, 1933)

Ulrich Schurmann, *Central Asian Rugs* (Frankfurt: Verlag Osterrieth, 1969)

—'The Pazyryk: Its Use and Origin', *Symposium of the Armenian Rug Society*, New York, September 1982

Hillel Schwartz, *The Culture of the Copy: Striking Likenesses, Unreasonable Facsimiles* (Cambridge MA: MIT Press, 1998)

Oleg Semenov, 'Oriental Carpets and the Russian Interior in the 19th Century', *Oriental Carpet and Textile Studies*, 1, 1985

Gottfried Semper, *The Four Elements of Architecture* (1851), Harry

Francis Mallgrave and Wolfgang Hermann trans. (Cambridge University Press, 2011)

Satadru Sen, *Disciplined Natives, Race, Freedom and Confinement in Colonial India* (Delhi: Primus Books, 2012)

'The Shimabara Rebellion', *In Our Time*, BBC Radio 4 podcast, 11 May 2023

Larry Shiner, *The Invention of Art: A Cultural History* (University of Chicago Press, 2003)

Victor A. Shnirelman, 'Archaeology, Nationalism and "The Arctic Homeland"', in *Selective Remembrances: Archaeology in the Construction, Commemoration and Consecration of National Pasts*, Philip L. Kohl, Maria Kozelski and Nachman Ben-Yehuda (eds.) (University of Chicago Press, 2007)

Elizabeth Simpson (ed.), *The Spoils of War, World War II and its Aftermath: The Loss, Reappearance and Recovery of Cultural Property, Conference Proceedings* (New York: Harry N. Abrams and Bard Graduate Center, 1997)

St John Simpson and Svetlana Pankova (eds.), *Scythians: Warriors of Ancient Siberia* (London and St Petersburg: Thames and Hudson, British Museum and Hermitage Museum, 2017)

Ganda Singh, *The Indian Mutiny of 1857: The Sikhs* (Delhi Sikh Student Federation, 1969)

Aleksandr Solzhenitsyn, *Gulag Archipelago* (London and New York: Harper Collins, 2007); *Cancer Ward* (London: Bodley Head, 1968)

Muriel Spark, *A Far Cry from Kensington* (London: Constable, 1988)

Laura Spinney, 'Ukraine's Museums Keep Watch over Priceless Gold in Bid to Halt Russian Looters', the *Guardian*, 18 December 2022

Frederick Spotts, *Hitler and the Power of Aesthetics* (London: Hutchison, 2002)

Friedrich Spuhler, 'Chessboard Rugs', *Oriental Carpet and Textile Studies*, vol. 2, 1986

—*Carpets and Textiles: The Thyssen Bornemisza Collection* (London: Philip Wilson Publishers, 2003)

Rexford Stead, *The Ardabil Carpets* (Malibu: The J. Paul Getty Museum, 1974)

Edward Stebbing, *The Holy Carpet of the Mosque at Ardebil: A Monograph* (London: Robinson and Company, 1892)

Bram Stoker, *Dracula* (London: Vintage, 2019)

Sanjay Subrahmanyam, *The Portuguese Empire in Asia 1500–1700: A Political and Economic History* (Oxford: Wiley-Blackwell, 2012)

Ronald Grigor Suny, 'The Hamidian Massacres, 1894–1897', *Études Arméniennes Contemporains*, vol. 11, 2018

Carlo Maria Suriano, 'Mamluk Blazon Carpets', *Hali*, issue 97, 1998

David Sylvester (ed.), *Islamic Carpets from the Collection of Joseph V. McMullan* (London: Arts Council of Great Britain, 1972)

—and Donald King (eds.), *The Eastern Carpet in the Western World: From the 15th to the 17th Century* (London: Arts Council of Great Britain, 1983)

Roya Taghiyeva, 'The Art of Azerbaijani Carpet Weaving in the Context of Intercivilisational Dialogue', *Geo-Culture*, vol. 3, no. 2–3, 2009

Richard Tapper and Jon Thompson (eds.), *The Nomadic Peoples of Iran* (London: Azimuth, 2002)

Johann Baptiste Tavernier, *Les Six Voyages de J.B. Tavernier en Turquie en Perse et aux Indes* (Paris: 1676)

Ghoncheh Tazmini, 'The Persian–Portuguese Encounter in Hormuz: Orientalism Reconsidered', *Iranian Studies*, vol. 50, no. 2, 2017

E.L. Thompson, 'J. Paul Getty's Motivations for Collecting Antiquities', *Adalya*, 19, 2016

Jon Thompson, *Carpets from the Tents, Cottages and Workshops of Asia* (London: Barrie & Jenkins, 1988)

—and Harald Bohmer, 'The Pazyryk Carpet', *Notes in the History of Art*, vol. 10, no. 4, 1991

—and Sheila R. Canby (eds.), *Hunt for Paradise: Court Arts of Safavid Iran 1501–1576* (Milan: Skira Editore, 2003)

—*Milestones in the History of Carpets* (Milan: Moshe Tabibnia, 2006)

Ronald P. Toby, *State and Diplomacy in Modern Japan: Asia in the Development of the Tokugawa Bakufu* (Stanford University Press, 1991)

John Train, *Oriental Carpet Symbols: Their Origins and Meaning from the Middle East to China* (London: Philip Wilson, 2001)

A.S. Travis, *The Rainbow Makers: The Origins of the Synthetic Dye-stuffs Industry in the West* (London and Toronto: Associated Universities Press, 1993)

Stephen Turnbull, *Toyotomi Hideyoshi: Leadership, Strategy, Conflict* (Oxford: Osprey Publishing, 2010)

—*The Samurai* (Oxford: Osprey Publishing, 2016)

Richard W. Unger (ed.), *Shipping and Economic Growth 1350–1850* (Leiden: Brill, 2011)

E. Le Vane and J.P. Getty, *Collector's Choice: The Chronicle of an Artistic Odyssey through Europe* (London: W.H. Allen, 1955)

Gyula Vegh and Karoly Layer, *Turkish Rugs in Transylvania*, Marino and Clara Dall'Oglio (eds.) (Fishguard: The Crosby Press, 1977)

Stephen Vernoit and Doris Behrens-Abouseif (eds.), *Discovering Islamic Art: Scholars, Collecting and Collections 1850–1950* (London: I.B. Tauris, 2000)

Kurt Vonnegut, *Slaughterhouse Five* (New York: Delacorte Press, 1969)

—*Palm Sunday: An Autobiographical Collage* (New York: Delacorte Press, 1981)

Judith Vos (ed.), 'Josephine Powell (1919–2007): Traveller, Photographer and Collector in the Muslim World', *Bulletin of the Tropenmuseum*, 384, 2008

Edmund de Waal, *The Hare with the Amber Eyes* (New York: Farrar, Strauss and Giroux, 2010)

Kim A. Wagner, *Amritsar: An Empire of Fear and the Making of a Massacre* (New Haven and London: Yale University Press, 2019)

Bethany J. Walker, 'Rethinking Mamluk Textiles', *Mamluk Studies Review*, vol.4, 2000

Daniel Walker, 'Rugs in the Gion Matsuri Preservation Associations', in Nobuko Kajitani and Kōjirō Yoshida (eds.), *A*

Survey of the Gion Festival Float Hangings: Imported Textiles Section (Kyoto: Gion Matsuri Yama Hoko Rengokai, 1992)

—*Flowers Under Foot: Indian Carpets of the Mughal Era* (London: Thames and Hudson, 1998)

Chris Walter, 'Turkomans in Exile', *Oriental Rug Review*, vol. 9, no. 5, June/July 1989

Marina Warner, 'Freud's Couch: A Case History', *Raritan*, vol. 31, no. 2, 2011

—*Stranger Magic: Charmed States and the Arabian Nights* (London: Chatto and Windus, 2011)

James Waterson, *The Knights of Islam: The Wars of the Mamluks* (London: Greenhill Books, 2007)

Oliver Watson, 'Authentic Forgeries', in *Creating Authenticity: Authentication Processes in Ethnographic Museums*, Alexander Geurds and Laura van Broekhoven (eds.) (Leiden: Sidestone Press, 2013)

Jennifer Wearden, 'The V&A Ardabil: The Early Repairs', *Hali*, issue 80, 1995

Max Weber, *The Protestant Ethic and the Spirit of Capitalism, 1904–5* (London: Unwin Hyman, 1930)

Alyson Wharton-Dugaryan, '"I have the honour to inform you that I have just arrived from Constantinople": Migration, Identity and Property Disavowal in the Formation of the Islamic Art Collection at the V&A', *Museum and Society*, July 2020

Francis Wheen, *The Soul of Indiscretion: Tom Driberg, Poet, Philanderer, Legislator and Outlaw* (London: HarperCollins, 2001)

M.C. Whiting, 'A Report on the Dyes of the Pazyryk Carpet', *Oriental Carpet and Textile Studies*, 1, 1985

D. Woodward (ed.), *The History of Cartography: 1806–1851*, vol. 3, part 2 (Chicago University Press, 2015)

Richard E. Wright, 'Caucasian Carpets', Carpets XV, *Encyclopaedia Iranica*, vol. 5/1

Feliccia Yacopino, *Threadlines Pakistan* (Karachi: Ministry of Industries, Government of Pakistan and United Nations Development Programme, 1977)

Aki Yamakawa, 'Japanese Warriors' Surcoats (Jinbaori) in the Age of Exploration', *ICOM Costume Committee Proceedings*, Kyoto, 2019

Suga Yasuko, 'Designing the Morality of Consumption: "Chamber of Horrors" at the Museum of Ornamental Art, 1852–53', *Design Issues*, vol. 20, no. 4, Autumn 2004

Arthur Campbell Yate, *England and Russia Face to Face in Asia: Travels with the Afghan Boundary Commission* (Edinburgh: Blackwell, 1887)

Fred H. Young, *A Century of Carpet-Making 1839–1939* (Glasgow: Collins, 1943)

M. Hakan Yuvuz and Michael Gunter (eds.), *The Nagorno-Karabagh Conflict: Historical and Political Perspectives* (London: Routledge, 2022)

Eberhard Zangger, 'Facts, Fantasies and Forgeries: Discussing James Mellaart', *Talanta: Proceedings of the Dutch Archaeological and Historical Society*, vol. 50, 2018

Agnes Ziegler and Frank-Thomas Ziegler, *In Honour of God, for Adornment and Use by the Honourable Guild* (Braşov: Printed privately, 2019)

Emile Zola, *Ladies' Delight*, trans. April Fitzlyon (London: John Calder, 1957)

Acknowledgements

In 2011 I first dipped my toe in the waters that became this book. I'd like to thank everyone who gave me the courage to swim in them.

An incomplete list includes my colleagues, students and mentors at the School of Oriental and African Studies, the Victoria and Albert Museum, the Royal College of Art, Edinburgh University and its College of Art, Oxford University and its Ashmolean Museum; in particular Christine Guth, Sarah Cheang, James Ryan, Spike Sweeting, Yun Wang, Artun Ozguner, Xueqing Xi, Swati Venkat, Hatice Yildiz, Jennifer Wearden, Melanie Gibson, George Manginis, Jas Elsner, Farniyaz Zaker, Francesca Leoni and Sue Stanton. The *Under the Carpet Collective* of Myriem Naji, Anna Portisch, Ludovica Matarrozo, Aida Balafkan and Jonathan Cleaver has been a source of inspiration and laughter. I think I would have lost faith in the effort to look down at the floor had it not been for Jonathan. Many of these people have become close and much-appreciated friends. Other encounters were like lightning strikes – brief but illuminating the whole landscape: Jon Thompson, Robert Hillenbrand, Walter Denny, Moya Carey, Giorgio Riello, Pennina Barnett, Anne Gerritsen, Ulinka Rublack, Yuka Kadoi, Stephen Cohen, Partha Mitter. I am grateful to all of you. Carpet enthusiasts are a congenial community, and I'd like to thank the Oxford Asian Textiles Group, the Oriental Rug and Textile Society in London, the Haji Baba Club in New York and Andrew Haughton of the Nomad's Tent in Edinburgh for their invitations to speak and their hospitality.

335

During my decade of research, I was grateful to receive funding from the Nicholas Berwin Charitable Trust, Dr Theodora Zemek, the Abdullah Al-Mubarak Al Sabah Foundation, the British Institute of Middle Eastern Studies, the V&A Gardner and Wainwright Funds and the Trustees of the May Beattie Archive at the Ashmolean Museum. Thank you for the chance you took on me.

Writing history is the work of many hands. Noorah Al-Gailani at the Burrell Collection in Glasgow, Anna Beselin at the Pergamon Museum in Berlin, Avalon Fotheringham and Tim Stanley at the V&A all took time out of their busy curatorial schedules to help me and I'm grateful. The study room teams of the Eastern Art Department at the Ashmolean Museum and at Glasgow Libraries and Special Collections were endlessly patient and helpful. Historians depend on archivists, and I thank those at the National Archives in the UK, the State Department in the US, the Royal Academy in London, the Bodleian Libraries in Oxford and the V&A Archives. I also thank the archivists and librarians at the British Library, who worked hard to help even as their globally important collection came under cyber-attack. Special thanks to Suke Wolton and the family of Georgie Wolton for access to Georgie's carpets and papers and to the Ashmolean Museum and its Beattie Archive.

Behind this book stand all those carpet writers who have gone before who, like me, did their best with sometimes scant information. I am grateful for their often-pioneering work. I am also deeply grateful for the support of my agent Adam Gauntlett and his team at Peters, Fraser and Dunlop, and for the brilliant conversations that sparked the book. I am more than thankful for the care and inspiration I have received from my editors Ed Lake and Lily McIlwain at Weidenfeld & Nicolson, and Michael Flamini at St Martin's Press. I have been blessed in my publishers.

All errors are of course my own.

Finally, to my nearest and dearest – Leo, Ellie, Ned, Zoe, Madeleine, David, Peter, Jan, Harriette, Robin, Vikki, Philip, Susan, Jeremy, Nicholas, Neil, Theo and the latest but certainly not the least, the next generation of Mila, Noah, Esmae and Rowan – thank you for a lifetime's affection and support.

Picture Credits

Plate Section 1

Page 1
One of the oldest rugs in existence, the Pazyryk carpet can be found at the Hermitage Museum in St Petersburg. *Knotted wool pile, fifth to fourth century BCE, place of making unknown, 183cm x 200cm, 6ft x 6ft 7in. Find spot: horsechamber, Pazyryk barrow number five, Altai Territory, Pazyryk Boundary, the Valley of the River Bolshoy Ulagan, Southern Siberia, excavation by S.I. Rudenko, 1949.* (CPA Media Pte Ltd / Alamy Stock Photo)

Page 2
Top – In this detail of the Pazyryk carpet, the internal organs of animals important to the way of life of its makers and users are picked out in different coloured knots. (The Picture Art Collection / Alamy Stock Photo)
Bottom – Russian archaeologists recovered the Pazyryk carpet from the frozen tomb of a Scythian chieftain in the remote Altai mountains of Siberia in 1949. *Sergei Rudenko's team excavate Pazyryk barrow number five.* (S.I Rudenko, *The Frozen Tombs of Siberia: The Pazyryk Burials of Iron Age Horsemen*, University of California Press, 1970)

Page 3
Top – There is mystery around where and when so-called chequerboard carpets were made. They are often associated with the Mamluk slave empire centred in Cairo. This example is in the Burrell Collection, Glasgow. *Knotted wool pile carpet, currently attributed to Damascus, Syria, or eastern Anatolia c.1500-1600, 155cm x 122cm, 5ft x 4ft.* (Burrell Collection, Glasgow)
Middle – For seventy-five years, the curators of the Burrell Collection have repeatedly changed their mind about where and when the chequerboard carpet was made. *Object file for Burrell carpet 9-67.*

337

Bottom – The chequerboard carpet demonstrates the skills of both its original weavers and later restorers, like these in a workshop in early twentieth-century Glasgow. *Asian women at work restoring carpets in the Carpet Repairing Department, Victor Behar Carpet Dealers, Sauchiehall Street, Glasgow.* (Glasgow School of Art Library)

Page 4
Left – 'Singular perfection…the finest I have seen'. The late-nineteenth-century judgement of William Morris has helped determine the modern reputation of the V&A's Ardabil carpet. *'Ardabil' carpet, wool knots, silk warps and wefts, Safavid Iran, 1540 CE, AH 946, 1044cm x 530cm, 34ft 3ins x 17ft 6ins.* (The Picture Art Collection / Alamy Stock Photo)
Right – The twin to the V&A's Ardabil was cannibalised to repair its tattered borders. The borderless carpet became a rich man's trophy until it was given by John Paul Getty to the Los Angeles County Museum of Art in 1949. *Borderless Ardabil carpet, wool knots, silk warps and wefts, Safavid Iran 1540 CE, AH 946, 718cm x 399cm, 23ft 7ins x 13ft 1in.* (MCLA Collection / Alamy Stock Photo)

Page 5
A war vest, or jinbaori, belonging to Toyotomi Hideyoshi, leader of Japan in the later part of the sixteenth century. The vest was made from a silk kilim imported from Safavid Persia and is currently held at the Kodaiji Temple in Kyoto. *Vest tailored late sixteenth century Japan, possibly Kyoto. Original kilim woven sixteenth century Iran, possibly Kirman.* (The Asahi Shimbun / Getty Images)

Page 6
Top – Satiric cartoon showing Japan's sixteenth- and seventeenth-century leaders jointly making the cake of a unified Japan. At the front the warlord Nobunaga grinds the rice, in the centre the 'bald rat' Hideyoshi bakes the cake, and in the upper right, the first Tokugawa Shogun Ieyasu, eats it. (Historic Collection / Alamy Stock Photo)
Bottom – May Beattie was one of the leading carpet scholars of the twentieth century. She asked many penetrating questions about the carpets in this book, including Hideyoshi's jinbaori. (Beattie Archive, Ashmolean Museum, University of Oxford)

Page 7
Top – A rug of diverse spiritual potential. Woven as an Islamic prayer rug, collected by the devout Lutheran churches of Transylvania between the

sixteenth and eighteenth centuries, and used as a prop in sacred paintings by
Roman Catholic artists such as Tintoretto during the Renaissance. This rug
is in the collection of the Black Church in Brasov, Transylvania. *Knotted wool
pile carpet, sixteenth or seventeenth centuries, Ushak, Anatolia, 113 x 162cm,
3ft 8ins x 5ft 4ins.* (Evangelical Church A.C. of Romania – Brasov Parish;
image courtesy of Stefano Ionescu)
Bottom – Within the austere interiors of the Lutheran churches of Transylvania, Anatolian prayer rugs hang like bright postage stamps as seen here
in the Black Church, Brasov. *Photograph, interior of Black Church, Brașov,
Transylvania.* (Dr Ned Wontner)

Page 8
Top – A carpet made either in India or in Persia, in either the seventeenth
or the nineteenth centuries. The ambiguity about this type of rug creates
difficulties for collectors of high-status carpets. The carpet is now in the
collection of the Getty Museum, California. *Knotted-pile carpet, wool and
silk, 305cm x 792cm, 26ft x 10ft, attributed to Herat, late-sixteenth-century
Safavid Iran.* (The J. Paul Getty Museum, Los Angeles, 78.DC.91)
Bottom – Weavers have used samplers for centuries. This example contains
motifs from more than fifteen different carpet designs, from wide-ranging
periods and locations. The mobility of designs and their persistence over time
make it difficult to identify when and where a carpet is made. *Knotted-pile
carpet sampler or wagireh, wool and cotton, attributed to Bijar, western Iran,
early twentieth century.* (Oturn carpets)

Plate Section 2

Page 9
Main image – The author and a colleague unroll an Anatolian kilim from
the collection of Georgie Wolton, now in the Ashmolean Museum, Univer-
sity of Oxford. *Flatwoven wool kilim, Anatolia, possibly Haymana, late
eighteenth or early nineteenth century, 109cm x 355cm, 3ft 7ins x 11ft 8ins.*
(Suke Wolton)
Top left – One woman inspires another. As she worked on the Wolton
Collection, the Ashmolean's textile conservator, Sue Stanton, was moved to
recreate their designs on pottery boxes. *Sue Stanton, earthenware boxes with
Wolton kilim patterned glaze, 2022.* (Sue Stanton)

Page 10
Top – The victors of the Second World War celebrate their division of the
spoils, their feet planted on a white ground Persianate carpet laid over the

soil of the Livadia Palace gardens, Yalta. *Photograph, Winston Churchill, Franklin D. Roosevelt and Joseph Stalin at the end of the Yalta Peace Conference, Crimea, 4-11 February 1945.* (PJF Military Collection / Alamy Stock Photo)

Bottom – The style of carpet may have been a favourite of Stalin, influencing its choice for the iconic Yalta image. The recreation of his study at the Stalin Museum in Gori uses a similar rug. *Photograph, white ground Persianate carpet, recreation of Stalin's study, Stalin Museum, Gori, Georgia.* (Dr Ned Wontner)

Page 11

Top – Jail labour in colonial India gave the British the opportunity to re-invent the idea of the Indian carpet. This rug is in the V&A, London. *Knotted wool pile carpet, Lahore Central Jail Punjab, 1880-1881, 250cm x 300cm, 8ft 2ins x 9ft 10ins.* (Victoria and Albert Museum, London)

Bottom right – The British re-invention turned to Persianate styles rather than to India's own Mughal tradition, like the whole plant style shown here. This example is in the Metropolitan Museum of Art, New York. *Knotted-pile carpet, Mughal India, Kashmir or Lahore, seventeenth century, wool, silk and cotton, 155cm x 103cm, 5ft 1in x 3ft 4ins.* (Metropolitan Museum of Art, New York)

Bottom left – The weavers of jail carpets have no voice in history, but images can give an insight into their experience, Karachi Jail, 1873. *Photographic print, Karachi jail weavers. 1873, Michie and Company.* (Archaeological Survey of India, 1000/52 (4906), British Library, London / Bridgeman)

Page 12

Left – Highly skilled and knowledgeable forgers waged war against the expertise of museum curators, dealers and collectors. This rug is now attributed to the twentieth century workshop of Teodor Tuduc but was sold to the V&A as the famous seventeenth-century Schwarzenberg carpet. It can still be found in the V&A. *Chintamani design carpet, knotted wool pile, Romania, 1920s, 297cm x 192cm, 9ft 9ins x 6ft 3ins.* (Victoria and Albert Museum, London)

Right – A clue to a forgery is sometimes that it is too perfect, Tuduc's weavers tidied up the corners of the Schwarzenberg original. The original Schwarzenberg carpet shown here is in the collection of the Prague National Museum. *Schwarzenberg Chintamani carpet, wool, Ottoman Anatolia, Selendi, seventeenth century, 297cm x 192cm, 9ft 9ins x 6ft 3ins.* (Prague National Museum)

Page 13

Top – The 'Bokhara' carpet has become a global commodity, sold at modest prices by international retailers. This carpet was made recently in Peshawar, Pakistan. *Knotted-pile 'Bokhara' carpet, Pakistan, twenty-first century.* (Imago / Alamy Stock Photo)

Middle – Modern Bokhara rugs are based on the weaving tradition of the Turkmen nomadic tribes of Central Asia and Iran. The medium of knotted-pile textiles was used by the Turkmen to make domestic objects they needed, like this woven builders' strap used to brace the structure of a yurt. Everyday objects show great artistry. This example is in the Textile Museum, Washington. *Detail of Turkmen tent band, knotted wool pile, Tekke tribe, Central Asia, first half of nineteenth century, 13.8m. x 21.5cm, 45ft 4ins x 8ins.* (Textile Museum Washington)

Bottom – Modern Bokhara rugs borrow the guls, or abstract floral motifs, found in Turkmen weaving. Tribes each have their own traditional guls. The weaver of this rug used that of the Tekke tribe. It may have been woven by a bride-to-be and her mother-in-law. This is a treasured rug from the author's collection. *Tekke Turkmen carpet, knotted wool pile, Central Asia, late nineteenth century, 122cm x 122cm, 4ft x 4ft.* (Author's collection)

Page 14

This carpet was destroyed in RAF attacks on Berlin in 1945. It inspired the work of the father of carpet studies, Wilhelm von Bode, and was Inventory No I.1 in the famous Islamic Art Collection in Berlin. When it burned, the work of a team of great artist-weavers was lost, along with a foundation-stone of carpet scholarship. *Bode Animal Carpet, knotted wool pile, Safavid-dynasty Iran, early sixteenth century, 604cm x 365cm, 19ft 10ins x 12ft.* (Museums für Islamische Kunst – Staatliche Museen zu Berlin)

Page 15

Like the Ardabil, the Bode Animal Carpet was one of a pair. The surviving rug, which can be found at the Los Angeles County Museum of Art, allows us to conjure up the lost carpet. *'Coronation Carpet', knotted wool pile, Safavid-dynasty Iran, early sixteenth century, 701cm x 365cm, 23ft x 12ft.* (LMA/AW / Alamy Stock Photo)

Page 16

The 1945 Berlin Mint fire stimulated the development of the art and technique of conservation in Germany. This carpet smouldered in the attack but did not completely burn. Conservators have now brought it back to numinous life and it is on display at the Museum of Islamic Art in Berlin. *Remains of 'Dragon' carpet, knotted wool pile, Caucasus, sixteenth century, 572cm x 268cm, 18ft 9ins x 8ft 10ins.* (Staatliche Museen zu Berlin, Museum für Islamische Kunst / Johannes KramerCC BY-SA 4.0)

Index

350 THREADS OF EMPIRE

Plutarch 34
Poland 201–2
'Polonaise' carpet 144, 146, 156
Pope, Arthur Upham 47, 75–6
Portugal 107–10, 113
Powell, Josephine 184
prayer niches 116
prayer rugs 115–16, 123, 124, 126, 129, 135
printing presses 118–19
Pripyat Marshes massacres (1941) 202
Protestantism 112, 114–15, 122, 125, 127, 132
Punjab exhibition (1881–82) 206–7, 210–11, 214, 217–19, 220–1, 223
Purdon Clarke, Caspar 78, 80, 221–4, 225–6
Putin, Vladimir 38, 39, 270

Qaytbay, Sultan 58
Qing throne 77
Quranic script 116

Radlov, Vasily 31
Reagan, Ronald 203
Reformation 111, 114, 115, 118, 126–7, 130, 136
Remarque, Erich Maria 238
Renaissance 52, 57–8, 63, 78, 130–1
restoration 42–4, 124, 237, 238, 272–3
Rhodes, Greece 49
Richard the Lionheart 55
Riegl, Alois 140, 229, 240
Robinson and Company 79
Robinson, Vincent 211
Rogers, Richard 167
Romania 120–1, 122, 126, 138, 228–45
Romanov family 188, 190
Roosevelt, Franklin Delano (FDR)

186–91, 192, 200, 201, 204
Royal College of Art, London 220
Rudenko, Sergei 16–22, 23–6, 29, 30–1, 38–9, 176
Russia 36–8, 121–2, 201, 204–5, 269–70
    Pazyryk carpet 19–21, 23, 26
Russian Empire 189, 194, 198, 231, 252–6
Rustam 230

Sadik, Shaik Gulam 212
Safavid carpets 74, 75–6, 144–5
Safavid dynasty 86–9
    Britain and 91
    carpets 79, 84, 113
    early 100, 105, 248
    peak of 69, 213
Safavid Iran 53, 80–1, 133, 152, 159
Safaviyya 81, 86
Safi al-Din Ardabili, Shayk 81, 87
Said, Edward 52
Sakoku ('closed country') 110–12
Saladin 54–6
Salomon, William 156
Samarkand, Uzbekistan 231
Sanguzsko knotted-pile carpet 113
Sarıkeçili, Anatolia 180, 182
Sarre, Friedrich 53, 74, 229, 240
Sawabi refugee camp, Kyber Pakhtunkhwa 260
Saxons, Transylvanian 120–1, 123–4, 126–7, 130, 135–6, 239
Schmutzler, Emil 137, 240–1
Schoene, Richard 264
Schwarzenberg collection 229, 235–6
Science and Art Department (V&A) 220–4, 226
screens, Japanese 108–9
Scythians 16–20, 24–39, 252

About the Author

Dr Dorothy Armstrong is a historian of the material culture of South, Central and West Asia. For more than a decade she has tried to penetrate the mysteries of Asian rugs, and the hidden stories of their participation in global history. As well as publishing, podcasting and lecturing widely on carpets, she has taught at the School of Oriental and African Studies, the Royal College of Art, Edinburgh College of Art and Oxford University. From 2021 to 2022 she was the Beattie Fellow in Carpet Studies at the Ashmolean Museum, University of Oxford, and is now Honorary Research Fellow in the Eastern Art Department at the Ashmolean.